AF580352

Indiana University *and the* World

A Celebration of Collaboration, 1890–2018

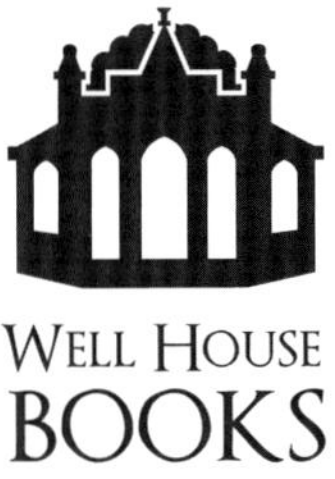
WELL HOUSE
BOOKS

Indiana University *and the* World

A Celebration of Collaboration, 1890–2018

Patrick O'Meara *with Leah K. Peck*

INDIANA UNIVERSITY PRESS

This book is a publication of

Indiana University Press
Office of Scholarly Publishing
Herman B Wells Library 350
1320 East 10th Street
Bloomington, Indiana 47405 USA

iupress.indiana.edu

This book is printed on acid-free paper.

Manufactured in Canada

Library of Congress Cataloging-in-Publication Data

Names: O'Meara, Patrick author.
Title: Indiana University and the world : a celebration of collaboration, 1890-2018 / Patrick O'Meara, with Leah K. Peck.
Description: Bloomington, Indiana : Indiana University Press, [2019] | Series: Well House Books | Includes bibliographical references and index.
Identifiers: LCCN 2019011002 (print) | LCCN 2019014177 (ebook) | ISBN 9780253044310 (ebook) | ISBN 9780253044280 | ISBN 9780253044280 (hardback : alk. paper)
Subjects: LCSH: Indiana University, Bloomington—History. | Indiana University—History.
Classification: LCC LD2518 (ebook) | LCC LD2518 .O44 2019 (print) | DDC 378.772/255—dc23
LC record available at https://lccn.loc.gov/2019011002

1 2 3 4 5 24 23 22 21 20 19

The book is dedicated to the generations of IU leaders, faculty, and students who believed that the university needed to be part of the wider world.

Contents

Preface

SINCE THE NINETEENTH CENTURY, GENERATIONS OF international students have attended Indiana University, many of whom returned to their home countries, where they became leaders in politics, the arts, business, academia, and other professions. Thousands of American students have gone abroad to learn about other societies and cultures and to perfect their language skills.[1]

The university has also been home to well-known programs for Africa, Asia, Latin America, the Middle East, Russia and East Europe, Central Asia, and Global Change. This book, however, looks at IU's remarkable achievements in serving the wider world through international development projects. The twenty-two chapters reflect in-depth commitments by the university and by individuals for more than a century on nearly every continent. The focus is on Indiana University abroad rather than on providing detailed descriptions of the individual projects.

In chronicling IU's far-reaching activities, it was not always possible to go back to the past to find conclusive data or interview participants. However, IU's rich archival holdings, detailed minutes of meetings, applications for funding, technical reports, budgetary information, correspondence with funding sources, faculty and student comments and records, and IU news reports have enabled me to be more than anecdotal. When possible, I interviewed participants in particular projects; recordings of these interviews are now housed in the IU Archives. My personal memories and reflections are also woven into the chapters. Juxtaposing and aggregating the various sources have enabled me to reconstruct and interpret the historical events. The chapters are in narrative form; they attempt to describe the choices, problems, and successes of faculty, students, and administrators who went to other parts of the world to offer guidance and assistance and to learn from institutions and colleagues in different parts of the world.

Why did presidents and other academic leaders choose to venture beyond the boundaries of Indiana? For them, it was the fundamental awareness that the international, in its many forms, was a central part of the teaching and research identity of a great university. For faculty and students, there were opportunities to conduct comparative academic research while collaborating and assisting with developing nations. In doing so, they were able to acquire new skills that benefited them in their teaching and research.

Acknowledgments

I am most grateful for Leah Peck's dedicated commitment to this book. Her insights, guidance, and skills were invaluable in developing and implementing key themes and ideas. She was a sounding board for what to include, exclude, or clarify, and her knowledge of higher education institutions and her international expertise led to innovative directions and approaches. She was responsible for writing sections of each chapter, and ultimately also for the overall review of the content, style, and other details of the entire book.

Edda Callahan was an amazing resource because of her firsthand experience with many of the places and projects discussed in the book. Over the years, she has interacted with countless colleagues from Indiana University and from different parts of the world, and she was vividly aware of details, events, and personalities. Her careful review and proofing of the chapters proved to be an essential part of the project.

Leah and Edda not only worked well together but also were a formidable team, never daunted by the scale of the project. I would have accomplished very little without them.

I am thankful to Judith Rice, who meticulously reviewed the manuscript and made thoughtful and constructive comments.

In so many of the projects in this book, Charles Reafsnyder wrote the applications, budgets, and final reports, and he carefully selected participants. Traveling to different overseas sites was challenging, and at the same time, fulfilling. All of his accumulated knowledge was an essential part of this book, and is gratefully recognized.

Kelly Kish and the Bicentennial Committee provided valuable support and guidance. Kelly's vision for the Bicentennial Celebration as a whole was an inspiration for countless projects, and she carefully nurtured a wide range of contributors and books, including this volume.

Lynn Schoch, Director of Information Resources, Office of the Vice President for International Affairs (OVPIA), generously provided comments, insights, and background information. The detailed files that he has preserved for the OVPIA office were an invaluable resource and an inspiration.

Dina Kellams, Director, Office of University Archives and Records Management, was supportive from the beginning of the project. She promptly provided access to materials, made boxes of documents appear often with the shortest notice, and made excellent suggestions.

Bradley D. Cook, Curator of Photographs, Indiana University Archives, was always willing to delve into the Archives' photographic collections and frequently found new images for us to consider.

Kristin Browning Leaman, Bicentennial Archivist, Indiana University Archives, offered us support and guidance as we continued our research.

From our first meeting, Gary Dunham, Director, IU Press and Digital Publishing, understood the purpose, relevance, and core ideas of the book; with skill and imagination, he guided its direction and structure. Our meetings with him, and with Peggy Solic, Acquisitions Editor, Bicentennial Publications Project Manager, were always lively, creative, and constructive.

Indiana University *and the* World

A Celebration of Collaboration, 1890–2018

INTRODUCTION

It is surprising that a campus, which originally operated out of a small town in southern Indiana, should not only seek out opportunities in foreign countries but that it should do so with eagerness and enthusiasm.

BY EARLY IN THE TWENTIETH CENTURY, INDIANA UNIVERSITY HAD become increasingly involved in different parts of the world. It is surprising that a campus, which originally operated out of a small town in southern Indiana, should not only seek out opportunities in foreign countries but that it should do so with eagerness and enthusiasm. How and why IU made these choices is the underlying theme of this book. Visionary presidents and academic administrators, increasing numbers of faculty who valued international ideas, and generations of students who were ready to explore the wider world, became part of IU's academic culture and legacy. There were many successes, and only a few setbacks; there were always risks and rewards. As IU began to celebrate its bicentennial, acknowledging IU's global and international accomplishments was more relevant than ever before, but this outlook also demanded greater resources and enterprise than in the past. The chapters in this book show that while the historic contexts differed, such needs were always there; it took courage and far-sightedness to meet them.

It is with Herman B Wells in the 1950s that guiding principles for international engagement became a central part of the mission of the university. Wells believed that the university should bring the world to the students from the towns and cities of the state; they should encounter firsthand the art, languages, ideas, and people from different countries: "We have been fortunate through

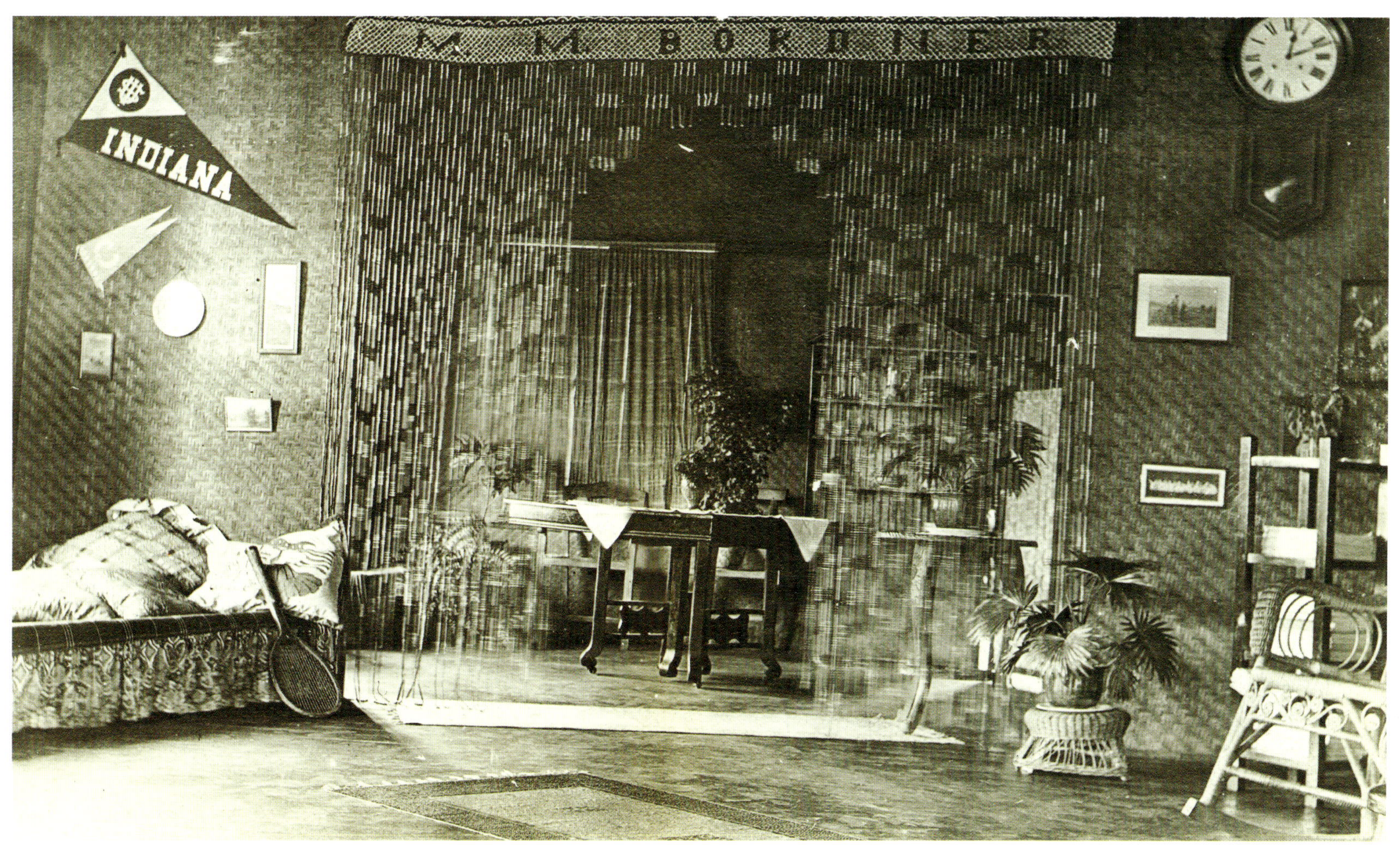

"Salon and Dining Room, Spring 1910," residence of Harvey Bordner (note the Indiana University pennant). *IU Archives (P0054332).*

the years also to have on our campus the rich resource of many students from overseas. . . . Thus any student in the university, regardless of how small or provincial the town from which the student came, can become acquainted with students from various places throughout the world, and through their eyes and through their minds come to gain a new appreciation and new understanding of the world in which we live."[1]

IU frequently became involved in countries that were going through conflicts, fundamental changes, or transitions, or that were in the midst of renewing or redefining their social, economic, and political structures.

In turn, Wells saw IU serving the world by mutually sharing knowledge, skills, and resources. He himself became an active and formative participant in the university's overseas projects. Generations of faculty and administrators followed in his footsteps. "In the early days of its development, Indiana University, along with other American universities, had been greatly assisted by older European universities. . . . So the American university, now among the strongest anywhere, had an obligation to repay the debt to the world of scholarship through extending assistance to new universities in the developing lands."[2]

In 1945, soon after the end of World War II, Wells represented the American Council on Education at the founding conference of the United Nations in San Francisco. This was an era that witnessed the ending of colonial power, the emergence of new nations, and the need for expanding access to higher education internationally.

The 1950s and 1960s marked the beginning of a new international order; one of the directions was toward the building or enhancement of institutions and the technical assistance, skills, training, and organizational structures needed to run them. At the heart of these programs was the need to provide better governance, alleviate poverty, and improve people's lives.

Overseas development projects, which are the primary focus of this book, were always grounded in this key mission of the university. At their heart was the connection to departments, schools, or international programs and centers; they have never been major sources of revenue, nor were they seen as such. When they flourished, they benefited countless lives in developing countries and, at the same time, provided opportunities for the intellectual growth of IU faculty and students.

IU frequently became involved in countries that were going through conflicts, fundamental changes, or transitions, or that were in the midst of renewing or redefining their social, economic, and political structures. An interesting pattern emerges of the university's assistance at times of upheaval—from Herman Wells in a decimated Berlin after World War II to countries such as Liberia, Macedonia, South Sudan, and South Africa in moments of rebuilding and reconstruction. At the same time, there were tangible returns to the state of Indiana, the United States, and various other countries because of the real economic impact resulting from improving the education of a larger number of people.

The history of these projects provides a vivid depiction of a university in the world. Indiana University faculty, administrators, and graduate students became increasingly involved in bilateral and mutually beneficial projects in Africa, Asia,

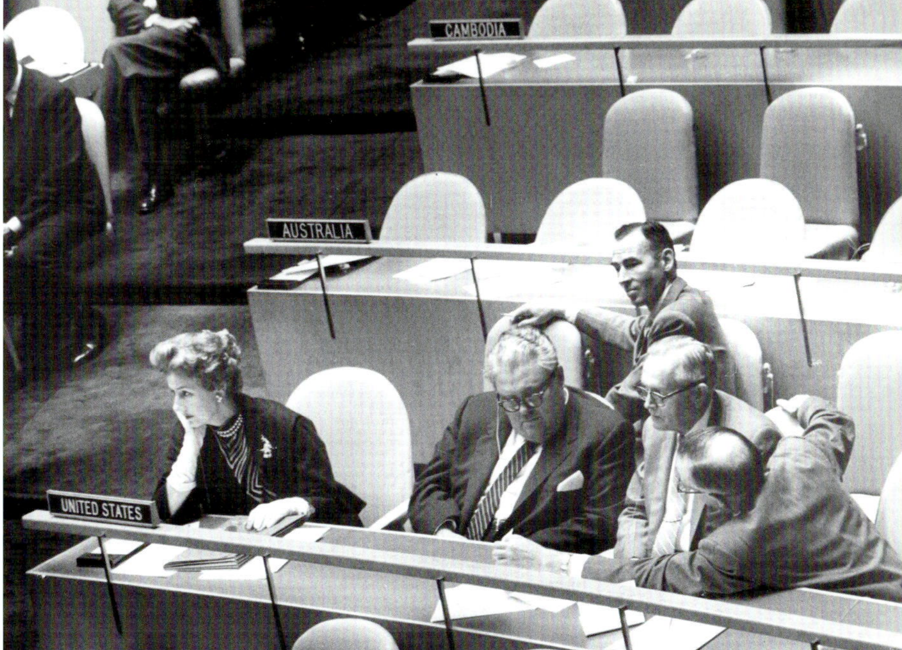

Herman B Wells at the 12th General Assembly of the United Nations, 1957. *Left to right:* American film actress and singer Irene Dunne, Herman B Wells, Albert Sidney Johnson Carnahan (US representative from Missouri), and Walter Henry Judd (US representative from Minnesota). *Photograph by Leo Rosenthal. IU Archives (P0023785).*

Central Asia, the Balkans, Latin America, and Europe. Funding for these development projects was awarded by foundations, government agencies, private enterprise, and overseas governments. In all these projects, IU staunchly adhered to its academic integrity and independence, the free exchange of ideas, and the strict fiscal guidelines and authority of the university.

The intellectual and pedagogical benefits of the international development projects were enormous. New knowledge was generated, faculty expanded their expertise, and students were drawn into unique opportunities.

The university insisted on its jurisdiction and autonomy in selecting those who participated in these projects. The applications for funding were competitive, and, at the national level, they underwent peer reviews and project outcomes were publicly available. In most cases, there were strong connections between overseas projects and IU's highly ranked language and area studies programs that were concerned with Africa, Russia and East Europe, Central Asia, East Asia, the Middle East, and West Europe. Beginning in the 1950s, IU had expanded and enhanced these programs by hiring outstanding scholars and attracting highly qualified graduate students.

The intellectual and pedagogical benefits of the international development projects were enormous. New knowledge was generated, faculty expanded their expertise, and students were drawn into unique opportunities. In these projects, faculty members and key administrators shared knowledge and technical know-how; junior faculty from the partner institutions received advanced degrees; graduate and undergraduate students completed degrees; computers and library materials were put in place. At the same time, IU faculty and staff were challenged to bridge theory and practice in cross-cultural contexts.

Less tangible and more difficult to measure were positive changes in the fostering of tolerance, democratic ideals, minority rights, and peacekeeping. There were very real, but less quantifiable, outcomes that were probably of greater importance than buildings, physical plant, or even courses and administrative structures. The long-term ripple effects, however, were substantial; for example, countless lives in the cities and towns of countries were improved because of better teachers, doctors, and public servants.

As with all human endeavors, these programs came to an end when their purposes were achieved; the expectation was that there would be self-sustained growth after the departure of IU. Principles of international engagement have become part of the culture of Indiana University; indeed, they are woven into the very fabric of the institution through visions and commitments of presidents such as Herman Wells, John Ryan, Thomas Ehrlich, and Myles Brand. Michael McRobbie's presidency reflected his deep commitment to the university's international and global mission. Immediately after his appointment, he established the university's first vice presidency for international affairs. When McRobbie came to IU, he already had an extensive network of colleagues in different parts of Asia. Once at IU, he expanded these connections. He initiated the university's first international plan and indicated that he would seek to create a new school of global and international studies. He also announced that there would be a major new international building on the Bloomington campus. He began to travel to every continent to meet with IU alumni and to explore new linkages and relationship. A direct outcome was the creation of innovative IU Gateways in India, China, and Germany. McRobbie also reaffirmed the ongoing relevance of overseas development projects: "Drawing on our long and rich tradition of international engagement, we must remember that education and research—IU's two fundamental missions—are the seeds for success in a world growing increasingly flat and seamless. Global literacy and collaboration have never been more important than they are now."[3]

New choices characterized the early years of the twenty-first century, an era of rapid technological innovation. IU was uniquely poised to transcend time and geographic differences by using new modes of communication and teaching with universities, colleagues, students, and alumni throughout the world.

David Zaret, former vice president for international affairs at IU, reflects, "What I admire about Michael is the passion and enthusiasm as well as the insight that informs his commitment to IU's engagements around the world. He positively delights in working to advance them. He is a leading voice in this country for international engagements by America's top research universities."[4]

The context in which the university operates in the twenty-first century, however, has required IU to change some of the ways that it engages with the world. The global and international opportunities and constraints that Indiana University faced at the beginning of the twenty-first century were dramatically different from those after World War II. While nation-states and geopolitical regions remained important, the impact of trade, energy, access to water resources, information technology, population movements, and religious fundamentalism were becoming increasingly global. These required new intercultural and international skills, understanding, and competencies. New choices characterized the early years of the twenty-first century, an era of rapid technological innovation. IU was uniquely poised to transcend time and geographic differences by using new modes of communication and teaching with universities, colleagues, students,

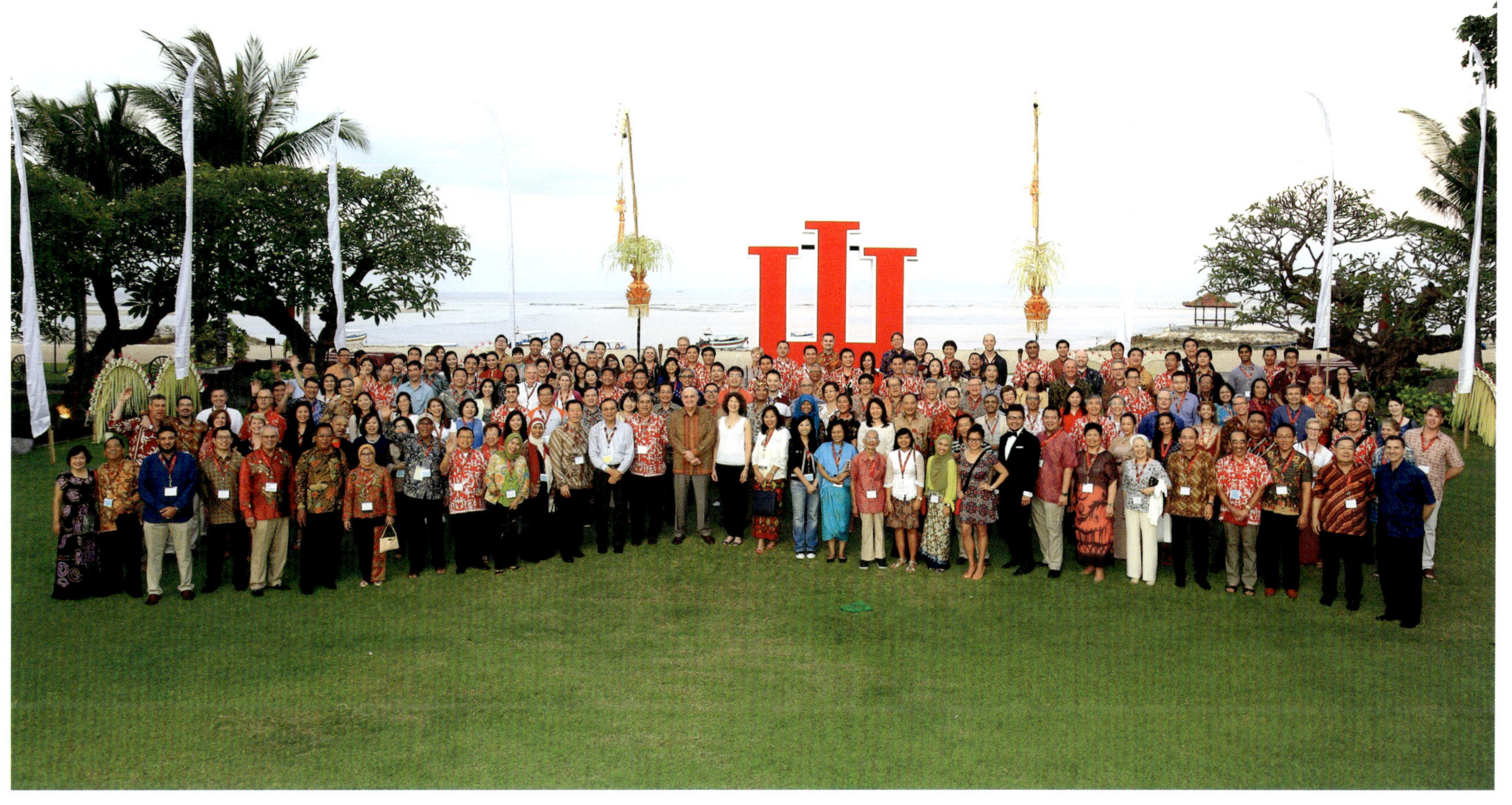

Indiana University president Michael McRobbie and first lady Laurie Burns McRobbie with IU alumni at the Asia-Pacific Alumni Conference in Bali, Indonesia, May 2015. *Photograph courtesy of Indiana University.*

and alumni throughout the world. To address this new milieu, IU also became more purposeful by continuing to foster international development, transitional, and renewal projects that are linked to the mission of the university; insisting that exchange agreements should only be with prestigious partners in regions of the world that had been predetermined in order to meet long-term research, teaching, service, and fundraising opportunities; and establishing IU overseas footprints abroad through the IU Gateway offices around the globe.

1 | History

The first significant international activity at Indiana University began in 1879.

Soon after its founding in the nineteenth century, Indiana University began to engage in international activities when faculty members and students from abroad found their ways to Bloomington. The first significant international activity at Indiana University, in the form of a study abroad trip, began in 1879. At first, this was an untried academic venture. There were no study abroad offices or advisers; purchasing of tickets and planning had to be done by mail. The logistics must have been daunting. Students had to travel by train to the East Coast, board a steamship for Europe, and then travel from country to country, often by foot.

The study abroad program was a great success, and each year, for the next ten years, faculty organized and led a series of summer "tramps" to Europe with twenty to thirty students and some professors. The groups studied natural history, language, and culture in Switzerland, Germany, Italy, France, and England. Archival material indicates that in 1881, there were twenty-eight participants, eleven women and seventeen men.

An 1879 advertisement for the 1880 tramp reads as follows:

INDIANA UNIVERSITY SUMMER TRAMP
Thuringia, Switzerland, Provence.
Daily instruction in German and French. Special attention to Natural History.

PRELIMINARY ANNOUNCEMENT.

Indiana University Summer Tramp.

Thuringia, Switzerland, Provence.

Daily instruction in German and French. **Special attention to Natural History.**

THE PARTY for 1880 leave Indianapolis about June 15th, take steamer from New York to Germany, visiting Berlin and Dresden.

A Walk of 50 Miles through Saxon Switzerland and Thuringia,

visiting Weimar, then via Nuremberg and Munich to Switzerland.

A WALK OF 250 MILES,

through the Bernese Oberland, by Lake of Lucerne, St. Gotthardt, Tosa Falls, Simplon Pass and Matterhorn to Italy; by rail to Milan and Genoa; by steamer to Marseilles. **A Tour through Provence,** then via Avignon to Geneva; Mt. Blanc; by rail to Paris; a week in England, returning about September 20th.

Fee, $30. **Total Expenses, $300.**

DAVID S. JORDAN, *Prof. of Natural Science,*
HERMANN B. BOISEN, *Prof. of Modern Languages,* } *Indiana State University.*

Bloomington, Ind. PROGRESS PRINT.

Announcement for the 1880 "Summer Tramp." *IU Archives (P0073785).*

The Party for 1890 leave Indianapolis about June 15th, take steamer from New York to Germany, visiting Berlin and Dresden.

A Walk of 50 Miles through Saxon Switzerland and Thurlagia, visiting Weimar then via Nuremberg and Munich to Switzerland.

A walk of 250 miles, through the Bernese Oberland, by Lake of Lucerne, St. Gotthardt, Tosa Falls, Simplon Pass and Matterhorn to Italy; by rail to Milan and Genoa; by steamer to Marseille. A Tour through Provence, then via Avignon to Geneva; Mt. Blanc; by rail to Paris; a week in England, returning about September 20th. Fee, $30. Total Expenses, $300.[1]

These early study abroad ventures recognized the importance for faculty and students to know and teach about other societies; to learn languages; to acquire new knowledge through direct experiences; and to be sensitive to other cultures. From these early beginnings, principles were woven into the international fabric of the university. Indeed, Indiana University's international roots include an instructor from Ireland who came to Bloomington in the middle of the nineteenth century and the first international student, who came from Japan around 1890.

Early in the twentieth century, Indiana University faculty members in education started the university's long and substantial history of assisting with overseas projects. In 1901, Professor Elmer Burritt Bryan accepted the appointment as principal of the Insular Normal school in the Philippines. Two years later, he became superintendent of education for the islands. In this capacity, he directed an educational system that employed eight hundred American teachers—many of them graduates of Indiana University. These teachers became known as the "Thomasites," named after the first ship to carry American teachers to the Philippines—the USS *Thomas*. Professor Bryan also encouraged many Filipino students to further their education in the United States and, in particular, at Indiana University.[2]

Early in the twentieth century, Indiana University faculty members in education started the university's long and substantial history of assisting with overseas projects.

IU had another connection to the Philippines. IU graduate and later law school dean, Paul V. McNutt, served as high commissioner to the Philippines from 1937 to 1939, after he was governor of Indiana. When McNutt Residence Quadrangle was completed on the Bloomington campus in 1964,

EDUCATION IN PHILIPPINES.

Elmer B. Bryan of Indiana Succeeds Superintendent Frederick Atkins.

Special to The New York Times.

WASHINGTON, Jan. 1.—Frederick Atkins of Massachusetts retires from the position of Superintendent of Education for the Philippines to-morrow, and will be succeeded by Elmer B. Bryan of Indiana. The place is one of importance in view of the policy of the Government in sending instructors from this country to teach the Filipino children and Americanize the islands.

Mr. Bryan was one of the first American teachers to go to the Philippines. He had taught for several years in Indiana. For a time he was Principal of the Normal School in Manila and Acting Superintendent of Education.

Above, The January 2, 1903, edition of the *New York Times* announced the appointment of IU alumnus and faculty member Elmer B. Bryan as the superintendent of education for the Philippines. During his appointment, Bryan employed nearly eight hundred American teachers. After his time in the Philippines, he went on to be president of Franklin College, Colgate University, and Ohio University.

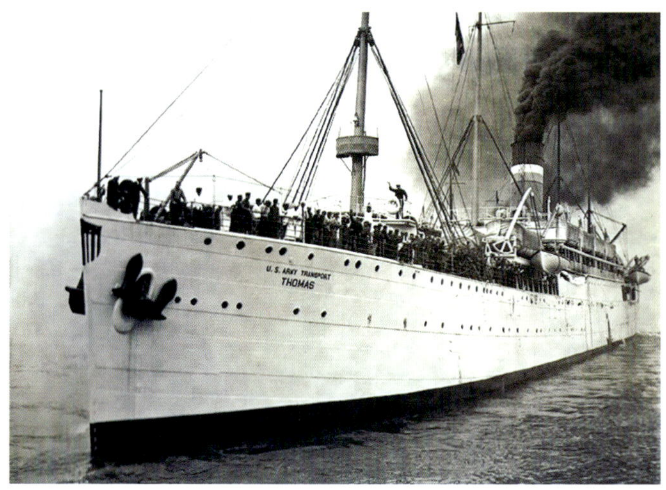

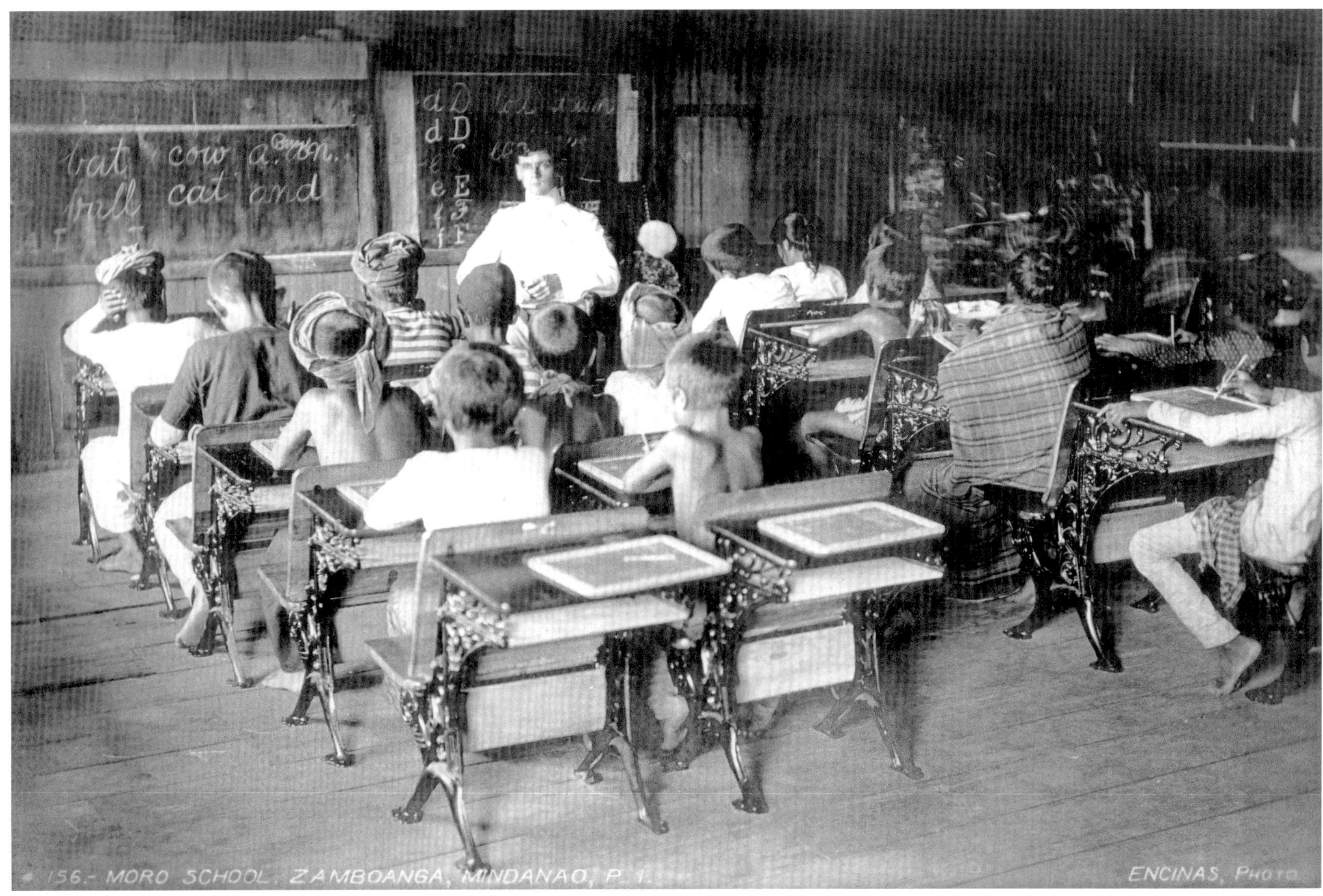

Facing bottom, US Army Transport *Thomas,* which brought the first group of American teachers to the Philippines in 1901. *Photograph courtesy of Jonathan Klinghorn, www.atlantictransportline.us.*

Above, An American schoolteacher in a classroom at the Moro School, Zamboanga, Mindanao, Philippines, 1901 or 1902. *Duke University Archives.*

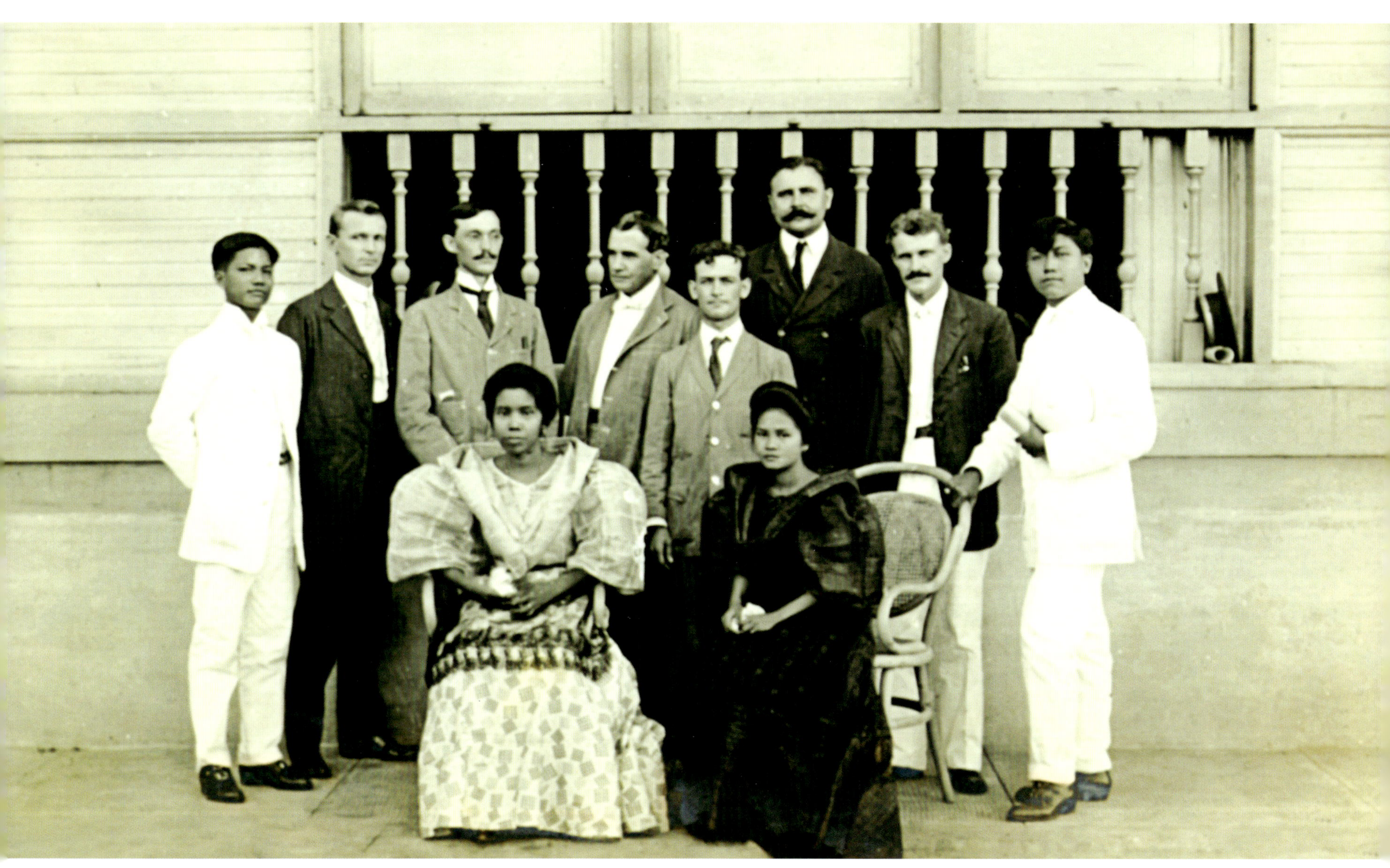

Instructors in the Bulacan Normal School, 1910.
From the collection of Harvey Bordner. IU Archives (P0025053).

six residence halls in the complex were named for Thomasite teachers.[3]

One other noteworthy effort took place in 1929, when students went to Munich, Germany, for a six-week for-credit summer school to study music, art, and languages. Of course, with the outbreak of World War II, such activities were on hold.

While the rich history of Indiana University's global development efforts dates back to these early activities, sustained and substantial institutional activities abroad began with the presidency of Herman B Wells. In the 1950s and 1960s, a new era began; the direction was toward the building or enhancement of institutions and the technical assistance, skills, training, and organizational structures needed to run them. For Wells, such programs also had a direct benefit on the academic mission of the university: "Of course, the more interest the administration evidenced in the international dimension, the more pervasive was its influence throughout the university and, to some extent, the state."[4]

Initiating the modern era of IU's increasing global and international engagement, Wells traveled far and wide, and his international vision and planning set the course for the university's future. Under his leadership, international activities began to flourish. "By our taking an active part in these international projects, the benefits would be two way: while lending whatever help we could to institutions abroad, we would be greatly enriching the store of experience, knowledge, and professional competence of our faculty participants in the assistance programs who, upon their return, would bring to the campus a comparative view that would stimulate the atmosphere of learning in the university."[5]

Thus, for Wells, the campus in Bloomington was not confined to Indiana but needed to look outward to the wider world. It was his belief that these contacts not only contribute richly to the development of their respective countries but also serve to spread the fame and name of Indiana University throughout the world.[6]

For Wells, the campus in Bloomington was not confined to Indiana but needed to look outward to the wider world.

By the mid-1960s, it had become clear that the growth of international activities on the Bloomington campus called for an administrative structure to coordinate and facilitate existing programs and to assist in finding new opportunities for the university. Over the next ten years, various approaches were implemented—including the creation of a center and a committee—until in 1975, a formal office was established. These new administrative structures reflected the increasing sophistication of the university's overseas commitments; indeed, they are an interesting reflection on how a major university refines and expands its international mission.

At the Indiana University Board of Trustees meeting in May 1965, Vice President Lynn L. Merritt presented a proposal for the establishment of an International Affairs Center, and on July 1, history professor and Russian specialist, Robert F. Byrnes, became its director.[7]

The center had three divisions—international studies, international development research, and international activities—each chaired by a faculty member. Soon after its creation, John M. Thompson, associate professor of history, was appointed as associate director of the International Affairs Center.[8]

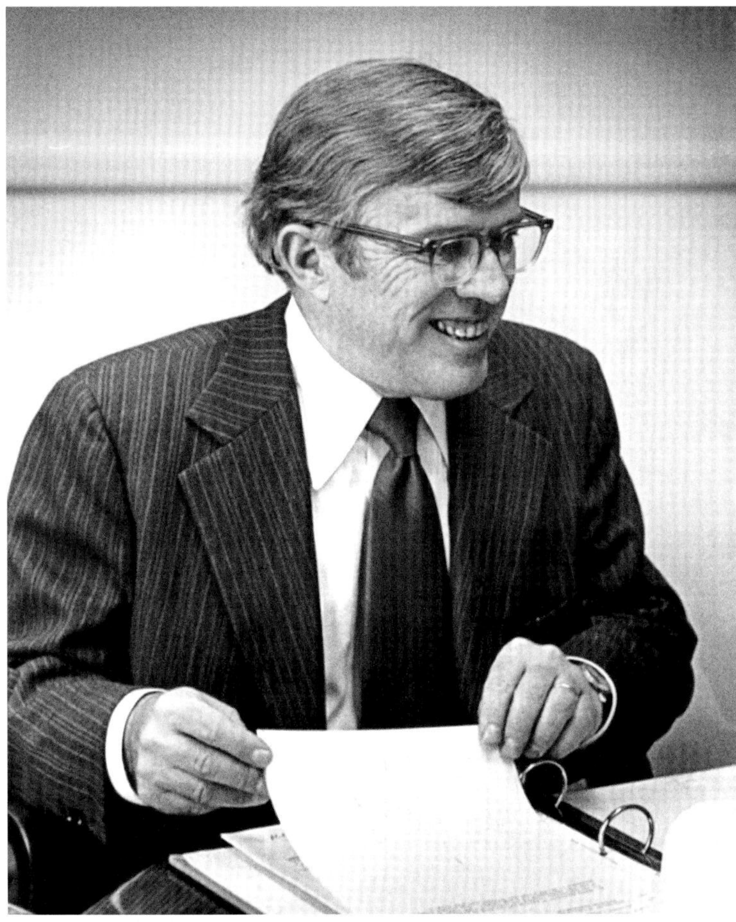

J. Gus Liebenow, founding director of African Studies at IU. *IU Archives (P0023192).*

At the July 1966 meeting of the board of trustees, Vice President Merritt and Chancellor Wells detailed the many areas and projects in international programs for which the university had responsibility, including study abroad at the universities of Hamburg, Strasbourg, Madrid, Bologna, and San Marcos. They also referred to the high school honors language program for intensive summer training abroad, which they saw as "having a great influence in the teaching of languages throughout the high school system in the state." In referring to contracts supported by the United States Agency for International Development and by the Ford Foundation, Wells and Merritt emphasized that IU was represented widely throughout the world. Chancellor Wells spoke about the operation of the International Affairs Center with special reference to the importance of American leadership in education and business, which he saw as the major developmental factors in bringing the two great areas of the world, old and new, into closer relationship.[9]

In May 1967, Robert Byrnes and John Thompson decided that they wanted to return to full-time teaching and research. Instead of replacing them, a committee was formed with Merritt as chair and Byrum Carter, College of Arts and Sciences dean, as co-chair.

In February 1970, J. Gus Liebenow, director of the African Studies Program and professor of political science, was appointed associate dean for research and advanced studies in Merritt's office. In addition, he was appointed associate dean for international programs in the office of Byrum Carter, who, by this point, had become chancellor of the Bloomington campus. At this time, IU began a process of reorganizing the structure of the university, taking into account the emergence of six smaller IU campuses in different parts of the state and the growing importance of the Indiana University–Purdue University Indianapolis (IUPUI) campus.[10]

In February 1972, Liebenow became acting vice president and dean for academic affairs, and George M. Wilson, associate professor of history, was appointed as associate dean for research and advanced studies and associate dean for international programs on the Bloomington campus.

Because of the university's increasing international activities, the Office of International Programs (OIP) was created in 1975, and the office was to be headed by a dean who reported directly to the president. In July 1975, Wilson became the first dean for overseas study in the OIP. When the deanship was officially launched, it brought together overseas study programs to serve faculty and students on all campuses; the International Student Office, sometimes referred to as the Foreign Student Office and later called Office of International Services, which served all campuses; and other system-wide international activities such as faculty and student exchanges and small grant programs. The Office of International Services and the Office of Overseas Study reported directly to the dean. OIP soon became an important resource for many of the university's international activities, and the dean was expected to advise and assist departments, schools, and other units. While most of the subject and area centers or programs were part of the College of Arts and Sciences, their directors, faculty, and students intersected with OIP on many different levels. When President Wells named Leo R. Dowling as IU's international student adviser in the mid-1940s, there were

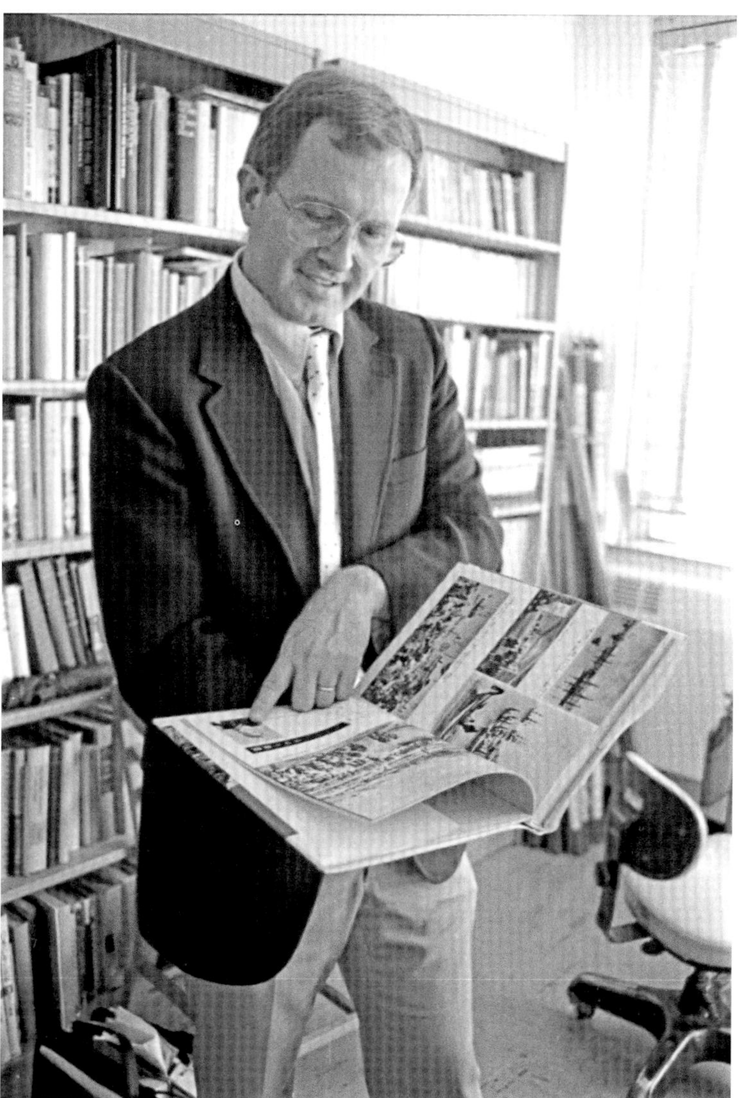

George M. Wilson, dean for overseas study in the Office of International Programs, December 1986. *IU Archives (P0056892).*

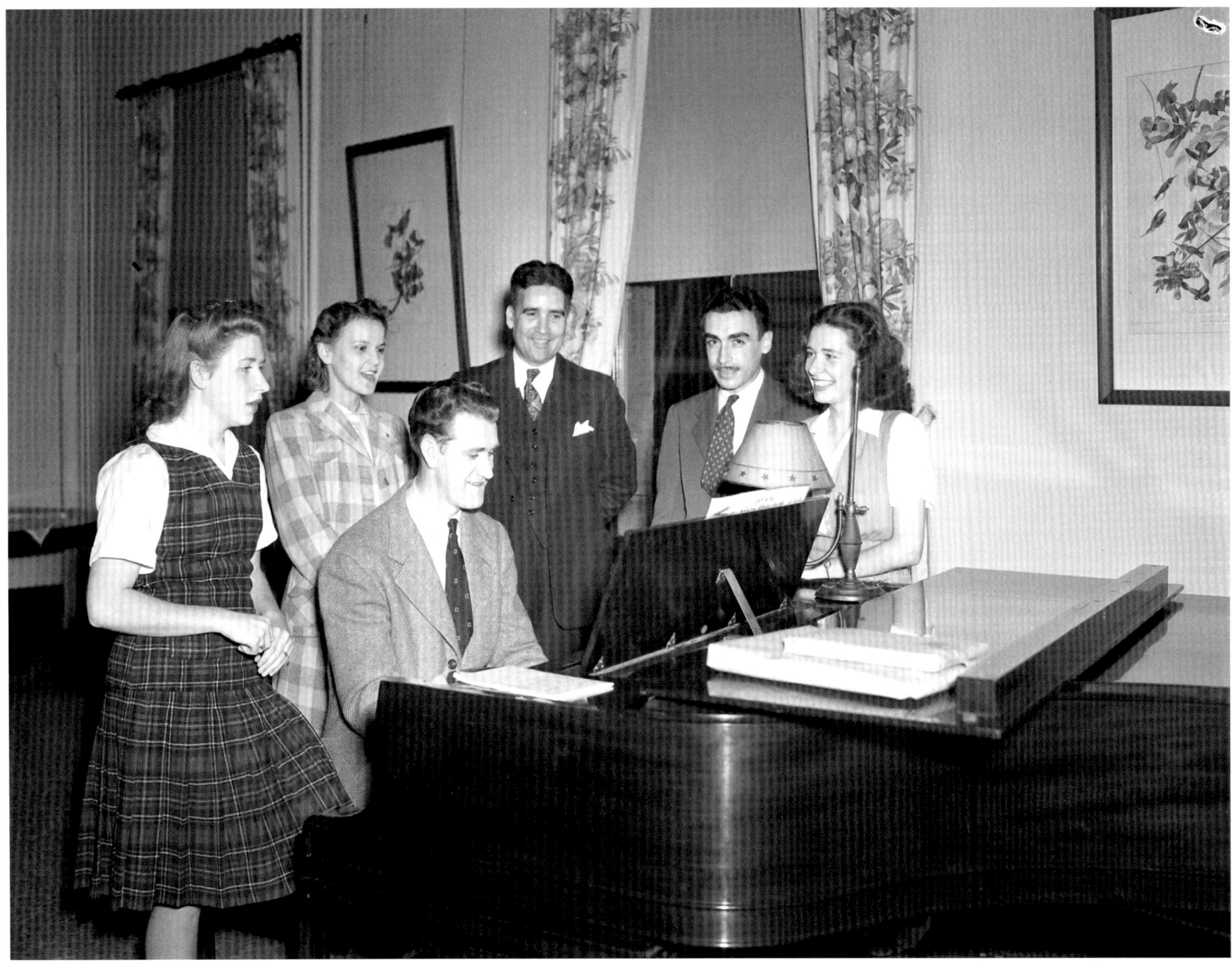

only fifty-eight foreign students on campus. When Dowling retired in 1972, there were fifteen hundred. The Office of International Services had primary responsibility for advising, visas, and student services for the foreign students at Indiana University. IUPUI also began to admit increasing numbers of international students and had its own international student adviser; however, the associate dean for the Office of International Services was the university's representative for foreign student concerns. Leo Dowling was succeeded by Kenneth Rogers, who remained in the position for twenty-five years.

The Office of Overseas Study provided study abroad programs of varying duration in different parts of the world. The associate dean chaired the Committee on Overseas Study, which developed policies for overseas study courses and approved programs designed to offer students university credit for study abroad.

In addition to these offices, a number of presidential initiatives were started. For example, the President's Council on International Programs was responsible for international policies on all campuses and provided competitive funding opportunities for tenured and tenure-track faculty for research abroad. Preference was given to those early in their careers who wanted to enhance their international reputation in research or teaching.

In 1986, President John Ryan asked Alexander (Alex) Rabinowitch to serve as dean of the Office of International Programs. Rabinowitch had received his BA from Knox College in 1956, a master's degree from the University of Chicago in 1961, and a PhD from Indiana University in 1965. From 1975 to 1984, Rabinowitch directed the Russian and East European

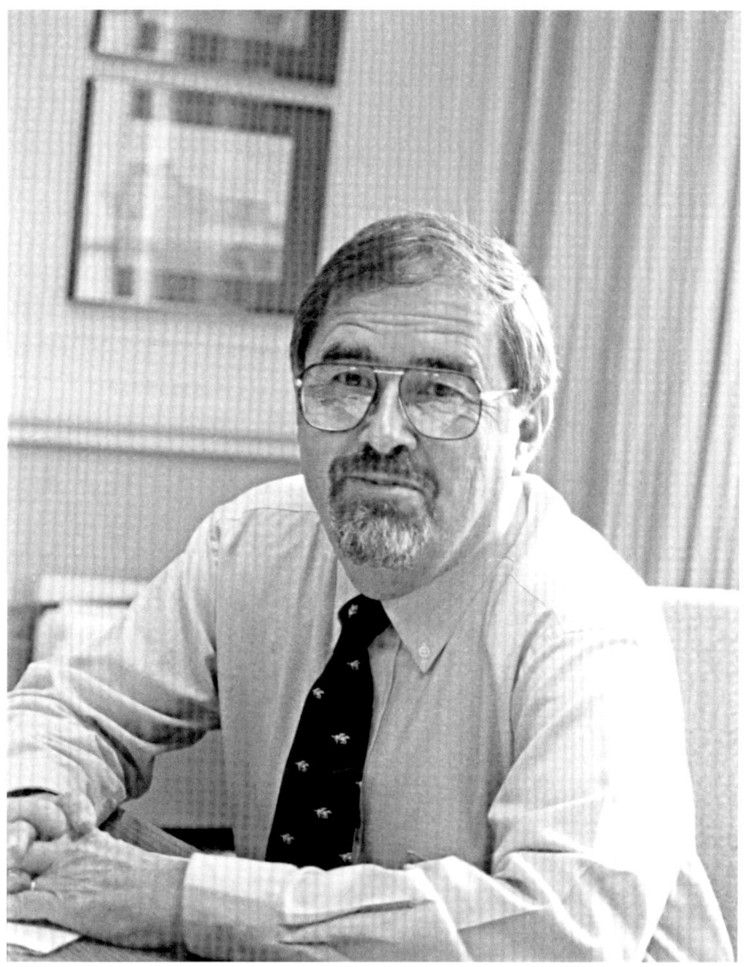

Above, Alexander Rabinowitch, dean for International Programs, October 1988. *IU Archives (P0056889).*

Facing, The IU Cosmopolitan Club, October 1, 1943. *Left to right:* Pat Bancroft, Libby Sosim (Russia), Leo Dowling (faculty adviser and class of 1935), Antonio Rodrigues (Puerto Rico), Julio Pazmino (Ecuador), and Peggy Thomas (India; Cosmopolitan Club president). *IU Archives (P0039559).*

Institute, playing a key role in attracting private foundation support and increasing the institute's Title VI federal funding. A renowned scholar of modern Russian and Soviet history, his books included *Prelude to Revolution: The Petrograd Bolsheviks and the July 1917 Uprising*; *The Bolsheviks Come to Power: The Revolution of 1917*; and *The Bolsheviks in Power: The First Year of Soviet Rule*. Rabinowitch worked to broaden contacts and provide opportunities for international faculty at the IU campuses and established a fully staffed international affairs office at IUPUI. In addition, he prepared the grant proposal to the MacArthur Foundation to establish the Indiana Center on Global Change and World Peace (ICGCWP), which focused on creating an interdisciplinary community of young scholars to study and research critical issues of change and peace at the global level. The ICGCWP identified and supported ten graduate students per year with annual stipends and participation in a variety of dedicated programs, workshops, and classes. Under Rabinowitch's leadership, overseas study opportunities for IU undergraduate and graduate students were greatly expanded, and he effectively continued the administration of the project in Malaysia.

Kenneth Rogers continued to serve as associate dean for international programs and director of international services. In 1989, Rabinowitch asked Dick Stryker to serve as associate dean and director of overseas study. In 1993 Charles Reafsnyder, who had directed the Malaysia Program, was appointed associate dean for international programs.

Patrick O'Meara was appointed dean for international programs in 1993 by President Thomas Ehrlich. O'Meara, a professor in the School of Public and Environmental Affairs and in the Political Science Department, had been director of IU's prestigious African Studies Program. A naturalized US citizen, O'Meara was born in Cape Town, South Africa, where he earned a bachelor's degree at the University of Cape Town; his PhD in political science was from IU. He became widely known for his books and publications on Africa.

His first book, *Rhodesia: Racial Conflict or Co-existence?* was published by Cornell University Press. Subsequent books include *Southern Africa in Crisis*; *First Twenty-Five Years*; *International Politics in Southern Africa*; and a textbook, *Africa*, which has been adopted by nearly one hundred universities and colleges throughout the United States and abroad. Other books include *Globalization and the Challenges of a New Century* and *Changing Perspectives on International Education*.

In July 2007, President McRobbie announced that he had appointed O'Meara to the newly created position of vice president for international affairs. McRobbie said he was creating this new position because of the rapidly increasing importance of the international and global dimension in higher education.

With this promotion, O'Meara continued to have oversight over international programs at all eight IU campuses, and he was asked to implement and develop a university-wide international strategic plan. As vice president, O'Meara provided leadership and coordination for all international directions and initiatives. McRobbie saw the historic new position as a central one for the future of Indiana University: "It is essential that we move all of our international activities into a higher gear if we fare to keep graduating students well prepared to work in an increasingly borderless world and to become even

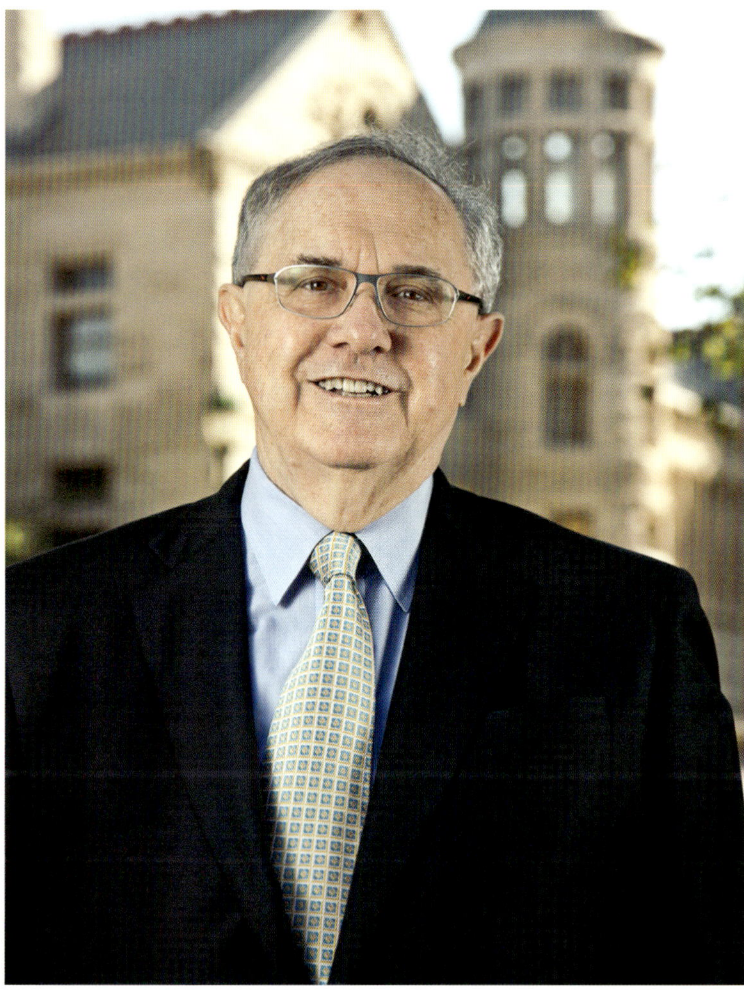

Patrick O'Meara, dean for International Programs, 1993–2007; vice president for International Affairs 2007–2011.
Photograph courtesy of Indiana University.

more competitive in recruiting the best faculty in a truly global marketplace."[11]

In choosing O'Meara for the position, McRobbie stated: "Patrick O'Meara has given Indiana University a well-earned reputation around the world as a place that truly welcomes and nurtures international students and scholars, and he understands deeply the importance of the global aspects of education. He has laid an excellent foundation for IU as we move to an even higher level of international engagement. I can think of no one more qualified to take on these new responsibilities."[12]

The strategic plan had several goals, including attracting and recruiting the very best international students and faculty members from around the world; implementing cooperative research and exchange agreements with top-tier universities, especially in Asia and the Pacific Rim; and developing more overseas study opportunities for IU undergraduates. The Office of the Vice President for International Affairs worked closely with McRobbie as he expanded IU's global and international commitments. Visits to Europe, Asia, and the Middle East took place to meet with university partners, alumni, and decision makers; a major alumni reunion was organized in Korea; exchange partnerships were reexamined and new criteria implemented. As dean for international programs, O'Meara had overseen externally funded exchange and technical assistance programs for the US Department of State, the United States Agency for International Development, and a variety of foreign governments, international businesses, and foundations. With the change in the status of the office, Associate Dean Charles Reafsnyder, who held primary responsibility for these activities, became an associate vice president. His portfolio included providing training and institution-building assistance through federal grants to Angola, Burmese refugees, Indonesia, Liberia, Macedonia, Malaysia, Kazakhstan, Kyrgyzstan, and South Africa. He also became an important resource for other academic units and individuals at Indiana University who were interested in exploring projects overseas.

Chris Viers, who was associate dean with responsibility for international scholars and students, became an associate vice president, as did Associate Dean Kathleen Sideli, whose office dealt with undergraduate study abroad. Susan Sutton, associate dean for international affairs at the Indianapolis campus, became associate vice president of international affairs at IUPUI.

When O'Meara retired in 2011, his service was recognized at Indiana University and by many countries overseas. He was the recipient of several international awards, including the Cross of Saint George awarded in Spain; the Warsaw University Medal; the Amicus Poloniae from the Embassy of Poland; an honorary doctorate from the National Institute of Development Administration in Thailand; and the Gold Cross of Merit of the Republic of Hungary. Indiana University has awarded him the Thomas Hart Benton Medal, the IU John Ryan Award, and the IU Distinguished Service Award. In 2014, a Senate resolution on behalf of the state of Indiana formally recognized O'Meara's life and accomplishments at the Indiana Statehouse. In 2011, the year of O'Meara's retirement, he was appointed as special adviser to the president, and the O'Meara International Lecture Series was created to celebrate his international legacy.

In July, 2011, President McRobbie asked David Zaret to serve as vice president for international affairs. Zaret had served in the IU Bloomington College of Arts and Sciences as executive associate dean and then as interim dean, and also for the Office of the Provost and Executive Vice President, where he worked as senior adviser to the provost. He received a doctor of philosophy degree from the University of Oxford and held visiting appointments at Oxford and at Heidelberg University in Germany. He held academic appointments in the Department of Sociology and the Department of History. His published work includes *Origins of Democratic Culture,* which explores the role of public opinion in British politics, and *The Heavenly Contract: Ideology and Organization in Pre-Revolutionary Puritanism.* Zaret's other publications address the topics of religion and social change, human rights, and methodological issues in cross-cultural research.

Zaret soon set out an agenda for his vice presidency, including more opportunities for undergraduates to study abroad and more resources to defray the additional expenses of international study: "We will continue our efforts to attract top international students, and we will continue to seek and enhance agreements with the best universities around the world. Our overseas alumni are a valuable resource in these efforts, and I look forward to cultivating deeper ties with them. Our long history of institutional development has already made a difference to universities in Africa, Latin America, Europe, Central Asia, and Southeast Asia; this work too must continue."[13]

In 2015, Zaret introduced a second International Strategic Plan, which emphasized the need to broaden and increase participation in undergraduate study abroad programs, student

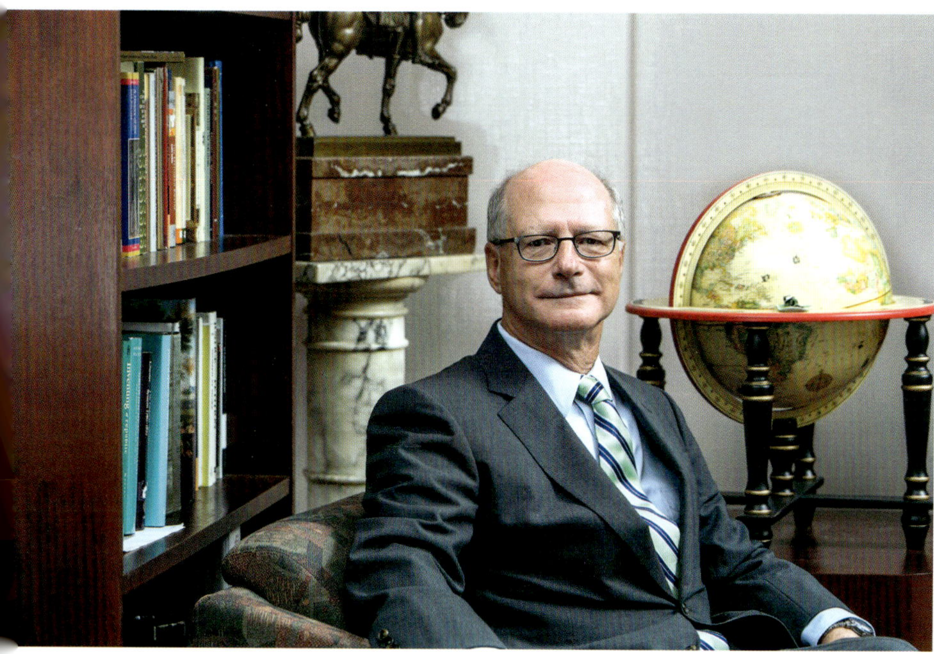

David Zaret, vice president for International Affairs, 2011–2018. *Photograph courtesy of Indiana University.*

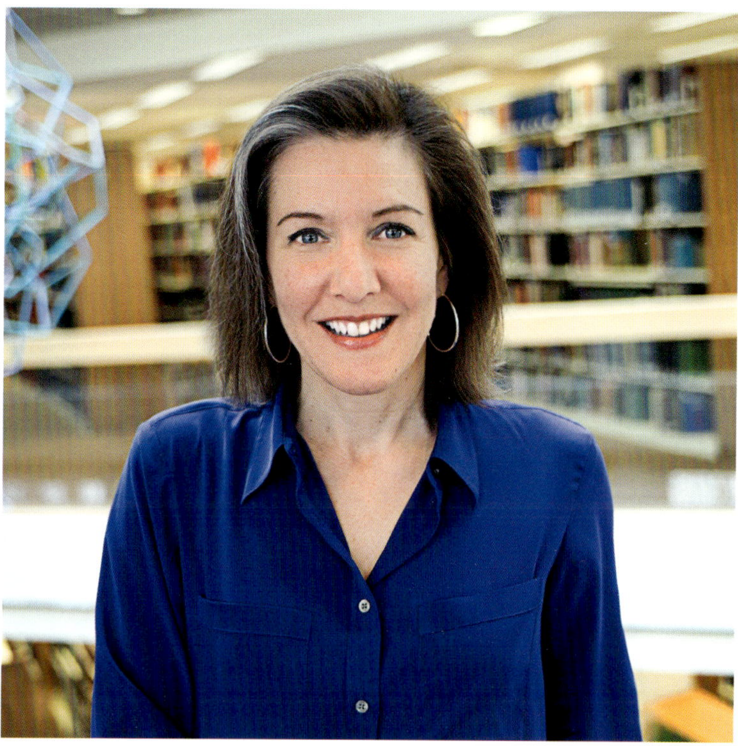

Hannah Buxbaum, vice president for International Affairs, 2018–present. *Photograph courtesy of Indiana University.*

internships, and service learning. It also aimed at increasing participation in exchange programs and the recruitment and retention of top-quality students from overseas. Other priorities were to create the capacity to obtain and manage institutional development projects, to work with the Indiana University Alumni Association, and to establish an international network of gateway offices to serve the needs of IU academic and nonacademic units in different parts of the world. The gateways served as Indiana University's front door in culturally dynamic parts of the world and were an innovative direction for the office.

In November 2017, the Indiana University Board of Trustees confirmed that Hannah Buxbaum would succeed David Zaret as vice president for international affairs when he retired in June 2018. In announcing her appointment, President Michael McRobbie commented that "Hannah's background and extensive international experience make her the ideal candidate to serve as IU's next vice president for international affairs."[14]

Professor Buxbaum's international background and expertise eminently equipped her for the appointment. After completing a bachelor's degree and subsequently, a law degree, at Cornell University, she finished a master's degree in law at the University of Heidelberg. She became a faculty member in the Indiana University Law School in Bloomington in 1997, after working in international securities transactions in the New York and Frankfurt offices of Davis Polk & Wardwell. In the Maurer School of Law, she was appointed to the John E. Schiller Chair in Legal Ethics. Her research has investigated private international law, and international litigation and jurisdiction, and she has taught courses on conflict of laws, contracts, international business transactions, and international litigation. Her visiting appointments have been at several foreign universities, including Humboldt University, the University of Cologne, and Université Paris II, Panthéon-Assas. She has also had overseas teaching assignments on international regulatory law at The Hague Academy of International Law, and in Buenos Aires.[15]

Buxbaum has published in leading US and European journals. Her recent research has been on the jurisdictional issues presented in cross-border securities and antitrust litigation. She is also the coauthor of a leading casebook on international business transactions. It is noteworthy that in doing her research, she received several research fellowships including one from the Alexander von Humboldt Foundation.

Buxbaum served as an active member in a number of national organizations, including the American Society of International Law, the American Society of Comparative Law, and the Association of American Law Schools. She was elected to the American Law Institute, where she advised on the Restatement of Foreign Relations Law, Jurisdiction, and Judgments. She was also a member of the International Academy of Comparative Law. In 2016, she joined the advisory board of the Max Planck Institute for Comparative and International Private Law in Hamburg.[16]

From January 2012 to December 2013, she served as the Maurer School's interim dean. From 2015 to 2018, she was the inaugural academic director of the Indiana University Europe Gateway in Berlin.

A time line of selected major projects demonstrates the depth and range of IU's international reach. They will be elaborated on in the individual chapters.

1879 IU establishes its first three-month overseas study programs in Europe for undergraduate students.

1891 First international student, Takekuma Okada, arrives from Japan.

1901 Education professor Elmer Burritt Bryan accepts appointment as principal of the Insular Normal school in the Philippines. Other IU education faculty members also go there.

1929 Summer program for IU students to study music, art, and languages takes place in Munich, Germany.

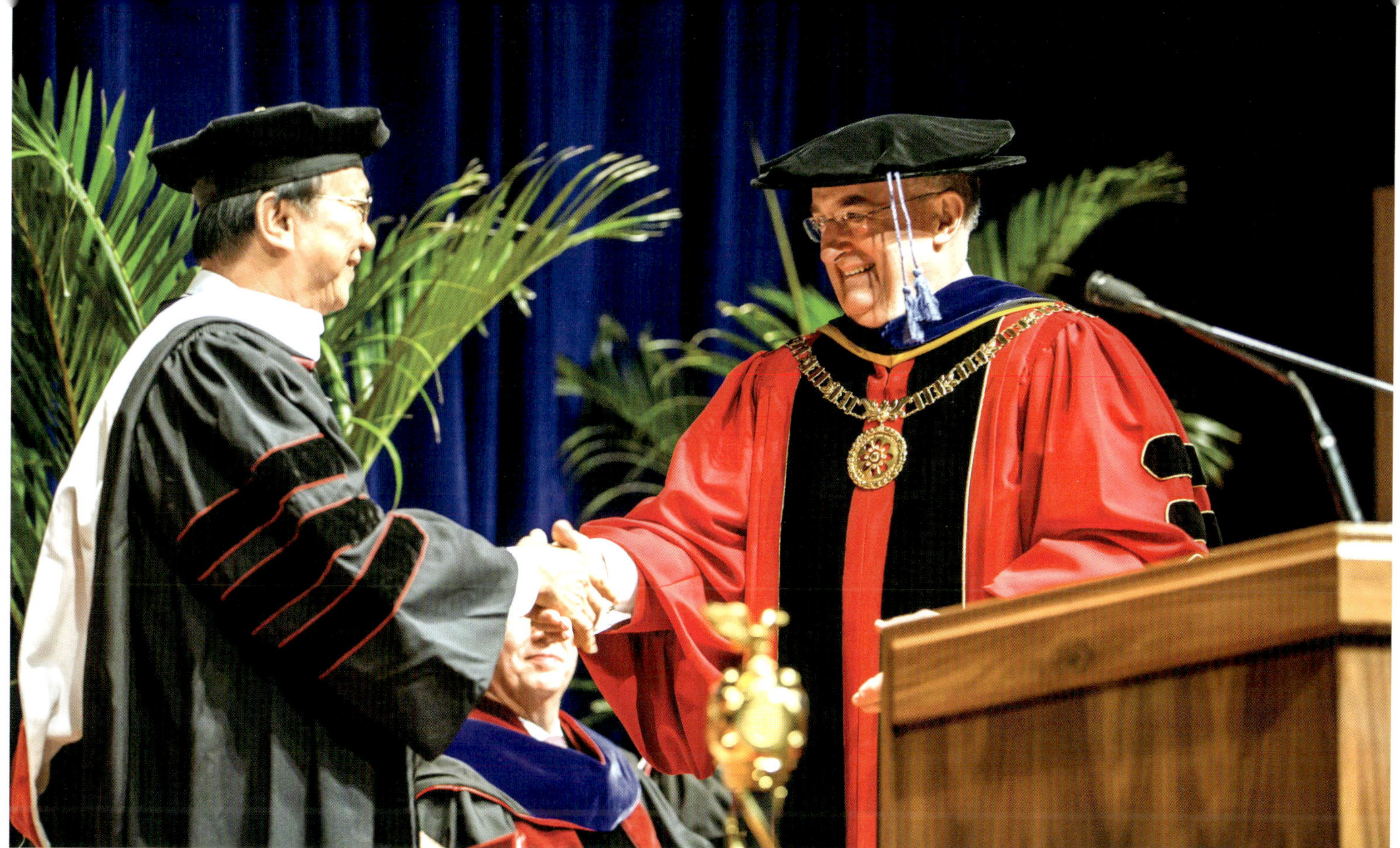

Indiana University president Michael A. McRobbie congratulates National Institute of Development Administration president Sombat Thamrongthanyawong. *Photograph courtesy of Indiana University, 2013.*

1948 Herman B Wells goes to Berlin for six months to work on the reconstruction of Berlin. He plays a formative role in the establishment of the Free University of Berlin.

1954 An agreement is reached between the IU School of Education, the Prasan Mitr College of Education, Bangkok, and the Thai Ministry of Education to develop a four-year program.

1966 IU assists in the creation and building of a national university for graduate students in Islamabad, Pakistan.

The National Institute of Development Administration is established in Thailand.

1976 Indiana University becomes actively involved with the study of Poland with Polish Studies in Bloomington and the American Studies Center at the University of Warsaw.

1982 An agreement is signed with Hangzhou University in China.

1984 IU assists Khanya College in South Africa to provide better access to higher education for disadvantaged black students.

1985 IU is the lead institution working with Institute Teknologi MARA in Malaysia to establish a two-year undergraduate program.

IU administers the first La Caixa Fellowship Program for outstanding students from Spain.

1988 IU School of Medicine launches AMPATH (Academic Model Providing Access to Healthcare) in Kenya.

1994 IU's School of Education and Ryazan State Pedagogical University in Russia engage in a two-year effort.

The Parliamentary Development Program launches in Ukraine.

1995 The Burmese Refugee Scholarship Program is established for Burmese refugees from India and Thailand to come to the United States.

1999 IU receives a grant for the American University in Kyrgyzstan to develop into a top regional institution.

2001 South East Europe University is established in Macedonia to increase higher education opportunities for disadvantaged ethnic Albanians.

2002 IU collaborates with University of Pretoria faculty of law to organize a Legislative Drafting Workshop in South Africa.

A project is undertaken to improve the Northern Campus of the University of Namibia.

2006 The Afghanistan Higher Education Project is funded to improve institutional administration and pre-service secondary teacher education.

2008 IU receives a grant to assist the Center for Excellence in Health and Life Sciences at the University of Liberia and address a national shortage of health care workers.

Robert P. McKinney School of Law (IUPUI) operates master of laws degree program at Cairo University and Alexandria University.

2009 An agreement is signed for the creation of an IU–Australian National University (ANU) Pan Asia Institute.

2011 A Higher Education Leadership and Management project strengthens management systems in Indonesia's higher education.

2012 A School of Education project addresses problems in higher education in South Sudan.

2013 Gateway office opens in Delhi.
Gateway office opens in Beijing.

2014 Office of International Development granted US State Department contract to develop and administer a program for Burmese youth leaders.

2015 Gateway office opens in Berlin.
IU Kelley School of Business awarded US State Department grant to partner with Bethlehem University, Palestine, to develop entrepreneurs and support Palestinian economic development.

2018 Gateway office opens in Mexico City.

2019 Gateway office opens in Bangkok, Thailand.

2 | INDIANA UNIVERSITY *in* Germany

AT THE END OF WORLD WAR II, HERMAN B WELLS WAS CALLED ON to play an important role in the reconstruction of a devastated Berlin. In the tenth year of his presidency, he embarked on a major overseas effort as the director of the educational and cultural affairs branch of the Office of Military Government, United States (OMGUS), in postwar Berlin. Wells's months in Berlin enhanced his understanding of the importance of international research and teaching, and this was to have an impact on the future of Indiana University. He had already emerged as an innovative university president, but he had limited international experience. His involvement in the renewal and reconstruction of Germany and his formative role in the establishment of the Free University of Berlin influenced him deeply. The impact of this experience was evident in the speeches he gave on his return to the United States and in letters he sent to IU friends and colleagues.

In early May 1947, a representative of OMGUS in Germany contacted Wells with the request that he consider heading its education and cultural affairs branch for a year in Berlin. General Lucius Clay, the military governor of the American sector in Germany, had requested Wells for the job. Clay had been

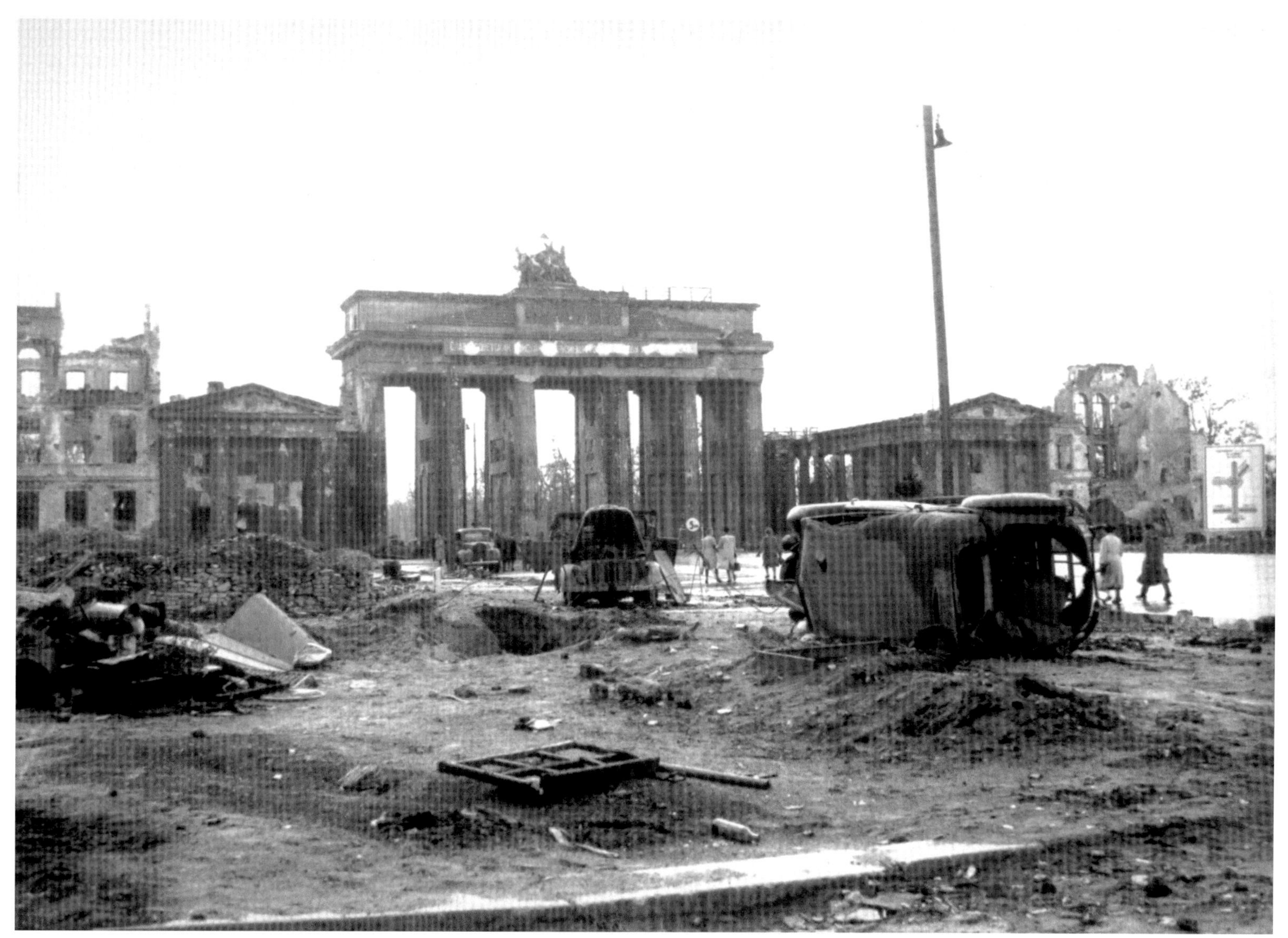

Destruction near the Brandenburg Gate, Berlin, circa 1945.
Photograph by Keystone/Getty Images.

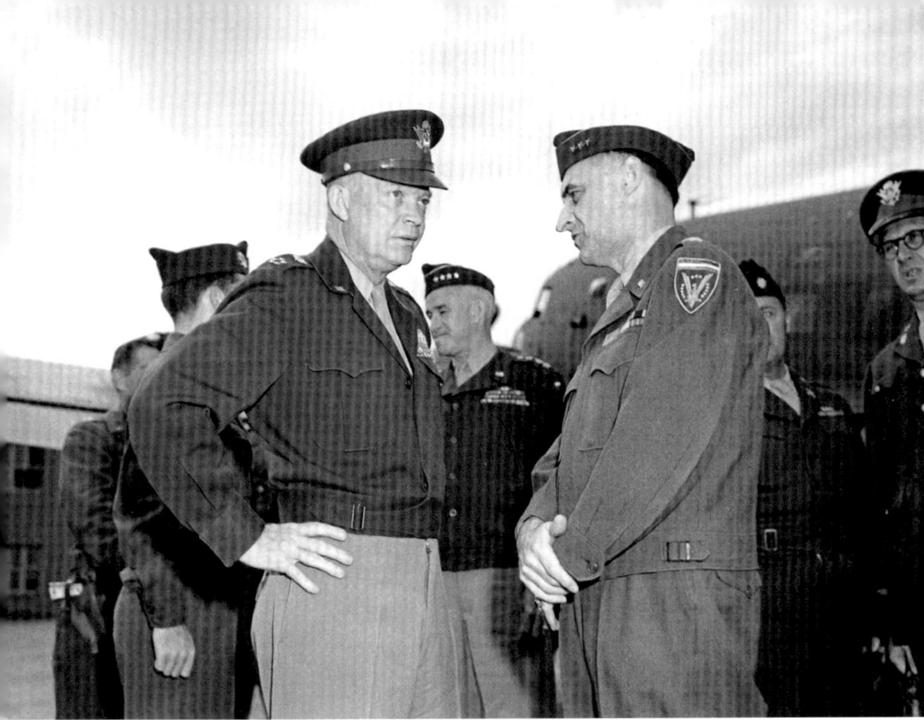

General Dwight D. Eisenhower (*left*) talks with Lieutenant General Lucius B. Clay at Gatow Field, Berlin, attending the Potsdam Conference, 1945. *Photograph courtesy of United States Army Signal Corps, Harry S. Truman Library and Museum.*

promoted to general in March 1947 and succeeded General Dwight D. Eisenhower as the military governor of occupied Germany, or the head of OMGUS. His responsibilities included social issues related to Germany's recovery from the war.[1]

With the permission of the Indiana University Board of Trustees, Wells traveled briefly to Germany in mid-1947 to survey the state of affairs in the OMGUS Berlin office and to get a sense of the immediate needs of the organization and of conditions within Germany in general. When he reported his impressions to Clay, the general asked him to return to Berlin as his personal cultural adviser. Wells wanted to accept the position, but the board of trustees, as well as Governor Ralph F. Gates, had reservations about his absence from IU.[2] This was a time of growth and change as well as a surge in enrollments at Indiana University because of the large number of war veterans who were taking advantage of the GI Bill to further their education. Both Governor Gates and the board felt that a long international appointment for Wells would take him away from Bloomington at a time when he was most needed.[3]

To support his position, Wells created a list of pros and cons for the board of trustees, which he presented to them in September 1947:

Pro

Job is great importance
If successful will redound to reputation of the University.
A good year to be away.
The year ahead is expected to be a normal one.
No great problems are to be expected.
Plans for the future year are laid and will be presented to Faculty shortly after opening.
Have a full admin. Staff.
This kind of absence in future years probably will not be possible

Con

Psychology—lack of realization on the part of people that we are thru the worst. The critical time is behind us rather than ahead.
Possibility that something might go wrong here.
Possibility that I might fail on the mission.
Extra responsibilities that might be put on my colleagues.
Some opportunities for advancement might be lost.

Personal consideration
The task is appealing because it is so different and so challenging.
Involves financial sacrifice.
The year ahead promises to be the easiest in the 10 that I have been president—Reluctantly, I would forgo it.
Discomfort of Germany
Such a booming year regret not to be in on it.[4]

After some negotiating and with telegrams from General Clay to both the Indiana University Board of Trustees and Governor Gates, Wells was granted a six-month leave. His appointment as director of education and cultural affairs in Berlin was to last until late May 1948, when he was expected to return to Bloomington in time for the early June commencement ceremony. In his absence, his duties at IU would be shared among five board members, and he agreed to keep in regular contact with Bloomington. Wells set off for Germany with crates of carefully selected supplies, food, and materials.[5]

On arrival, he saw his task as challenging: "My assignment as Cultural Affairs Adviser to General Clay is proving to be one of the most interesting experiences I have had. I am charged with responsibility for coordinating the American reorientation effort in Germany in all its many phases: education, press, radio, publications, music, theater, motion pictures, and religious affairs, among others."[6]

In Berlin, Wells was assisted by Peter Fraenkel, a recent IU graduate who was then studying for his master's degree in physics at Harvard University. Fraenkel's family background was German, and he was able to advise and translate for Wells.[7] Fraenkel would later return to Indiana University, where he had a long career as an administrator.[8]

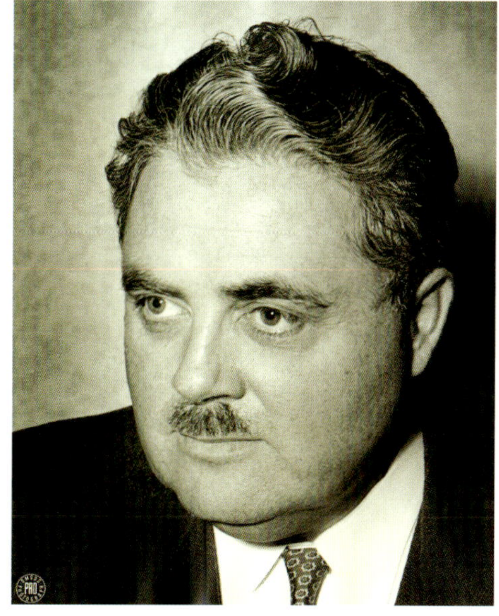

This portrait of Herman B Wells was taken by the Office of Military Government, United States, in 1947, probably for identification purposes.
IU Archives (P0041669).

After Wells arrived, he wrote to the board of trustees and to the *Indiana Daily Student* to explain his work and to share his impressions of German higher education. He vividly and frankly expressed what he encountered in Berlin. In speeches that he gave when he returned to the United States in the late spring of 1948, Wells reflected on what he had seen as barriers to progress in German higher education. These included collateral damage from World War II such as food and housing shortages, the role of the professors in German society, and the elite nature of higher education. He also noted that many Germans were fearful, or at best uncertain, about the very idea of democracy. Frank Banta, a young US Army Intelligence officer who was stationed in Berlin at the time and who later

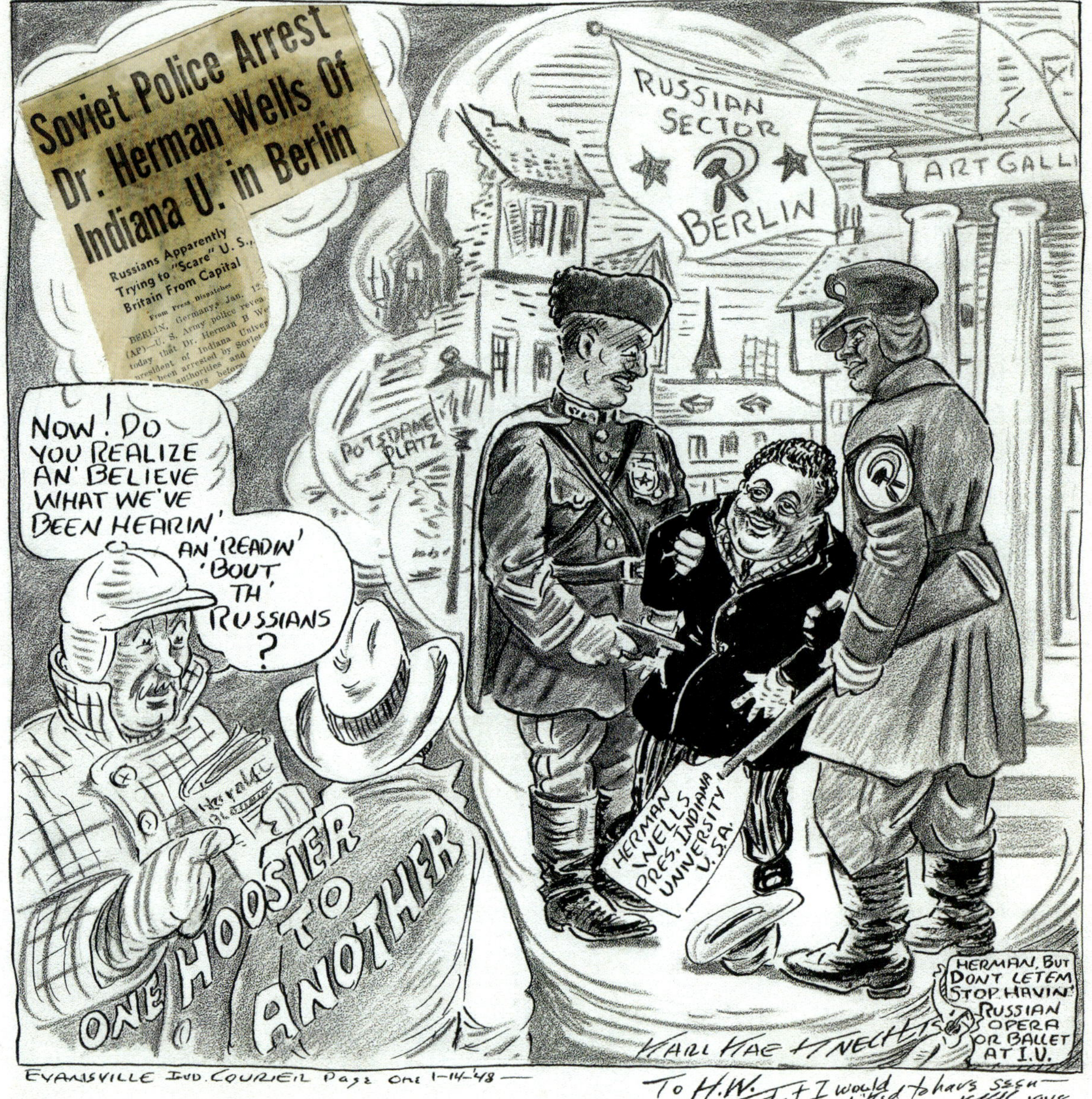

Karl Kae Knecht, cartoonist for the Evansville Courier, captured Wells's arrest in Berlin in 1949.

IU Archives (P0031151).

became a professor of German at Indiana University, referred to the prevailing perspective on democracy by quoting a German colleague:

> The conception of democracy as a balance of freedom and responsibility was incomprehensible to her, as to many. "Do you know what democracy is?" she asked me once. "A crowded train pulls into a station. A man in the middle of a coach wants to get off, but cannot force his way through the aisles. Just as he is about to reach the door, new passengers begin to board, and he is pushed back into the middle of the coach. The train starts off again. As it picks up speed, he reaches up in desperation and pulls the emergency break. The train screams to a halt, passengers are flung about the coach, and the man in the middle walks over them to reach the door and leaves the train. That is democracy."[9]

At the time, the Soviets, who occupied the eastern part of Germany as well as the Russian Sector in Berlin, reintroduced communism to Germany. The overall German population was wary of the occupying forces, and the general mood of the country after World War II was low. Wells had a personal incident with Soviet power when he strayed by accident into the Soviet sector of Berlin and was detained for several hours. A cartoon in the Indianapolis press documents the event, with the punch line, "Don't let 'em stop havin' Russian opera or ballet at I.U."

Wells vividly described the incident:

> I had an unpleasant brush with the Russian military. On one Sunday afternoon, Peter Fraenkel and I had driven into the Russian sector of Berlin to deliver a CARE package to Peter's childhood nurse . . . enroute home . . . we saw a brightly lit shop in the otherwise dark Potsdamer Platz . . . I asked our driver, PFC Wade Ferris, to take us over to see what was going on. Later we learned that it was a fence run by Russian soldiers for antiques taken from German houses. All innocent, Peter asked a Russian solider nearby if the store was open. The solider shook his head and, as Peter returned to the car, detained us with an order to halt, reinforced by a gun. . . . The soldier accused us of driving round and round Potsdamer Platz taking pictures in a manner unfriendly to the Soviet Union. Though it was evident that the charge against us was fabricated because we had no camera, it was two hours before we were released into the custody of an American Military Police captain.[10]

Wells wanted to talk with many people and to see as much of Germany as possible to advise General Clay. A photograph shows Wells, accompanied by Banta, engaged in discussions with young students and their teacher in a classroom.

The condition of higher education in Germany was no better than the state of its cities. In a letter to the *Indiana Daily Student*, Wells mentioned that many university buildings had been partially or completely destroyed and that materials—including textbooks, paper, pens and pencils, and library materials—were scarce. In the Western Occupied Zone, only five of the twenty-three universities and technical institutes remained undamaged by the war.[11] Frank Banta explains the state of German universities while he was in Berlin: "I was given a bicycle and a list of institutes of various kinds and was asked to check whether they still existed. Some of them did and some did not. I enjoyed very much doing that because it took me all over Berlin at that time, and Berlin was a big city. I was certainly not over all of it—it is 29 miles one way and 30 miles the other way—I found some of the institutes still in existence. Some places were just another pile of bricks."[12]

He goes on to describe how difficult it was for students to find suitable places to live and study: "Most German universities were not residential prior to the war. Students did not have access to dormitories, so the challenge to find adequate student housing in university towns led to crowded student living conditions in areas where many were already homeless."[13] Indeed, he wrote that the lives of many students were far from idyllic: "Students were frequently required to do manual labor to clear building rubble on campus for mere pennies an hour as part of their enrollment requirements. . . . Disease was also widespread: 25–30% of university students were tubercular."[14]

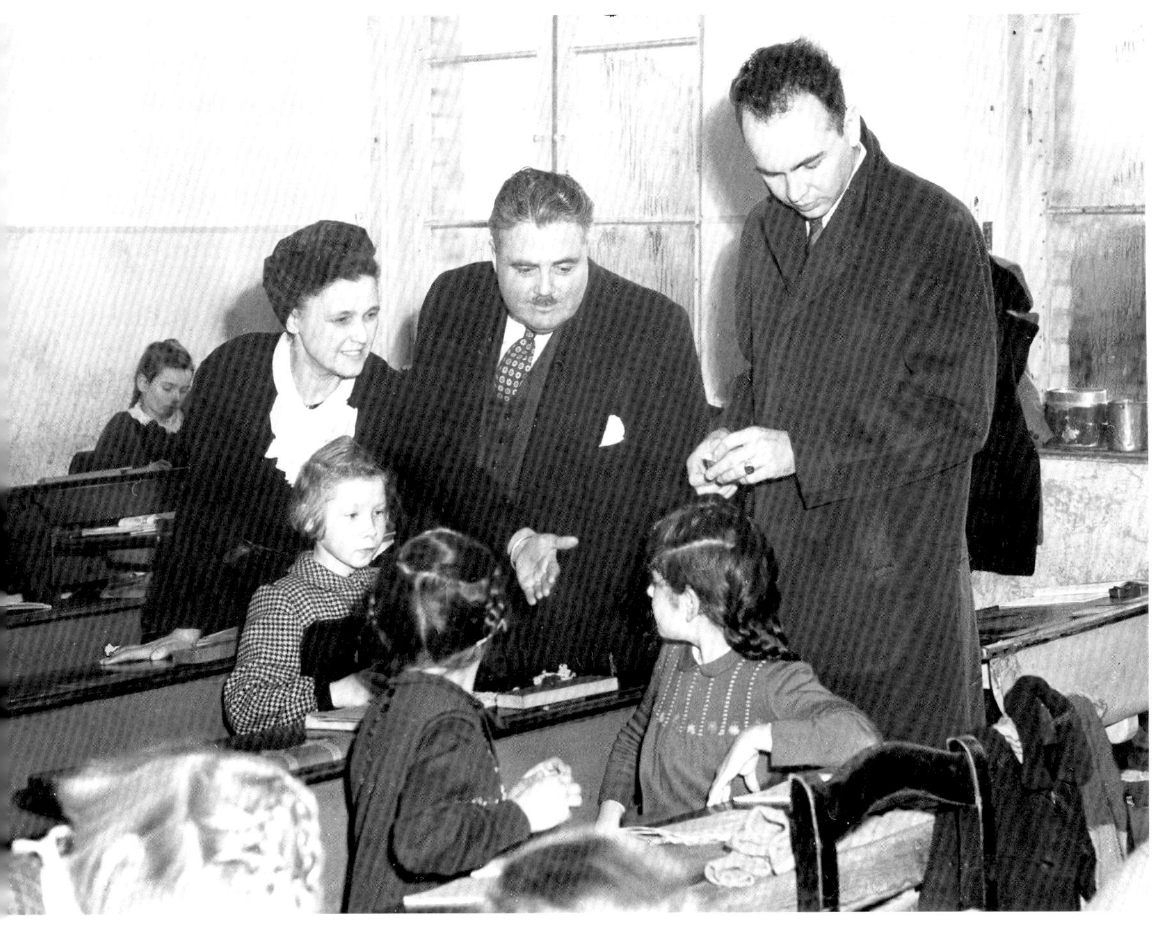

Herman Wells (*center*) and Frank Banta (*right*) in a German classroom, 1948. Wells was the adviser on cultural affairs to the military governor and acting chief of educational and cultural affairs for the US Occupied Zone in Germany, and Banta was the chief of the cultural exchange section, Educational and Cultural Relations Division, Office of Military Government, United States. Banta later became a member of the faculty of Indiana University. *IU Archives (P0041668).*

It is in this environment that Wells came to make a major contribution to German higher education; he was to be instrumental in the establishment of the Free University of Berlin. In mid-April 1948, a handful of student protestors from the University Unter den Linden were dismissed from the university after calling for educational options other than the higher education institution that had come under communist Soviet control at the end of the war. Kendall Foss, an American staff writer for the *Neue Zeitung*, an American newspaper for Germans, covered the story and befriended the student protestors. Foss was a Harvard-educated journalist from New York who began his career at United Press International's London office in 1927. From there, he worked as a foreign correspondent for the International News Service and a variety of publications, including the *New York Times*, the *Washington Post*, and *Time* magazine. In 1944, Foss became a contributing editor of *Time* magazine while simultaneously working for the *New York Post* as a foreign correspondent and political columnist.[15] Foss suggested that the students call on OMGUS to see whether the military government might support democratic higher education in Berlin.

After meeting with Foss, Clay suggested that he contact Wells to see if anything could be done. Wells frequently opened his home to visitors on the weekends for social calls, and knowing this, Foss took the student protestors to meet with him the very afternoon after he had spoken with Clay. Wells received Foss and the students and listened to them with great interest. He was impressed by the group's determination to find new educational options in the Western sector and promised to take the group's specific request to Clay.[16]

Clay worked in his office early on Sunday mornings, and Wells went to speak with him about the request the day after the group had come to see him. To Wells's surprise, Clay was highly enthusiastic about supporting a new university and even suggested that it should open that same year. Wells cautioned that this would be a complicated undertaking and difficult to achieve in such a short time; it would need a faculty, and this seemed formidable. Nonetheless, with Clay's support, Wells began to set it up. Acting quickly, his first move was to hire Kendall Foss as his special assistant to help with the possible creation of a new university in the American sector, and he asked his staff to do a feasibility study for a possible new university.[17] Wells cautioned, "The new university should be a German university developed by German leadership," and "The enterprise would have to be carried out well if it was to be carried out at all."[18]

Wells came to make a major contribution to German higher education; he was to be instrumental in the establishment of the Free University of Berlin.

Wells spent the short remainder of his time in Berlin working with OMGUS officials and academics to establish an "academic philosophy and principles of university governance."[19] Historian James Tent writes that Wells was "a catalyst for the creation of the Free University of Berlin" and "was probably the most vital link in the American chain of officialdom" leading to the university's founding.[20] In his own words, Wells described his final weeks in Berlin as follows: "It was from this initiative that the Free University of Berlin sprang. I did not stay long enough to do more than start the machinery to establish it, but the university opened the following fall after I had returned to Bloomington. It started with almost two thousand students and became a powerful influence for freedom and democracy in German higher education for a number of years."[21]

The founding motto of the Free University Berlin—"Truth, Justice, Freedom"—has shaped its history since 1948. It is the largest university in Germany's capital and one of the largest in the nation. Over the years, Indiana University and the Free University have maintained a strong relationship; generations of students from both universities have been part of a continuing exchange.

During his stay, Wells also played a role in opening up Germany for scholarly exchanges. His staff had become increasingly aware of the need for a major exchange of students and scholars. In *Being Lucky*, he wrote that, in 1946, George Zook, then president of the American Council on Education had led a delegation that called for these exchanges, and their revival became official policy in 1947. However, there were only limited funds for the exchanges. Wells recalls: "It was against this background that I undertook to express to Clay the belief of our staff that the time had come for widespread introduction of German-American exchanges of student scholars, which would of course require appropriation of funds to finance the movement of the Germans to the United States and of the Americans to Germany. I took this idea to Clay early one Sunday morning and found him quite interested in it, but skeptical of its practicality. In fact, he said he believed it was too soon to begin such exchanges."[22]

Over the years, Indiana University has maintained strong ties with Germany.

However, Wells was determined to do something about this. On a trip to Washington, DC, with the help of colleagues at the American Council on Education, he was able to get an appropriation to begin the process: "Clay wrote on my report of the trip to Washington: Dr. Wells: "A lot done in a short time. Thanks again. Please follow Washington developments closely and let me know if you receive any 'flac.'"[23]

Wells goes on to write, "When the Federal Republic of Germany did me the honor of conferring upon me the Commander's Cross of the Order of Merit in 1960, that recognition came in part, I am convinced, because of this initiative."[24] At the end of his six-month appointment, Wells returned to Bloomington. There is evidence that he, or perhaps General Clay, requested an extension of his OMGUS appointment by another six months, but the board of trustees unanimously voted it down in the spring of 1948.[25]

Wells's time in Berlin provides a brief glimpse into US efforts to democratize Germany as well as a unique lens through which to examine his future agenda for higher education; his observations and reflections are a testament to his particular style of leadership. His time in Germany and his involvement in the establishment of the Free University contributed to his growing international experience and was an inspiration for increasing Indiana University's international activity.[26]

Over the years, Indiana University has maintained strong ties with Germany. Many faculty in the sciences, arts, music, languages, humanities, and law have studied and conducted research there on IU grants, Deutscher Akademischer Austausch Dienst (German Academic Exchange Services), the Fulbright US Student Program, and other awards. Beginning in the 1960s, IU created study abroad opportunities for undergraduate students in Germany. A program was established with Hamburg University in 1965 which operated for more than three decades. In the summer of 1997, the location shifted to Freiburg University, because the ambience of the town near the Black Forest in the *Baden-Württemberg* area of southwest Germany appealed to many students.

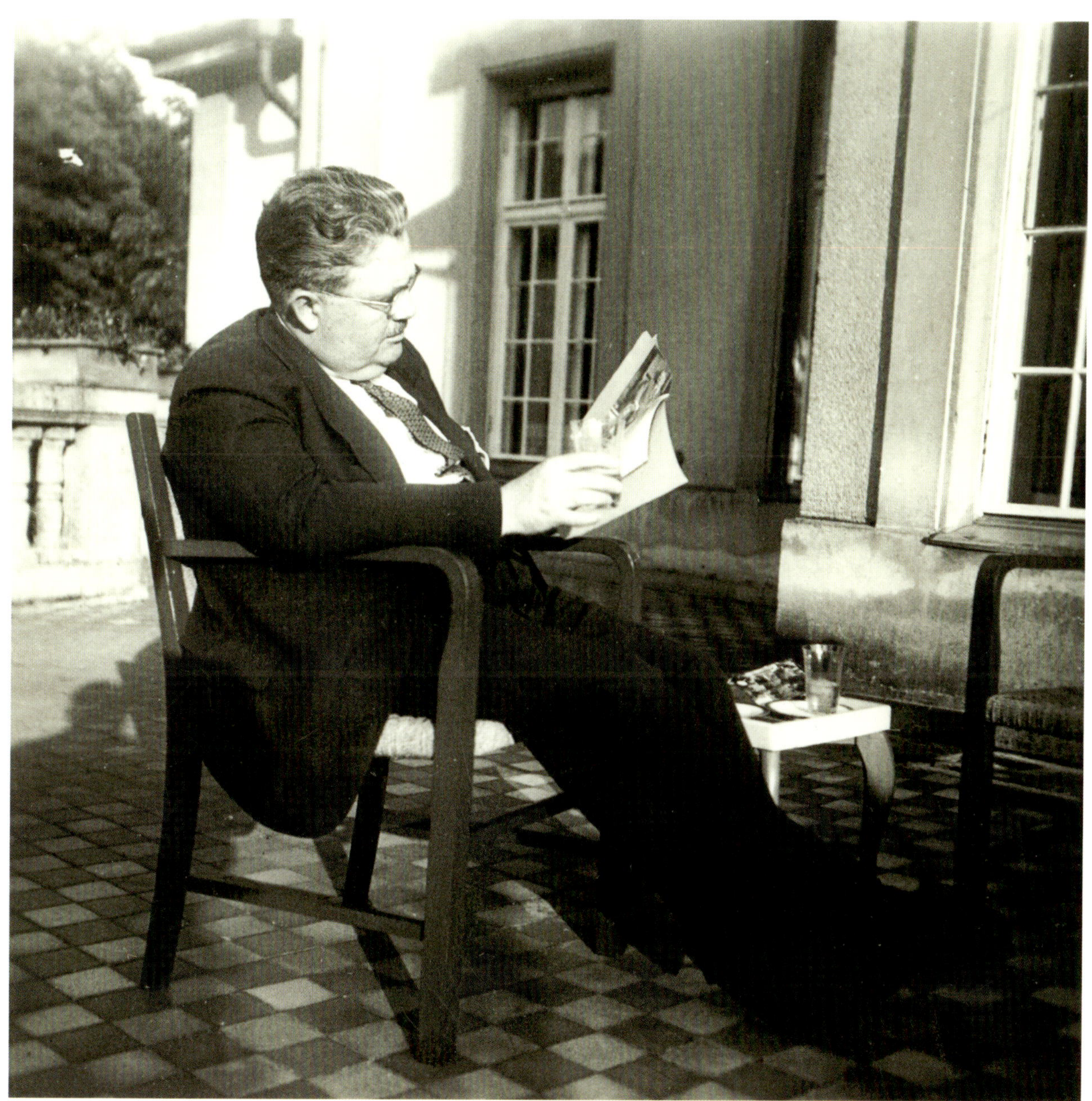

Herman Wells on the terrace of his house in Germany, 1947/1948.

Photograph by Peter Fraenkel. IU Archives (P0050221).

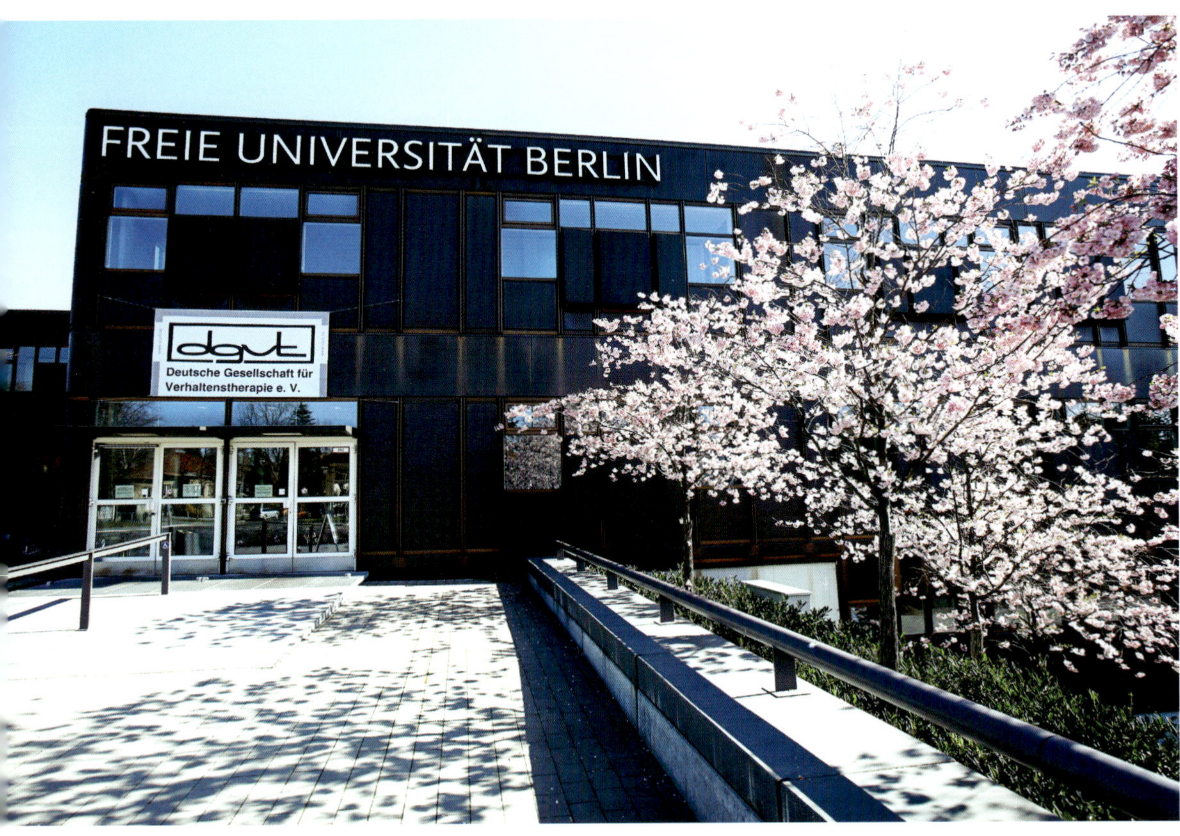

In the 1950s, a special student exchange was created with the University of Kiel due in large part to the work of Jost Delbrück. Delbrück first came to the Indiana University School of Law in the 1950s. After earning his LLM degree from IU in 1960, Delbrück later served as the dean of the law school at the University of Kiel and as the university's president from 1985 to 1989. Delbrück fostered strong new ties between IU and the University of Kiel by creating further opportunities for IU law school graduates to study at Kiel and for students from Germany to come to IU. Many law faculty members also benefited from the relationship. Delbrück received an honorary IU doctorate in 2002.

On a visit to Germany in 2010, President Michael McRobbie reaffirmed ties with the Free University of Berlin and signed an agreement with the University of Freiburg.

Dr. Wells played an important role in rebuilding war-torn Germany. In particular, he helped establish the Free University of Berlin, which provided a generation of art scholars their academic home. He also transformed Indiana University into an institution with an international reputation for excellence.

—Michael McRobbie

In December 2010, McRobbie visited the Free University and met with the rector to reaffirm Indiana University's long history and friendship. The two men met in a reception room on campus that had been the meeting room for the leaders of the Allied Forces after the war. In November 2011, McRobbie returned to Berlin as head of a delegation that was returning a fifteenth-century painted panel, *The Flagellation of Christ*, to the Jagdschloss Grunewald, where it was housed before the war. After World War II, some British and American soldiers carried home small items from collections; such was the case with this panel. In 2004, the IU Art Museum was contacted by the Stiftung Preußische Schlösser und Gärten about this panel. After careful research, curators discovered that this work had apparently been taken from Jagdschloss Grunewald and ultimately purchased in good faith by Herman Wells from a reputable gallery in London in 1967.[27]

In 1985, Wells donated the panel to the IU Art Museum, where it was on display. In 2006, Heidi Gealt, director of the IU Art Museum, announced that, based on the evidence collected by IU and the German museum, the painting would be returned to Berlin.

At the repatriation ceremony in Berlin, McRobbie remarked: "In voluntarily returning the painting, we are very pleased to be restoring this work of art to its rightful place. All institutions, worldwide, have a moral responsibility to repatriate property of this kind that can be proved to have once been the property of people or institutions in Germany, irrespective of whether this is legally necessary."[28]

At the ceremony, McRobbie also reflected on IU's relationship with Berlin: "Dr. Wells played an important role in rebuilding war-torn Germany. In particular, he helped establish the Free University of Berlin, which provided a generation of art scholars their academic home. He also transformed Indiana University into an institution with an international reputation for excellence."[29]

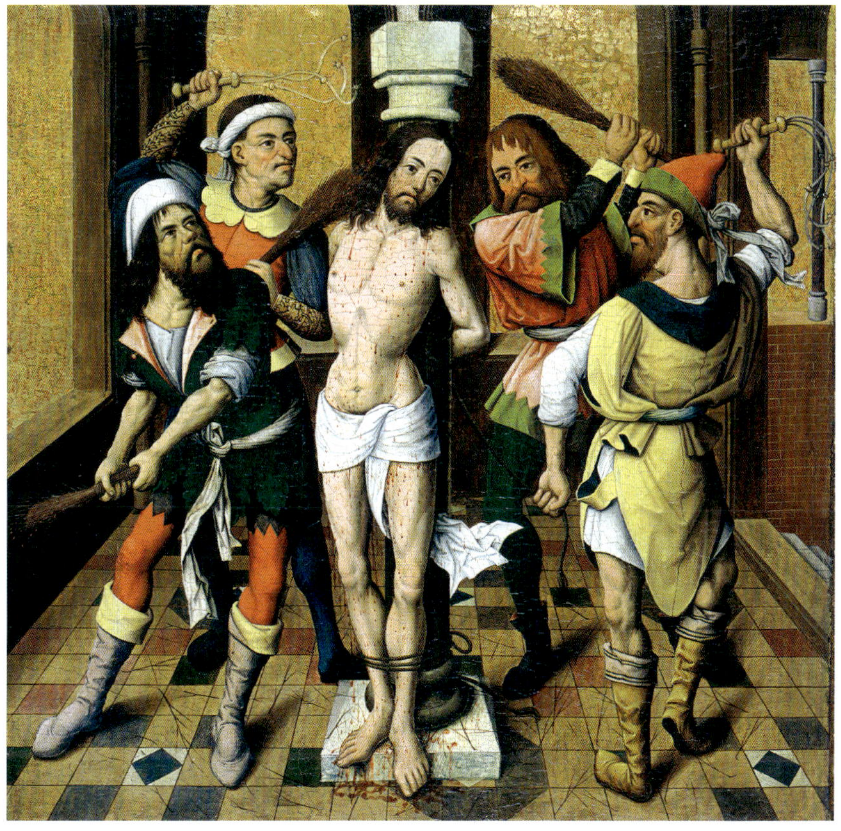

Above, A photo of *Flagellation of Christ*, purchased by Herman Wells at the Gallery Lasson on a 1967 trip to London. Wells donated the painting to the IU Art Museum (now the Eskenazi Museum of Art) in 1985. The original collector's mark on the back of the painting provided some of the strongest evidence of the painting's rightful home. *Photograph courtesy of the IU Eskenazi Museum of Art.*

Facing, Philological Library of the Free University of Berlin. *Photograph by Reiner Zensen/ullstein bild via Getty Images.*

3 | INDIANA UNIVERSITY *in* Thailand

Over the years, Indiana University has had a long, sustained, and highly productive relationship with universities in Thailand. In addition, generations of Thai students have come to Indiana, and many returned to positions of leadership in government or higher education. The first major venture took place in the 1950s, when the Thai government saw the need to improve the quality of the country's teacher training institutions and at a time when the US government had begun to focus on the development needs of Southeast Asian countries. The International Cooperation Administration, a precursor to the United States Agency for International Development, recruited Willis Porter, a professor at a state teacher's college in New York, to go to Thailand to review teacher training. Porter's report recommended that the IU School of Education should help to build a national school of teacher education for the whole of Thailand. Walter Laves of the IU Department of Government later went to Bangkok to negotiate a possible contract.

In 1954, an agreement was drawn up between IU's School of Education, the Prasan Mitr College of Education in Bangkok, and the Thai Ministry of Education, with funding provided by the US Foreign Operations Administration, which was beginning to fund technical assistance programs to strengthen government infrastructures in different countries; it had a particular interest in establishing institutes of public administration.[1]

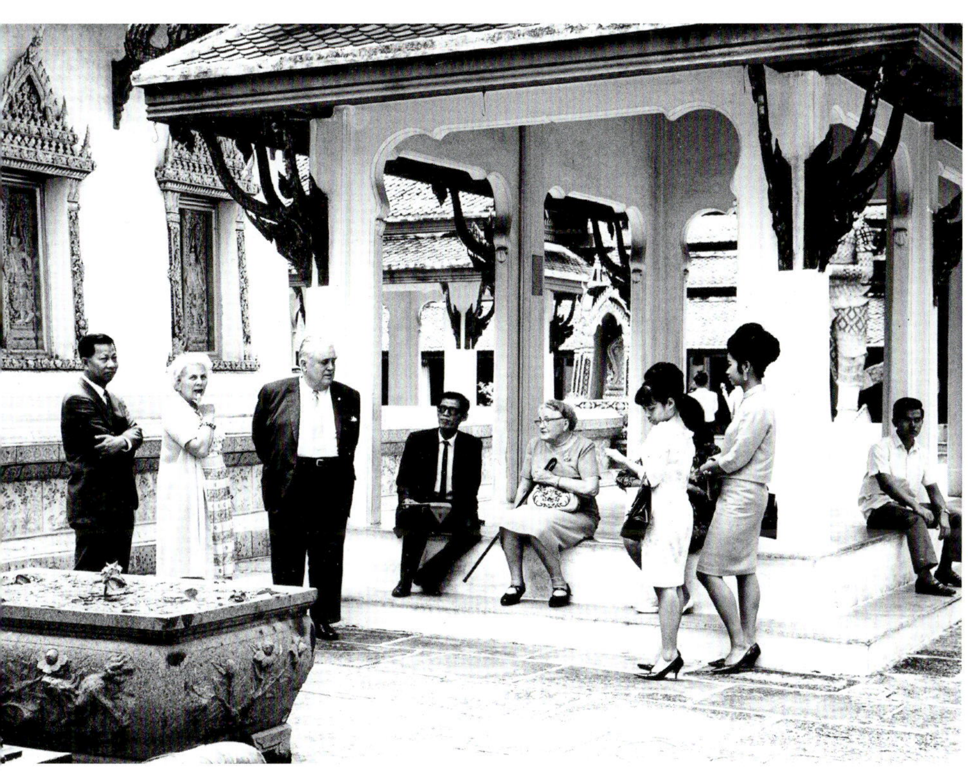

Herman Wells (*third from left*) and his mother, Anna Bernice Harting Wells (*seated center*), at Thammasat University, September 1965.
IU Archives (P0033119).

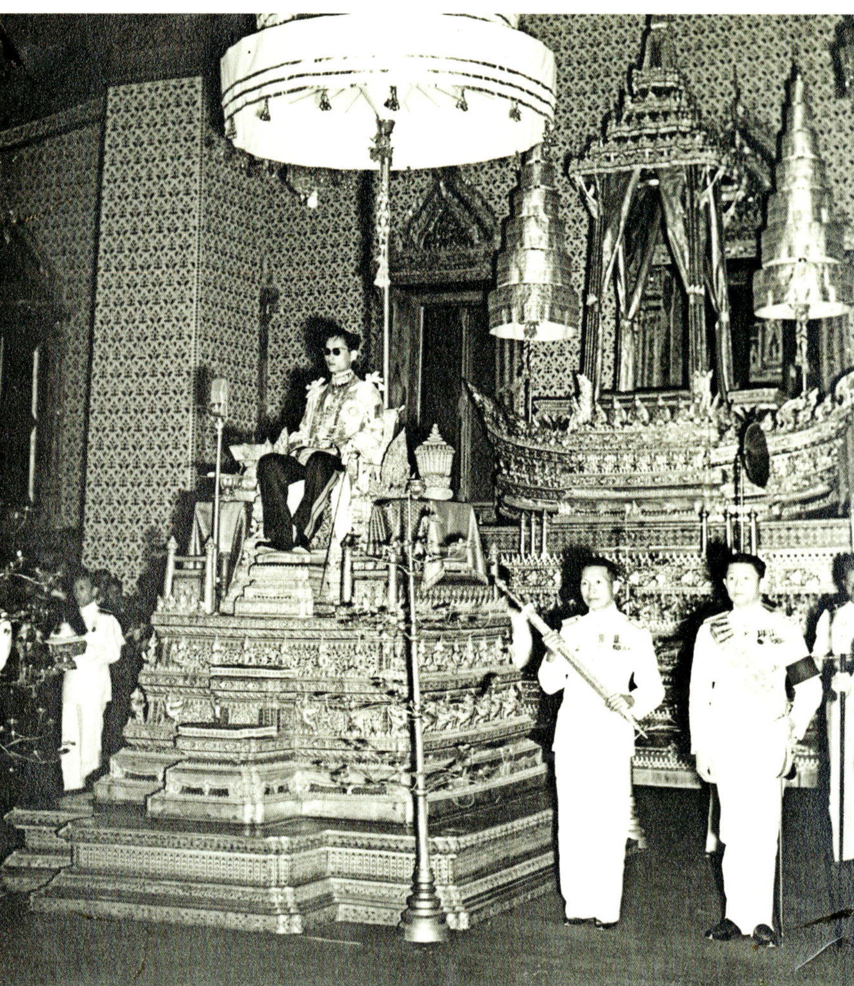

King Bhumbiol Adulyadej of Thailand in the Baisal Daksin Thorne Hall, Grand Palace, Bangkok.
IU Archives (P0077666).

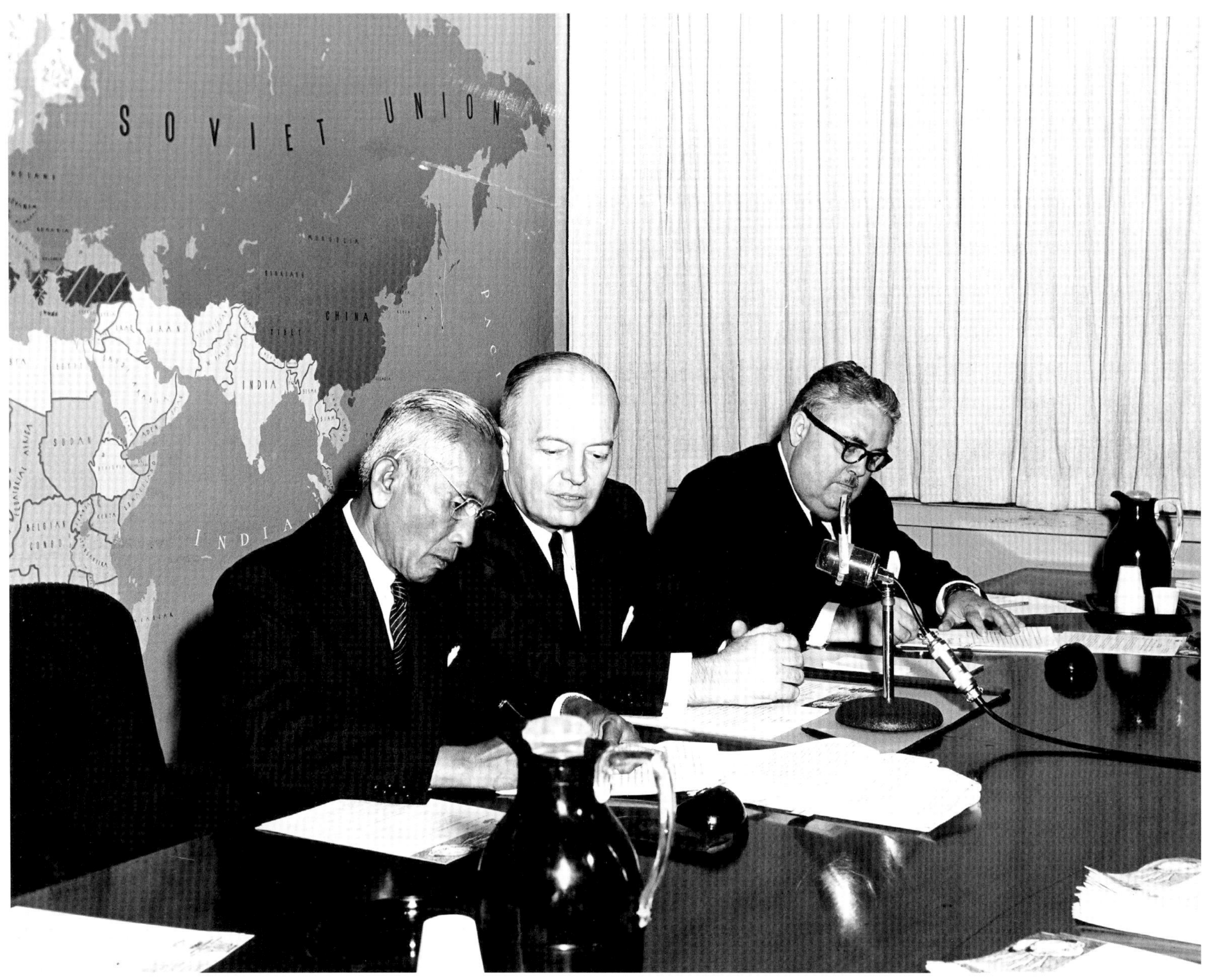
SOVIET UNION
CHINA
INDIA

Once an agreement was in place, IU's dean of the School of Education, Wendell Wright, spent several weeks in Thailand to develop a relevant bachelor's degree. For the eight years of this contract, many professionals and staff members, mostly senior faculty members from IU, went to Thailand for different lengths of time.[2]

During its involvement with the College of Education at Prasan Mitr, IU began discussions with the Thai government about a new institute of public administration. In May 1955, Indiana University signed a $1.5 million contract, funded by the US Agency for International Development and by the government of Thailand, to establish an Institute of Public Administration (IPA) at Thammasat University in Bangkok, which would train graduate students for a master's degree in public administration. The contract was signed in Washington, DC, by IU president Herman B Wells and by Thailand's prime minister P. Pibulsonggram, who was also rector of Thammasat University; the rector was in the United States on an official visit at the invitation of President Eisenhower. The objectives of the contract were to strengthen the academic program of Thammasat University in public administration; expand the research, extension, and staff training programs of the university; develop in-service training programs and facilities at the university for government officials; and provide training in the United States for a number of Thai students.[3]

IU's Walter Laves, chair of the Department of Government, who had been in Bangkok two years earlier to explore possibilities for public administration training, was responsible for preparing the agreement and directing the program. Under the terms of the contract, Thai graduate students would come to IU for special training, and IU would send specialists in various fields to Thammasat for stays of up to nine months. IU welcomed the opportunity to join Thammasat University in strengthening the latter's program in public administration. It was thought that manifold benefits would accrue to both the participating universities and the governments involved.[4]

IU's chief of party at Thammasat was Joseph Sutton, a professor of government who later became president of IU from 1968 to 1971. Lynton Caldwell, a professor of public administration and political science, served as coordinator of the program on the Bloomington campus. Between 1955 and 1962, forty-five people from IU went to Thailand, thirty-one on two-year assignments and ten on short-term consultancies.

A small number of advanced graduate students also went to Bangkok to assist with the work at the IPA and to conduct research for their doctoral degrees. John W. Ryan, who became president of IU in 1971, went there between 1955 and 1957 to finish his PhD dissertation on Bangkok government and administration.[5]

Political science professor William Siffin also served for three years from early 1957 to the end of 1959, teaching and

Facing, On May 3, 1955, Indiana University and the Thai government entered into an agreement, funded by USAID, to establish the Institute of Public Administration at Thammasat University in Bangkok. The contract was signed in Washington, DC, by IU president Herman B Wells (*right*) and by Thailand's prime minister and rector of Thammasat University, P. Pibulsonggram (*left*), who was in the United States on an official visit at the invitation of President Dwight Eisenhower. Also pictured is Harold E. Stassen (*center*), former governor of Minnesota and director of Foreign Operations for the Eisenhower administration. *IU Archives (P0033240).*

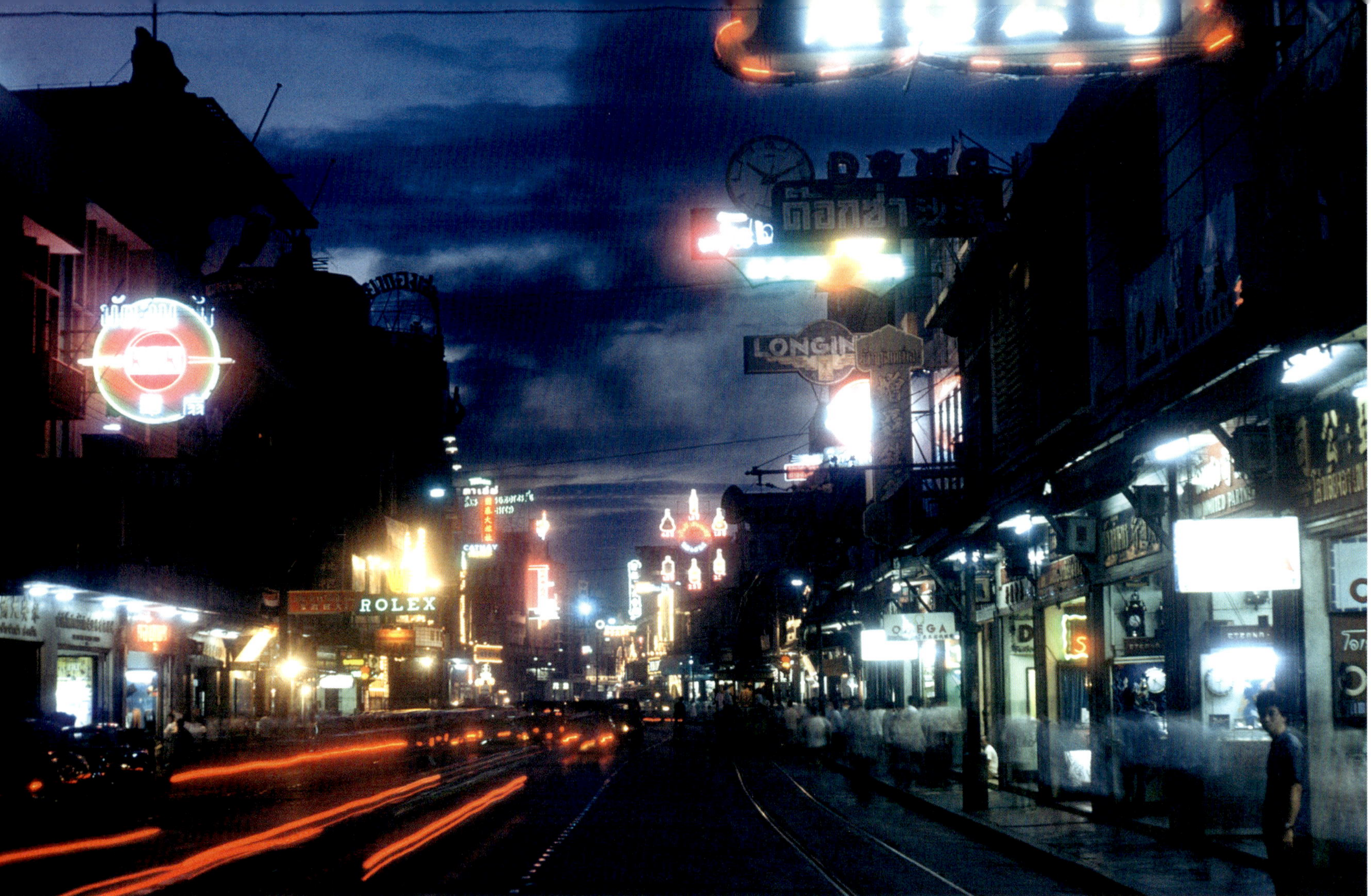

advising at both the IPA and Chulalongkorn University; in 1966, he wrote an important study on Thailand's bureaucracy and administrative structures.[6]

During this period, forty-one selected Thai students were sent to the United States for advanced training in public administration and related fields—thirty-five of them to Indiana University. By 1962, the staff of the IPA had grown to seventy-one, and seventeen of the nineteen professional staff were Thai. At that time, thirteen members of the Thai faculty held US graduate degrees.[7]

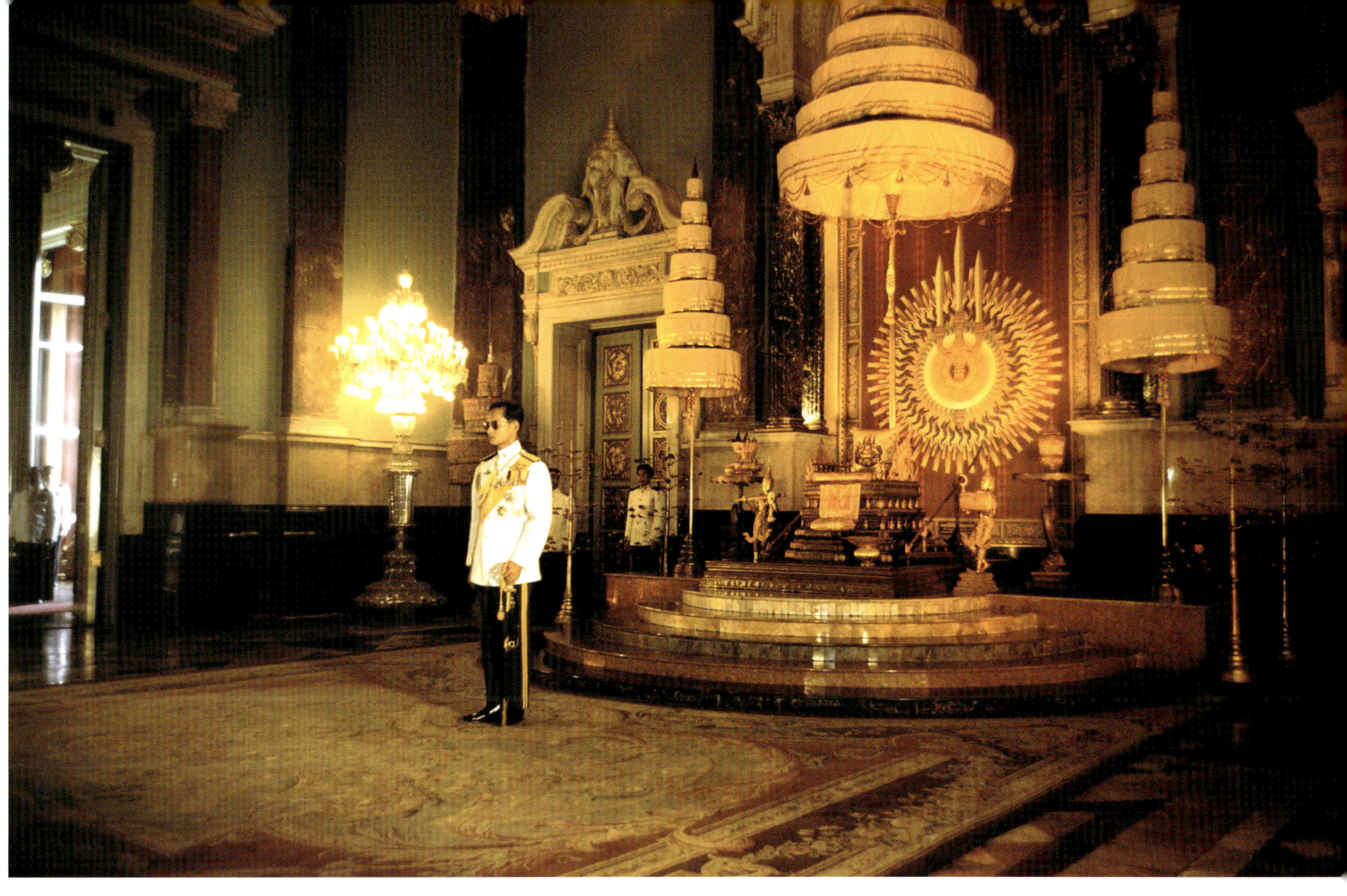

The private palace of King Bhumibol Adulyadej and Queen Kirikit, Bangkok, Thailand, 1961.

Photograph by Jack Garofalo/Paris Match via Getty Images.

Facing, Bangkok, Thailand, June 6, 1961. Signs are in Thai, Chinese, and English.

Photograph by W. Robert Moore/National Geographic/Getty Images.

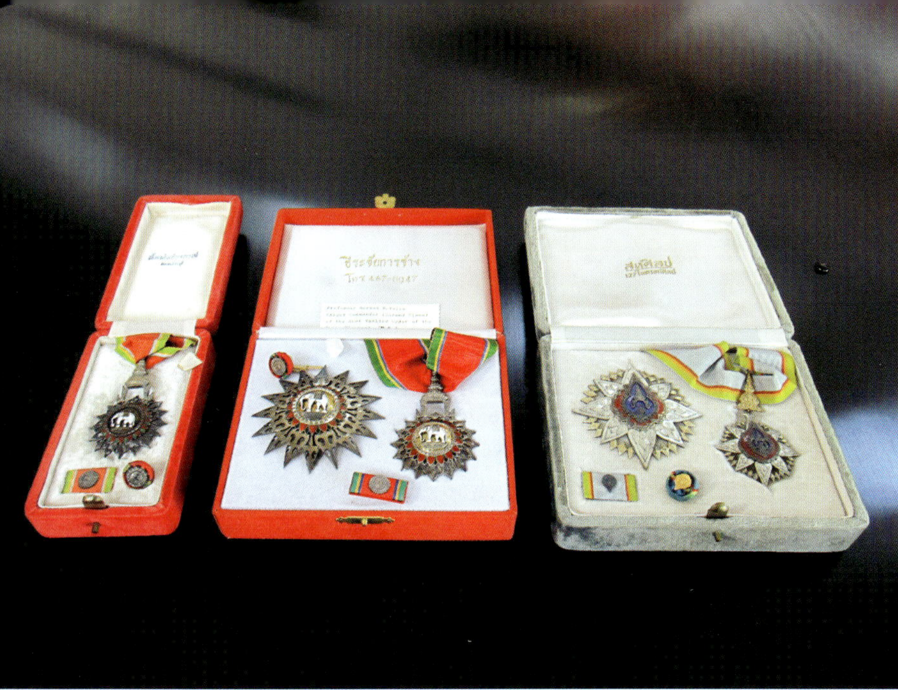

Knight Commander of the Most Exalted Order of the White Elephant, gifted to Herman Wells from a Thailand minister in October 1962. *Photograph courtesy of Lynn Schoch, IU International magazine.*

Facing, Herman Wells (*left*) calls on H. E. Field Marshall Thanom Kittikachorn (*right*), the prime minister, at Government House, September 1965. *IU Archives (P0033125).*

In 1962, IU's president Wells was recognized by the Thai government for his leadership with the programs at Prasan Mitr and Thammasat University; he received the Thailand government award of Commander of the Most Exalted Order of the White Elephant, one of Thailand's highest decorations.

Wells made several trips to Thailand, and in 1968, he was named a Knight Commander of the Most Noble Order of the Crown.[8]

In the early 1960s, US government support was declining due to changing national priorities in regard to Thailand. In this context, various significant events led to the establishment of the National Institute of Development Administration (NIDA). In 1963, King Bhumibol Adulyadej spoke with David Rockefeller of the Rockefeller Foundation about his vision for Thailand's development, which included establishing an advanced educational institute that would produce graduates who could serve the country. Thailand needed to produce graduates with a greater ability to respond to the social and political context in the service of national development.

In July 1963, deputy minister of the Ministry of National Development, Bunchana Attakor, wrote to the Ford Foundation's representative in Southeast Asia to request that the foundation appoint a preliminary team to work out, in collaboration with the Governing Council, a comprehensive plan for a National Institute of Development Administration. The foundation responded by appointing a team. It saw the idea of such an institute to be basically sound in the existing Thai setting.[9]

Nearly two years later, the Ford Foundation offered a multiyear technical assistance grant to the Midwest Universities

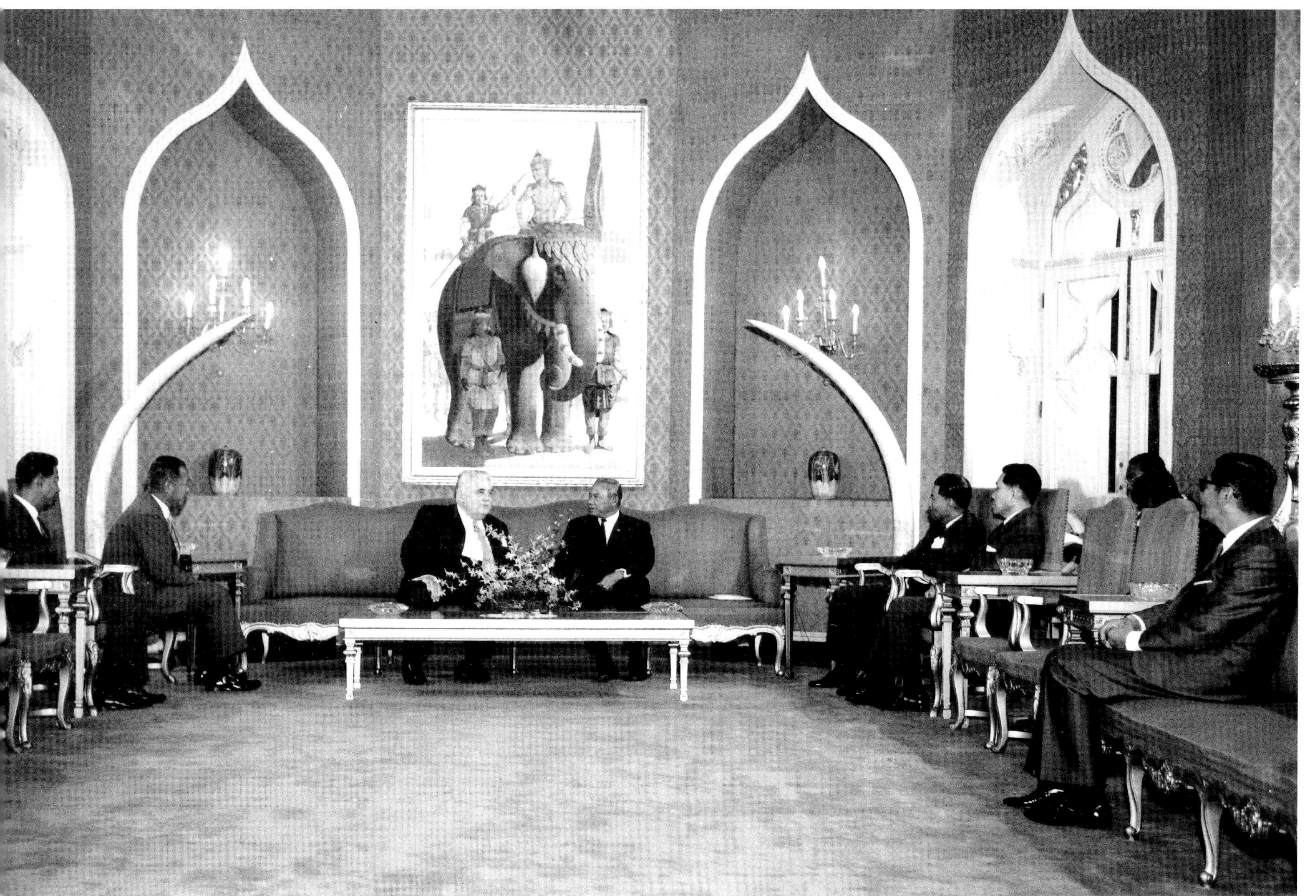

Consortium for International Activities (MUCIA) to create a national institute. Because IU had worked closely with the Thai government in achieving the goals of NIDA's predecessor, the IPA, it was chosen to be the lead institution on the new project. IU political science professor Woodworth Thrombley arrived in Bangkok at the end of 1965 to assist in drafting the NIDA Enabling Act, which was approved by the Thai government in March 1966.

The National Institute of Development Administration was established on April 1, 1966, by a royal proclamation. With Ford Foundation support, its mission was to teach and conduct research on administration and development.

The National Institute of Development Administration was established on April 1, 1966, by a royal proclamation. With Ford Foundation support, its mission was to teach and conduct research on administration and development; Dr. Bunchana Attakor was its first rector.[10]

Four schools were established within the institute: public administration, business administration, development economics, and applied statistics. In a 1969 review, the core curriculum received special recognition. The institute devotes attention to the specific problems and procedures of economic development and to the Thai system for accelerating development by national planning.[11]

NIDA's continuing expansion included publication of the *Journal of Public Administration*, the inclusion of special training programs for thousands of participants, and a library to serve the research and teaching needs of all four schools. From the beginning, NIDA emphasized instruction in English, which was seen as essential for students entering graduate studies in public administration. Many of the textbooks were written in English, and the language was necessary for graduates hoping to advance to higher levels in the Thai government and bureaucracy.[12]

Between 1965 and 1973, faculty from IU and MUCIA went to NIDA to teach, develop curricula, and select faculty and staff for fellowships to the United States for advanced training.[13] In 1973, near the end of the project, twenty-five NIDA staff members had returned with advanced degrees in fields ranging from business, economics, education, political science, public administration, statistics, and sociology; twenty more had completed their degrees by 1976.[14]

In September 1986, an article for the *Indiana University Alumni Magazine* celebrated the thirtieth anniversary of the IU partnership. IU alumni and NIDA administrators Amara Raksasataya and Chirawan Bhakdibutr noted that during one year in the 1980s, three-fifths of the governors of Thailand's seventy-two provinces held degrees from NIDA. The institution has more than thirty-three hundred master's graduates and has trained fifteen hundred of the Thai government's top executives, including the prime minister, and more than a thousand of its diplomats.[15]

In 1973, near the end of the project, twenty-five NIDA staff members had returned with advanced degrees in fields ranging from business, economics, education, and political science to public administration, statistics, and sociology; twenty more had completed their degrees by 1976.

As part of that thirtieth anniversary, the IU Alumni Association of Thailand set up an office in Bangkok. To celebrate the occasion, IU president John Ryan traveled to Thailand with W. George Pinnell, executive vice president, and Howard Schaller, executive dean of the business school.

In 1986, King Bhumibol Adulyadej awarded royal decorations to eleven IU administrators and faculty members who were important in shaping public administration education in Thailand. Among the recipients were IU chancellor Herman B Wells and IU president John Ryan.[16]

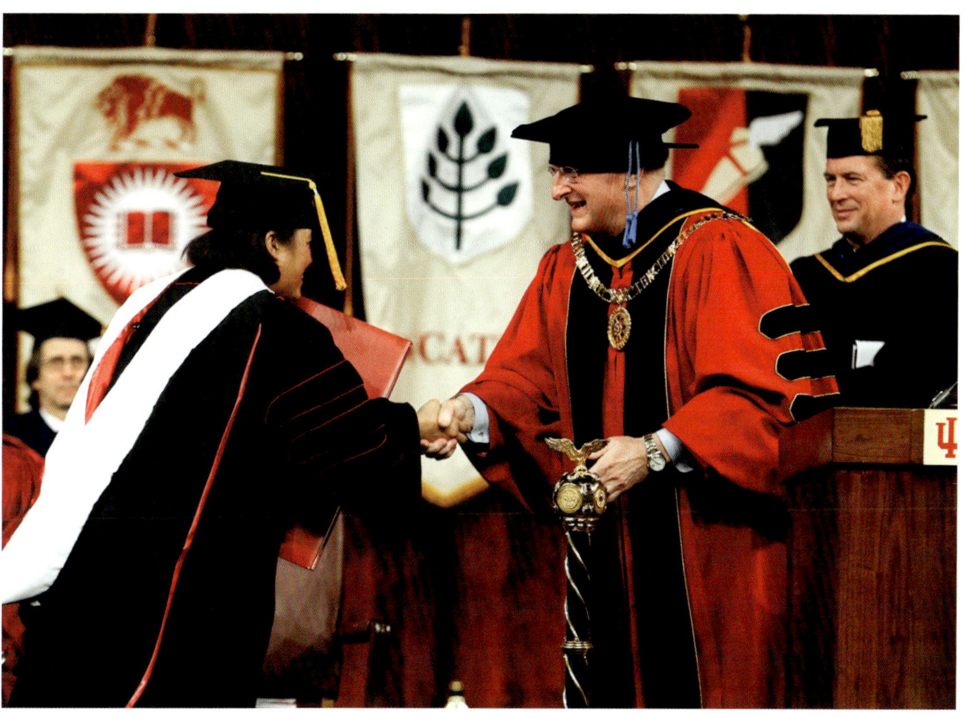

Her Royal Highness Princess Maha Chakri Sirindhorn (*left*) shakes hands with Indiana University president Michael McRobbie (*right*) after receiving an honorary degree from IU, December 2010. *Photograph courtesy of Indiana University, 2010.*

The presidency of Michael A. McRobbie sustained and enhanced IU's presence in Thailand. In 2010, he conferred an honorary doctorate on Her Royal Highness Princess Maha Chakri Sirindhorn at the Bloomington December commencement. The princess was recognized for her efforts to expand and improve public education across Thailand, especially in remote and rural areas. In 2014, President McRobbie and First Lady Laurie Burns McRobbie had a private visit with the princess in Bangkok.[17]

On a trip to Thailand in May 2012, McRobbie presented the Thomas Hart Benton Medallion to NIDA president Dr. Sombat Thamrongthanyawong, and in April 2013, he conferred an honorary doctorate to Dr. Thamrongthanyawong at a ceremony on the Indiana University–Purdue University Indianapolis (IUPUI) campus. Because of IU's close ties with NIDA, honorary doctorates had also been awarded to NIDA former presidents—Amara Raksasatya in 2000 and Juree Vichit-Vadakan in 2007. In turn, NIDA presented honorary doctorates to former president John Ryan in 1991, vice president Patrick O'Meara in 2005, and executive vice chancellor William Plater in 2010.

In a speech given at NIDA in March 2016 in celebration of the fiftieth anniversary of its founding, McRobbie remarked: "NIDA has made enormous contributions to the personal and academic development of many thousands of students. It has

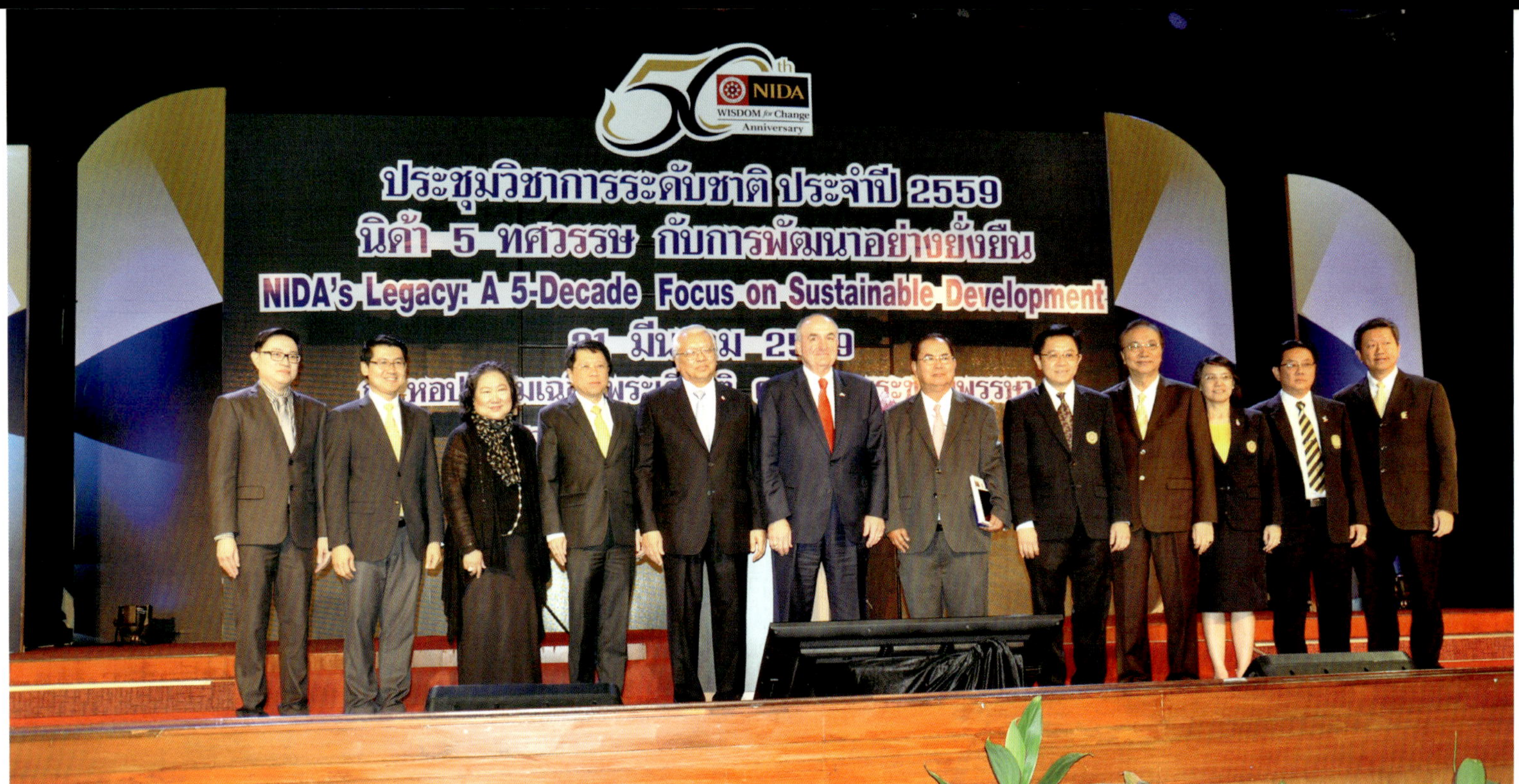

Indiana University president Michael McRobbie (*center*) delivers a keynote address at the fiftieth-anniversary celebration of Thailand's National Institute of Development Administration, March 2016.
Photograph courtesy of Indiana University.

contributed greatly to the economic and social development of Thailand. And it will, I am certain, continue to prepare students to successfully serve Thailand, Southeast Asia, and the world for many more decades to come."[18]

In addition to the activities on the ground in Thailand, a memorable exhibition took place on the Bloomington campus in 1960. The event, which was organized by art history professor Theodore R. Bowie, was the first major exhibit of Thai art in the Western Hemisphere and toured major US, European, and Asian museums after its Bloomington opening. Other sites included the Metropolitan Museum of Art, the Museum of Fine Arts in Boston, the Los Angeles County Museum of Art, the California Palace of the Legion of Honor in San Francisco, and the Honolulu Academy of Arts. The catalog for the show was published by IU Press. The IU Archives have photographs of the pieces arriving, the setup, the installation, and Herman Wells with a high-level Thai delegation at the opening ceremony.[19]

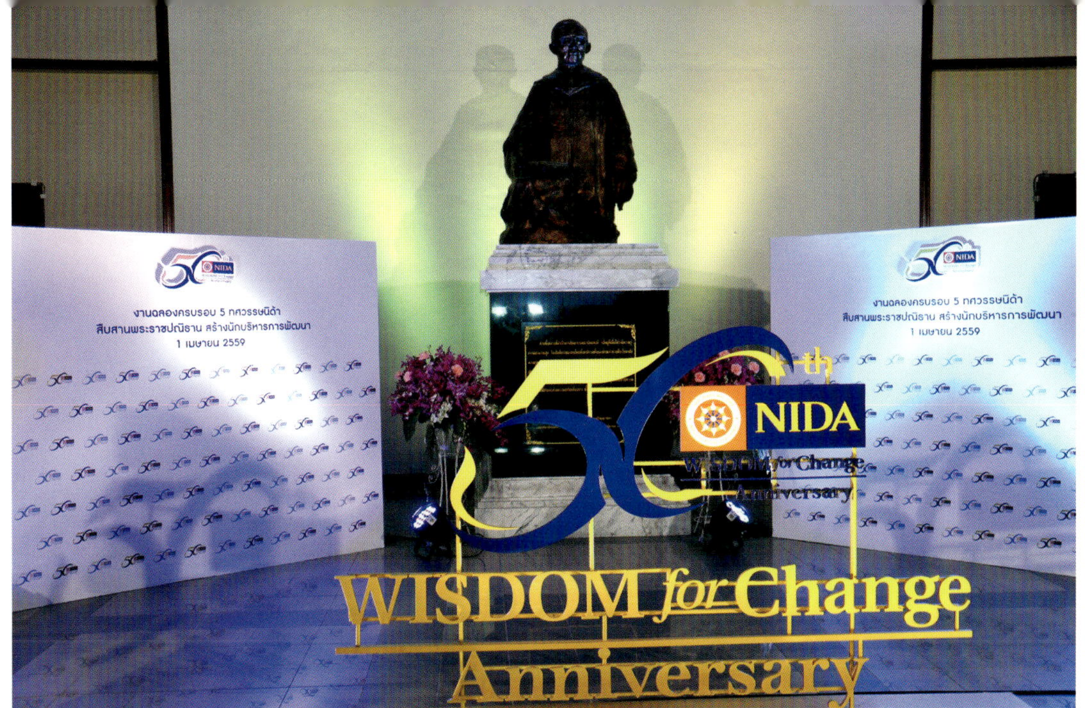

National Institute of Development Administration's fiftieth-anniversary celebration, March 2016.

Photograph courtesy of Indiana University.

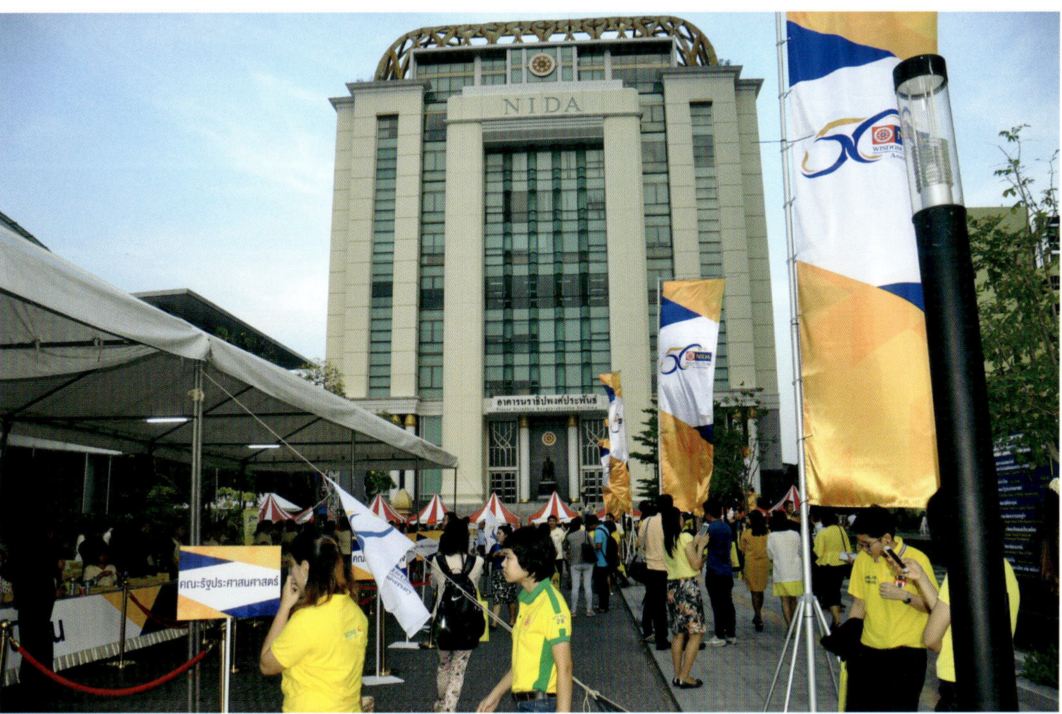

National Institute of Development Administration campus during its fiftieth-anniversary celebration, March 2016.

Photograph courtesy of Indiana University.

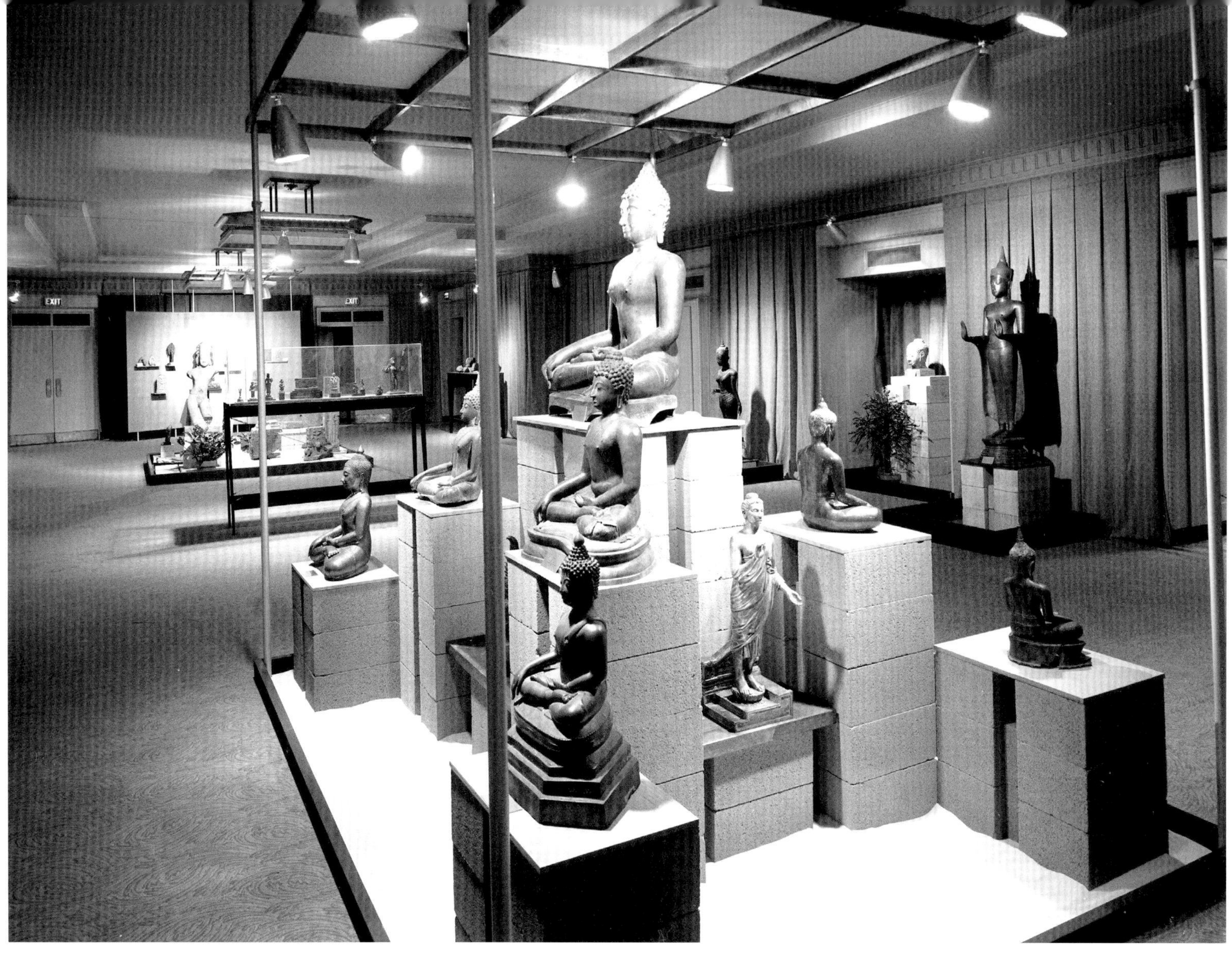

"The Arts of Thailand" exhibition, Indiana University Bloomington, September 1960.
IU Archives (P0033177).

Facing, Professor Theodore "Ted" R. Bowie (*right*) takes delivery of artifacts for display at "The Arts of Thailand" exhibition, Indiana University Bloomington, August 1960.
IU Archives (P0033169).

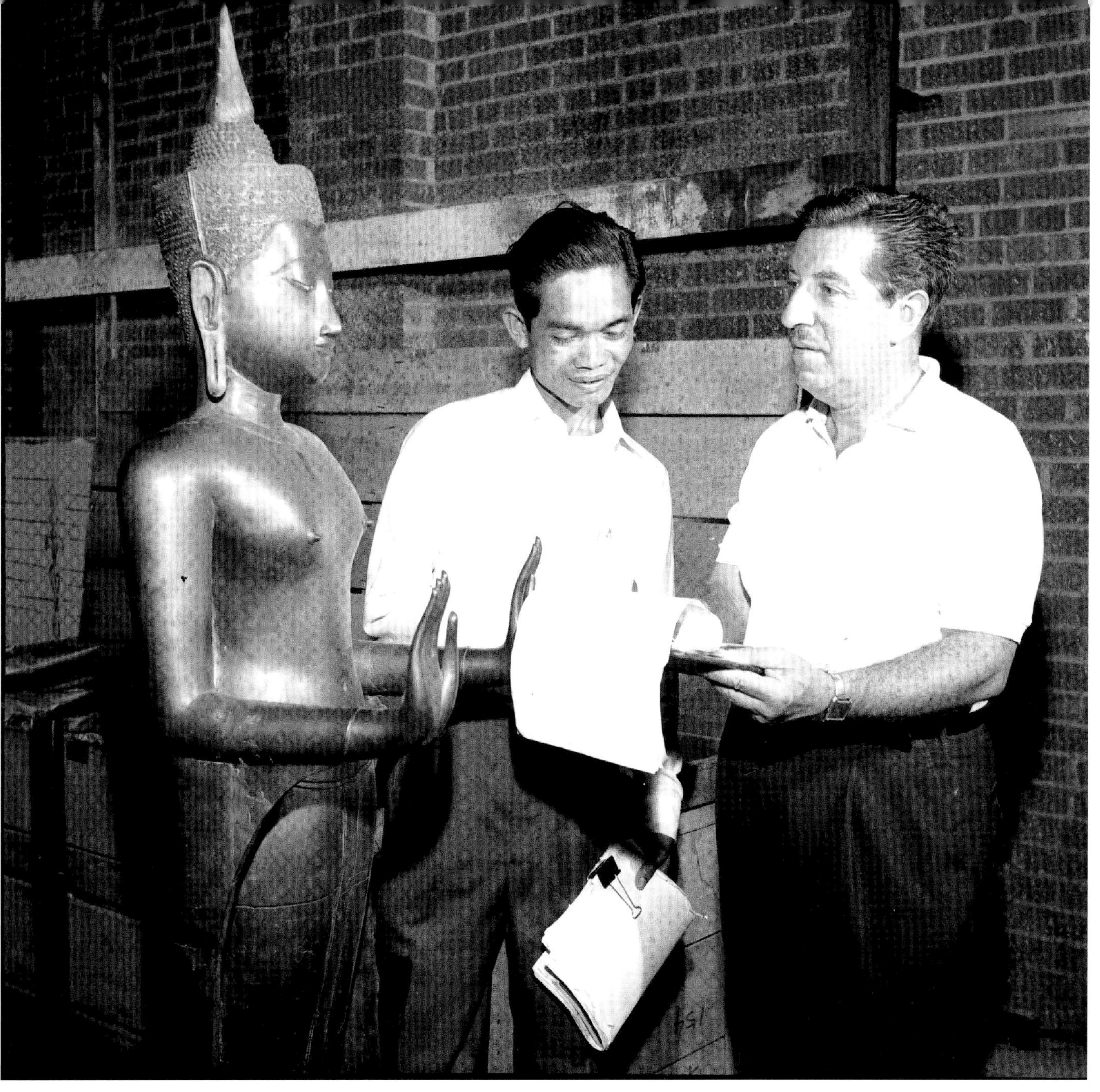

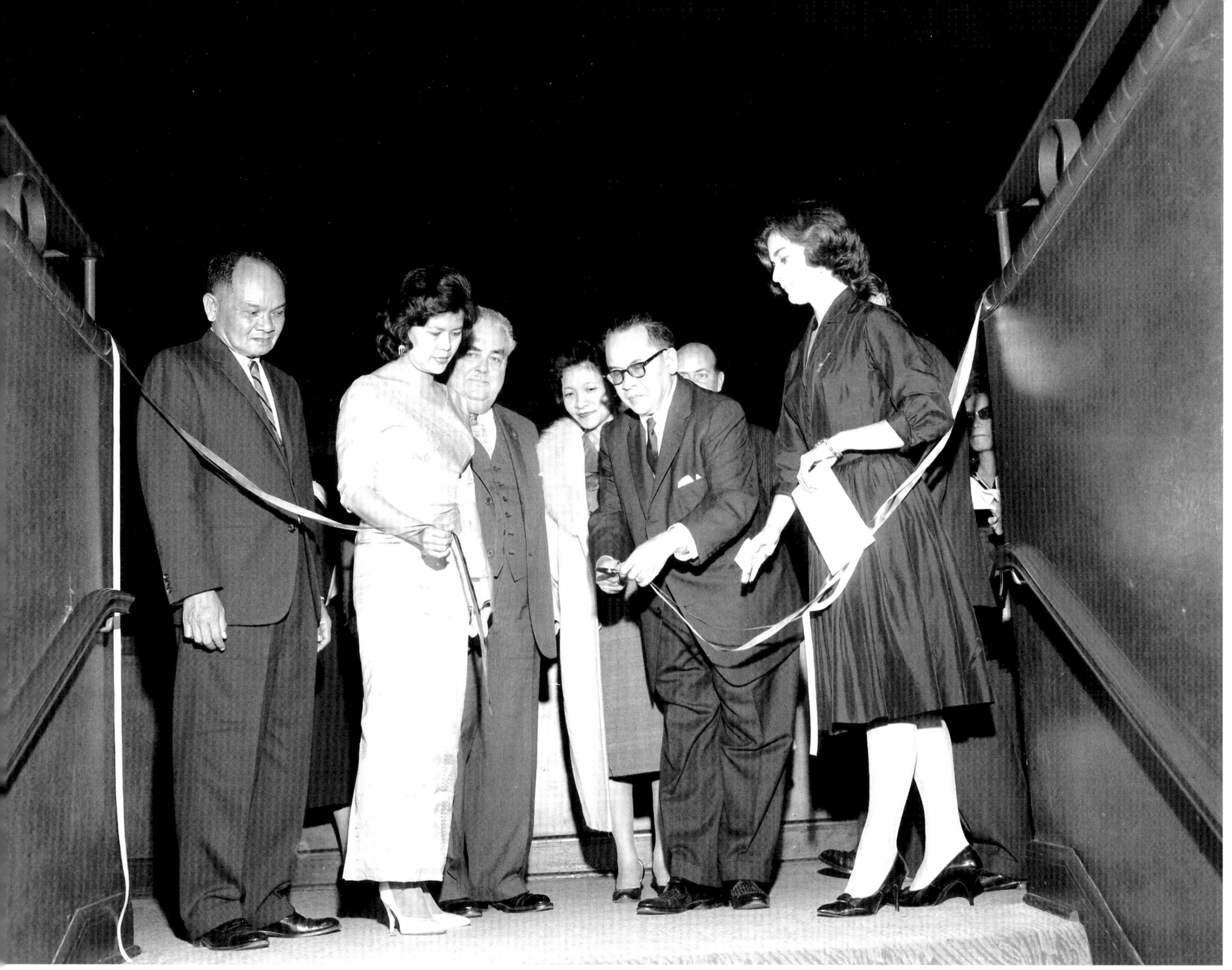

NIDA has made enormous contributions to the personal and academic development of many thousands of students. It has contributed greatly to the economic and social development of Thailand. And it will, I am certain, continue to prepare students to successfully serve Thailand, Southeast Asia, and the world for many more decades to come.

—Michael McRobbie

Herman Wells (*third from left*) and Thai dignitaries open "The Arts of Thailand" exhibition at Indiana University Bloomington, October 9, 1960.

IU Archives (P0033173).

4 | INDIANA UNIVERSITY *in* Pakistan

The partition of India into two entities, one Hindu India and the other Muslim, Pakistan East and West, created one of the great social upheavals of modern times.

The educational system that the Pakistani inherited had been instituted by the British in the 18th century and was designed to produce civil servants to manage the country under the direction of their British rulers.

—Herman Wells

BEGINNING IN THE 1950S, INDIANA UNIVERSITY BECAME INVOLVED in development activities in Pakistan. There was an urgent need for technical assistance after the partition of India and the emergence of the state of Pakistan in 1947; in particular, existing educational institutions, many of them created by the British, were antiquated or inadequate to serve the new nation. The partition of India into two entities, one Hindu India and the other Muslim, Pakistan East and West, created one of the great social upheavals of modern times. There was extensive migration of Hindus from the Pakistan areas into India and, conversely, migration of Muslims from India outward to Pakistan Territories.

Wells adds, "In education, the situation was especially critical. The educational system that the Pakistani inherited had been instituted by the British in the 18th century and was designed to produce civil servants to manage the country under the direction of their British rulers."[1]

In 1957, the IU Office of Research and Advanced Studies received funding from the International Cooperation Administration, the predecessor of the United States Agency for International Development to work with the Jinnah Postgraduate Medical Center at the University of Karachi. The purpose of the grant was to increase the quality and quantity of medical education in Pakistan through the development of a postgraduate master of science degree for

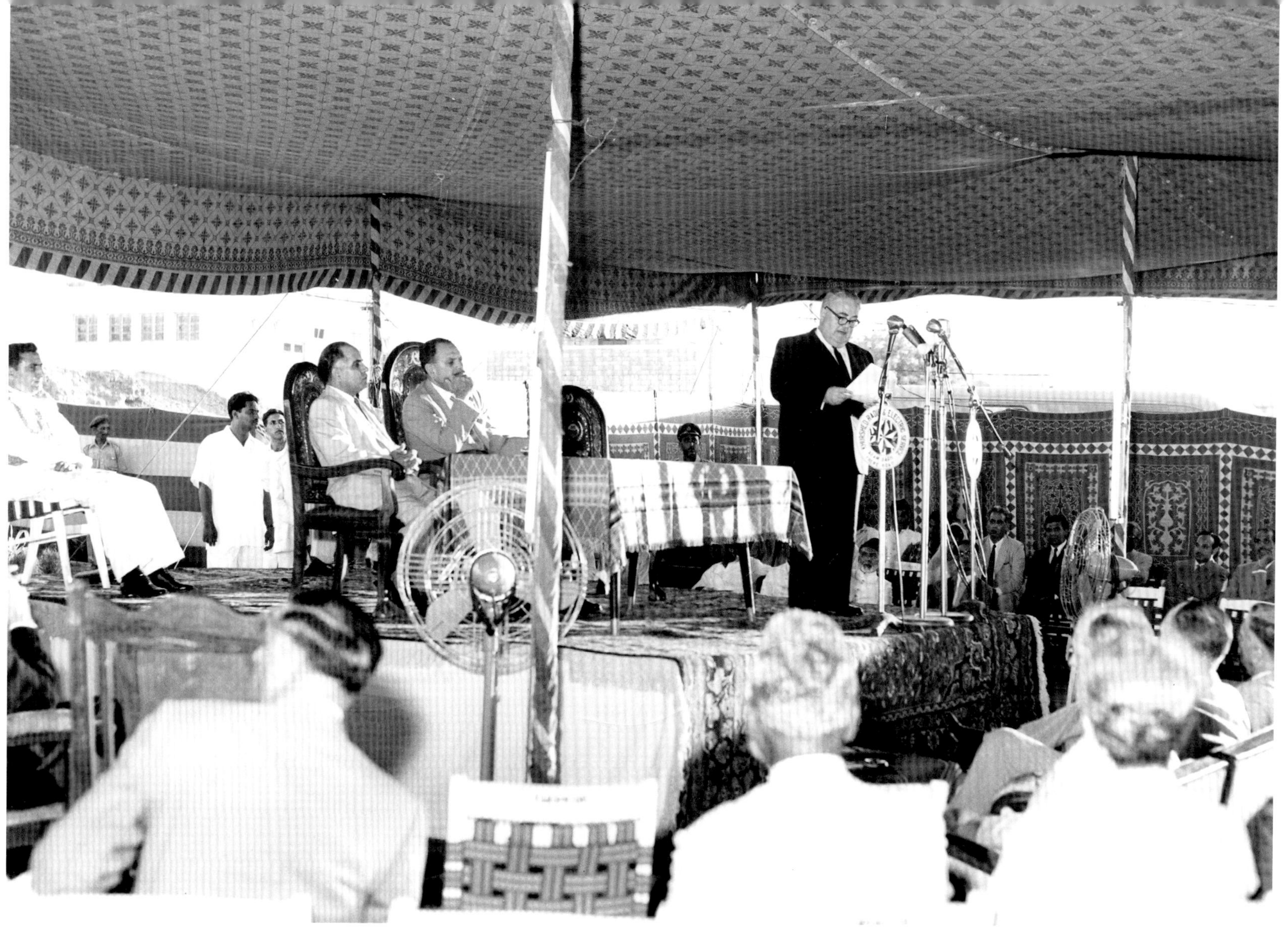

Herman B Wells speaking at the opening of the Basic Medical Institute in Karachi. On platform, *left to right:* Colonel M. Jaffer, director general of health of Pakistan; General Mohammed Ayub Khan, president of Pakistan; and Herman B Wells, April 1959. *IU Archives (P0022053).*

those who might become faculty members at medical colleges throughout Pakistan. The first students were admitted to the institute in 1959. Paul A. Nicoll served as the initial chief of party, followed by Harold Margulies and Sherman A. Minton Jr. Many other faculty members were instructors and advisers in pharmacology, biochemistry, anatomy, microbiology, and pathology. William Hugh Headlee from the Indianapolis campus was contract coordinator, and John Ashton, vice president for graduate development and dean of the Graduate School, led the program. In 1965, Lynne L. Merritt, dean of research and advanced studies, took over Ashton's role. In addition to developing an academic curriculum and degree program, twenty-one Pakistani students, nineteen of whom attended Indiana University, were sent to the United States to continue their education in advanced specialties. The project also focused on building library collections in basic medical sciences and in clinical specialties.

All of the Indiana University project members left Karachi at the end of 1965, but the contract was extended until March 1966 because of the conflict between India and Pakistan, which caused delays. By that time, a master of science degree, a clinical training program, a bachelor of science degree program in medical technology, and a PhD program were in place.[2]

A smaller project during this period was one that involved advising on the formation of a medical college at the new University of Peshawar. Another endeavor was the University of Dacca Institute of Business Administration project in East Pakistan, which was funded by the Ford Foundation and run by the IU School of Business from 1966 to 1970. The project was designed to establish graduate-level training, research, and consulting services in modern management methods. It offered an MBA, diploma programs, short courses in management, research studies on business problems, and consulting services for the business community. Conflict in the region forced the project to end when East Pakistan seceded from Pakistan to become the independent state of Bangladesh in 1971.[3]

The Teacher Training Program at the University of the Panjab in Lahore operated from 1959 to 1967, funded by a grant from the International Cooperation Administration and administered by the School of Education. Its purpose was to develop the Institute of Education and Research, a graduate-level institution for training current and future teachers. This initiative included providing advisory personnel and technical assistance to aid in the building, staffing, equipping, and operating of the institute. It focused on curricula and degree programs, hiring faculty and staff, creating a research library, and promoting academic research and publishing in the field of education.[4]

In January 1958, the president of Pakistan, General Mohammad Ayub Khan, established the President's Commission on National Education to look into necessary reforms in education and find new directions for Pakistan's educational system.[5]

The commission concluded, "Pakistan itself is not producing gifted scientific personnel needed for the task of national development. In all the twenty years since Independence, Pakistan has not domestically produced one PhD in science. Such superior talent as Pakistan has been produced in foreign universities. No developing country can afford this sort of drain on foreign exchange indefinitely. . . . Islamabad University will meet the national need by providing an institution of excellence which can carry out fundamental and applied scientific research, and train people to staff the colleges, universities, research councils, industries and business."[6]

Herman Wells was appointed to the commission, and from mid-March to mid-April 1959, he attended its hearings in Pakistan. One of the commission's key findings would lead to the creation of the University of Islamabad.

Thus, IU's most substantial involvement in Pakistan began in 1966, when it played a major role in the creation and building of a national university for graduate students at Islamabad, the new capital of Pakistan. Wells worked closely with Muhammad Raziuddin Siddiqui, a Pakistani theoretical physicist and mathematician who had been involved in Pakistan's education system.

During his distinguished career, Siddiqui served as the vice chancellor of four Pakistan universities; from the perspective of IU, Siddiqui's role as the first vice chancellor of the University of Islamabad was of major importance. After independence in 1947, the government of Pakistan asked Siddiqui to move to Karachi from India. In 1953, he was simultaneously appointed to two key positions, vice chancellor of the University of Sindh and of the University of Peshawar. In 1964, Siddiqui moved to Islamabad, where he joined the Pakistan Atomic Energy Commission, and in 1965, he was appointed as vice chancellor of the University of Islamabad.[7]

Funding was received from the Ford Foundation, which had selected Pakistan as one of the developing countries where it wished to concentrate its efforts, and the project was administered by the Office of the Dean of Research and Advanced Studies at IU. Herman B Wells, who was then president of the Indiana University Foundation, took a very active role in the planning and management of this project. Wells traveled to Pakistan to monitor the project's progress. He was in frequent contact with Vice Chancellor Siddiqi. Wells and Lynne L. Merritt visited Pakistan on different occasions. Indiana University's contributions included providing consultants for the organization and development of the university and for the planning of its campus; hiring visiting professors to teach short-term appointments; recruiting Pakistani teachers residing abroad; and purchasing library books, journals, and equipment.[8]

Because Indiana University's initial role in the project revolved around managing the construction and staffing of the University of Islamabad, most of the work was conducted from the United States rather than in Pakistan. A site overlooking Islamabad was selected for the new campus, and the distinguished American architect Edward Durrell Stone was chosen to design the buildings on the campus. He was asked to provide master drawing plans for buildings for mathematics, physics, chemistry, biology, earth sciences, social sciences, and Islamic studies; a library and administration building; an auditorium and community center; and student hostels and staff residences.[9]

The Indiana University Foundation signed an agreement with the architect, and Wells wrote in a letter to Siddiqi: "Dean Merritt and I visited with Mr. Edward Durell Stone and his associates Saturday, September 28, in New York. I am very pleased with the concept that Mr. Stone has developed for the University of Islamabad. . . . It should be very beautiful, indeed."[10] A 1967 article from the Christian Science Monitor reported on the construction of the campus: "The Islamabad University campus, whose first phase is scheduled to be completed by mid-1970 at a cost of $10 million, promises to be an architectural masterpiece. Its American architect has woven into the design some striking characteristics of the Muslim style of architecture."[11]

Dean Merritt and I visited with Mr. Edward Durell Stone and his associates Saturday, September 28, in New York. I am very pleased with the concept that Mr. Stone has developed for the University of Islamabad. . . . It should be very beautiful, indeed.

—Herman Wells

Several members of the Indiana University faculty and staff—including Harold Jordan, Cecil Byrd, Lynne L. Merritt, and Stanley Hagstrom—acted as consultants in planning the facilities. On the academic level, IU was a formative influence. The University of Islamabad project focused on establishing a residential postgraduate university with an emphasis on advanced teaching and research in science and technology.[12]

Edward W. Najam, executive secretary of the Committee on International Affairs and associate professor of French and Italian, helped recruit outstanding faculty in the United States, the United Kingdom, and Europe.[13]

The initiative included developing academic programs for master's and doctorate degrees for graduates who might go on to become scholars, teachers, and researchers at universities in Pakistan. The goals were to create a university to reduce Pakistan's dependence on foreign countries for advanced scientific training and to bring Pakistani scientists back to teach and conduct research with the promise of a high-ranking university position, competitive salary, prestige, and a professional work environment.

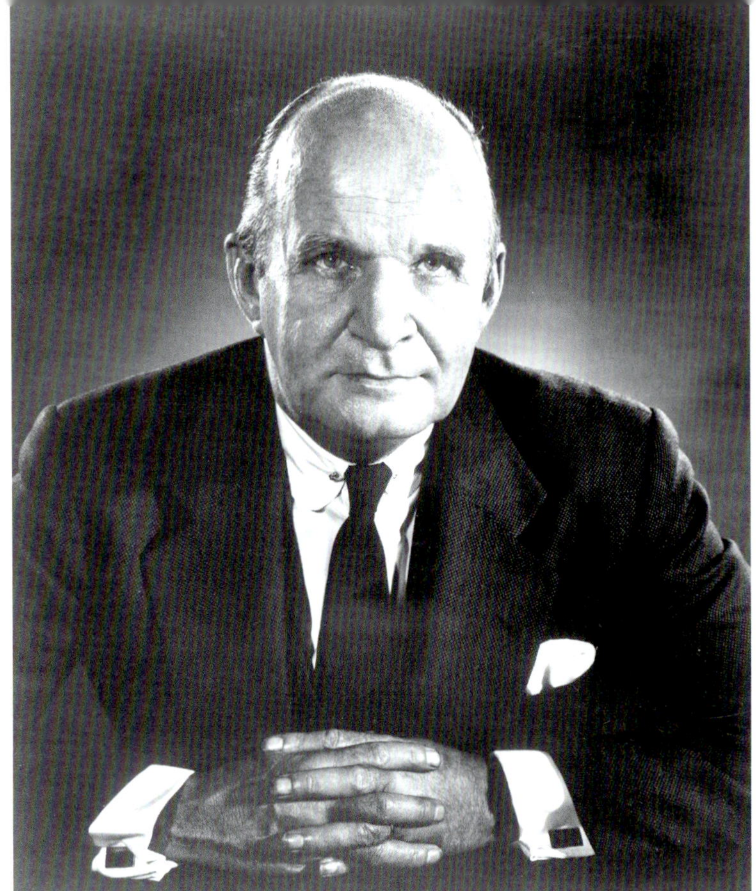

Edward Durell Stone, architect of the library of Quaid-i-Azam University in Islamabad. *Photograph by Bettmann/Getty Images.*

The Ford Foundation provided financial assistance to attract six imminent American, British, French, and German scientists as visiting professors during the academic year beginning September 1, 1967. Chancellor Wells helped in the selection of this team of visiting professors and their teaching and research assignments. Describing the process, he explained: "Part of our responsibility in the Islamabad contract was to do contacting of various scholars, academic leaders throughout the world and persuade them to come to Islamabad. I worked on that; Ed Najam did the detail and I would sometimes write or I would telephone. For instance, I would say '. . . would you go out?' We'd pay their way and pay them an honorarium and so forth. That, of course, was one of the most fascinating parts."[14]

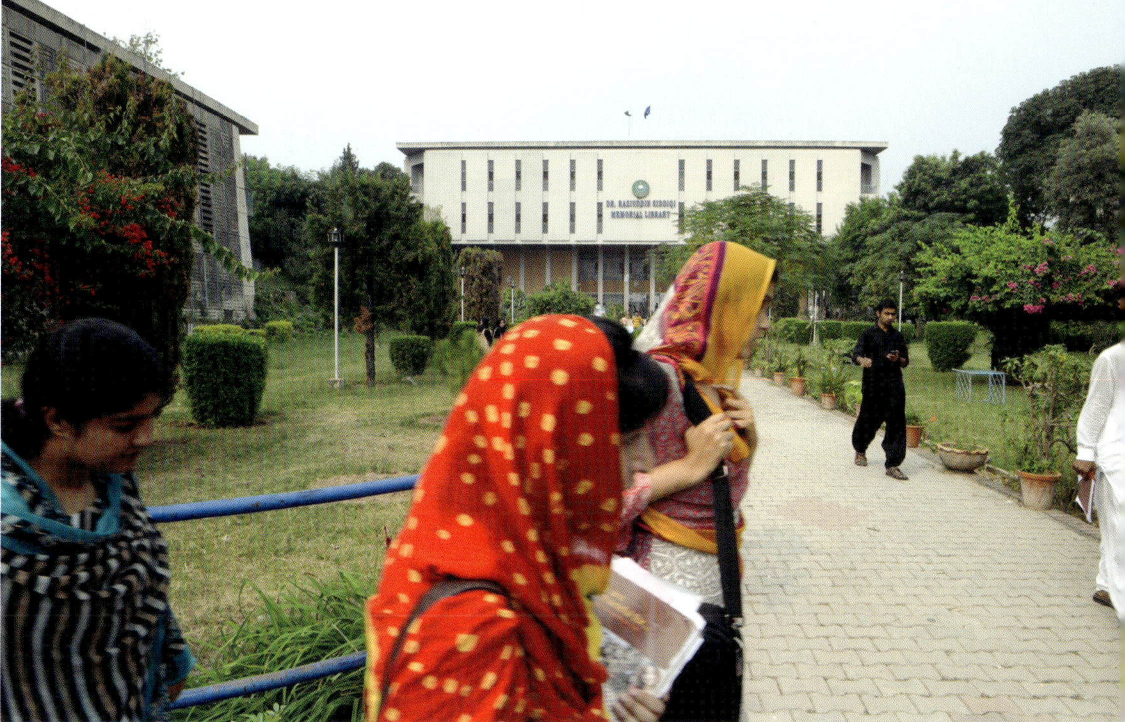

Quaid-i-Azam University in Islamabad with Edward Durrell Stone–designed library in the background.
Photograph by Aamir Qureshi/AFP/Getty Images.

Visiting faculty and consultants from Indiana University included Vaclav Hlavaty from the Mathematics Department, Walter John (W. J.) Moore from the Chemistry Department, and F. B. Malik and Don Lichtenberg from the Physics Department. In 1968, Stanley Hagstrom from the Chemistry Department served as a consultant for the installation of computers purchased for the university and the training of staff.[15]

The grant also supported visits to the United States and the United Kingdom for select Pakistani faculty and administrators to observe how universities managed their institutions. Select students were also sent abroad to obtain PhDs, with the understanding that they would later return to Pakistan and join the faculty at the University of Islamabad.

IU remained in Pakistan until the 1970s; by then, many goals had been accomplished, including completion of the construction of a new campus, significant faculty recruitment, and the development of master's and doctorate programs in the sciences. In 1976, the university's name was changed to Quaid-i-Azam University, the name by which it is currently known.[16]

5 | INDIANA UNIVERSITY *in* Afghanistan

Over a forty-year period, Indiana University was involved in Afghanistan on different occasions. In 1966, there was no indication that this country would become part of a regional and international conflict that would result in US military engagement and far-reaching worldwide consequences.

OVER A FORTY-YEAR PERIOD, INDIANA UNIVERSITY WAS INVOLVED in Afghanistan on different occasions. In 1966, there was no indication that this country would become part of a regional and international conflict that would result in US military engagement and far-reaching worldwide consequences.

Kabul University president Touryalay Etemadi, who had completed an MA at Indiana University in 1954, requested support from United States Agency for International Development (USAID) to modernize his university's academic programs. USAID contacted Herman B Wells and asked him to review the needs of Kabul University and to consider whether IU might engage in a project. In May of 1966, Wells and Lynne Merritt, vice president for research and dean of advanced studies, went to Kabul, the capital of Afghanistan, to meet with university officials. USAID agreed to fund the project, and IU and Kabul University signed a contract on October 22, 1966; the Office of Research and Advanced Studies in Bloomington was designated to administer the project.[1]

Chris W. Jung of the IU School of Education served as chief of party, and Thomas C. Schreck, dean of students, served as adviser to the Kabul University Administration Program in Student Affairs. Several additional faculty members, including Willis Porter, served as short-term consultants. At the start of the program, four Afghan faculty members came to IU to complete degrees in

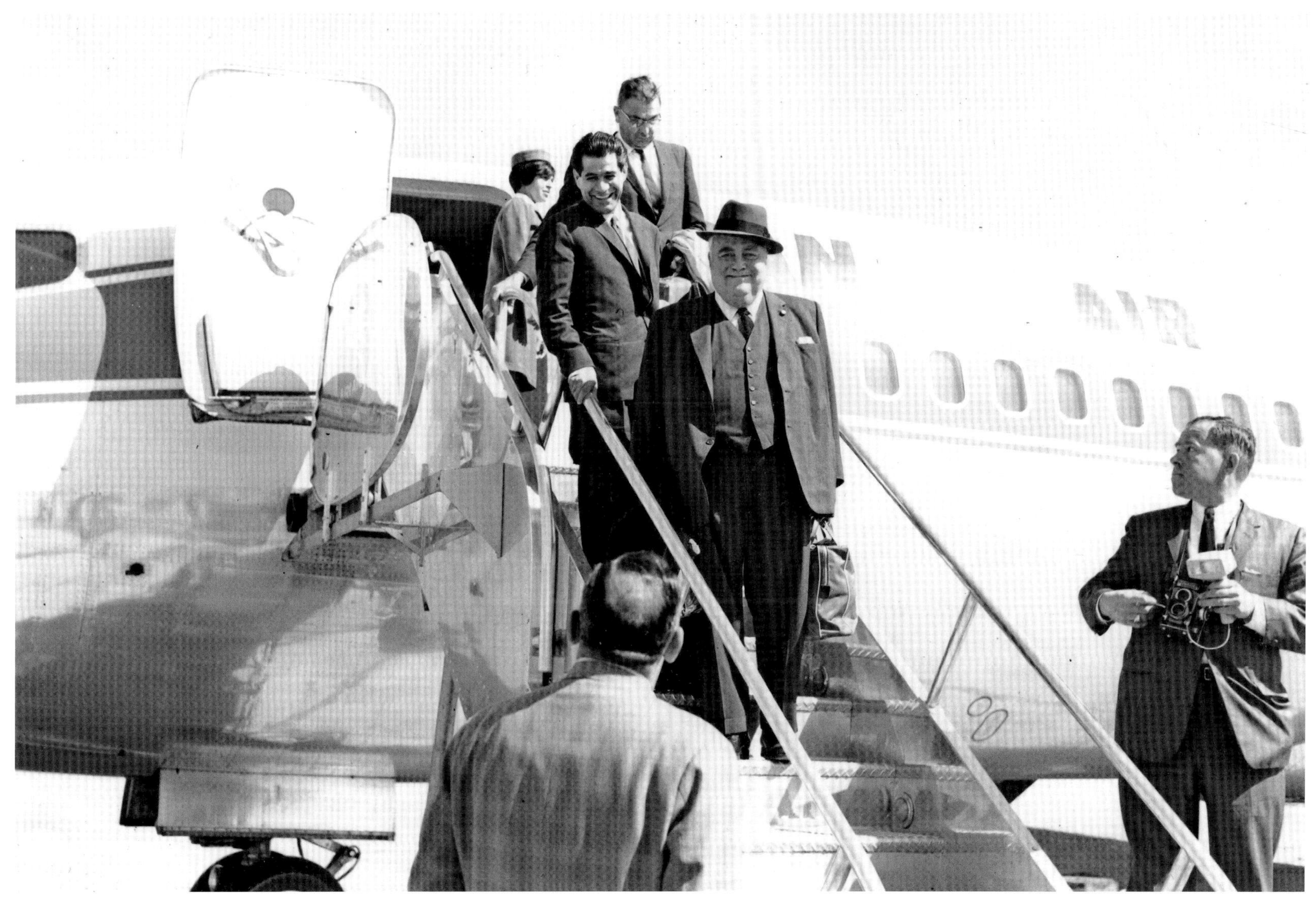

Herman B Wells arrives in Kabul, Afghanistan, May 1966.
IU Archives (P0023772).

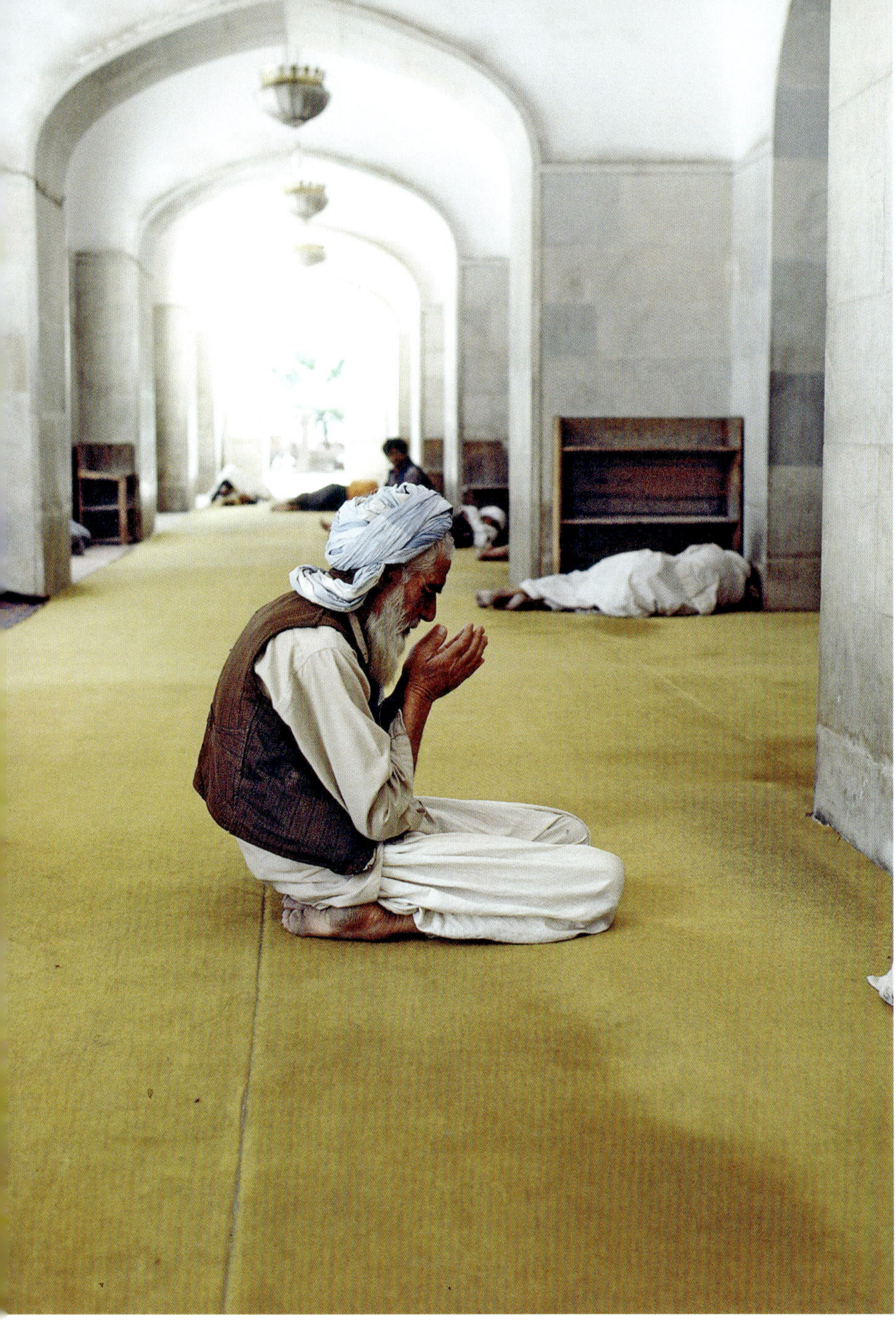

management, and four more did training in Kabul. Over the next few years, others from Kabul were sent to IU to earn masters degrees and, in some cases, doctorates. It is noteworthy that the project instituted advances for women students, for whom there were inadequate housing, advising, and curriculum options. A 1967 Field Study Report commented: "Promotion of feminism is the second program. Free the women from second-class citizenship. An educated mother is an obvious asset to her children."[2]

In the last couple of years of the project, there was unrest on the Kabul campus. On a few occasions in 1971, protests among students from dissenting religious groups escalated into violence. Despite these problems, the project's final report indicated that progress had been made on the university's administration and organization.

The second IU project in Afghanistan resulted from fundamental changes in the Middle East and international terrorism. US military forces entered Afghanistan in late 2001, a few months after the September 11 terrorist attacks on the World Trade Center and on the Pentagon. Efforts were made to expel from power the Taliban, an Islamic fundamentalist political movement, and to stop terrorist attacks from Al-Qaeda, a radical Sunni Muslim organization dedicated to the elimination of a Western presence in Arab countries and militantly opposed to Western foreign policy. Al-Qaeda had been founded by Osama bin Laden in 1988. The war was a costly one in terms of US resources and the death of more than two thousand US soldiers.

A conference in Bloomington in 2003 brought together Afghan and Afghan American scholars to discuss the

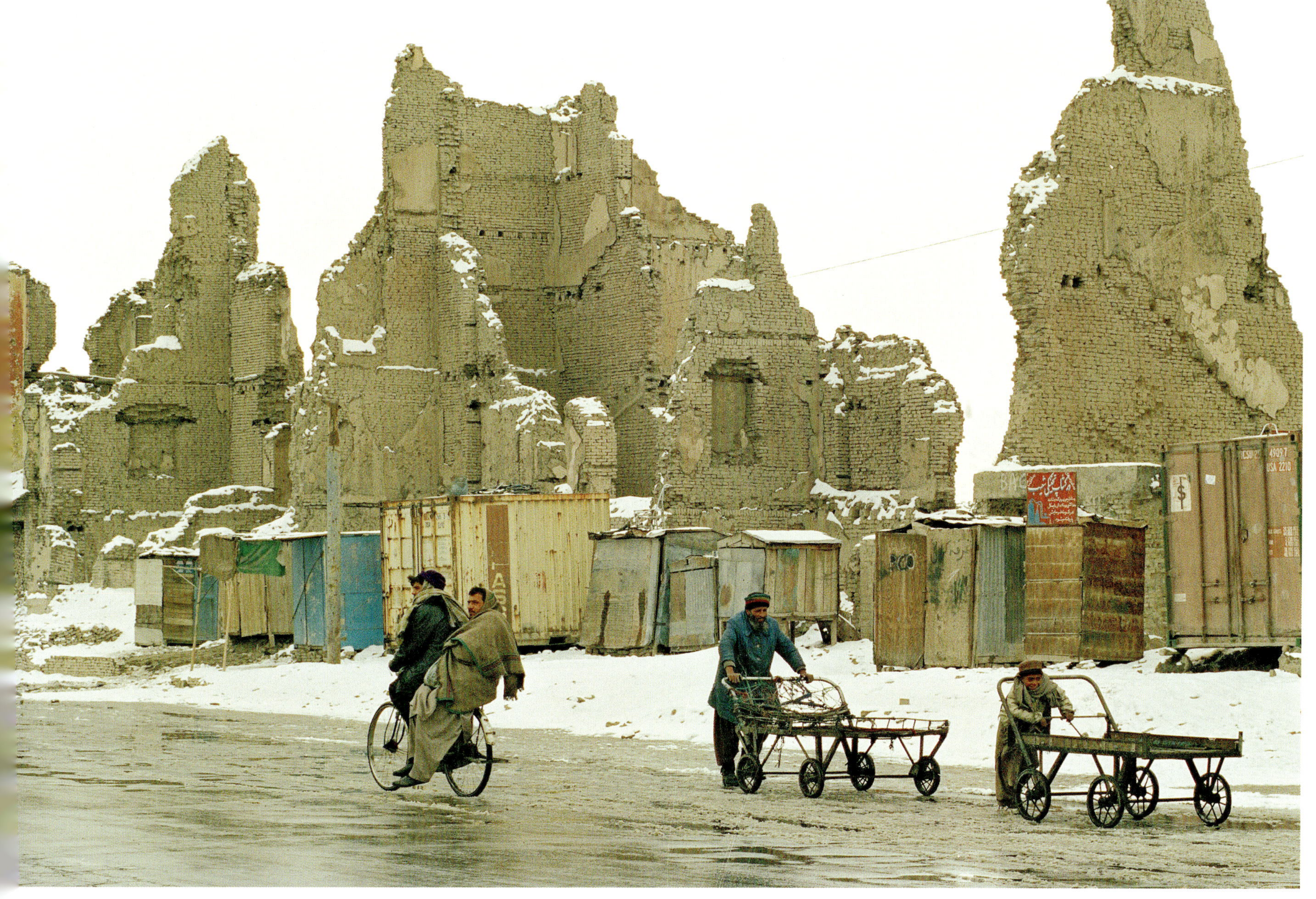

Facing, A man prays in a mosque in Kabul, Afghanistan, January 1988. *UN Photo/John Isaac.*

Above, Residents of Kabul amid destruction caused by Afghanistan's civil war, February 6, 2002. *UN Photo/Eskinder Debebe.*

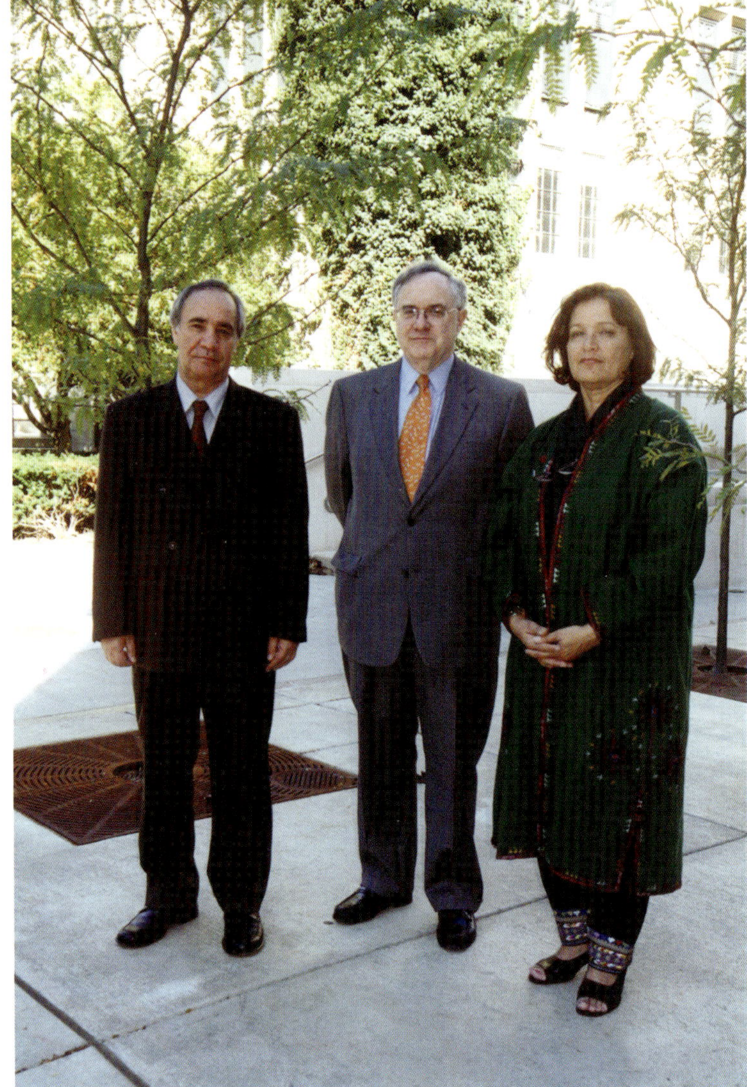

On the Indiana University Bloomington campus, October 2002. *Left to right*: Minister of Higher Education Sharif Fayez, Dean Patrick O'Meara, and Deputy Minister of Higher Education Maliha Zulfacar.

Photograph courtesy of IU International magazine/Roxana Newman.

reconstruction of higher education in Afghanistan. At the conference, the minister of higher education, Sharif Fayez, indicated that training in English was critical to rebuilding the nation's system of higher education.[3]

Many of the thirty participants had received degrees and training from IU during the 1960s and 1970s because of Herman B Wells's vision and influence in assisting Kabul University.

In 2004, the School of Education was awarded a two-year Fulbright Educational Partnerships grant through the US Department of State's Bureau of Educational and Cultural Affairs to collaborate with the Afghan Education University (AEU) in Kabul, which had recently been established with about 130 faculty and two thousand students.[4]

A team from IU trained Afghan educators using updated materials for the teaching of English as a second language (ESL) and engaged in curriculum development, faculty enhancement exchanges, teacher education workshops, and library development. In collaboration with instructors from the Center for English Language Training, the project included the drafting of a handbook of ESL materials. In April 2004, the first year of the grant, Mitzi Lewison, professor of literacy, culture, and language education, and Mary Beth Hines, chair of the language education department, went to Afghanistan to observe teaching at AEU and to conduct a needs assessment. Lewison recalls:

> When I was there with the group from University of Massachusetts and AEU, we interviewed the chancellors, the deans of education, and faculty members from the five major universities—from Kandahar, Nangahar, from Kabul Education,

Kabul University, and Herat University, and that went on for a couple of weeks, and we talked to them about their needs, and strengths, and what we could do to help. We already had the grant, but there was little contact with Afghans on the ground, so we spent the whole first month going around talking to everyone. I am so lucky that I am the person who was there, it was amazing to hear the stories.[5]

In the second year of the grant, two advanced IU graduate students from the Department of Literacy, Culture, and Language Education went to Kabul to team-teach and conduct workshops using the preliminary draft of the handbook, assessing its effectiveness and incorporating necessary revisions. The revised handbook was used in workshops to train 240 Afghan ESL teacher trainees. In endorsing the aims of the grant, Afghanistan's minister of higher education, Sharif Fayez, said: "The IU–AEU affiliation and collaboration will be a major step forward in our reform efforts to revitalize the higher education system in Afghanistan."[6]

This project was followed by another initiative, the Afghanistan Higher Education Project (HEP), an effort funded by USAID to improve institutional administration and preservice secondary teacher education at the eighteen higher education institutions across Afghanistan. IU received the funding in partnership with the University of Massachusetts Amherst and AEU. IU professors Terrence (Terry) and Mitzi Lewison led the project. The IU Center for Social Studies and International Education was the administrative base for the project. Although its primary mission was to improve education in the social studies in elementary and secondary schools, the center also met various international professional development needs through in-service training, content seminars, and curriculum workshops.

The goal of the project was to help reestablish teacher education programs in Afghan colleges and universities; later, it also included English courses for medical schools. Mason emphasized that cultural fluency would be important and challenging as US educators set out to address democratic themes, including enhancing the role of women in the educational system and creating greater equity and participation among the many ethnic and linguistic groups. Mason also pointed out the importance of English for international diplomacy and world commerce. Lewison comments on the scope of the project:

There were really three major areas I worked on as the English director. First of all, helping to develop the whole program, but also finding twelve people—we did a country-wide search, so they came from around Afghanistan, and they got master's degrees in the School of Education here, so what we had was twelve people whose English was good enough and their academics were good enough—now, these are all faculty members who teach in faculties of education around Afghanistan. There were also some really bright people whose English wasn't good enough, so we sent sixteen people, one from each of the universities we were working with, to Singapore, for a six-month intensive English and new methods program.[7]

The Center for Social Studies and International Education hosted a group of twelve Afghan teacher educators from 2007 to 2009 who completed master's degrees in education at IU; subsequently, a graduation ceremony was held for forty-one Afghans, including those who had studied at Indiana University.[8]

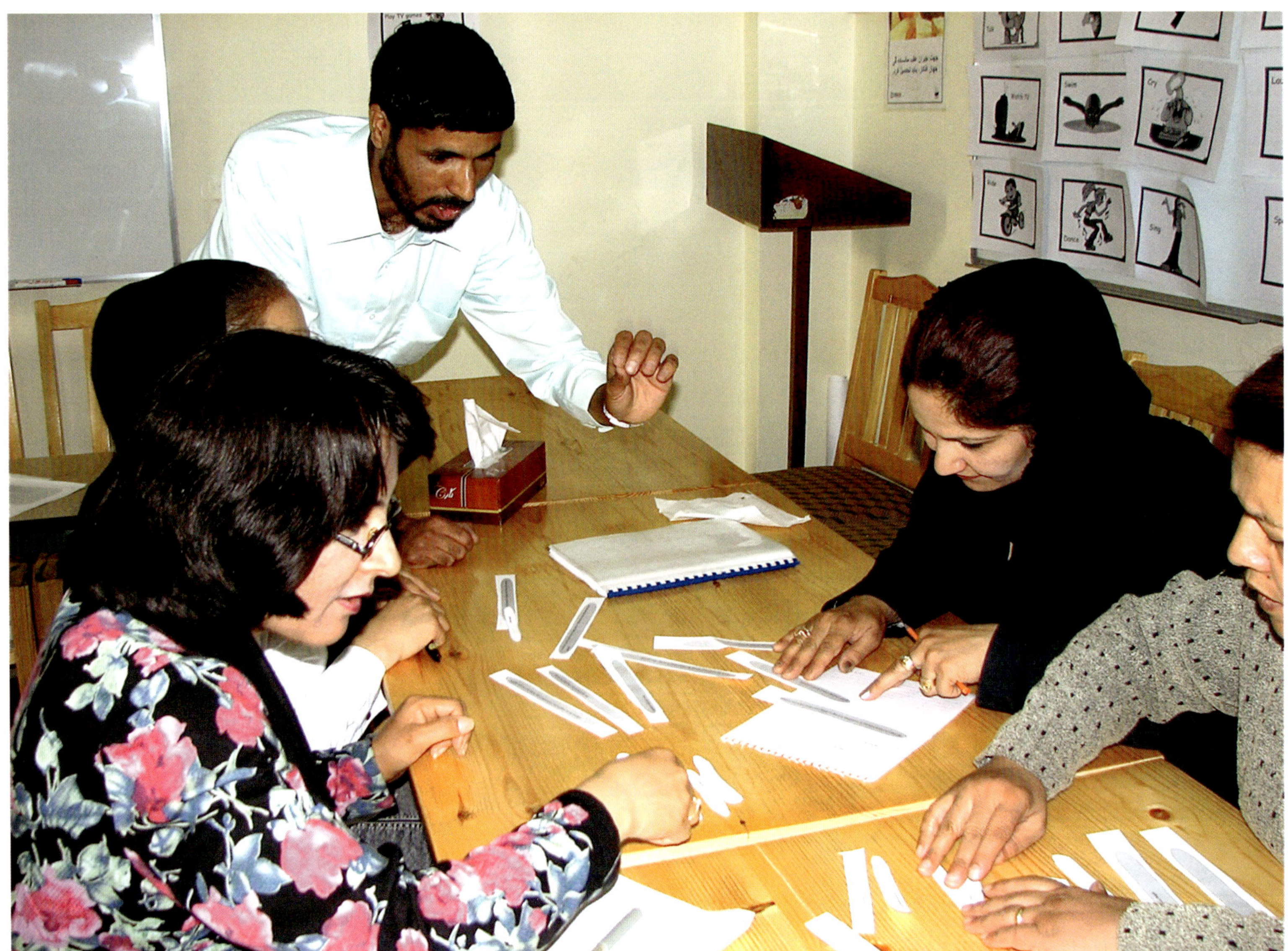

The Center for Social Studies and International Education at Indiana University was selected for a $3.5 million US State Department grant to create a new master's degree program in Afghanistan. *Photograph courtesy of Indiana University.*

When the project began, according to Mason, Afghan teacher educators had few usable teaching materials: "There were lecture notes left over from the Soviet era. They were based on antiquated teaching methods. They were often inaccurate and out of date."[9]

Lewison expands on this perspective: "Teaching notes were handed from professor to professor, and every faculty member I talked to said, 'We know what we're doing is out of date, we know our content is out of date. We want to become part of the world,' that is what they were saying, so it was quite amazing."[10]

Thus, Afghan education institutions, faced with these dire resources, turned to the United States for assistance as they developed education programs for secondary school teachers. A guiding principle, according to Mason, was respect for indigenous knowledge and education: "We knew from the start that it was essential, if the effort was going to work, to assure that training programs and materials were created within an Afghan context and approved by Afghan advisors."[11]

Mason's part of the project has focused on curriculum development for teacher education, emphasizing mathematics and science content. He also saw the situation in a broader context: "We hear a lot about the war. What people don't hear a lot about is the development work that's going on over there, and this is a great example of that."[12]

Educated in the United States, G. Omar Qargha, manager for standards and content development for the project, was an important contributor to IU's efforts. Qargha describes some of the ways that Western educational materials were successfully adapted for use in Afghan universities:

> We tried to include articles and scenarios that focused on the indigenous heritage of science and math in the region. This made participants more in tune with the ideas, rather than having them feel that all the information is from the West; during the European Dark Ages, Muslim scientists made great advances in their field. In math, we'd read several articles about the accomplishments of Muslim mathematicians, which also included research by a Harvard professor about the architectural marvels of this region, stressing the fact that the math needed to design and build some of these structures was not discovered in the West until the 1960s.[13]

We knew from the start that it was essential, if the effort was going to work, to assure that training programs and materials were created within an Afghan context and approved by Afghan advisors.
—Terry Mason

For Lewison, the education of women was a long-term major achievement: "The project affected women in a way I don't think we had done before. Half of our faculty who taught, and over half of the students, who were faculty at other places, were women. We had women telling us it was their golden opportunity, because while there were degree programs for example, in India, the women could not go there unescorted. So this was something they could do in their own country. This was really important. I didn't realize that that was going to be a big part of it when we started."[14]

Terry Mason sums up the personal value of such projects:

> When I was promoted and received tenure, ironically in 2001, the world was changing for all of us in that year in significant ways. I decided that since I now had the autonomy as an academic to make decisions about where my career was going to go,

> I said, well listen, I can do the traditional academic route, write articles, do research, and publish, etc. Or, I can reconfigure my academic trajectory in a way that might have an impact on some of the issues I saw emerging at that time. And the one to me was that the US needed to do a different kind of work in the world, one that it seemed to me, people at a university could do to help build capacity, help create educational institutions that would stabilize countries in ways that would be better for everyone—better for us, better for them, and so I made a conscious decision to redirect my work. When the call came to go to Washington, Mitzi and I went together to work with this group on the Afghanistan project, I was ready to go, because that was my commitment at the time.[15]

Between 2011 and 2014, another grant supported the development of a graduate degree program, taught in English, for public universities in Afghanistan. The aim was to collaborate with Kabul Education University in creating a master's degree program for the teaching of English to speakers of other languages. Mitzi Lewison and IU's Center for International Education Development and Research project manager Arlene Benitez, directed this project. Because of increasing conflicts in Afghanistan, and insecurity in Kabul, it was difficult to recruit for the program. With the help of the US embassy in Kabul, the program operated and ultimately was taken over by the university. Lewison and Benitez provided extensive support and monitoring through Skype and email as well as by spending a short time in Kabul.[16]

When the projects were administered, Afghanistan was a country first of uncertainty, and later of ongoing warfare. While Mason and Lewison recognized the deteriorating conditions, their focus always remained on improving educational opportunities rather than on the risks involved.

When the projects were administered, Afghanistan was a country first of uncertainty, and later of ongoing warfare. While Mason and Lewison recognized the deteriorating conditions, their focus always remained on improving educational opportunities rather than on the risks involved.

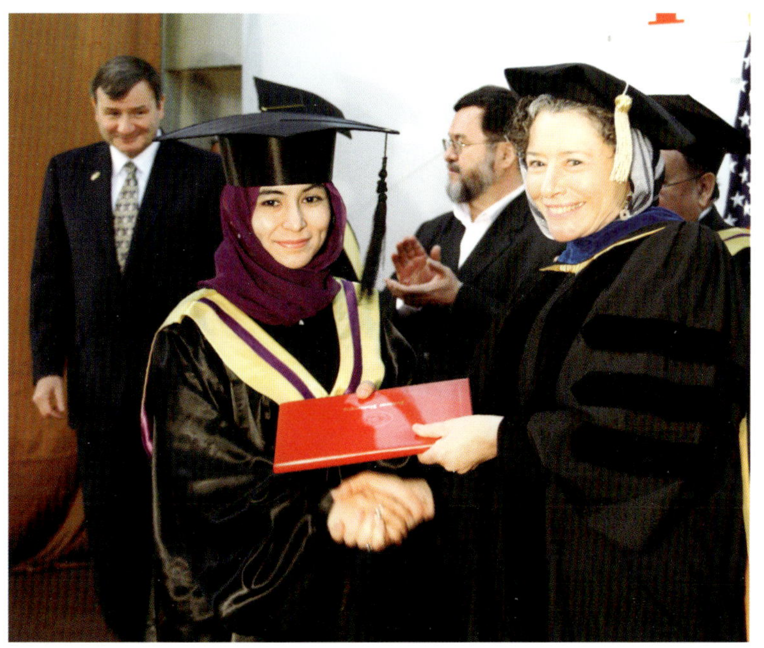

Graduation ceremony in Kabul, Afghanistan. Indiana University professor Mitzi Lewison (*right*) and Afghan graduate.
Photograph courtesy of Indiana University.

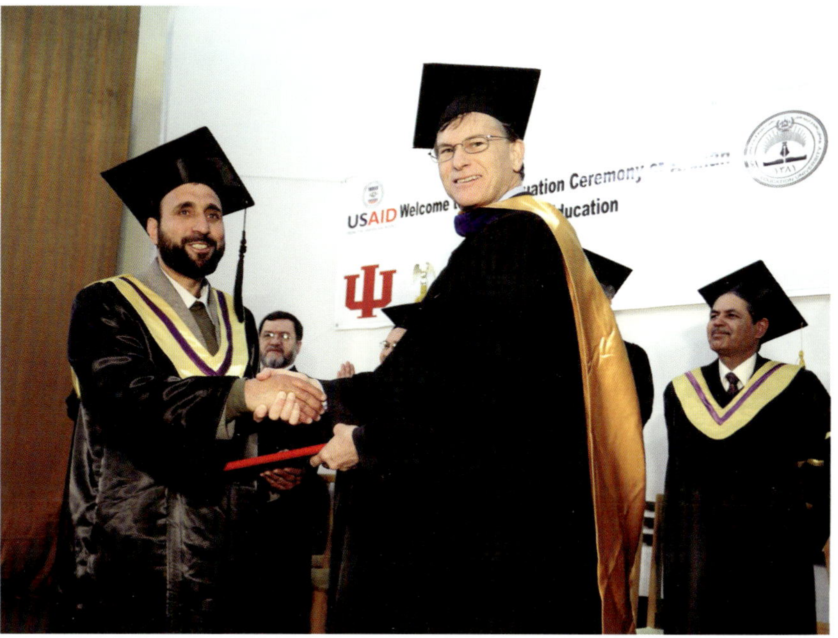

Indiana University faculty member Terrence (Terry) Mason (*right*) congratulates a graduate of the USAID-funded, IU-led project.
Photograph courtesy of Indiana University.

6 | INDIANA UNIVERSITY *in* Poland

This was a time of fundamental political and social transformation in Poland. Indiana University was privileged to be a participant in the country at this historic time.

IN THE 1970S, INDIANA UNIVERSITY BECAME ACTIVELY INVOLVED with the study of Poland and played a formative role with the American Studies Center at the University of Warsaw. This was a time of fundamental political and social transformation in Poland. Indiana University was privileged to be a participant in the country at this historic time. In the 1970s, the Communist government increased food prices at a time when wages were very low. This and other unpopular moves led to large-scale protests in June 1976. Because of these pressures, the government imposed heavy controls on opposition. In early September 1980, the Solidarity: Independent Self-governing Labor Union was organized. In 1981, martial law was imposed because the Soviet-backed government wanted to contain the increasing power and threat of Solidarity. All contact with the outside world was forbidden, and many academics and journalists were detained. The movement that evolved from this beginning was committed to nonviolence and had the support of the Catholic Church, especially of Pope John Paul II. By 1989, deteriorating conditions forced the government to engage in negotiations with the opposition, and, by 1990, Lech Walesa, Solidarity cofounder and leader had become president of Poland. Indiana University was an influential presence in Warsaw during these years.

The Polish Studies Center was established at Indiana University on October 30, 1977, while the counterpart American Studies Center at the University of

Facing, The original library building, University of Warsaw. During World War II, the Nazis established their occupation headquarters on the University of Warsaw campus, which consequently was spared complete destruction. *Photograph courtesy of Lynn Schoch.*

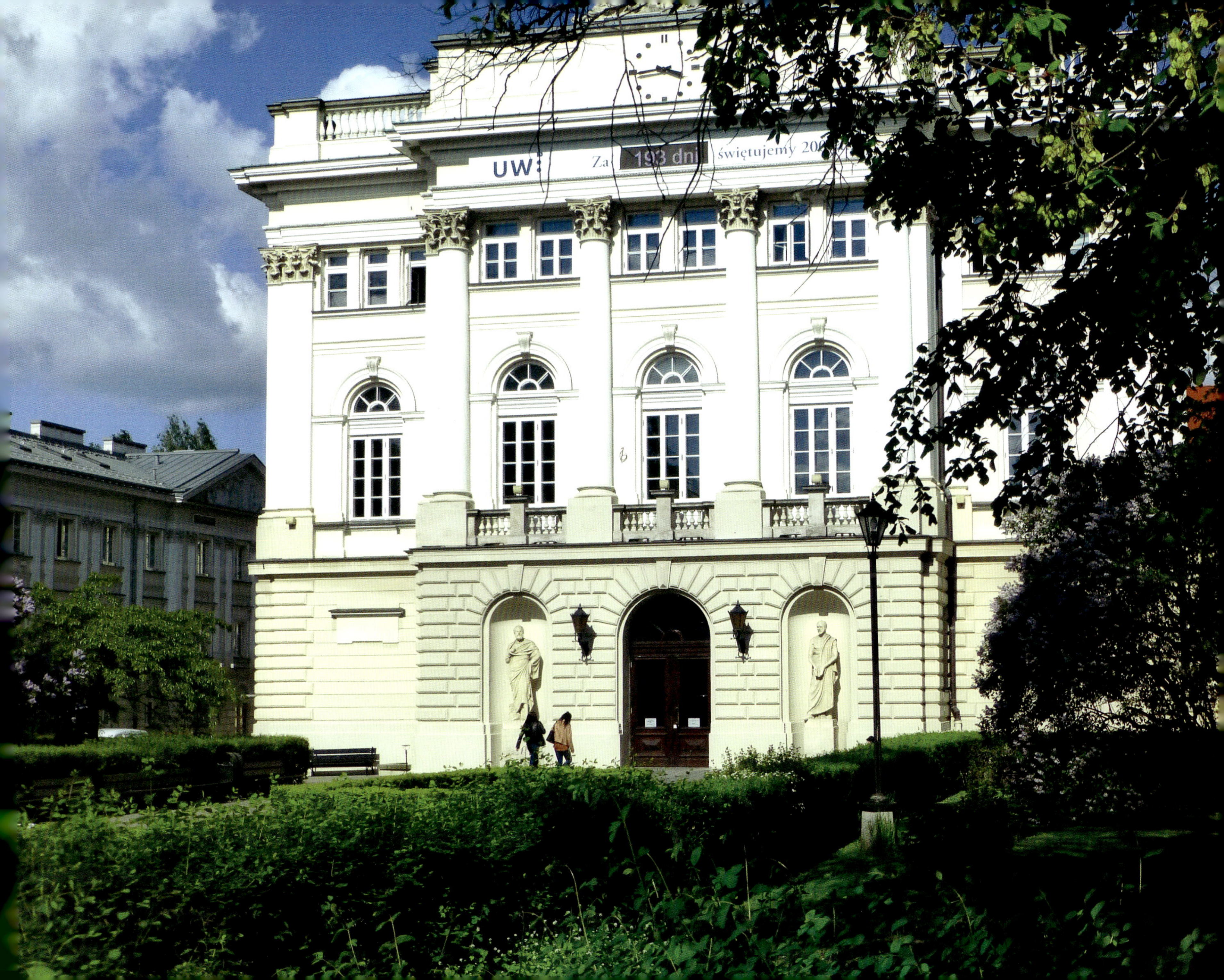
UW:
Za 193 dni świętujemy

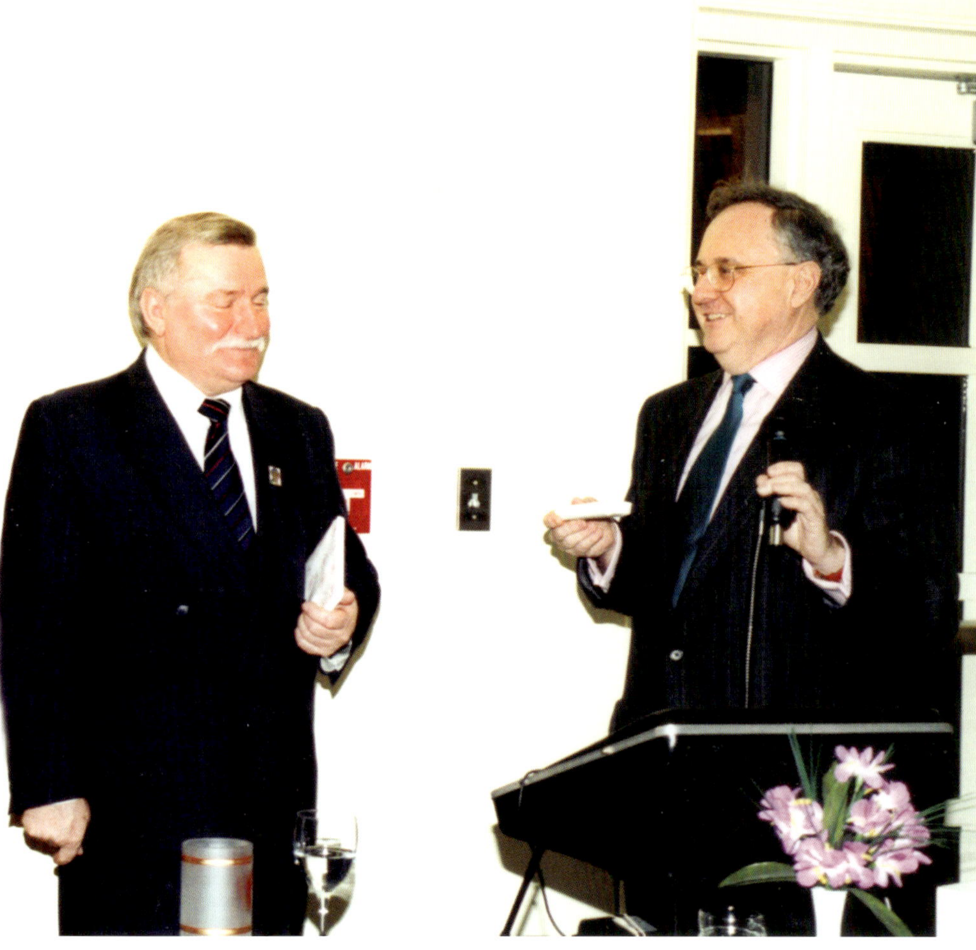

Lech Walesa (*left*) and Patrick O'Meara (*right*), 1998.
Photograph courtesy of IU International magazine.

Leonard J. Baldyga, who was public affairs officer with the United States Information Agency in Warsaw at the time, commented: "With the establishment of the American Studies Center at the University of Warsaw in 1976, one of the main cultural and educational objectives of the United States Government was achieved despite the uncertain political relationship that existed at the time between Poland and the United States." He went on to observe that:

> No formal exchange agreement existed between Poland and the United States, unlike the complex and tightly reciprocal agreements the U.S. had with other East European countries and with the then Soviet Union. Poland continued to be unique in that, despite official censorship and other restraints, we managed to establish university linkages, conduct cultural programs and engage in extensive English teaching and language programs, all without the benefits of a formal bilateral and reciprocal educational and cultural exchange agreement between the two governments. But the initiative to set up an American Studies Center, the first of its kind in Eastern Europe, went beyond any previous university affiliation program in Poland and, therefore, had to be carefully negotiated.[1]

Warsaw had opened in 1976. The purpose of the IU Polish Studies Center was to promote lectures, discussions, academic courses, and an exchange program with the University of Warsaw. It was hoped that these activities would increase the knowledge and cultural awareness of Poland and East Europe.

Historian and former director of the Polish Studies Center at IU, Padraic Kenney—a specialist on the experience of workers in early Communist Poland, gender and anticommunist opposition, and social movements in the fall of communism in

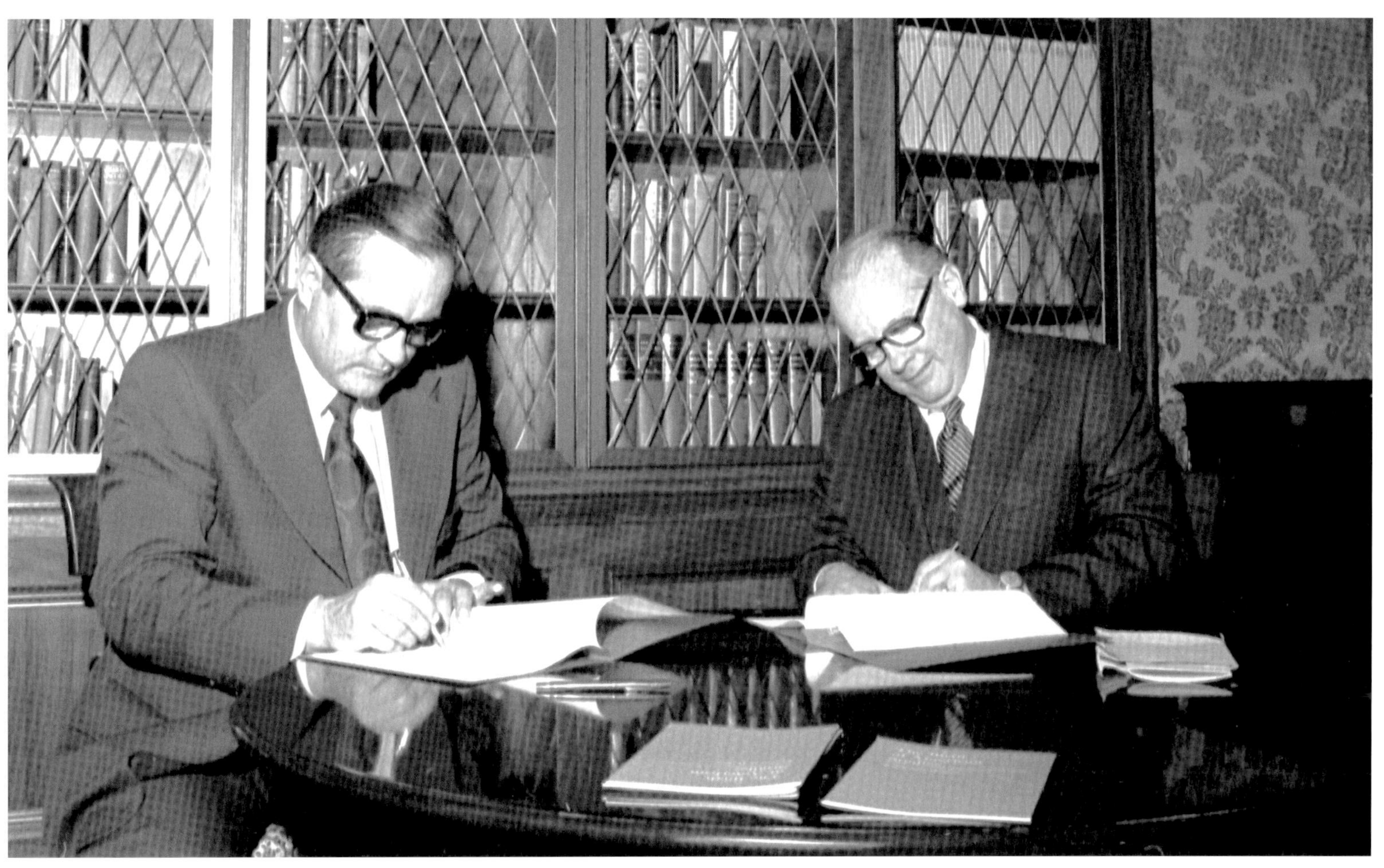

Zygmunt Rybicki (*left*), rector of the University of Warsaw, and John W. Ryan (*right*), president of Indiana University, sign an agreement of cooperation at the IU Lilly Library to create the American Studies Center at the University of Warsaw and the Polish Studies Center at Indiana University, October 31, 1977.

IU Archives (P0030596).

Central Europe—reflected on this important period and provided a similar perspective: "It is clear to me that by the 1970s, it was not impossible [in Poland] to be interested in American culture the way it would have been in the 1950s and 1960s. This is one of the kinds of openings that happened in those early years because, clearly, for Warsaw to even send a letter to the State Department, would have been impossible ten years before."[2]

Mary Ellen Solt, professor of comparative literature on the Bloomington campus, served as the inaugural director of the Polish Studies Center at IU, beginning in 1977. Under her leadership, the center organized numerous lectures, films, and panel discussions. She was also responsible for the exchange program with the American Studies Center at the University of Warsaw. Between 1976 and 1989, the American Studies Center was the only center of its type allowed to operate in a communist country.

In commenting about this period, Robert Gosende, at that time a US cultural affairs officer, wrote:

> President John Ryan also understood how important it was for U.S. universities to work closely with our federal government on international education. I first met him in mid-1970, while serving as Cultural Affairs Officer at the U.S. Embassy in Warsaw, Poland. Indiana University was asked by the Bureau of Educational and Cultural Affairs of the Department of State if it would be interested in partnering with Warsaw University for the establishment of an American Studies Center. Indiana University's Russian and Eastern European Studies Program was a leader in the field and, because of this, it was thought that Bloomington might be an ideal partner for this important initiative. That certainly turned out to be the case. President Ryan enthusiastically endorsed this effort.[3]

IU's relationship with the American Studies Center in Warsaw was the first of its kind between the United States and a partner institution behind the Iron Curtain, and it would become the focal point in East Central Europe for the study of the United States. During the Cold War, the center's library was influential in promoting American studies throughout East Europe. In a 1996 essay published to commemorate the twenty-year anniversary of the American Studies Center at the University of Warsaw, American diplomat Leonard Baldgya wrote:

> The fact that the American Studies Center was separated and essentially independent from the Press and Cultural Section of the American Embassy, enabled the Center to survive the difficult crisis years of Martial Law in the early 1980's. While it was virtually impossible for a Polish scholar to try to visit the small library collection located within the American Embassy in this period, he or she could more easily access the small American Studies Center unit at the University and, thereby, manage to keep up on developments in American economy, sociology, history and literature. While official relations were basically frozen, the intellectual and scholarly exchange envisioned in the original agreement between the two universities bore fruit and continued to function.[4]

IU's relationship with the American Studies Center in Warsaw was the first of its kind between the United States and a partner institution behind the Iron Curtain, and it would become the focal point in East Central Europe for the study of the United States. During the Cold War, the center's library was influential in promoting American studies throughout East Europe.

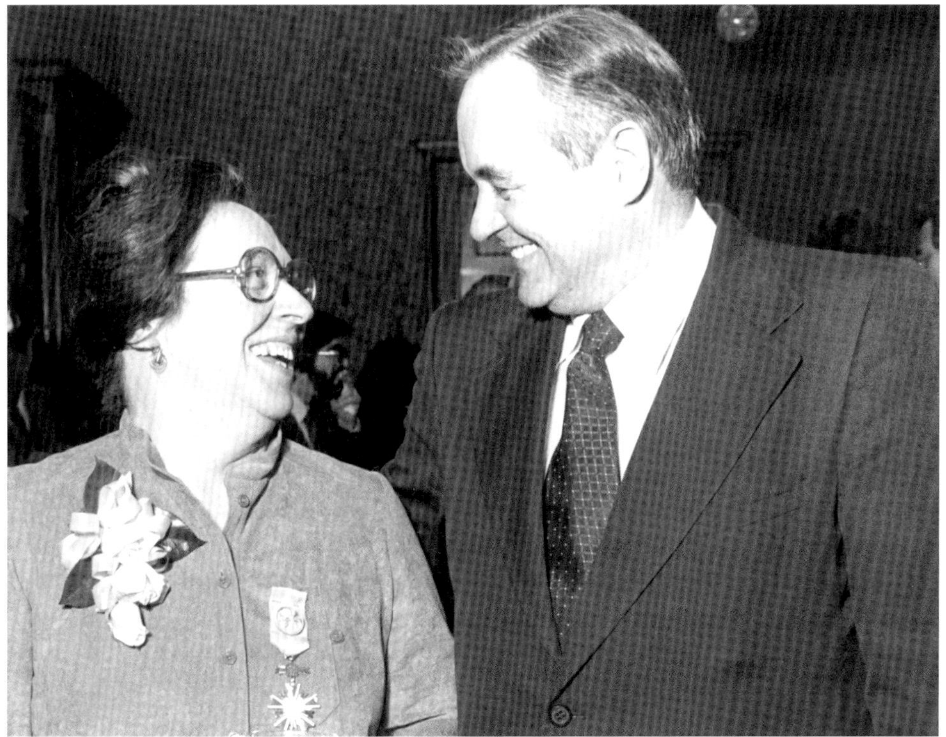

Indiana University faculty member Mary Ellen Solt (*left*), director of IU's Polish Studies Center, is awarded Poland's Gold Badge of Merit by Zygmunt Rybicki (*right*), president of the University of Warsaw, April 7, 1980. The award was for Solt's contributions in promoting Polish–American understanding and cultural relations.
IU Archives (P0030597).

Since the American Studies Center was part of the University of Warsaw and not the US embassy, it was possible for Polish dissidents to go there to read American newspapers, magazines, and journals that were unavailable in the country. The center even printed copies in Polish of important articles from these sources.

Mary McGann, who served as the associate director of the American Studies Center while she and her husband, IU professor Timothy (Tim) Wiles, were in Warsaw, reflects on the great importance of the center's achievements: "It really was not only the only one in Eastern Europe, except for Berlin, it was the only one in Europe; faculty, administrators, and embassy employees talked about the future of Poland and what was going to happen."[5]

Bill Johnston, a professor of comparative literature at IU, began his term as the director of the IU Polish Studies Center in 2001. His extensive list of major Polish authors whom he translated into English included works by leading poets, novelists, and twentieth-century authors. He provided his impressions on this time period:

> I think, there was a great gratitude amongst the Poles in the seventies and eighties for those countries and institutions that spent the time to invest resources and energy and personnel when Poland felt isolated from the world. It was, of course, cut off in terms of access—physical access. You had to have a visa, and that was hard; there were controls. It was difficult to get to physically, also; travel was harder and, again, with visas and passports, that made it even harder. There wasn't anything like the tourism one sees today; it was a much rarer thing for foreigners to be there at all, let alone living in the country. . . . Poland has always been very aware of and attached to the West and the West's

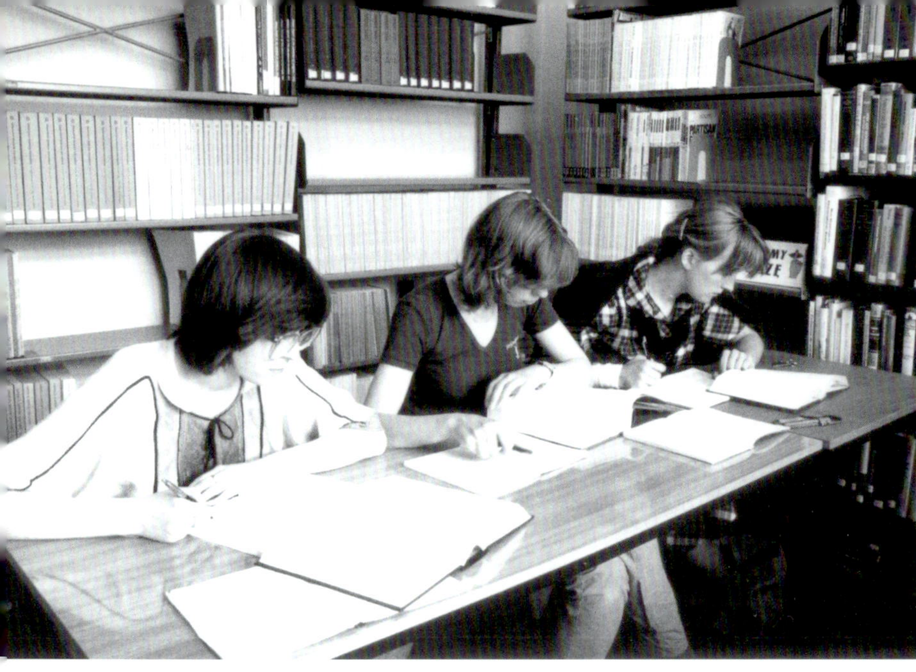

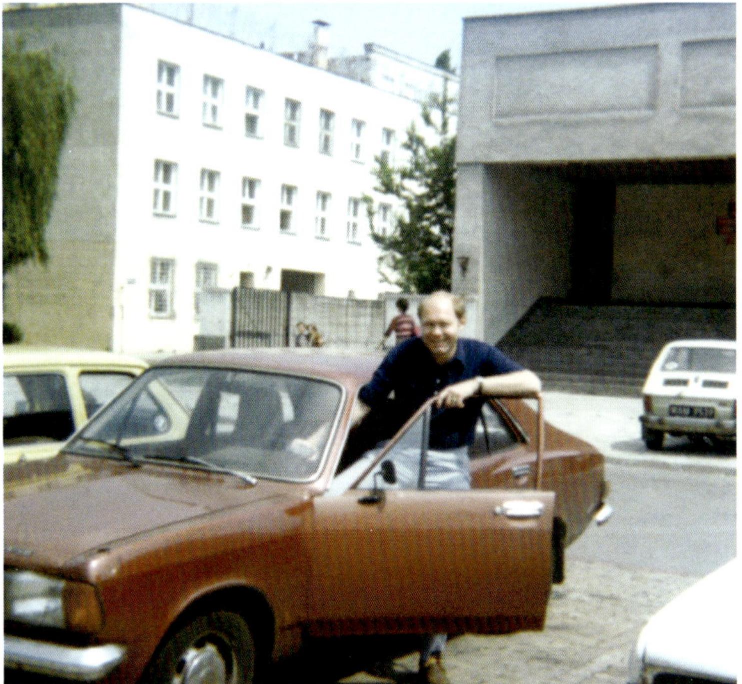

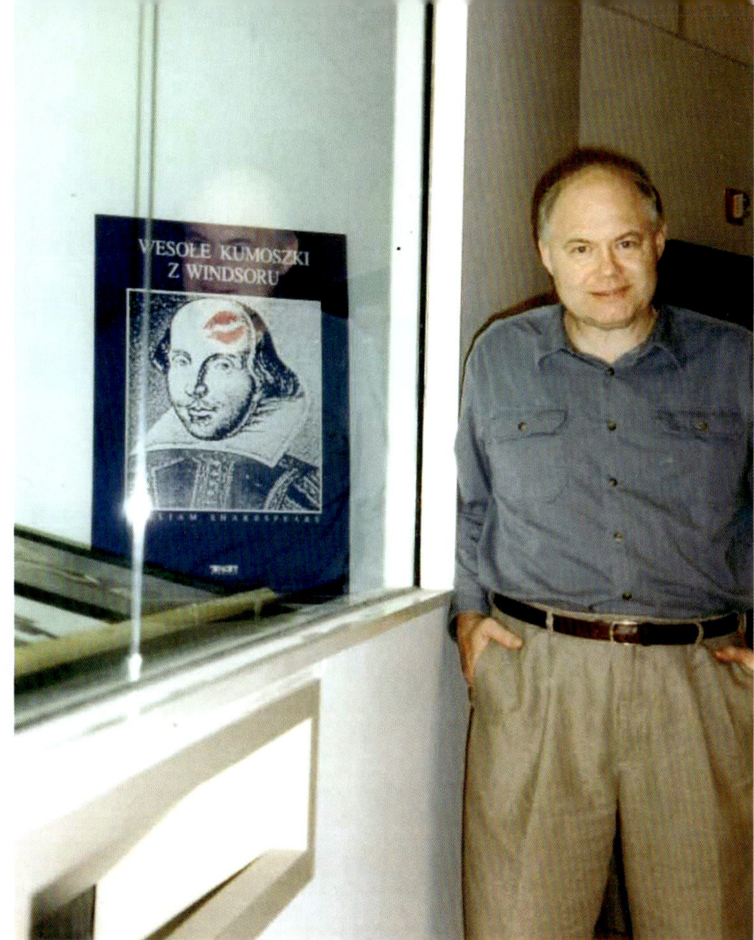

Above left, University of Warsaw students in the American Studies Center library. In 1975, Timothy (Tim) Wiles helped to carry books and journals from the US embassy to the American Studies Center. These books formed the core of a library that provided the main source of information about the West for Polish scholars during martial law, and to this day is a key repository of Western information.
Photograph courtesy of Mary McGann, IU International *magazine.*

Left, Timothy (Tim) Wiles, Warsaw, Poland, 1983.
Photograph courtesy of Mary McGann.

Above, Timothy (Tim) Wiles stands next to a Polish poster exhibit he curated at Indiana University, circa 1999.
Photograph courtesy of Mary McGann.

> ideas—its artists, writers, thinkers, concerts, ways of living . . . but after Solidarity and the clampdown, it got harder [to engage with Western culture]. So it was very hard to have access to those ideas; books were banned, obviously there was no internet, even telephoning someone was really, really hard. When I went out in September eighty-three, I think it was three months before I saw a single Western newspaper. And so, the places you could have access to, and for me in Krakow, that was the American Consulate, which had a library of newspapers and magazines—it was very precious. I can only imagine that when Tim [Wiles] and Mary [McGann] were in Warsaw, their institution would be very much the same kind of haven, both politically and intellectually, for the university and for the broader intellectual and academic community.[6]

Some critics of the exchange felt that IU should not work in a country with a communist regime. Today, it is clear that this was a bold and visionary decision for Indiana University. Those who used or studied at the center in Warsaw and those who visited or attended Indiana University went on to play senior roles in government, academia, and public affairs in Poland both before and after the fall of communism. Bill Johnston commented: "The academic community as a whole was not just very good at whatever work they did, but was deeply interested in world politics, in new literature and art and intellectual movements, in film, generally speaking, the life of the mind. The life of the mind has always been an absolute value among the Polish intelligentsia, and so the presence of these islands of openness and access to the West were an immense gift to that world."[7]

Tim Wiles and Mary McGann were formative actors in Poland and at Indiana University.

Bill Johnston recognized the contribution of Wiles:

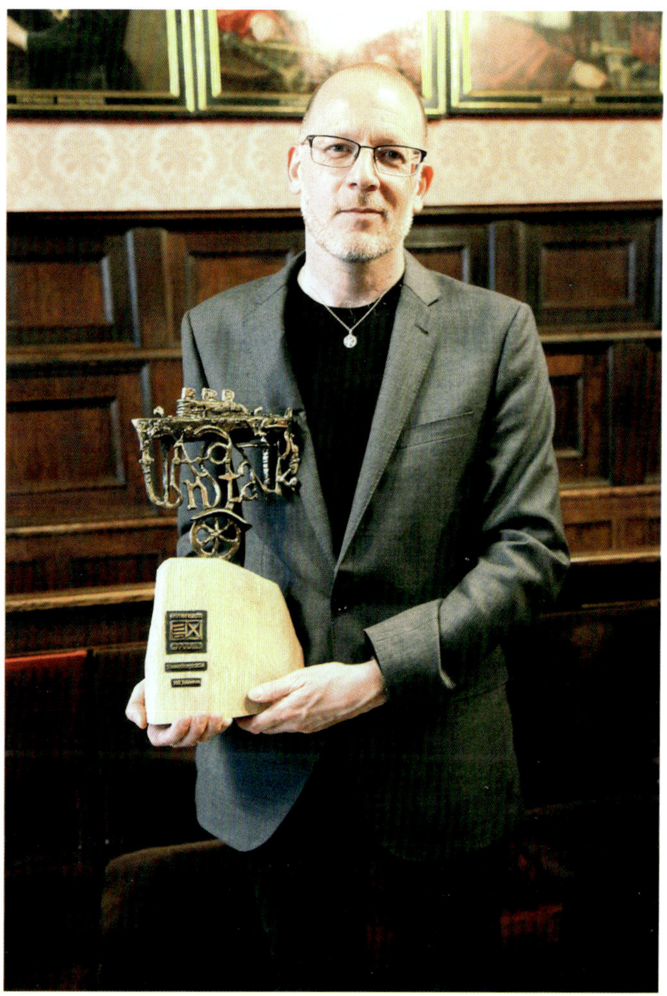

Bill Johnston, Indiana University professor of comparative literature, receiving the Transatlantyk Prize from the Book Institute in Kraków for his contribution to popularizing Polish literature abroad, 2014. *Photograph courtesy of Bill Johnston.*

> Tim was a very strong advocate for the fact that we have great commonalities between the two institutions, that we can learn from the faculty and scholars of Warsaw just as much as they can learn from us. It's a mutual thing, and he very much pursued that. Because I think the need for something like a Polish Studies Center was more immediately apparent in the eighties, and after eighty-nine, I think his great accomplishment was to solidify those contacts and ensure the exchange wasn't just big brother helping out little brother, but was on the basis of parity and one that was of mutual interest and ongoing interest to many, many scholars in both institutions.[8]

IU and the University of Warsaw continued to exchange students and faculty members as well as promote and enhance research, teaching skills, and study opportunities. The different Polish Studies directors at IU over the years—including Jack Bielasiak, Tim Wiles, Bozena Shallcross, Owen Johnson, Bill Johnston, Padraic Kenney, and Joanna Nizynska—enabled the center to reach new heights with a variety of unique programs and conferences. The Polish Studies Center at IU received funds from the United States Information Agency, which subsidized conferences, travel expenses for guest lectures, and visiting faculty members. Conferences included such topics as "In Transition: A Conference on Society, Politics and the Economy in East Central Europe" and "Central Europe and Russia: Alliances, Business, and Culture."

Conference participants were from Poland and from the United States. Many Polish scholars, artists, and political figures came to IU even during the period of martial law. In October 1999, there was a visit by Solidarity leader Lech Walesa, who became president of Poland in 1991 and was awarded the Nobel Peace Prize in 1983.[9]

IU president Myles Brand, wife of Myles Brand and IU women's studies professor Peg Zelin Brand, international dean Patrick O'Meara, Polish studies director Timothy Wiles, and vice president for government relations Christopher Simpson went on an official visit to Poland in 1996. Peg Zelin Brand delivered a lecture on feminist aesthetics to an audience of American and women's studies scholars. After the visit to Warsaw, the group went to Krakow to visit the Jagiellonian University, where they met Rector Aleksander Koj to discuss an exchange agreement between the two institutions.[10]

In February 1997, University of Warsaw rector Wlodzimierz Siwinski was the guest of Myles and Peg Brand in Bloomington. Siwinski had been the associate director of the American Studies Center in Warsaw from 1981 to 1983. At the time of his visit, a special ceremony was held at which Jerzy Kozminski, the Polish ambassador, awarded the Amicus Poloniae distinction to Timothy Wiles and to professor of Polish literature Samuel Fiszman. During the visit, the rector presented the University of Warsaw Distinguished Medal of Service to Timothy Wiles and Patrick O'Meara.

In June 2000, the Polish Studies Center organized a program for rectors and vice rectors of universities in Poland. The event—Strategic Planning for Polish Higher Education—was hosted by the University of Warsaw and funded by the US Department of State. While in Poland, Patrick O'Meara, who led the delegation, signed a renewed exchange agreement with the then rector Piotr Weglenski.

In December 2003, Przemyslaw Grudzinski, the Polish ambassador, conferred the Amicus Poloniae award to Patrick O'Meara and Bill Johnston in recognition of their promotion of better understanding through scholarly work and academic exchanges between Poland and the United States.

What was the outcome of IU's involvement in Poland at a crucial time in its history? Padraic Kenney commented on the historic impact of Indiana University and on its contribution:

> Indiana still has meaning, so if you walk in the door of the American Studies center and say "I'm here from Indiana University," people understand that. You meet a half dozen people who have been there, you meet people you recognize, and you think to yourself, "Where am I? This is remarkable!" We served our purpose, and we can feel that with confidence, because of the goodwill that was left behind. I recall when I first became director and had this idea of having a reception for exchange alumni in Warsaw, and you recognized the importance of this [event]. When this took place, June of 2008 or 2009, it was in this wonderful mirrored room in the rector's palace—I don't know how many people—maybe forty or fifty people gathered, including at least one former minister of education, a couple of former rectors, a number of leading academics, and to hear these people say, "Oh Dunn Meadow! Oh, Nick's!" You know they're not going to say, "How's the football team doing?" Wrong audience, but in this deeply Polish, academic context, to have a distinguished former rector or well-known scholar to mention Nick's or Dunn Meadow . . . it was incredibly meaningful to them.[11]

Mary McGann echoes this perspective:

> I would say in retrospect, the American Studies Center has grown to a point that IU can be extraordinarily proud of what has happened. It now has more applications from prospective students than any other unit in the university, except business, probably. It has a library that would be the envy of any university. The staff is . . . about eight staff members. They have, of course, the director, the assistant director—it's all Polish now, it's all been taken over by Warsaw University, and the students are top notch—they're excellent. And so, what I felt, when I was there was that we were present at the creation. We were there at the beginning—it was so cool! It really was. And then the other achievement IU had a direct influence on was the eventual establishment of the binational Fulbright. They have a Polish academic now, who is very good, I hear, and the numbers of Fulbrights going and coming are large, particularly the researchers coming from Poland.[12]

Indiana still has meaning, so if you walk in the door of the American Studies center and say "I'm here from Indiana University," people understand that.
—Padraic Kenney

In June 2016, IU president Michael McRobbie was in Warsaw to celebrate the fortieth anniversary of the American Studies Center in Warsaw. McRobbie and Rector Marcin Palys renewed the ongoing agreement of cooperation between the two universities, and the rector was awarded the Thomas Hart Benton Medal. In March 2017, the fortieth anniversary of the IU Polish Studies Center, under the leadership of Joanna Nizynska, was celebrated in Bloomington.

The past forty years of this exchange have seen many achievements and outcomes. The enormous importance and influence of the American Studies Center in Warsaw at a critical time in Polish history has become legendary. At the same time, the Polish Studies Center in Bloomington has kept Polish issues in the forefront through conferences, visits, and exchanges. The long-term continuity and viability of both centers, in changing political contexts, is testimony to their relevance.

7 | INDIANA UNIVERSITY *in* South Africa

The 1970s and the 1980s were a time when US educational and philanthropic interests had become seriously concerned with the tremendous educational deficits—especially the lack of access to higher education—facing black students at all levels of education in South Africa.

THE 1970S AND THE 1980S WERE A TIME WHEN US EDUCATIONAL and philanthropic interests had become seriously concerned with the tremendous educational deficits—especially the lack of access to higher education—facing black students at all levels of education in South Africa. Indiana University's African Studies Program had always had a strong academic focus on South Africa. In addition to Patrick O'Meara, director of African Studies and political science faculty member who specialized in political issues in Southern Africa, the university had on its faculty the distinguished African political scientist Gwendolen Carter from 1974 to 1984.

In 1981, Lawrence Keller of the IU School of Continuing Studies went to South Africa with a group of American university administrators who wanted to explore ways to improve educational opportunities for black South Africans. Keller was moved by what he saw.

In conversations with John Samuel, who was then executive director of the South African Committee for Higher Education (SACHED) Trust, the idea emerged that IU correspondence courses might be used, in some form, to meet the needs of African students. In a report published by the National University Continuing Education Association, Indiana University faculty members Frank Di Silvestro and Lawrence Keller described the need for expanding access to higher education in South Africa:

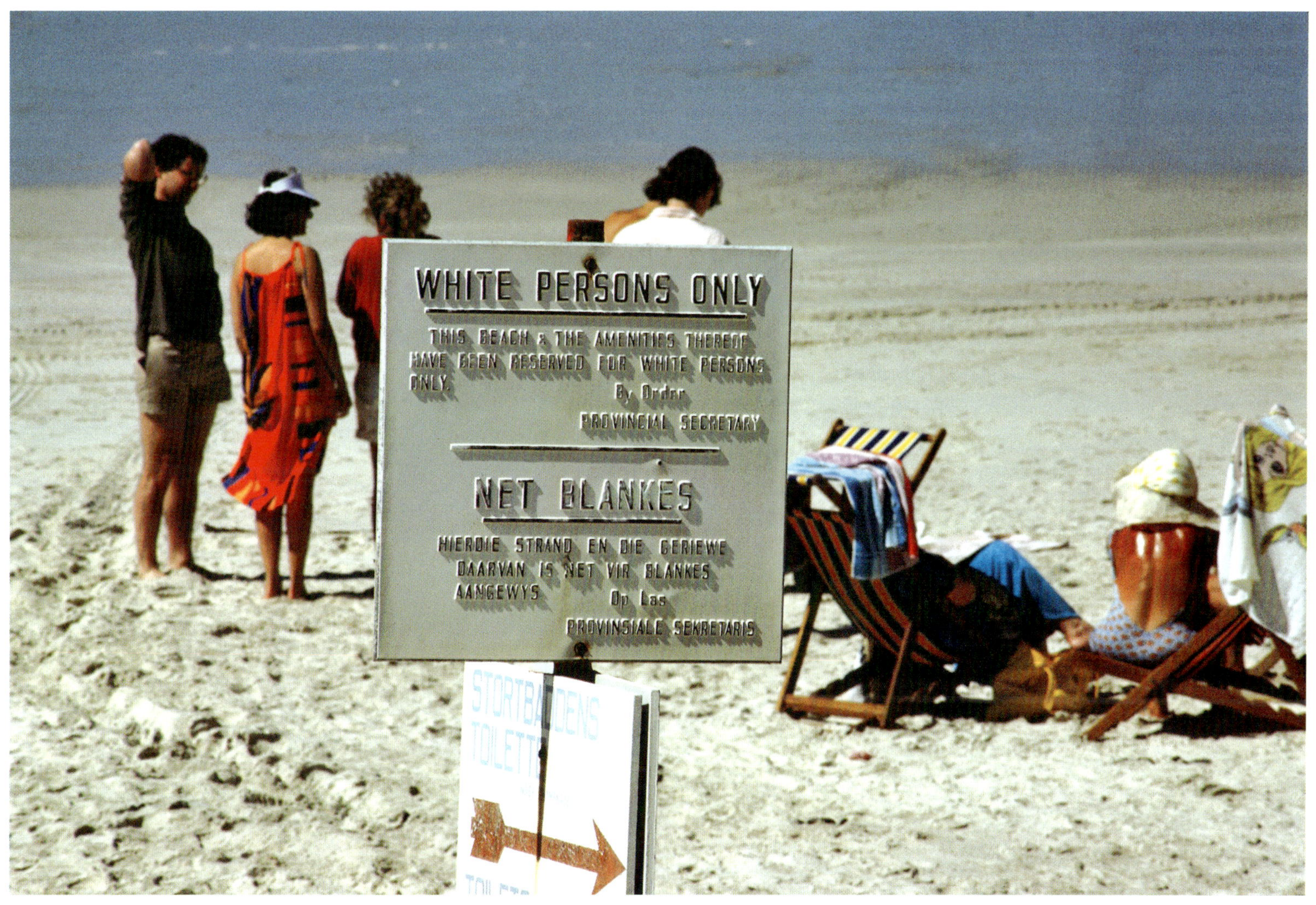

Segregated beach at Stranofontein near Cape Town, South Africa, January 1985.
UN Photo/A Tennenbaum.

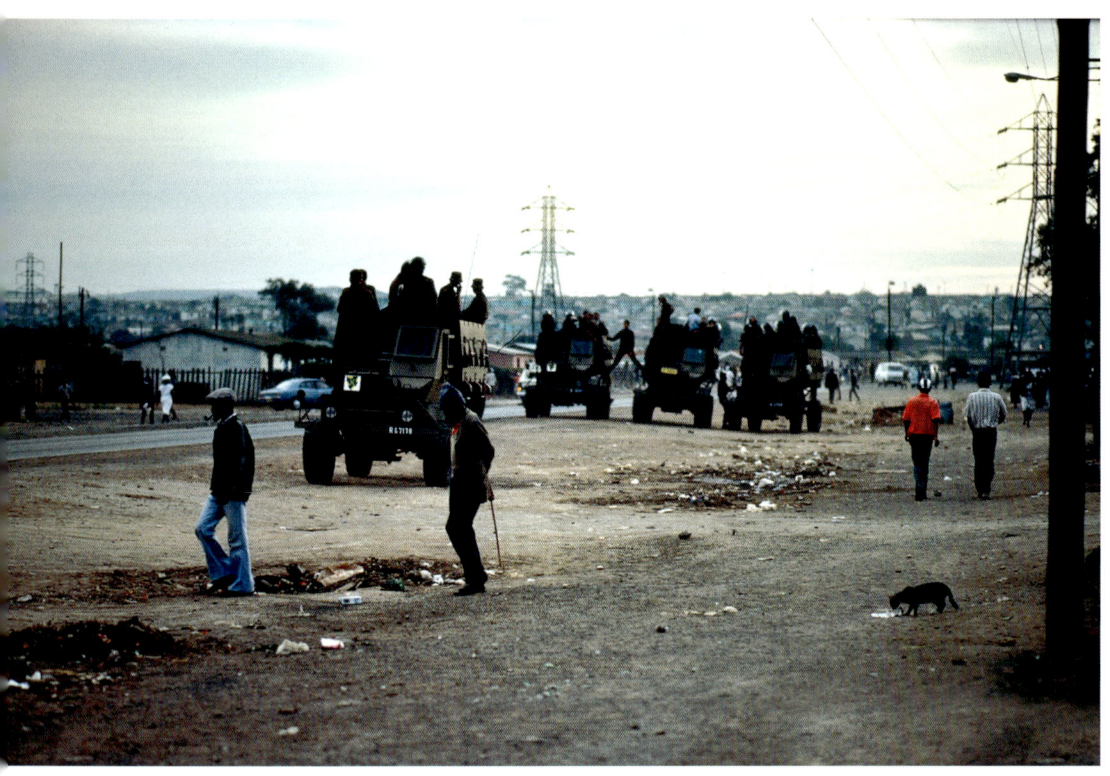

South African army at Port Elizabeth, March 1985. *UN Photo.*

> Most black students in South Africa struggled under appalling conditions to complete their schooling, and they also experienced serious economic and social deprivation in their homes and communities. As a result, these students were either unable to meet the requirements for entering universities or, if they were admitted, they were often unable to perform academic tasks expected of them. South Africa's apartheid educational system prevented black students from acquiring the skills they needed for university study: The ability to read selectively and critically; to take notes and structure essays; and to use research and reference libraries. A further problem was that many of these students have a very poor grounding in English, and for that reason, had great difficulty working in the English medium at the university.[1]

Khanya College (*khanya* means "education for liberation") in Johannesburg became the structure for the implementation of these goals. The intention was not only to provide solid academic training but to enable the students to transcend the personal constraints imposed by the apartheid system. In fall 1982, John Samuel made the first of several visits to Bloomington to further explore the possibility of collaboration with Indiana University.

In December 1984, the Ford Foundation announced financial support for this project and approved a grant directly to SACHED, which included a 1985 meeting in South Africa for Indiana University faculty who would be involved with Khanya College.

In April 1985, the IU School of Continuing Studies and SACHED signed an agreement that listed six IU courses that would be taught at Khanya College by South African academics. IU faculty would supervise syllabi and grade examinations and papers. Khanya students who successfully completed the one-year program would receive an IU transcript, which would enable them to transfer to the University of Witwatersrand in Johannesburg and the University of Cape Town, which were eager to open access to their institutions for more qualified African students.

Most black students in South Africa struggled under appalling conditions to complete their schooling, and they also experienced serious economic and social deprivation in their homes and communities.

—Frank Di Silvestro and Lawrence Keller

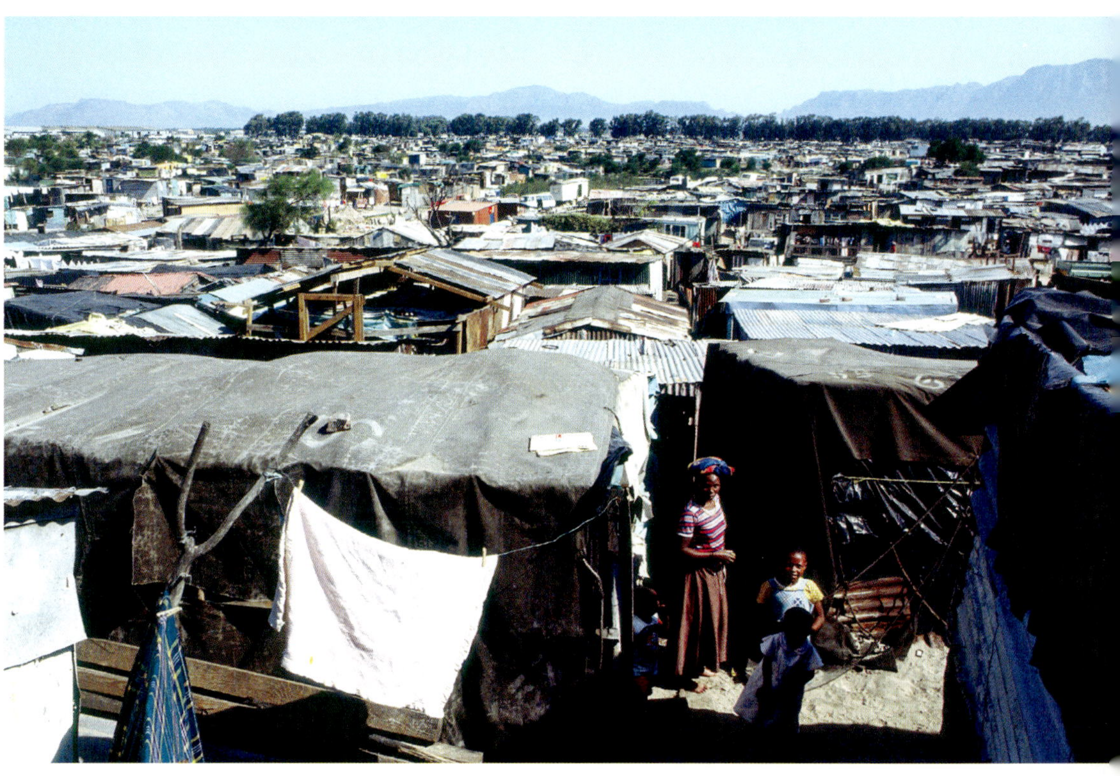

Shantytown at Crossroads, Cape Town, South Africa, April 1985. *UN Photo.*

James Kilgore, former Khanya instructor and, later, director of the college, recalls:

> We were on the fifth floor of a fairly rundown office block with an Allied Bank at the bottom. We had furniture that was kind of falling apart—the place was really minimal in terms of facilities. We also had a residence, which was around the corner, which was a very rundown apartment building. We probably had around 110 students. You know, the academic program at the time was geared towards getting students into the historically white universities, so we had six classes, and people took two, and they applied to Wits [University of Witwatersrand] and to other institutions, and if they passed, they got credits, and all the accreditation was arranged through Indiana—we had to send exams to Indiana, and things like that.[2]

By March 1986, there was enough academic and donor support for Khanya College to hire faculty and admit one hundred students at campuses in Johannesburg and Cape Town. The aim was to enable students to think independently, work in groups, think critically, and obtain the necessary credits for admission to the major universities. Thus, the founding of Khanya was based on one of apartheid education's many contradictions: a student had to earn credit from 10,000 kilometers away in order to enter a local university.[3]

John Samuel remarked on the importance of Khanya College's relationship with Indiana University: "We wouldn't have

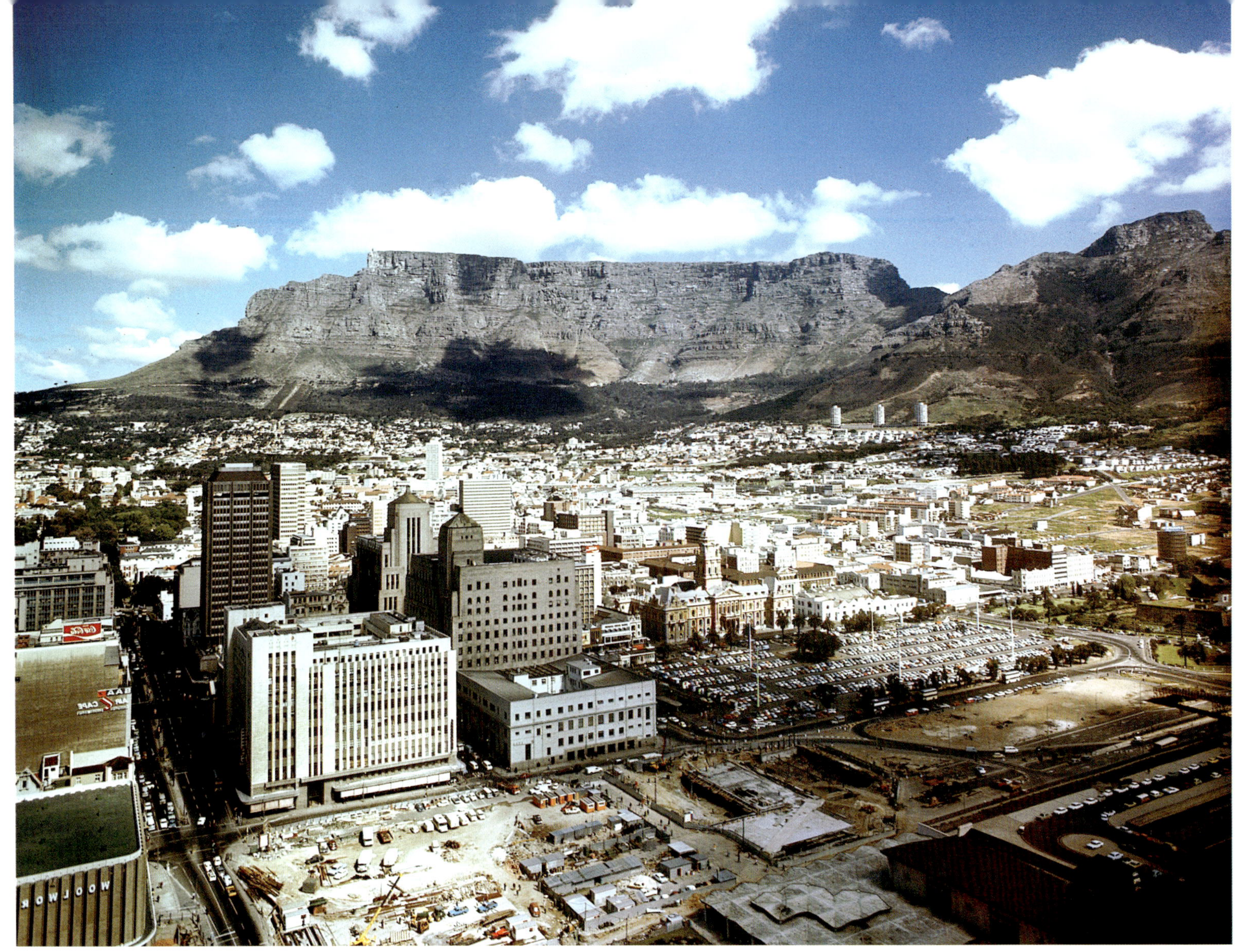

Cape Town, South Africa; Table Mountain in the background, January 1974.
UN Photo/Jerry Frank.

gotten anywhere without the Indiana link . . . but if it weren't for the sympathetic support of individuals at the university [in South Africa] it wouldn't have gotten anywhere . . . to some extent we were trading on the conscience of the university. They had some sense that this is what they should be doing."[4]

IU faculty members such as Ben Brabson in physics and Phyllis Martin from history praised the caliber and the dedication of the instructors at Khanya. After a visit in 1990, IU professor of English Albert Wertheim wrote: "Seeing the Khanya operations first hand, meeting my colleagues there, and talking with students proved to be far more beneficial than I had originally anticipated. I now feel I know the pressures each school is under, the capabilities and backgrounds of the students, and the personalities and commitments of the staff. I was inspired by the importance of what Khanya is. I was always pleased but now am proud to be connected to Khanya and its efforts."[5]

James Kilgore contributes to the Khanya perspective:

> The college itself had an incredibly vibrant culture; most of the students there came out of the democratic movement, out of the anti-apartheid movement—the majority of them were activists. The majority of them were older, at least in their late twenties, some even older than that. Some had been national leaders in organizations—we had someone who was a general secretary of the railway workers union. We had other people that had national positions in student organizations or religion—South African churches, etc. We also had people who had been outside the country in guerilla camps for the ANC and had come back and enrolled in the college, so it was a very unusual student body, and it was run according to the culture of the mass democratic movement, that is the idea of participatory democracy.[6]

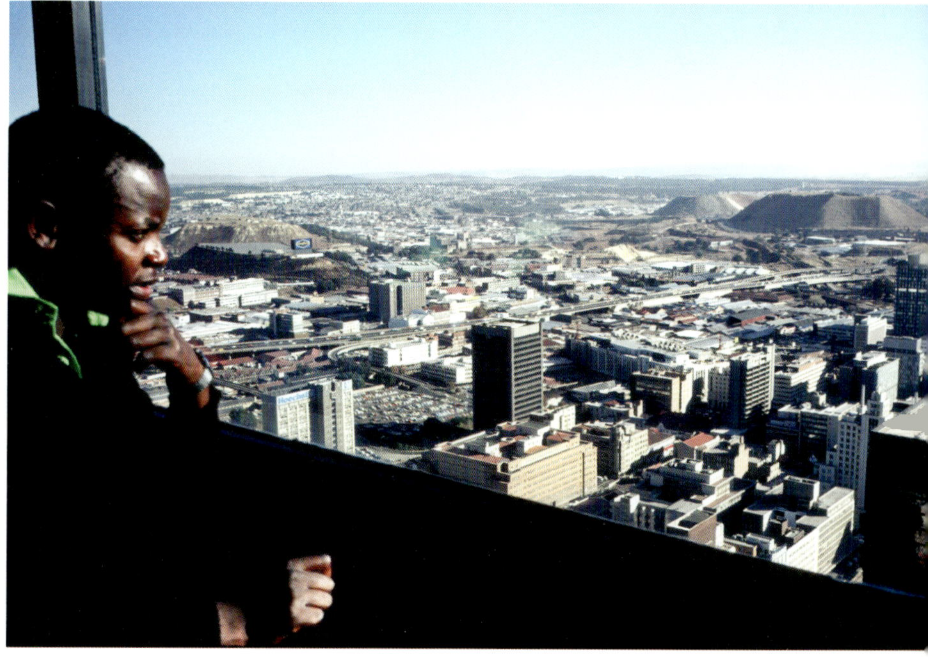

Johannesburg, South Africa, January 1982. *UN Photo/DB.*

An underlying philosophy of Khanya was based on premises of the Latin American political thinker Paulo Freire, expressed in his book, *The Pedagogy of the Oppressed.* James Kilgore discussed the context in which this ideology was applied:

> We wanted to provide an opportunity to become part of what we thought was going to be the new South Africa, and provide them with access to the education skills that they'd be able to compete academically, but ultimately be able to occupy positions of power in the government and civil society, post 1994. So, that was just broadly, that's how it was. So we operated—we tried

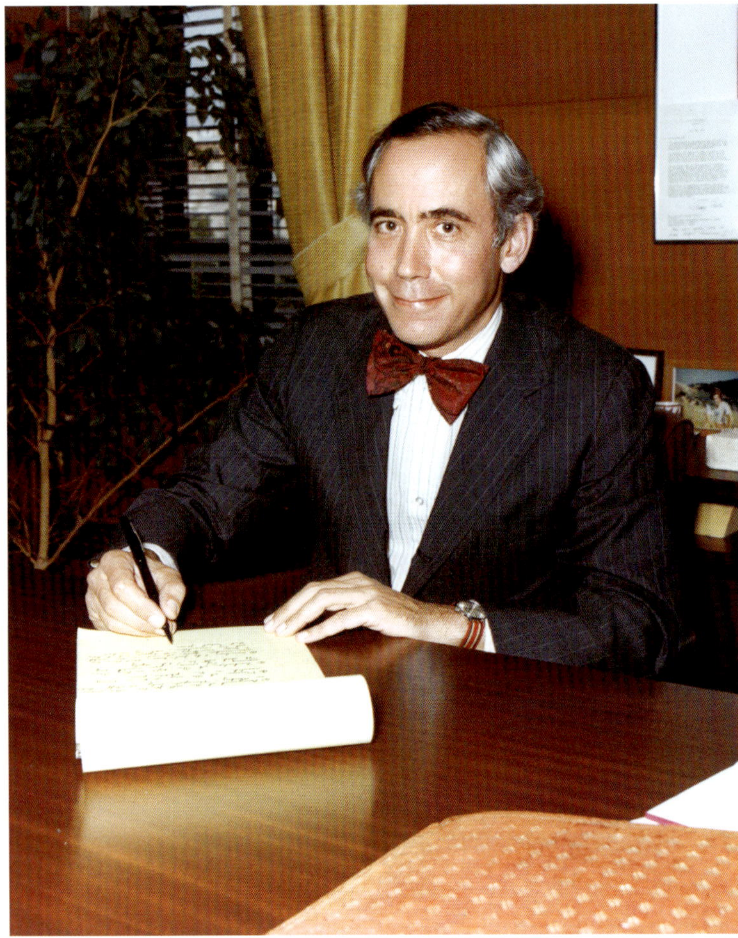

Tom Ehrlich, the fifteenth president of Indiana University, serving from 1987 to 1994. *IU Archives (P0040165).*

Facing, Newly elected president Nelson Mandela delivers his inaugural address from a balcony of the town hall, Pretoria, South Africa, May 1994. *UN Photo/Chris Sattlberger.*

> to operate it—along Paulo Freire's principles, so we did a lot of activities in classes, although we had to follow a syllabus, and it had to be approved by Wits University and by Indiana. Nonetheless, we played with that as much as we could, and so we tried to do a lot of activity-based stuff in the classroom.[7]

Kilgore goes on to discuss the challenges and limitations that were faced, mainly because of education for black South Africans under apartheid:

> People could debate things, especially political issues, historical issues, at a very, very high level . . . they would be at a higher level than the typical kind of graduate seminar . . . but because of their academic training, they couldn't write most of it. They could not write an essay. If you read what they wrote, you'd think they had a sixth-grade education. So one of the biggest tasks we found was building up people's writing skills. With dedication and personal attention, about half the class would make a qualitative leap in writing.[8]

In 1987, after its first year, the Indiana University–Khanya College program won national awards in the United States from the National University Continuing Education Association and the American College Testing Program. The collaboration was cited for its innovative design as well as for its contribution to building an unbiased and quality-based education for black South Africans.[9]

In the early 1990s, additional funding to support the IU–Khanya College program came from the Lilly Endowment, the Kellogg Foundation, and the US Agency for International Development. During that period, IU had established a three-way linkage with Khanya College and the University of the Witwatersrand for an exchange of faculty and administrators

We wanted to provide an opportunity to become part of what we thought was going to be the new South Africa, and provide them with access to the education skills that they'd be able to compete academically, but ultimately be able to occupy positions of power in the government and civil society.

—James Kilgore

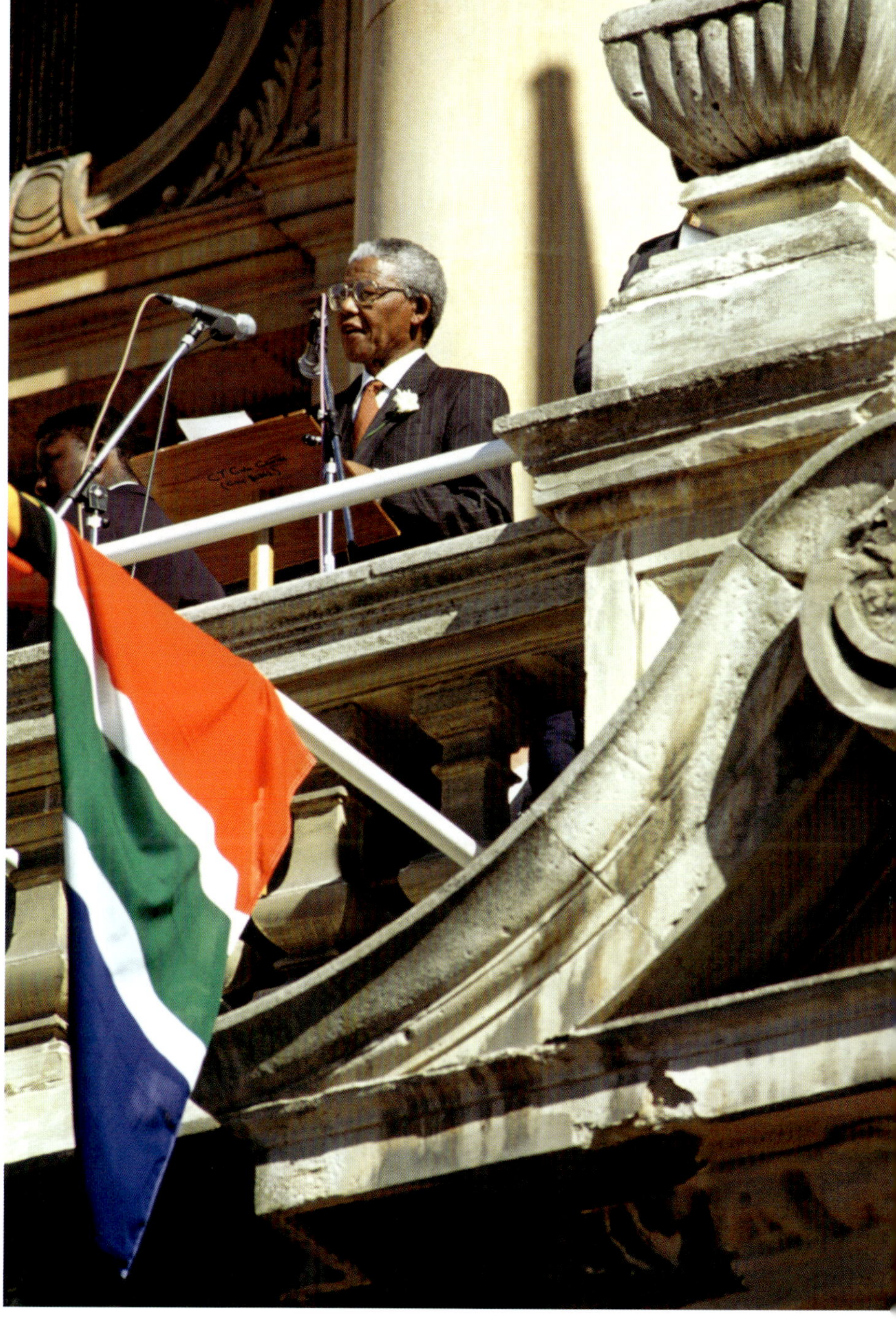

in the area of academic skills and learning resources. This three-way exchange was complementary with IU's mission at Khanya College. As Sharon Pugh, director of IU's Learning Skills Center, stated: "In order to design an effective transitional program [for Khanya College], we need to understand a great deal about both Khanya and the South African universities that take Khanya students."[10]

In 1990, Thomas Ehrlich, then president of Indiana University, also paid a visit to Khanya. He wrote: "My brief visit gave me a sense of strong hope in political terms and enhanced admiration for John Samuel and his colleagues who face incredible economic and social concerns. Education is key to so much of the future there. I very much hope—and expect—Indiana University can have a continuing and useful role."[11]

The following comments from Khanya students indicate the value of their learning experience:

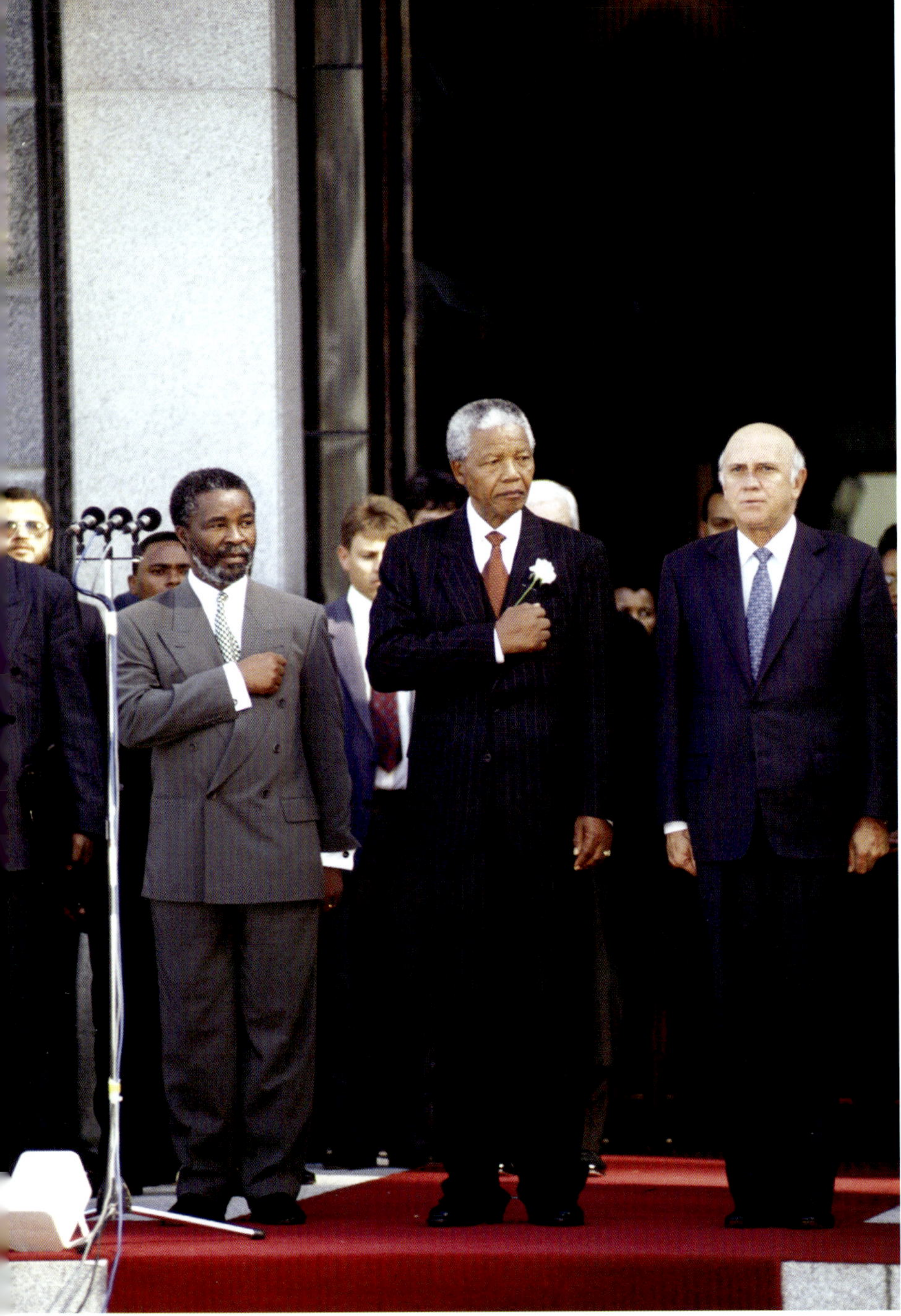

Every person belonged to a study group. Every week, a meeting was compulsory. Study groups forced people to work together. —Fana Jiyane, 1988

In my African Literature class at Wits, former Khanya students, myself included, occupied the top positions all the way. Even in my drama classes, I found myself sailing above the rest. While this may be a fact of my own ingenuity, I strongly suspect that Khanya contributed substantially to this desired end. —Kgafela oa Mogogbdi, 1993

My high point at Khanya was that I got a chance to do what I wanted to do, learn without being restricted . . . a chance to express what I felt about being black and being a woman . . . I got a taste of ideal education. Once you get a taste of it, you never forget it. —Rose Telela, 1987

Academically, we are far better off that most first year students in terms of taking notes and writing essays. There is less work here (at Wits) [University of Witwatersrand]. Tutorials are easy at Wits. —Silone Musapelo, 1994

We had freedom of expression, and I think the method is more learner centered unlike other institutions of higher learning, where we were not given a chance to interact with lecturers, especially when we left Khanya . . . And I think our views were respected because the lecturer always wanted to know about our opinions, that is, what are the things that we mostly need to learn more about and he/she would change the pattern according to our interest. —Thulani Majozi, 1993

I compared favourably to other students regardless of the schools they came from, multiracial or DET [Department of Education and Training schools].[12] The kind of tutorials we had were more rigorous than the ones at Wits. —Moosa Magubane, 1990[13]

In 1992, a new cooperative IU–Khanya College agreement was formed. South Africa had been undergoing rapid chances at all levels—political, social, and educational. John Samuel had resigned as director of SACHED; Robert Segall had taken over as project coordinator of Khanya and was able to meet with administrators in Bloomington. Under the new agreement, Khanya students would no longer receive IU transfer credit; instead, Indiana University faculty would serve as external examiners.

The Indiana University–Khanya College program played a part in the educational restructuring that took place as South Africa moved toward a more democratic society.

Kilgore concludes: "I really found it immensely rewarding, the overall experience of working in a democratic culture and working with people who would have this kind of history of political involvement and desire to change the nature of South Africa. Being in that place at that moment was quite an amazing experience."[14]

The Indiana University–Khanya College program played a part in the educational restructuring that took place as South Africa moved toward a more democratic society.

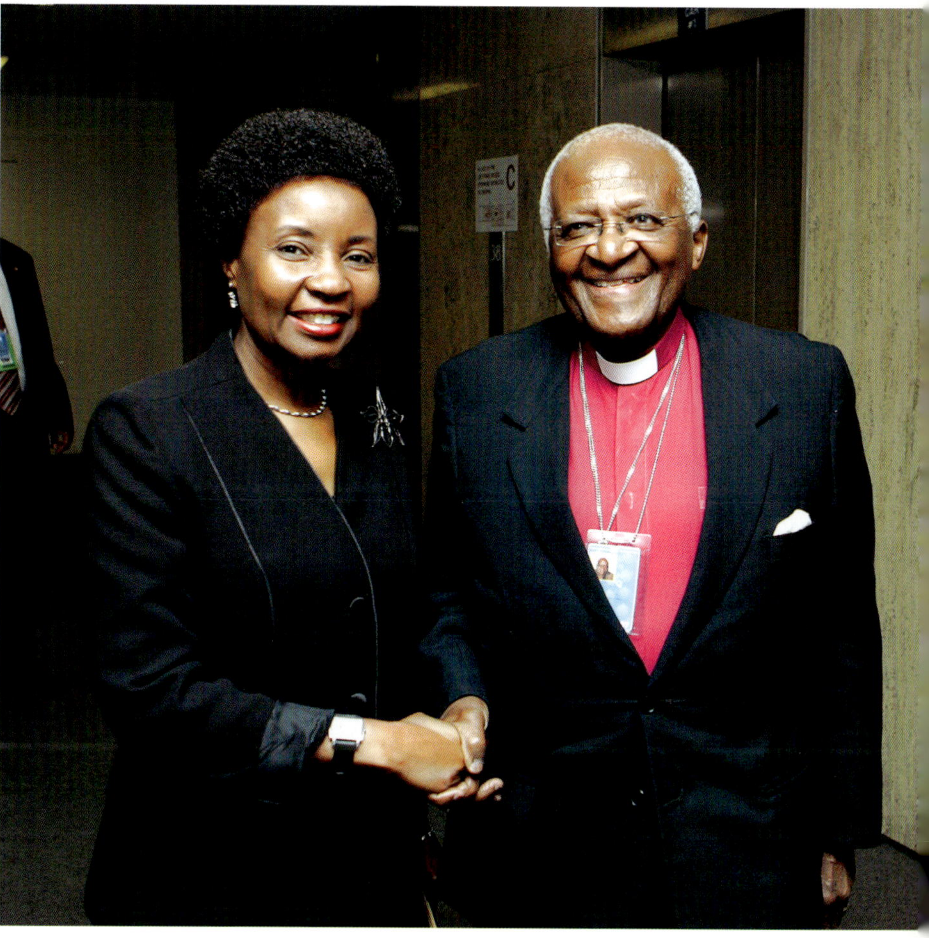

Deputy Secretary-General Asha Rose Migiro (*left*) meets with Desmond Tutu, Archbishop Emeritus of Cape Town, Republic of South Africa, at UN Headquarters in New York, September 2007. *UN Photo/Evan Schneider.*

Facing, Inauguration ceremony of South African president Nelson Mandela, Natal, South Africa, May 1994. *Left to right:* Vice President Thabo Mbeki, Mandela, and Vice President F. W. de Clerk, *UN Photo/Chris Sattlberger.*

8 | INDIANA UNIVERSITY *in* Malaysia

Educational barriers were among the most commonly mentioned obstacles to improvement in social and economic status. After independence, there was an impetus to remove educational barriers and to upgrade educational opportunities.

MALAYSIA IS A MULTIETHNIC COUNTRY. IN THE 1960S, MORE THAN 50 percent of the 16 million people were Bumiputra or ethnic Malays, 35 percent were Malaysian Chinese, and 10 percent were Malaysian Indian. Bumiputra had not benefited proportionally from the country's economic growth and rising personal incomes. By the time independence was achieved in August 1957, ethnicity, occupation, and social class were firmly established. As late as 1971, for example, Bumiputra owned just 4.3 percent of the corporate equity in the country, while other Malaysians owned 34 percent, the remainder being controlled by multinational corporations. The concentration of economy can be explained by many factors, but educational barriers were among the most commonly mentioned obstacles to improvement in social and economic status. After independence, there was an impetus to remove educational barriers and to upgrade educational opportunities for Bumiputra.[1]

The inequitable distribution of opportunity and wealth among the ethnic communities of Malaysia created by unbalanced growth that was seen as a threat to the country's stability. Moreover, increased industrialization required a rapid increase in the number of people with technical expertise. In 1971, with all major political parties participating, the National Consultative Council recommended that future development plans set as a goal the equitable participation in the economy by all members of Malaysian society. The result

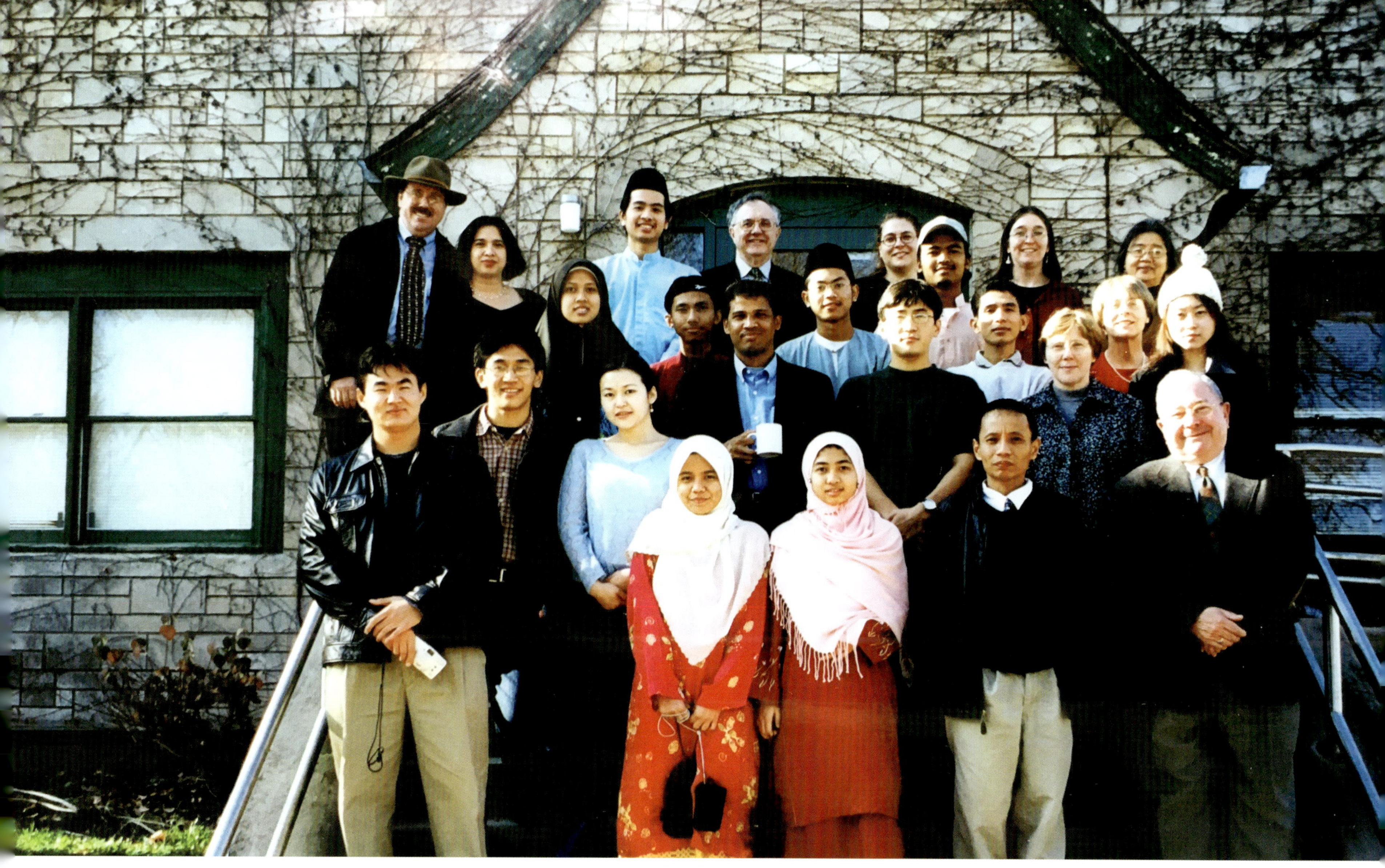

Malaysian students at Indiana University, with Charles Reafsnyder and Faridah Pawan (*top left*), Patrick O'Meara (*middle top*), Roxana Ma Newman (*top right*), Kay Ikranagara (*middle, second from right*), and Ken Rogers (*bottom right*). *Photograph courtesy of Charles Reafsnyder.*

was the New Economic Policy, embodied in the Second Plan, 1971–1975, and signed into law by parliament.[2]

At that time, the Malaysian government funded more than twenty thousand students in the United States, and it now wanted students to complete the first two years of their undergraduate studies in Malaysia and then to proceed to major US universities. The cost of sending students to the United States had become increasingly expensive because of the exchange rate with the US dollar. Other concerns were the need for improved placement for the students at American universities and ways to ensure success at top US institutions.[3]

Our task was to send American faculty members to Malaysia to deliver the first two years of an IU curriculum, with the idea that if you focused enough on the core education requirements, with perhaps some extra emphasis on mathematics for the people bound for engineering, you could serve lots of different majors.

—Tim Diemer

In 1985, the Institute Teknologi MARA (ITM) in Malaysia and the Midwest Universities Consortium for International Activities (MUCIA) agreed to establish a two-year undergraduate program in Selangor, Malaysia, to provide academic coursework for Malaysian students in business, computer science, and engineering. MUCIA was the oldest and most experienced of the several US consortia involved in international development and education. MUCIA was started in 1964 with Ford Foundation support and included four member universities: the University of Illinois, Indiana University, Michigan State University, and the University of Wisconsin. These were joined later by the University of Minnesota, Ohio State University, and the University of Iowa.

The Malaysia Student Program was a cooperative venture involving Indiana University, MUCIA, and ITM. ITM (now called Universiti Teknologi MARA), which operated under the Ministry of Education, was the postsecondary institution charged with the responsibility for developing this program.

An important consideration was the fact that, until 1974, most secondary and university-level teaching was still conducted in either English or Chinese, a practice going back to colonial British times. This placed the predominantly rural Malays, who generally did not speak English or Chinese, at a disadvantage in being admitted to Malaysia's universities and technical schools. After 1969, Bahasa was mandated as the national language of the country, and plans were implemented to phase out English and Chinese in courses at secondary and postsecondary levels of schooling.[4]

Thus, the ITM program was a key part of a general effort to increase the academic participation of ethnic Malays. All these factors led the Malaysians to explore alternative ways of providing government-sponsored students with higher education in the United States. Their solution was based on the establishment of a US equivalent two-year undergraduate program in Malaysia. On completion of the program, successful students would transfer to American universities to complete their undergraduate degrees. Thus, in 1982, the concept of "twinning" was articulated, in which US-bound students would receive the first two years of their overseas education in Malaysia taught by US professors who had been brought to Malaysia for that purpose.[5]

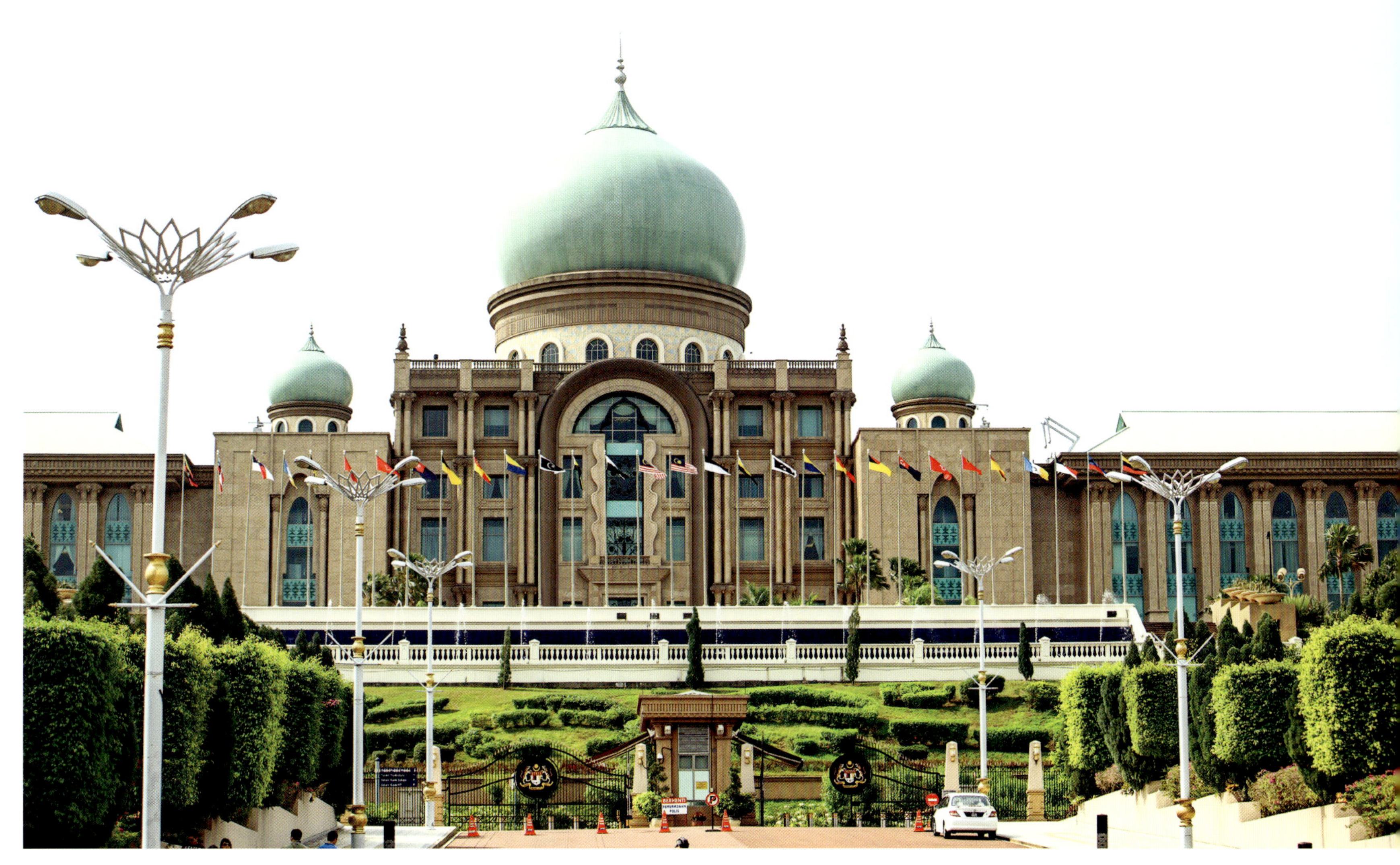

Malaysian prime minister's office, Putrajaya, Malaysia, June 2013.
Photograph courtesy of iStock.

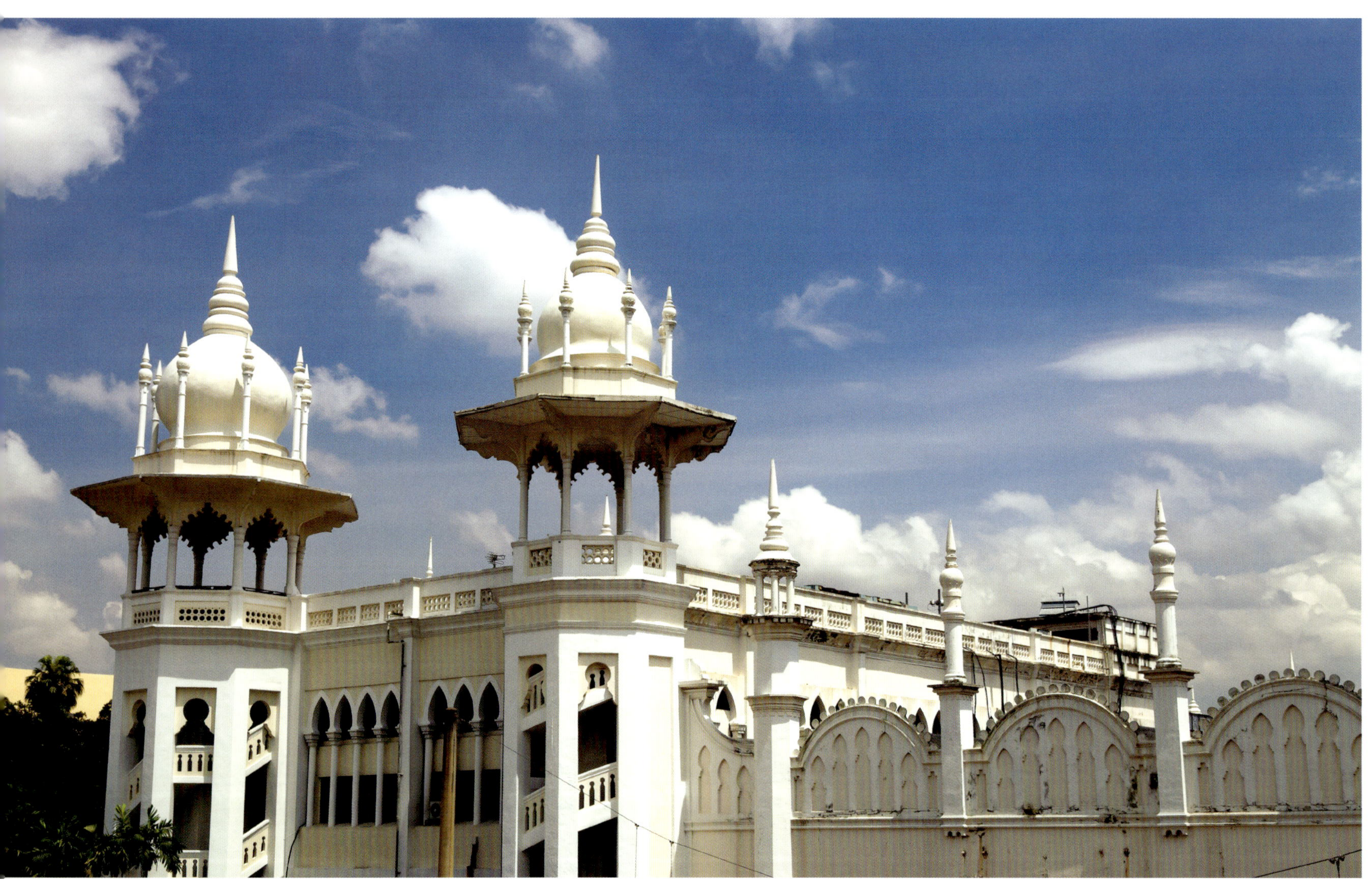

Old Kuala Lumpur railway station, Malaysia.
Photograph courtesy of iStock.

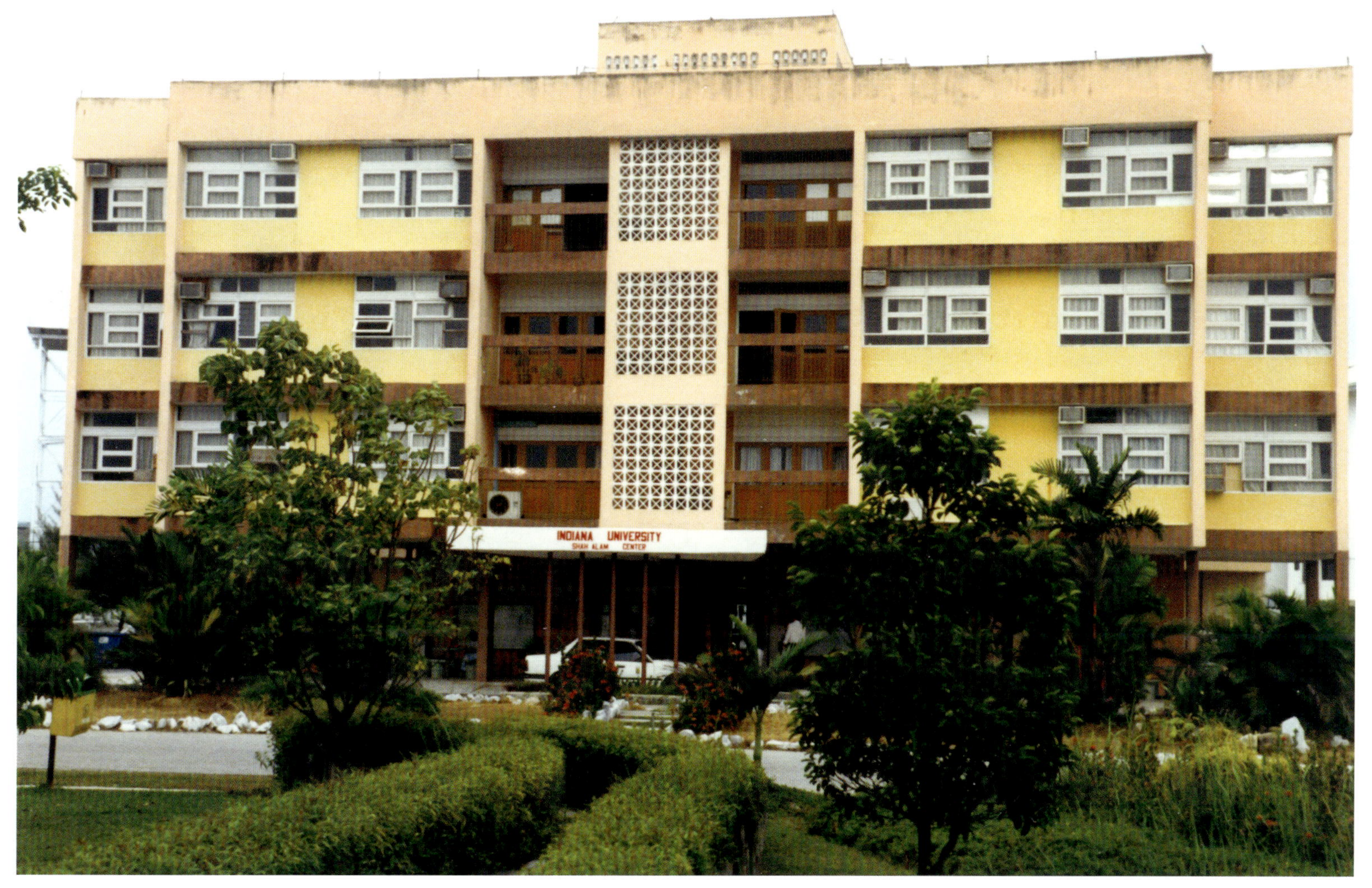

Indiana University offices in Malaysia.
Photograph courtesy of Charles Reafsnyder.

The Malaysians sent a team to the United States to discuss the plan with selected US colleges and universities. When the team came to Indiana University, they met people from the School of Continuing Studies, the School of Business, the School of Engineering at Indiana University–Purdue University Indianapolis (IUPUI), and other IU units. They learned that IU had the necessary expertise and institutional support to help develop the cooperative program they sought. They found that faculty and staff at IU understood their goals and offered concrete ways to address any difficulties inherent in their proposal. It was also clear that MUCIA and its member institutions would be valuable resources. In short, the Malaysians were impressed, and they asked Indiana University and MUCIA to develop a project document. They also provided funds for Robert Shaffer of the IU School of Education to visit Malaysia to carry out a feasibility study.[6]

More than four thousand students ultimately enrolled at Indiana University through ITM/MUCIA in Malaysia. Most of the students who came to the United States after completing their studies at the Shah Alam campus were placed at 174 of America's leading colleges and universities with a large number attending IU.

Key participants in writing this proposal included John V. Lombardi, dean for the Office of International Programs at IU, and James Weigand, dean of the IU School of Continuing Studies. Malaysian participants included Mohammed Thalha, Habbibah Salleh, Hazadiah Dahan, and Tan Sri Othman Malek, secretary general of the Malaysia Ministry of Education.

Visits to Malaysia by staff from the IU School of Continuing Studies, MUCIA, international programs, and IU president John Ryan, along with continuing negotiations led to an acceptable contract and plan of work. Special credit for the smooth relations was due to the long-term involvement of Ken Rogers in Malaysia; his many friends there gave the IU/MUCIA team a tremendous advantage.

The IU School of Continuing Studies proposed two years of undergraduate education focusing on pre-business and pre-science/technology coursework. In addition, the program would prepare students for an associate of general studies degree from the School of Continuing Studies, which they would receive on completion of the two-year program.[7] Regular Indiana University courses would be taught by faculty who had been approved and appointed by Indiana University. By the summer of 1985, the first group of faculty from IU campuses or member MUCIA institutions were in place in Malaysia. IU also agreed to facilitate the placement of students at universities in the United States. The on-site director of international services and IUPUI faculty member, Tim Diemer, recalls: "Our task was to send American faculty members to Malaysia to deliver the first two years of an IU curriculum, with the idea that if you focused enough on the core education requirements, with perhaps some extra emphasis on mathematics for the people bound for engineering, you could serve lots of different majors."[8]

All three US administrative units—MUCIA, the Indiana University School of Continuing Studies, and the Indiana University Office of International Programs—came together in the person of the provost of the ITM/MUCIA Cooperative

Program. The provost served both as the chief academic officer and as the chief of party of the ITM/MUCIA Cooperative Program. As the chief academic officer, the provost reported to the president of Indiana University. Roy Jumper, a faculty member and associate dean in the IU School of Public and Environmental Affairs, was provost at IU's Shah Alam campus from 1986 until he retired in February 1991. His successor was Herbert J. Davis, a senior fellow at MUCIA. Subsequent provosts were Jack Hopkins, a professor in the IU School of Public and Environmental Affairs, and Norman Overly, of the IU School of Education.

In June 1985, the first group of six hundred students arrived on the Shah Alam campus, twenty-four kilometers from Kuala Lumpur. The campus was equipped to ultimately offer instruction to more than two thousand students. Classrooms, laboratories, and other buildings were of high quality and included computer facilities for classroom and administrative use. The campus had a small library, but students had access to a larger library at the nearby Institute Teknologi MARA.

Project director Charles Reafsnyder became the driving force for the entire project. As an anthropologist, his respect of cultural sensitivity, his knowledge of other societies (including Malaysia), and his sensitivity to the complexities of this project were major factors in the success of this work. His devotion to detail and his long friendships with people in Malaysia were key factors, not only in the day-to-day operations, but in the planning and implementation of the whole project. Reafsnyder recalls: "In Malaysia, the project played a formative role; it insisted on strict standards, fixed curricula, and on appropriate academic credentials for faculty. It also helped to

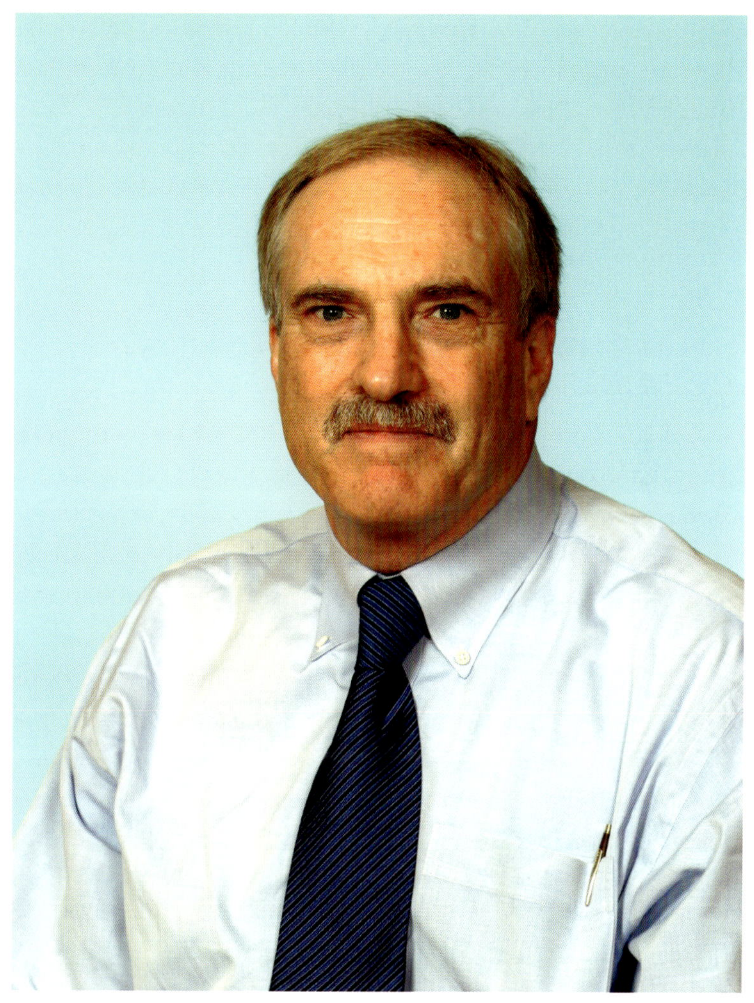

Timothy Diemer, director of international services, Indiana University–Purdue University Indianapolis.
Photograph courtesy of Timothy Diemer.

streamline administrative procedures."[9] Diemer remembers: "We had eighty ex-patriate faculty members, not only from MUCIA institutions but from outside MUCIA as well."[10] Reafsnyder adds: "Over the years, IU and the partner universities benefited from the experiences of faculty living and teaching in Malaysia, who might otherwise not have had an overseas experience. At IU, it also provided special opportunities for a number of faculty from smaller campuses."[11]

At IU, a Malaysia Program Advisory Committee was established and chaired by President John Ryan; the Office of International Programs served as the committee's secretariat. In early November 1985, Ryan made an official visit to Malaysia to meet with ITM, the Ministry of Education, and government officials. In July 1987, he returned there to preside over the first Indiana commencement ceremony of the cooperative program.

Initially, the IU School of Continuing Studies provided academic support for the program at the Shah Alam campus, but in 1991, academic responsibility shifted to the Undergraduate Education Center at Indiana University–Purdue University Indianapolis under the direction of Scott Evenbeck, associate vice chancellor. Charles Reafsnyder recalls: "For the first two years, the program was administered by Continuing Studies and then, because a large number of students attended IUPUI, the academic administration moved to Indianapolis."[12]

More than four thousand students ultimately enrolled at Indiana University through ITM/MUCIA in Malaysia. Most of the students who came to the United States after completing their studies at the Shah Alam campus were placed at 174 of America's leading colleges and universities with a large number attending IU. Others enrolled at MUCIA institutions such as the University of Iowa, Purdue University, and the University of Wisconsin–Madison.

Reafsnyder recollects: "The project brought a number of students to IU and to the other Big 10 universities as well as to other universities and colleges in other parts of the country. They were fully funded, and they were good students; in fact, their academic performance was above average wherever they went."[13] Diemer recalls: "I don't know what number of them were engineers, but probably twenty percent were bound for engineering degrees. There were a large number of arts and science degrees, and there were some business degrees. We'd take them for the first two years and deliver an IU curriculum with syllabi and faculty members approved through Bloomington—or, in the case of engineering, approved through Indianapolis—and deliver the curriculum on-site."[14]

For Diemer, there was a direct impact on individual faculty members: "Many of them told stories about their time there being the best year of their career, they learned so much about themselves as teachers, they learned more about what it meant to be an American, etc. We had people who had never been outside the country before—in Malaysia, they had to live in the culture—go to the night market, figuring out how to get a phone connected, etc. They lived it." He goes on to describe the broader impact of the project: "The preference in Malaysia has historically been education in the UK rather than the USA. We definitely had an impact in changing that, as well as the IU and IUPUI brands are now well recognized in Malaysia

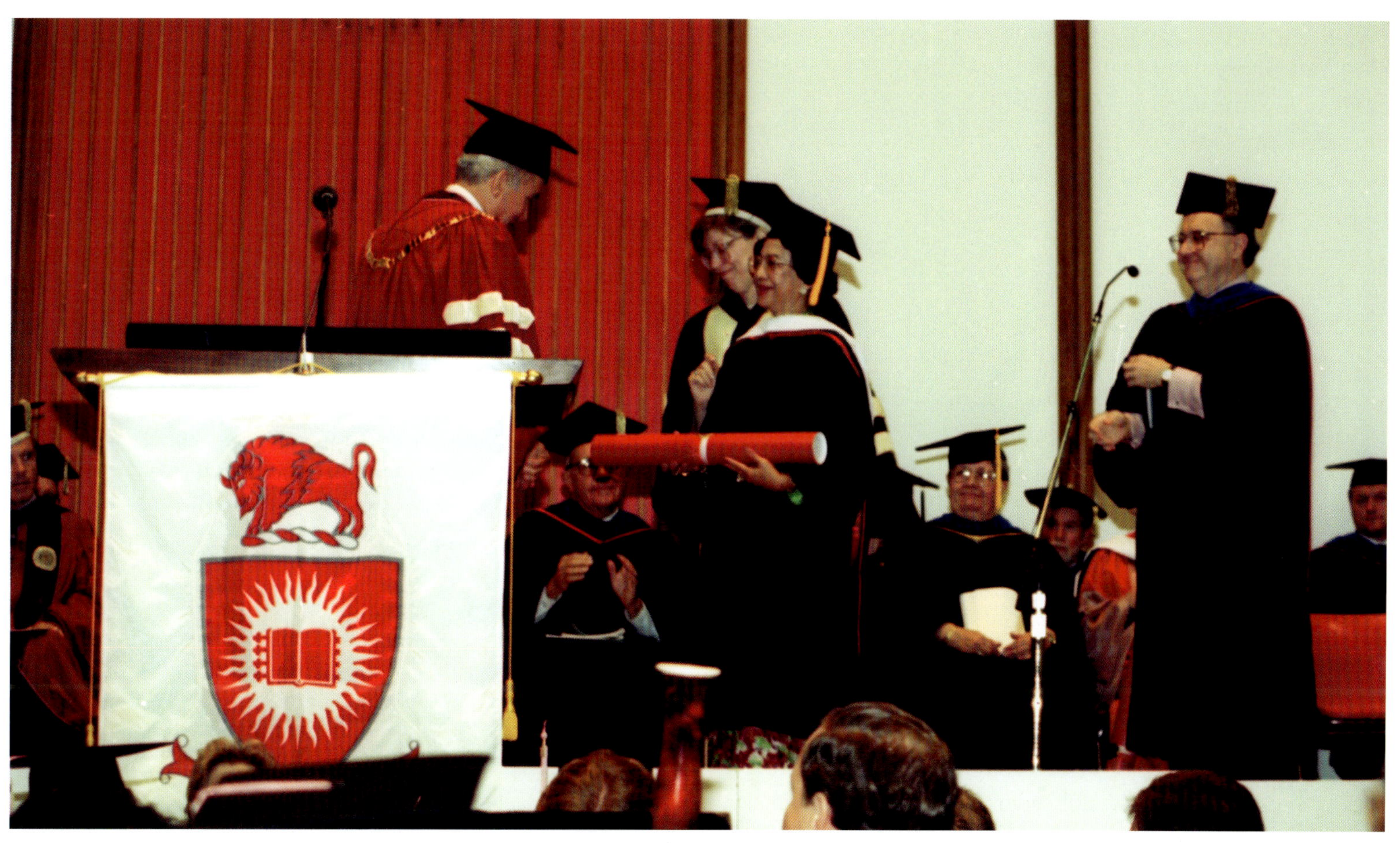

Tun Dr. Siti Hasmah binti Haji Mohamad Ali receives an honorary degree from Indiana University, May 7, 1994.

IU Archives (P0023153).

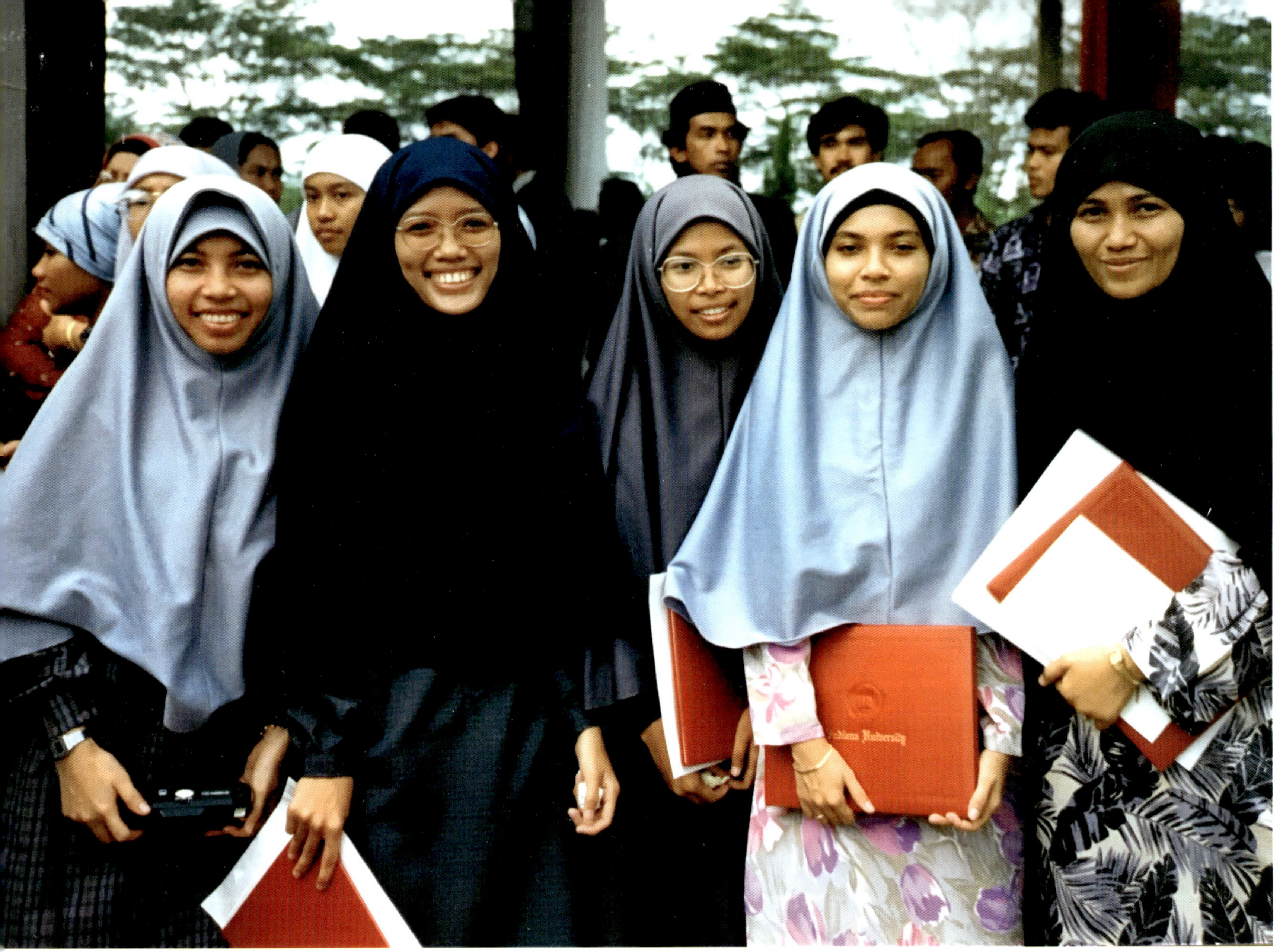

Malaysian students at graduation.
Photograph courtesy of Charles Reafsnyder.

in a way that wasn't possible before. I don't think that Indiana University had much of a footprint or name recognition before ITM, and now it has great name recognition."[15]

As with all projects of this type, a key question is: What was the long-term impact on Malaysia? Diemer reflects: "I think this was worth doing. It was a temporary program with a built-in end date. We did prepare, by my count, well over three thousand students for degrees in engineering, business, social science, who then subsequently earned degrees in the USA. We don't have good tracking, but there's no doubt in my mind that they're making a very positive contribution to Malaysian society and the economy."[16] Reafsnyder adds: "I think we set the standard for this kind of program. Not only did we consult the North Central Association [of Colleges and Schools] but they then involved us in their own planning of best practices for overseas programs."[17]

In 1994, in recognition of IU's involvement in Malaysia, an honorary doctorate was awarded to Siti Hasmah, the wife of Malaysian prime minister Mahatir Mohamed.

In May 1994, the IUPUI School of Engineering and Technology formalized a cooperative twinning agreement with Malaysia's Tenaga Nasional Institute of Engineering and Technology—the new educational training facility of Tenaga Nasional Berhad, a state-owned company undergoing privatization that provides 97 percent of the country's electric power.[18] Under the terms of the agreement, the IUPUI school assists the Tenaga Institute in the development of two-year preparatory programs in electrical and mechanical engineering. On July 11, 1994, Tenaga Institute's first group of fifty students began their engineering studies. Representing Indiana University at the July 9 opening ceremony for the Tenaga Institute were IUPUI's dean Alfred Potvin of the School of Engineering and Technology, Associate Vice Chancellor William Plater, and Associate Dean of International Affairs Giles Hoyt. The Tenaga program was based on IUPUI's curriculum and is partially taught by IUPUI faculty. Associate Dean Oner Yurtseven of IUPUI's School of Engineering and Technology served in Malaysia as the program's provost and chief academic officer, while Timothy Diemer was director of administration at the IUPUI campus.

9 | INDIANA UNIVERSITY *in* Russia

IN 1994, TO EXPLORE NEW OVERSEAS OPPORTUNITIES, THE IU SCHOOL of Education in Bloomington and Ryazan State Pedagogical University in Russia applied for, and received, a grant from the United States Information Agency for both universities to increase the international content of their programs. With an enrollment of six thousand students, Ryazan State was a teachers college that was about to become a comprehensive university. Because of its basic mission to prepare future educators, Ryazan State worked closely with secondary schools. Through the USIA grant, five Russian educators and administrators came to Bloomington in November and December 1994: two professors of English, a botanist, an instructor in in-service teacher training, and the dean of physics and mathematics. They were eager to learn about higher education in the United States and how an American university, such as Indiana University, functioned. As part of the program, they also observed primary and secondary schools in Monroe County as well as Valparaiso University, the College Board offices in Evanston, Illinois, and Ivy Tech Community College in Indianapolis.[1] Nina Ivanovna Demidova, Ryazan State's deputy rector of education, described the experience: "We imagine ourselves as 'freshmen' going through all stages of the learning process, from admission to graduation.[2]

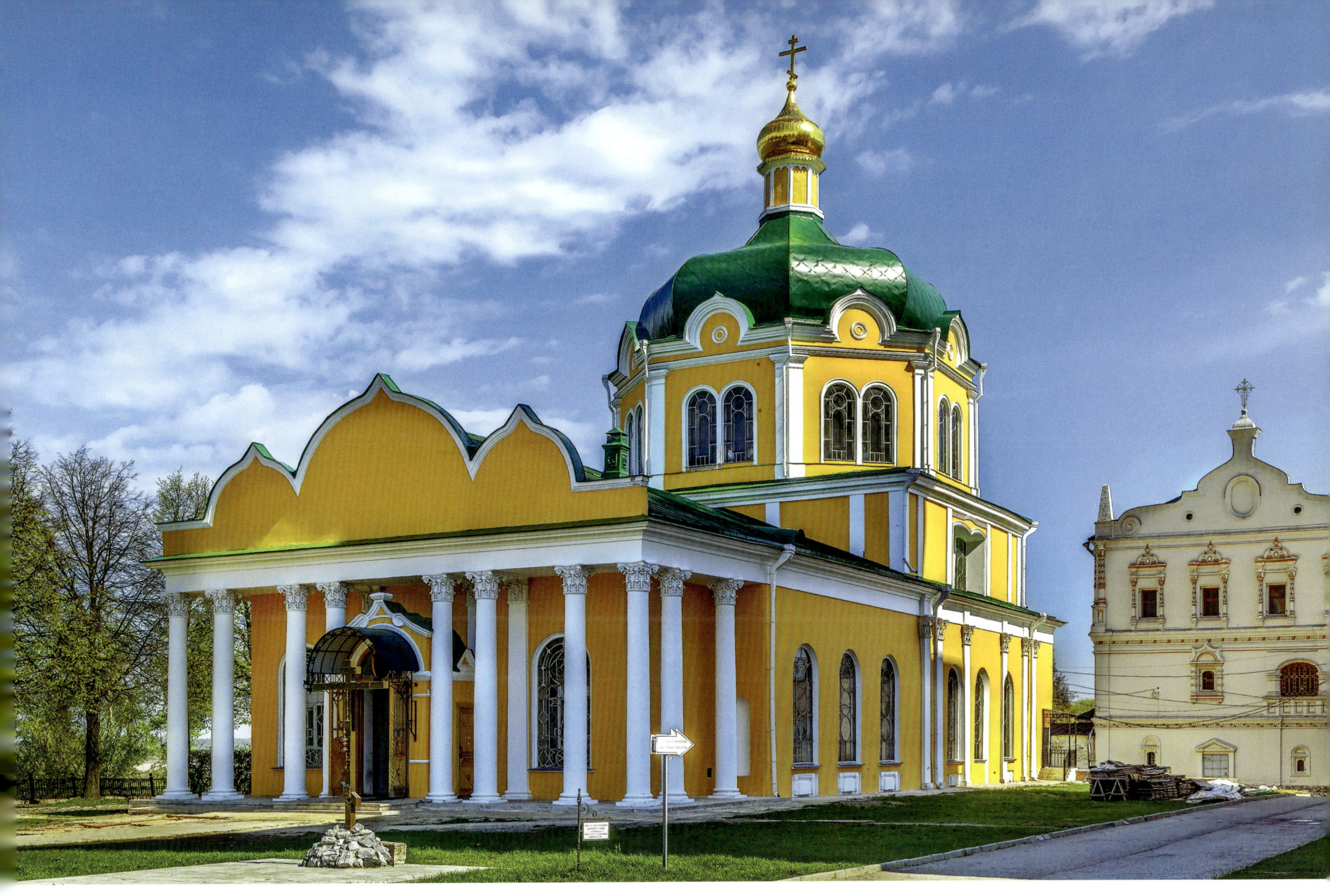

Church of the Nativity of Christ, Ryazan, Russia, 2017.
Photograph courtesy of iStock.

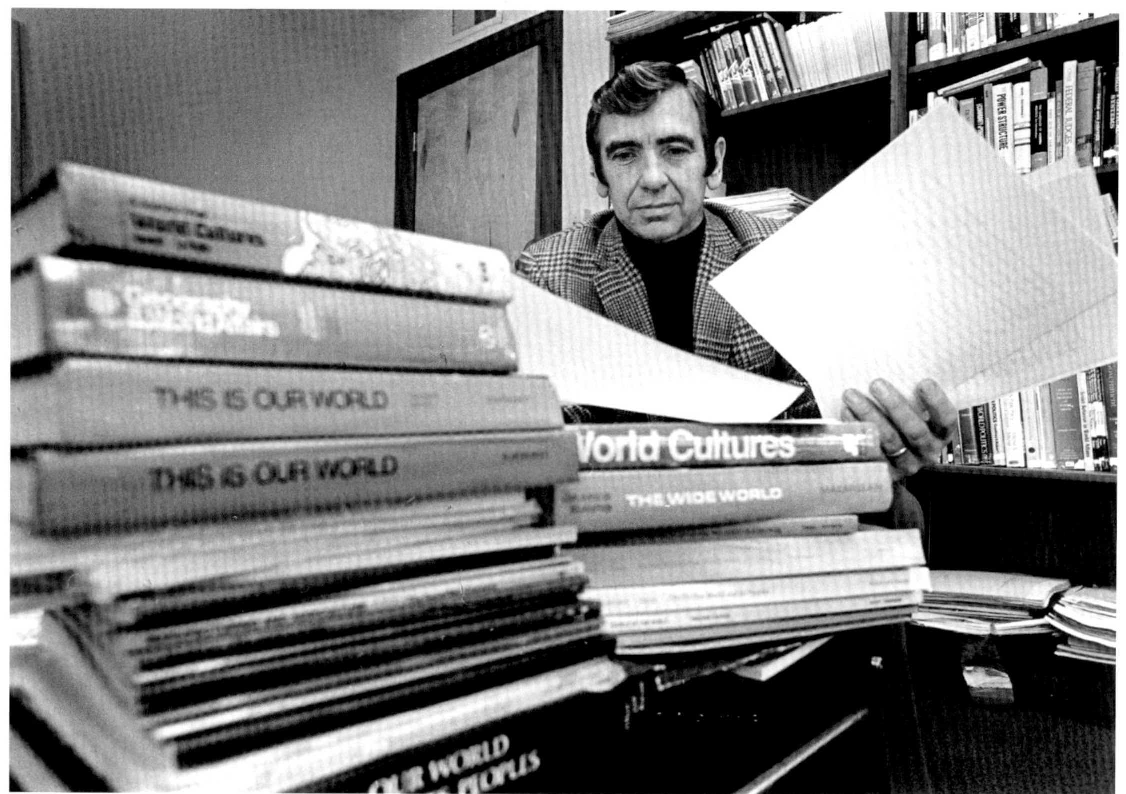

Howard Mehlinger, dean of the School of Education.
IU Archives (P0040173).

Howard Mehlinger, the project director, saw the visit in the broader context of Russia's efforts at educational reform. He had been dean of the School of Education from 1981 to 1989 and helped establish the Center for Excellence in Education, of which he served as director beginning in 1993. From 1977 until 1989, Mehlinger played a key role in the US/USSR Textbook Study Project.[3]

Mehlinger described the visit in the broader context of Russia's efforts at educational reform: "Ryazan State's partnership with IU should place it in a strategic position in the educational reform movement going on in Russia. Russia must incorporate fifty-three different languages and more than a hundred ethnic groups into its society. The issue is how to deal with creating the melting pot and yet recognize different ethnic groups. It's an overwhelming problem there, and here, and I think we have a lot to learn from how they handle that."[4]

IU's participation in the linkage was of value to the School of Education's Center for the Study of Russian Education, which was codirected by Mehlinger and Ben Eklof, as well

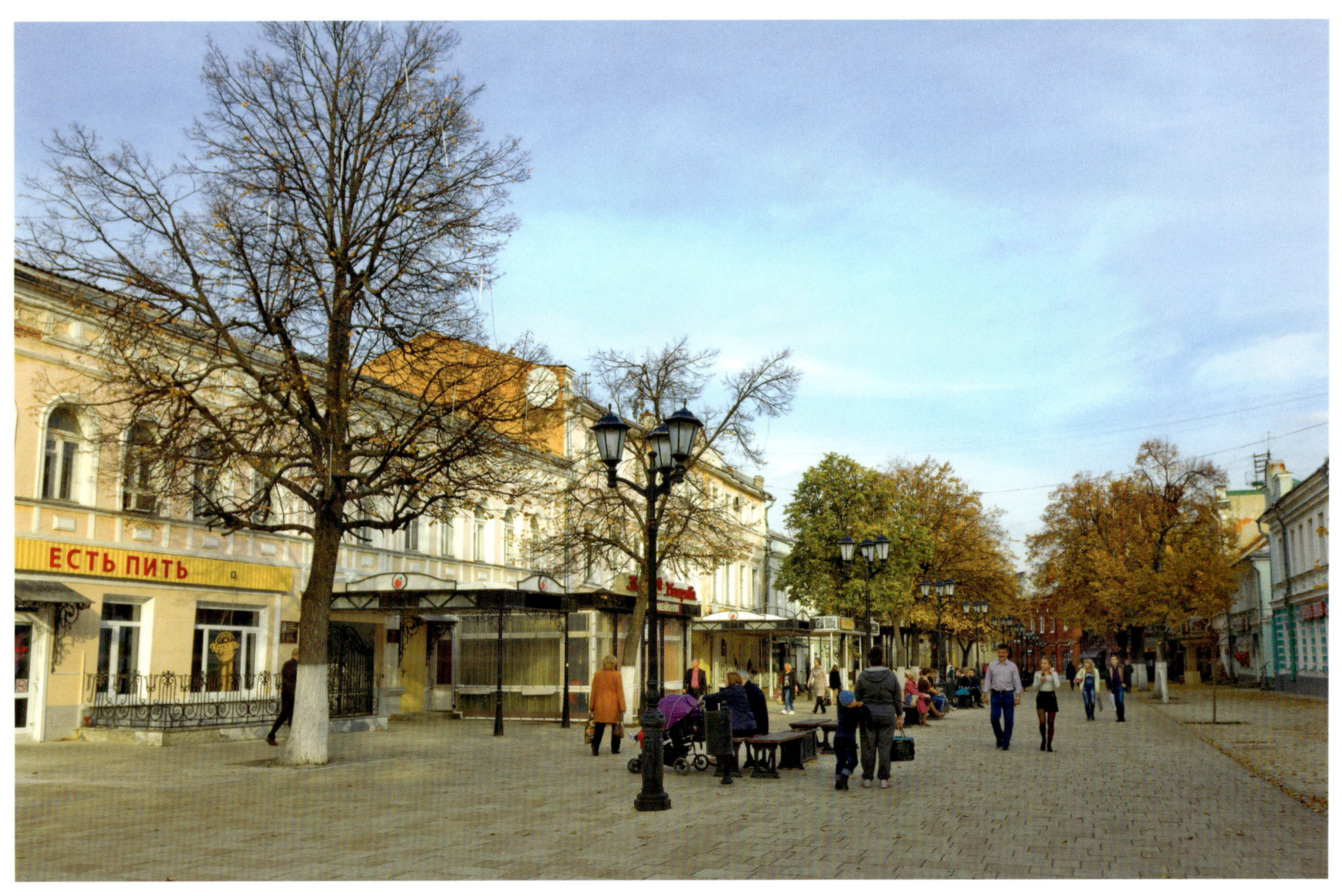

Pochtovaya Street, Ryazan, Russia, October 2016.
Photograph courtesy of iStock.

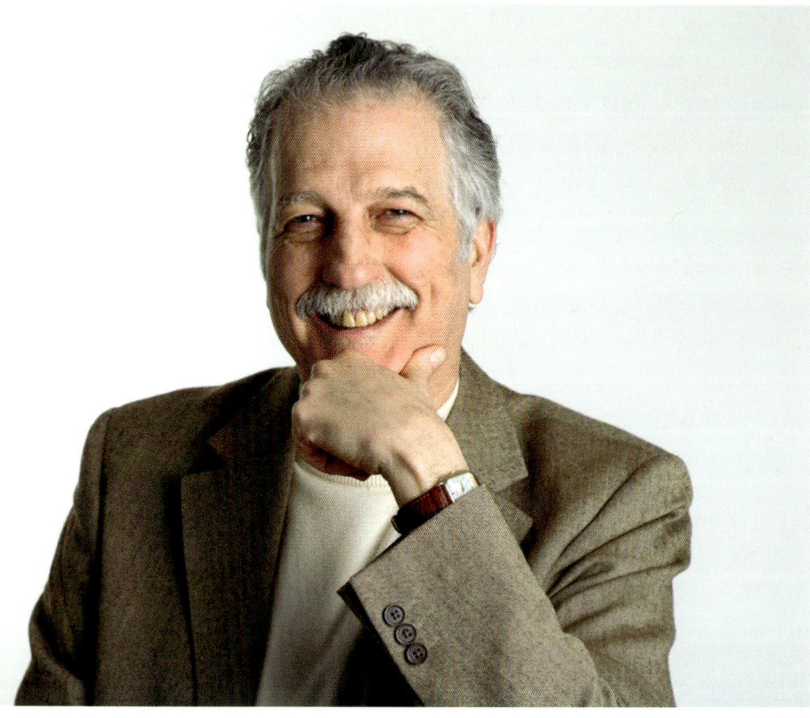

Don Hossler, distinguished provost professor emeritus in the Department of Educational Leadership and Policy Studies, Indiana University.
Photograph courtesy of Indiana University.

as to the Russian and East European Institute, which was directed by Owen Johnson.

Over the course of the project, other visitors came to Indiana University from Ryazan State, and IU participants went to Ryazan to consult on globalizing curriculum, administrative structures, library services, and options for distance education.

Don Hossler, emeritus professor of educational leadership and policy in the School of Education, reflects on the importance of the linkages between Russia and the School of Education: "From 1992 through 1997, I hosted nearly twenty visiting scholars from the former Soviet Union. After glasnost and perestroika, it was the hope of the United States that by bringing academics from the former Soviet Union to the US, this would in turn help to Westernize and modernize their higher education system, which would result in the development of a more representative government over time."[5]

Hossler also recalls his time at Ryazan, and the impact of IU there: "Along with hosting visiting scholars, I also lived in the city of Ryazan for four months as part of a USAID grant. Ryazan is the capital of the Ryazan region. It is approximately four hours by car, south of Moscow. I recall the hope voiced by an aging physicist working in the Ministry of Education. He hoped to introduce a US-style liberal arts general education program. He offered that the difference between the American and Soviet higher education systems was that Americans taught their students to think."[6]

In addition to the School of Education initiative, there had been an earlier project in Ryazan. In 1992, a group of academic, business, and government leaders from Ryazan met with

Mehlinger and two others from IU—Alexander Rabinowitch, then dean of the Office of International Programs, and Charles Bonser, director of the Institute for Developmental Strategies in the School of Public and Environmental Affairs—about ways that IU might assist with the economic and cultural growth of the region. In June 1994, Ryazan's mayor Vladimir Markov, Central Bank president Tamara Pigilova, and Rector Anatoly Liferov of Ryazan State Pedagogy University came to Bloomington for planning meetings. They also visited banks in Louisville, Kentucky, and Washington, DC, where they met with Representative Lee Hamilton, then chair of the House Foreign Relations Committee. In 1994, Michele Fratianni and Patricia Eoyang of the IU School of Business were awarded a grant from the Eurasia Foundation. The Ryazan business community provided a modest commitment to cover local expenses for an eighteen-month program. IU faculty members who went to Ryazan, in addition to Fratianni, included John Hill, Bruce Jaffee, William Sartoris, Robert Klemkosky, John Pratt, Mikel Tiller, and Juergen Von Hagen. The participation of practicing US bankers was a key component of the IU training program, and David Baer, president of Bloomington's Monroe County Bank, also went to Ryazan. By the conclusion of the project, top-level managers from twenty-eight business and financial institutions in the Ryazan region received training.[7]

Ryazan State's partnership with IU should place it in a strategic position in the educational reform movement going on in Russia. Russia must incorporate fifty-three different languages and more than a hundred ethnic groups into its society.

—Howard Mehlinger

10 | INDIANA UNIVERSITY *in* Kenya

Its humanitarian impact on the African country of Kenya was enormous, but its transformative effect on thousands of American doctors, nurses, and others has been equally significant.

Facing, Eldoret, Kenya, July 2008. *Photograph courtesy of Dreamstime.*

In 1988, colleagues at the Indiana University School of Medicine launched an overseas program that was to have far-reaching consequences. Its humanitarian impact on the African country of Kenya was enormous, but its transformative effect on thousands of American doctors, nurses, and others has been equally significant. Four faculty members at the School of Medicine began to explore the possibility of an international partnership: Charles Kelley, who had also spent time in Afghanistan; David Van Reken, who had been a missionary in Liberia; Joseph Mamlin; and Robert Einterz. Einterz was the prime mover of the initiative.

The four doctors decided they should visit several medical schools in developing countries and evaluate potential partners for Indiana University. They did not want a conventional exchange program, but rather a mission of service, research, and education. In November 1988, they received financial assistance from a small Indiana family foundation to visit the Institute of Medicine in Kathmandu, Nepal; Moi University in Eldoret, Kenya; and the School of Medical Sciences at the University of Science and Technology in Kumasi, Ghana. In Eldoret, they met with Dr. Haroun N. K. arap Mengech, the dean of a medical school that was being planned at Moi University at the time. They liked Mengech and were impressed with his vision and his enthusiasm. They also found the idea of working with a new medical school attractive, and so

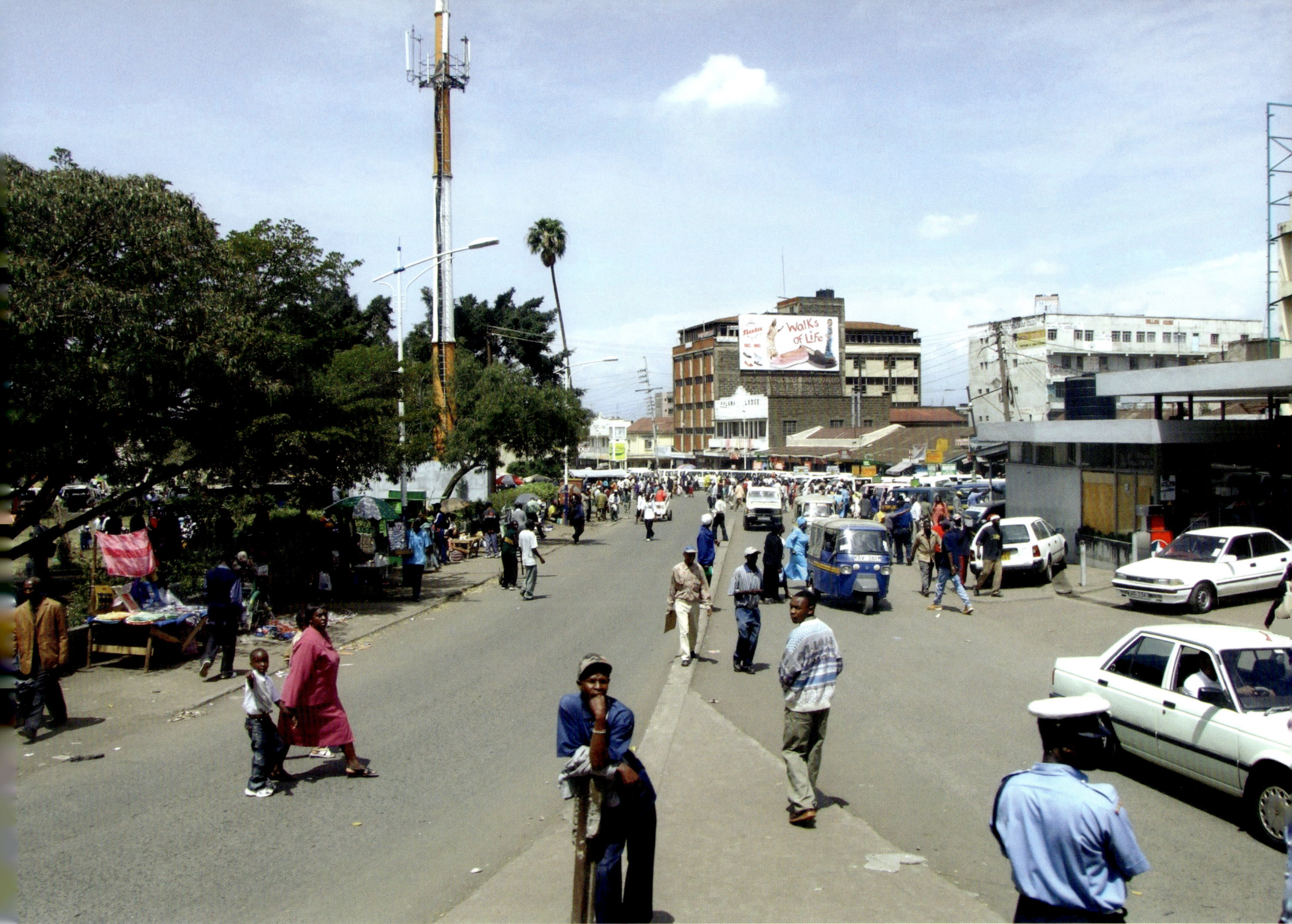
Walks of Life

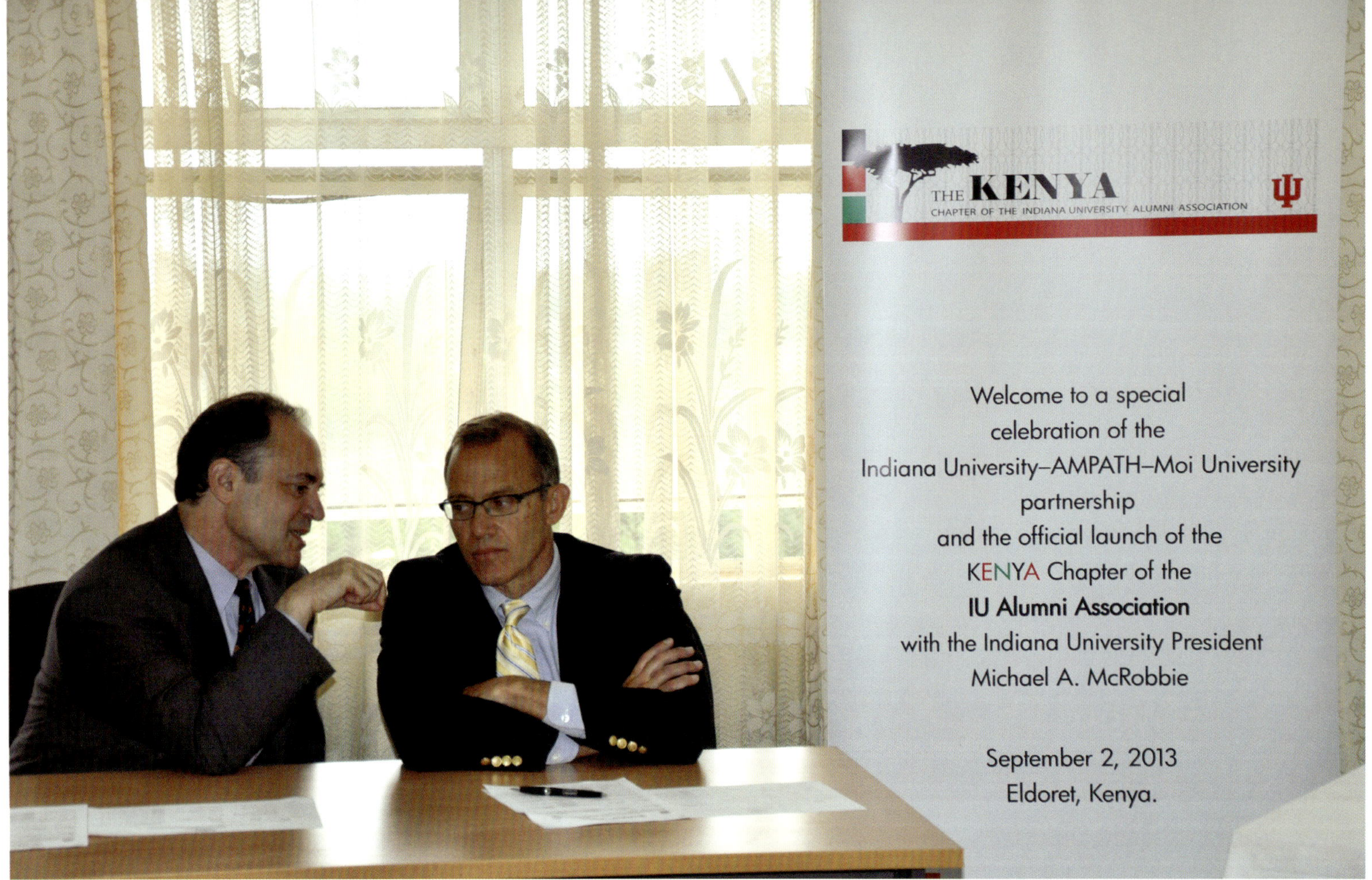

Indiana University–Purdue University Indianapolis associate vice chancellor for international affairs Gil Latz (*left*) and executive director of the Academic Model Providing Access to Healthcare consortium Robert Einterz (*right*) converse during a meeting with Moi University's senior management team, Eldoret, Kenya, September 2013.

Photograph courtesy of Indiana University.

they decided to form a partnership with Mengech and his institution.[1]

Mamlin, who was a professor of medicine at Indiana University and also chief of medicine at what was then Wishard Memorial Hospital, took the lead in setting up special neighborhood-centered health care systems in Indianapolis. Einterz was the first IU faculty physician to spend a full year in Kenya, in what was to become an annual rotation of team leaders who would practice medicine, teach at Moi University, and oversee Indiana University students and residents for a full year. By the time Einterz arrived, Mengech had hired a dozen faculty members, and the first Moi University medical school class of forty students began their studies that fall. Six Indiana University medical students and residents went to Kenya in that first year.[2]

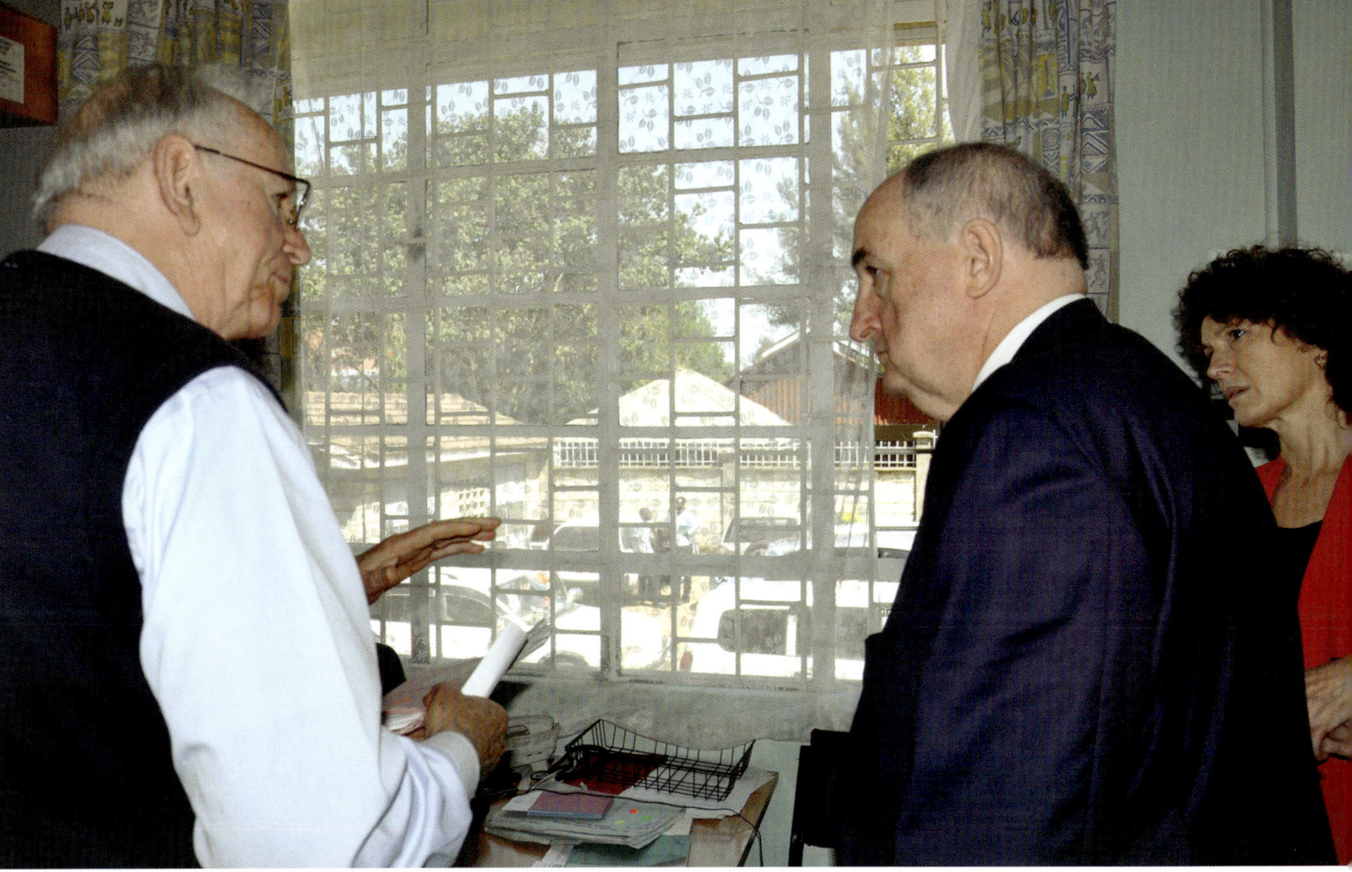

Joseph Mamlin (*left*), MD and field director of Academic Model Providing Access to Healthcare (AMPATH), talks to Indiana University president Michael McRobbie and first lady Laurie Burns McRobbie about AMPATH. Mamlin was one of the original four Indiana University School of Medicine faculty members who traveled to several developing countries and selected Kenya and Moi University as the partners for IU. *Photograph courtesy of Indiana University.*

Einterz was followed by Kelley and then Mamlin as team leaders for Indiana. Diana Meneya and Gabriel Anabwani were the first Moi physicians to travel to Indiana.[3] From this beginning, the IU partners helped build the Moi University Faculty of Health Sciences, which subsequently became the Moi University School of Medicine. It is noteworthy that from its inception, the partnership was bilateral; Kenyan faculty members and students, most on full fellowships or scholarships, traveled to Indianapolis for advanced training. In addition, joint research projects began; over the years, these were to number in the many hundreds. Einterz, who later became the associate dean for global health

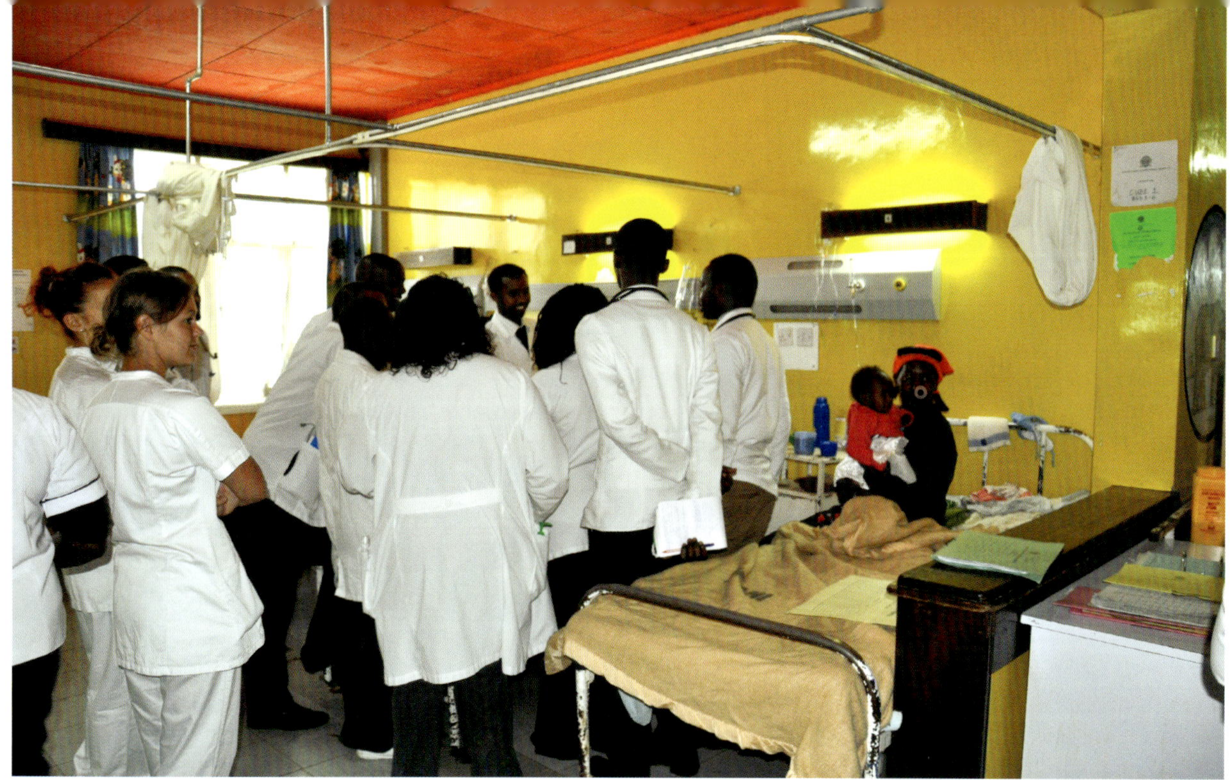

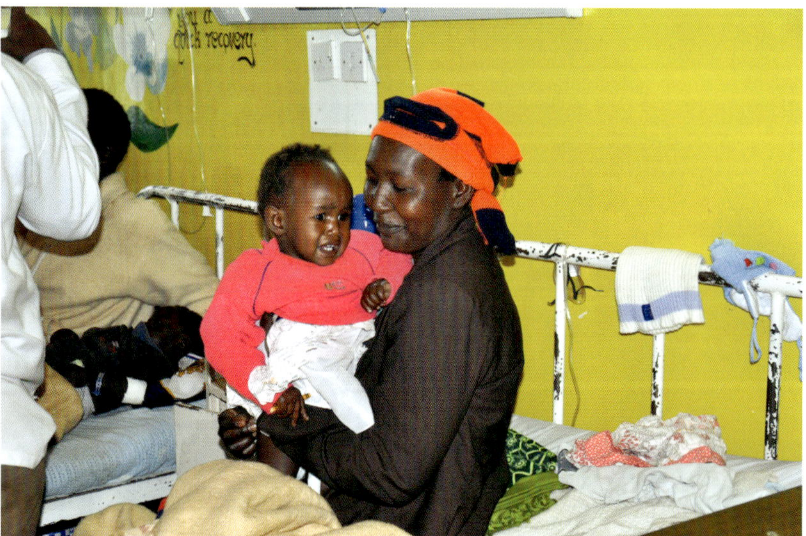

Above, Students on rounds at Moi Teaching Hospital, 2013.
Photograph courtesy of Indiana University.

Left, Just getting children to an Academic Model Providing Access to Healthcare (AMPATH) clinic is a huge achievement, because many families do not seek treatment due to the costs and stigma associated with having a child with HIV. AMPATH leaders believe that one of its main program pillars, called Find, Link, Treat, and Retain (or FLTR) can ultimately create a new, HIV-free generation in Kenya.
Photograph courtesy of Indiana University.

in the School of Medicine, coordinated the relationship between various IU departments and schools and the Moi University School of Medicine from this point on. The program enabled students and residents from IU and from Moi to enhance their understanding of medicine and improved their ability to care for patients in their different countries.

In 1992–1993, Mamlin, accompanied by his wife, Sarah Ellen, went to Eldoret to serve as a physician-in-residence. In 2000, when Mamlin retired from the School of Medicine, he returned to Eldoret to become field director for the Academic Model Providing Access to Healthcare (AMPATH) until 2012, when he was named field director for clinical services.

> Mamlin entered the Moi hospital one evening in 2000 and saw a fifth-year student from the Moi University School of Medicine sitting at the bedside of an HIV patient. When Mamlin asked the student what he was doing, the young man replied that he was trying to feed Daniel Ochieng, one of his classmates from Moi University. Mamlin was stunned and unwilling to let this student die. It is a shame it has to be a med student before you say, "Hey, I better treat one person," says Mamlin. But it was treating one patient that opened his eyes to the possibility of treating more.[4]

The HIV/AIDS epidemic had become devastating in sub-Saharan Africa, and Mamlin was deeply concerned by its spread. He wrote to Joe Wheat, who specialized in infectious diseases at IU: "'Joe, I would like for you to consider helping me with a tough problem.' 'I have seen more HIV in these three months I have been here than all the docs in Indiana combined,' Mamlin wrote, 'yet I have seen no one treated for HIV—we treat the TB, typhoid, pneumonias, etc. and let the retrovirus do its thing—which it does relentlessly.'"[5]

Mamlin wanted Wheat's help in guiding the regimen and finding the money to do it. He asked for $24,000 to treat Daniel, and soon received word from a School of Medicine faculty member who offered to cover the full amount. Slowly, Daniel began to heal. "Everyone was dying around us, and I saw one person come back to life. You can't help but say, 'If he came back to life, what about all these other people?' I suddenly had this rush of hope, because I realized something could be done instead of nothing."[6]

Mamlin contemplated the challenge of treating HIV/AIDS in Kenya and was able to draw on his experience, building a citywide clinical care system and university medical group in Indianapolis: "'I'm not scared of big numbers,' he says. 'At Wishard Hospital, we went from no outreach at all to twenty-one sites. We went from just me in the Indiana University Medical Group to one hundred physicians. I've learned that vision attracts funding. If it is the right idea at the right time, the funding will follow.'"[7]

Many Kenyans felt that the HIV/AIDS stigma, which blocked widespread testing and safe-sex practices, was less of a cultural phenomenon than a predictable reaction to the prevailing African view that the disease was the equivalent of a death sentence. In other words, treatment is prevention.

In the summer of 2002, the AMPATH clinic and the Indiana and Moi physicians finally were awarded their first large grant. The MTCT-Plus Initiative (MTCT stands for mother-to-child transmission of HIV/AIDS), a program sponsored by

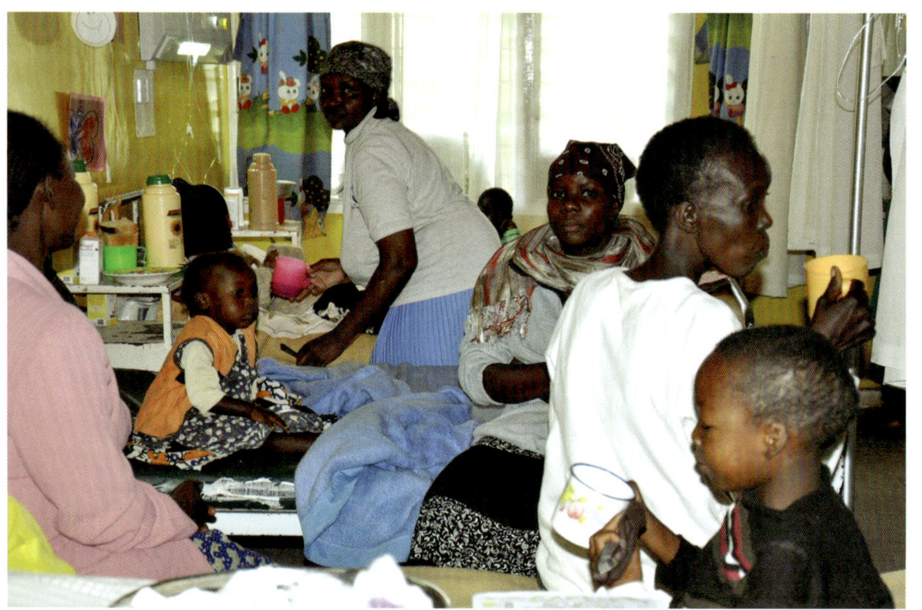

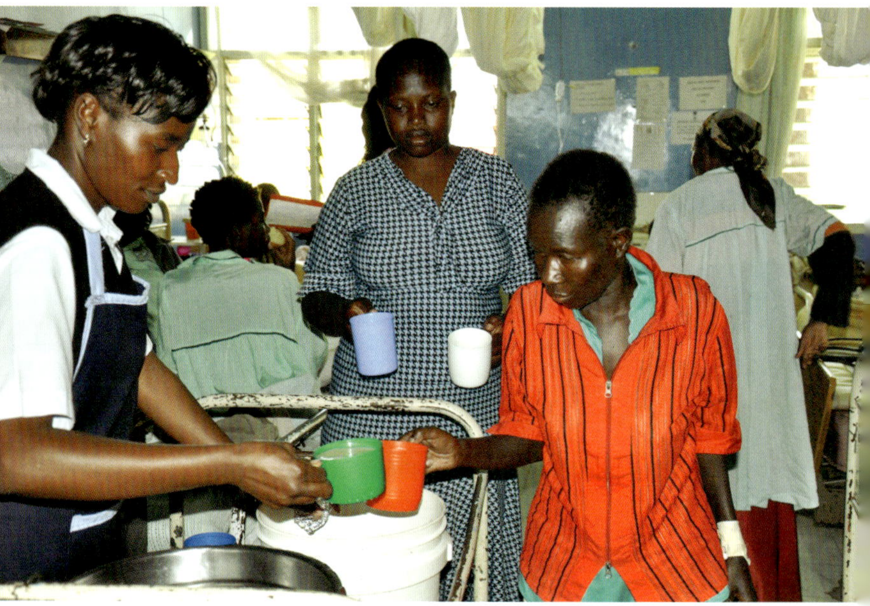

Patients receiving care at Moi Teaching Hospital, 2013.
Photographs courtesy of Indiana University.

a coalition of foundations, awarded the Indiana-Moi program one of just twelve international grants given in the developing world. The grant provided for HIV care and treatment for mothers, children, and other family members and included a commitment to lifetime treatment of enrolled patients. The Indiana-Moi team used the grant and other private donations to begin enrolling more HIV-positive patients. By early 2003, more than 80 percent of new mothers treated at the Moi hospital were agreeing to be tested for HIV, and Indiana-Moi surveys showed that many of the culture's deadly HIV myths were fading away. Over three-quarters of Kenyans surveyed knew that someone without symptoms can transmit HIV, and almost all knew there was no cure for the disease. As the Indiana-Moi program's treatment numbers increased, global health experts took notice. "There is a growing sense that devoting a lot of resources to treatment is necessary, but there is not a lot out there yet in how to do it responsibly," Tim Evans, director of health equity for the Rockefeller Foundation, told an Indianapolis newspaper in 2003. "That is why the IU–Moi model is so important. It is the best practice model, which importantly is not a Cadillac that no one can afford. It is a Toyota that is a good quality model of care that can be replicated in a lot of settings with constrained resources."[8]

AMPATH received significant support from the United States Agency for International Development, the President's Emergency Plan for HIV/AIDS Relief, the Centers for Disease Control and Prevention, and the Bill and Melinda Gates Foundation.[9]

While AMPATH had a significant impact on countless patients and medical practitioners in Kenya, it also influenced medical students, doctors, and others from Indiana. Their diagnostic skills and awareness of and sensitivity to medical treatment in an environment of poverty and their increased understanding of infectious diseases enhanced their skills and knowledge. "Dr. Einterz swears that Kenya is the best place to learn medicine, and I know what he, means now," Dr. Ben Wince, an Indiana University School of Medicine graduate, says his Kenya experience made him a better doctor: "I had a college background in biomedical engineering, and I used to think technology was everything. But the experience in Kenya, where literally all you have is patient history and an examination, forced me to learn that you need to treat the whole person, not just the disease. What I know now is that sometimes technology can interfere with the doctor-patient relationship."[10]

Wince and other students and faculty also expressed admiration for Moi University's models of problem-based medical education and the Kenyan school's emphasis on learning through community-based research and practice in underserved rural areas.[11]

The AMPATH group included medical school professors from Indiana and Brown Universities. The University of Utah has sent physician-professors and students to Eldoret, and the University of Toronto and Duke University added obstetrics and gynecology specialties to the America/Sub-Saharan Network for Training and Education in Medicine Consortium, which includes Lehigh Valley Hospital and Health Network and Providence Portland Medical Center.[12]

While AMPATH had a significant impact on countless patients and medical practitioners in Kenya, it also influenced medical students, doctors, and others from Indiana. Their diagnostic skills and awareness of and sensitivity to medical treatment in an environment of poverty and their increased understanding of infectious diseases enhanced their skills and knowledge.

In 2006, Indiana University–Purdue University at Indianapolis (IUPUI) established a formal relationship with Moi University to nurture academic partnerships in social sciences, engineering, informatics, and other disciplines.

The program served 3.5 million in over five hundred urban and rural clinics in western Kenya and enrolled more than 160,000 HIV-positive people.[13] "AMPATH has its own farms with support from the World Food Programme, a United Nations agency, headed by former IU trustee, Jim Morris, which supports economic and social development. Mamlin says the program's distribution system 'would be the envy of Wal-Mart.' Its food program is the first in the world to offer full food support along with HIV care for the patient's entire family."[14]

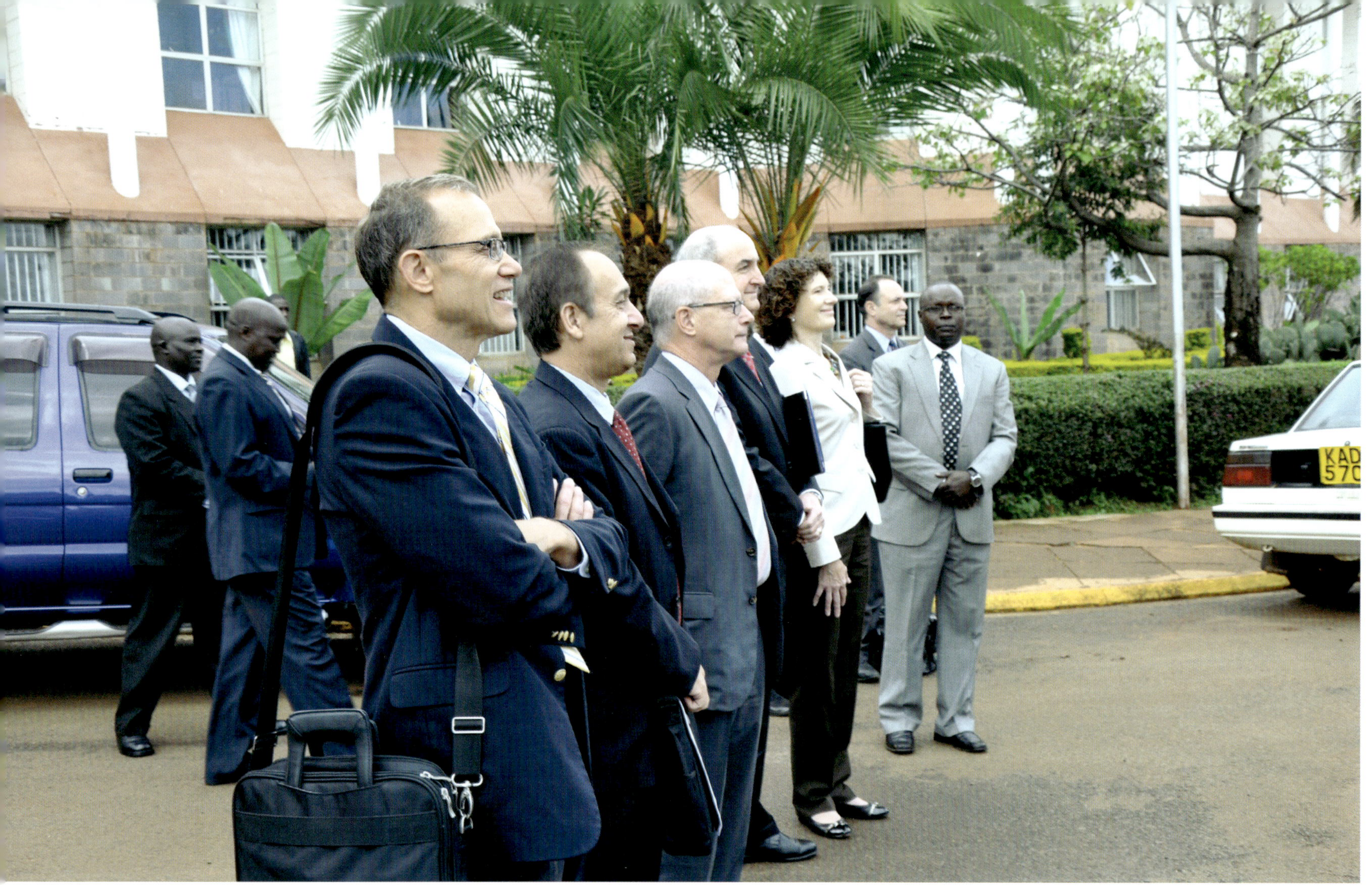

Members of the Indiana University delegation watch the Moi University Choir perform.
Photograph courtesy of Indiana University.

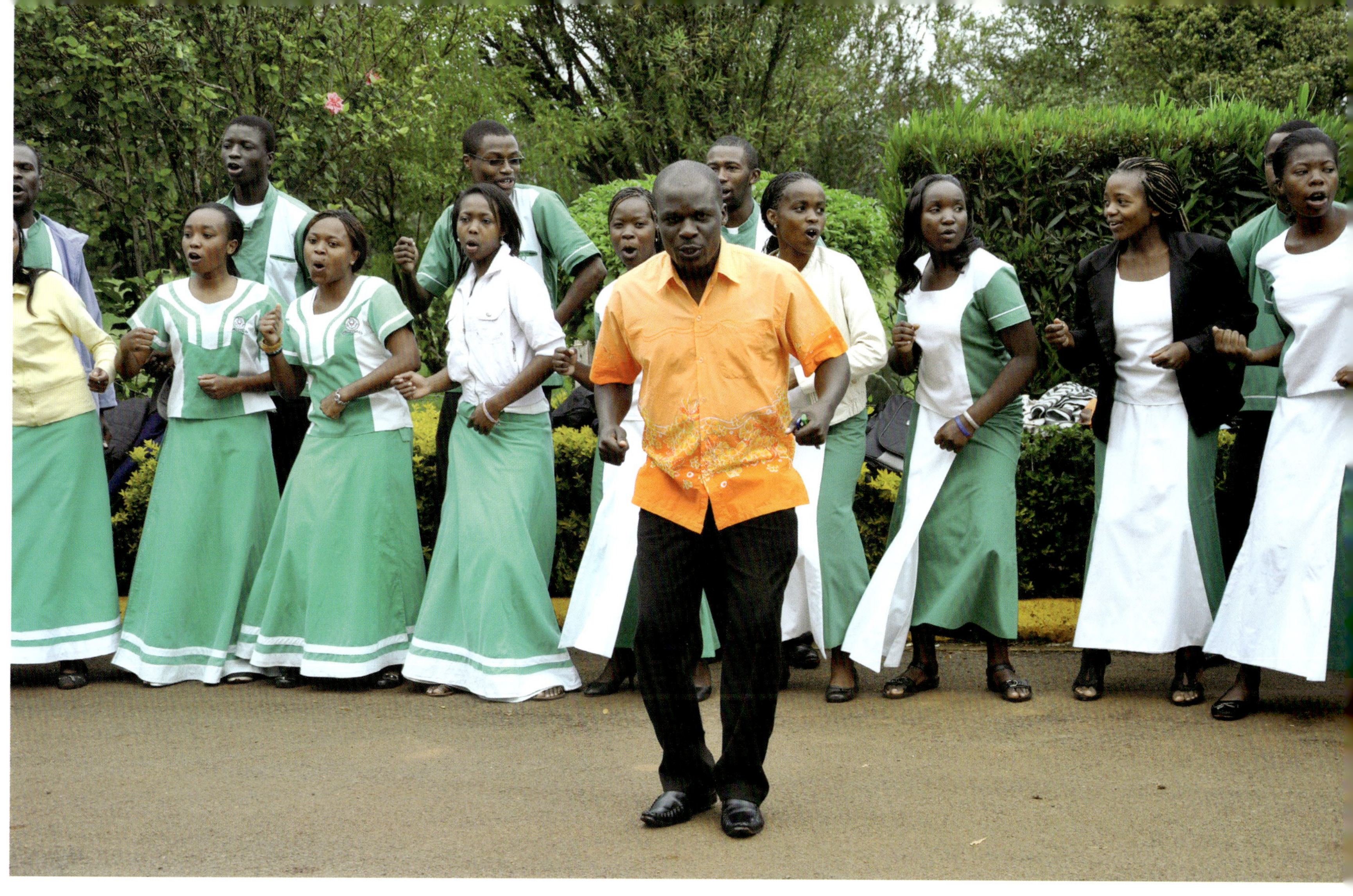

The Moi University Choir welcomes the Indiana University delegation to campus.
Photograph courtesy of Indiana University.

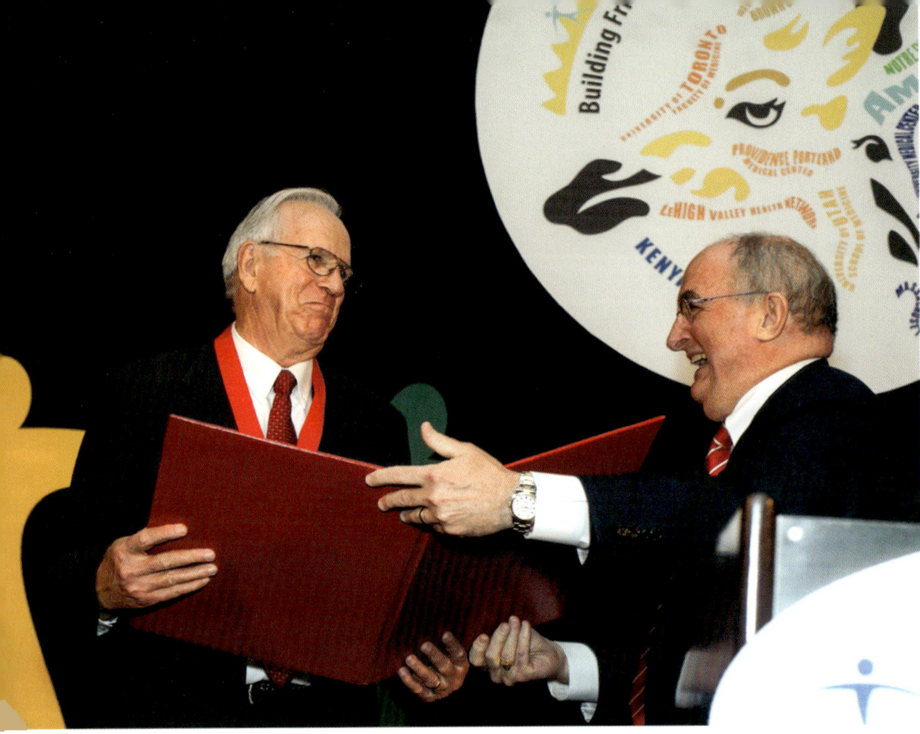

Indiana University president Michael McRobbie (*right*) presents Joseph Mamlin (*left*) with the President's Medal for Excellence, which is the highest honor an IU president can bestow, October 2013.
Photograph courtesy of Indiana University.

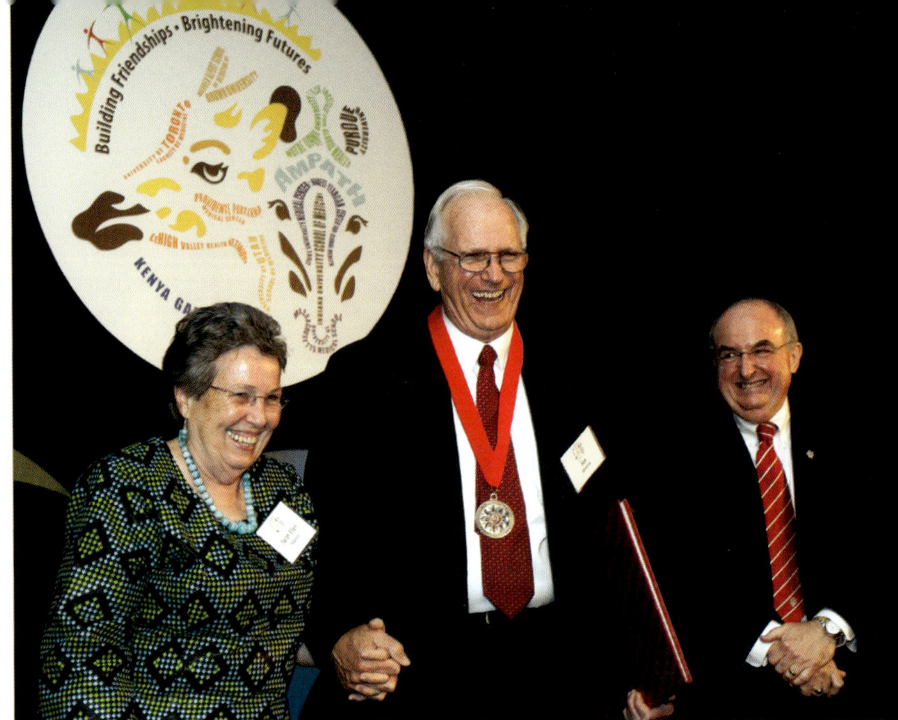

Joseph Mamlin (*center*) and his wife, Sarah Ellen Mamlin, stand together at the podium as Indiana University president Michael McRobbie (*right*) looks on.
Photograph courtesy of Indiana University.

What started as the germ of an idea nourished by four dedicated physicians in 1988 blossomed in many ways. Funding became available, which alleviated the suffering of countless Kenyans. Support came in from the President's Emergency Plan for HIV/AIDS Relief, the Centers for Disease Control and Prevention, the Bill and Melinda Gates Foundation, and gifts and donations from concerned individuals. The Indianapolis community embraced IU's work with AMPATH through the involvement of churches and faith groups, the legal community, and thousands of volunteers and supporters. Joe Mamlin was nominated for the Nobel Peace Prize in 2007. "Citing the widespread influence of AMPATH and Mamlin's role in the program, two Hoosier professors, Scott Pegg of IUPUI and David Mason, PhD'78, of Butler University, have nominated AMPATH for the 2007 Nobel Peace Prize. The professors suggested in their letter to the Norwegian Nobel Committee that it would be 'perfectly fitting to recognize [Mamlin] as a co-recipient of the peace prize.'"[15]

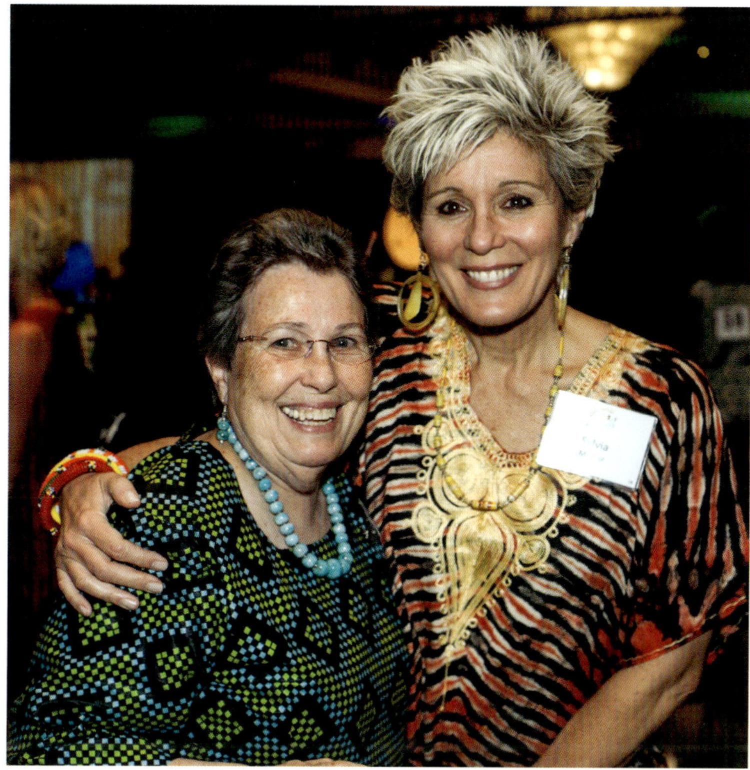

Sarah Ellen Mamlin (*left*) and opera singer Sylvia McNair at the 2013 Kenya Gala. Once every three years, the Indiana University Center for Global Health hosts an international gala to celebrate the work of the Academic Model Providing Access to Healthcare partners and their supporters. *Photograph courtesy of Indiana University.*

At the Kenya Gala in October 2013, Mamlin was awarded the President's Medal for Excellence by Indiana University president Michael McRobbie.

"'In gratitude for all that you have done to leverage the power and expertise of an academic health center in the interest of global health, I am privileged and honored to present you with the President's Medal for Excellence,' McRobbie said to Mamlin, whom he called 'one of the visionary founders of the IU-Moi partnership.'"[16]

The President's Medal for Excellence is the highest honor an IU president can bestow.

Eventually, the AMPATH program became Africa's largest and most comprehensive and effective HIV/AIDS control system. Over a million patients and hundreds of American doctors and students have been involved in AMPATH's activities since its inception—all of this from three medical students and a few residents who first went to Eldoret in 1990. According to Mamlin, "We just wanted to go where we had an opportunity for some Hoosier medical students to see another part of the world and vice versa. By accident, Indiana found itself in the epicenter of history's most powerfully destructive pandemic."[17]

11 | INDIANA UNIVERSITY *in* Ukraine

In the late 1980s, Mikhail Gorbachev began offering some autonomy to the republics that made up the Soviet Union, and in 1990, the Soviet Union permitted Ukraine, the second largest Soviet republic, to hold elections to create a parliament.

Facing, Ukrainian parliamentary delegation visits the School of Public and Environmental Affairs (SPEA), November 1993. *Left to right*: V. Makyenko, Y. Zbitniew, M. Shulha, interpreter W. Pechenuk, S. Dorohuntsov, M. Hryshko, associate dean of SPEA Charles Wise, Nadia McConnell of the US Ukraine Foundation, V. Nossov, S. Sobolev, A. Sukhorukov, interpreter M. Hryckowian, B. Radekjo of the US Ukraine Foundation, and T. Sinclair of SPEA. *Photograph courtesy of IU International magazine.*

IN THE LATE 1980S, MIKHAIL GORBACHEV BEGAN OFFERING SOME autonomy to the republics that made up the Soviet Union, and in 1990, the Soviet Union permitted Ukraine, the second largest Soviet republic, to hold elections to create a parliament. That body, known as the Verkhovna Rada, adopted independence and the priority of Ukrainian law over Soviet law.

In the spring of 1990, Charles Wise, a professor in the School of Public and Environmental Affairs (SPEA), contacted some of the new Ukrainian parliamentarians. He recalls the origins of his idea:

> This came out of a trip I made to Ukraine in the 1990s. I was having a conversation with some friends in Washington with whom I'd become acquainted when I was director of intergovernmental affairs for the Justice Department. This whole thing with Ukraine was . . . when Gorbachev initiated glasnost and they allowed the first competitive elections. There were a number of opponents of the Communist Party—several of whom had been imprisoned, they had gotten into parliament, and they were contacting people in the Ukrainian diaspora—they called them up and said, "Guess what? We got elected to parliament, but what do you do in parliament?"[1]

By April 1991, SPEA welcomed the first parliamentary delegation from the Republic of Ukraine to a conference designed specifically for their needs.[2] Wise has observed that, for "most of the thirteen delegates, this was their first

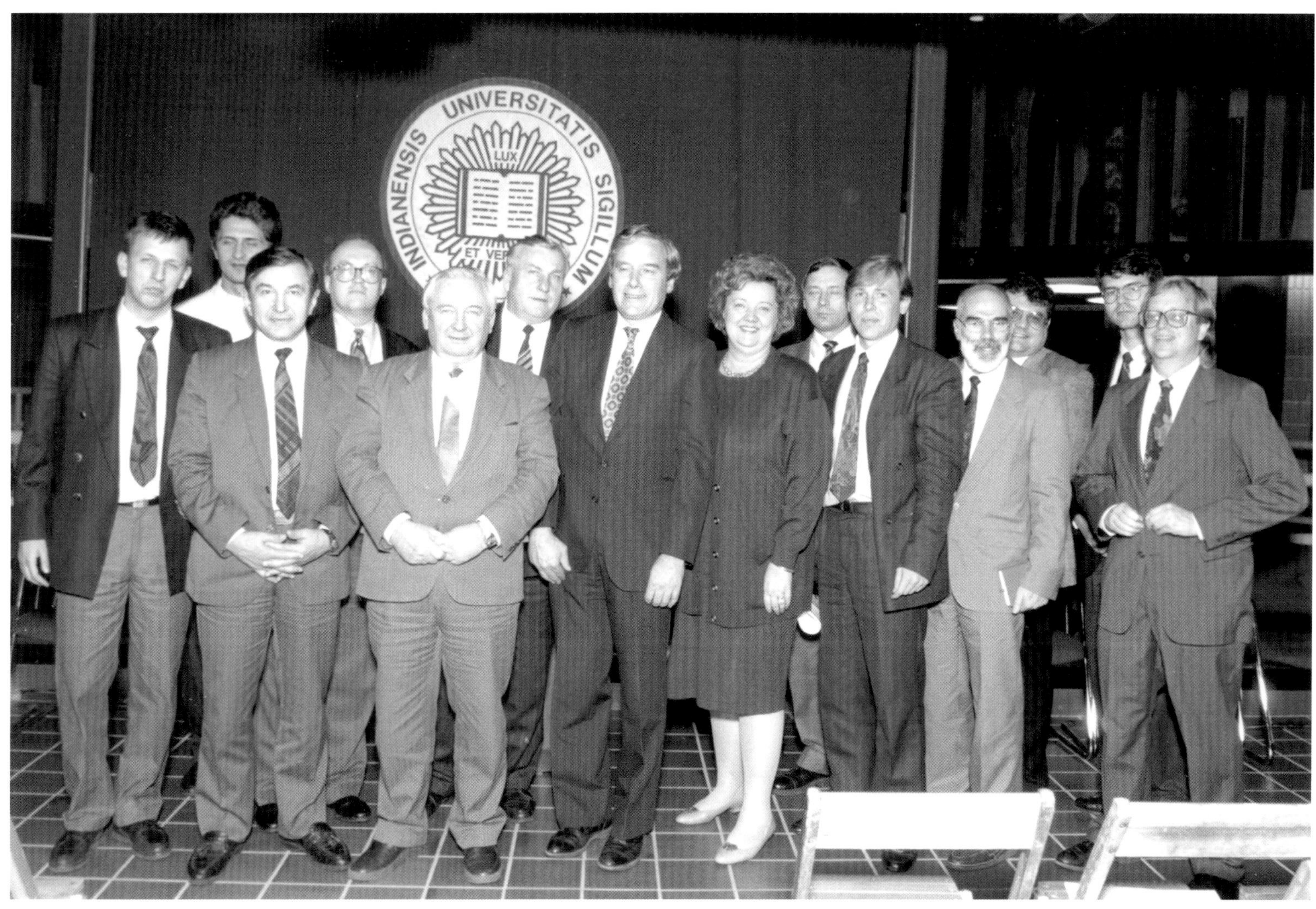
INDIANENSIS UNIVERSITATIS SIGILLUM
LUX

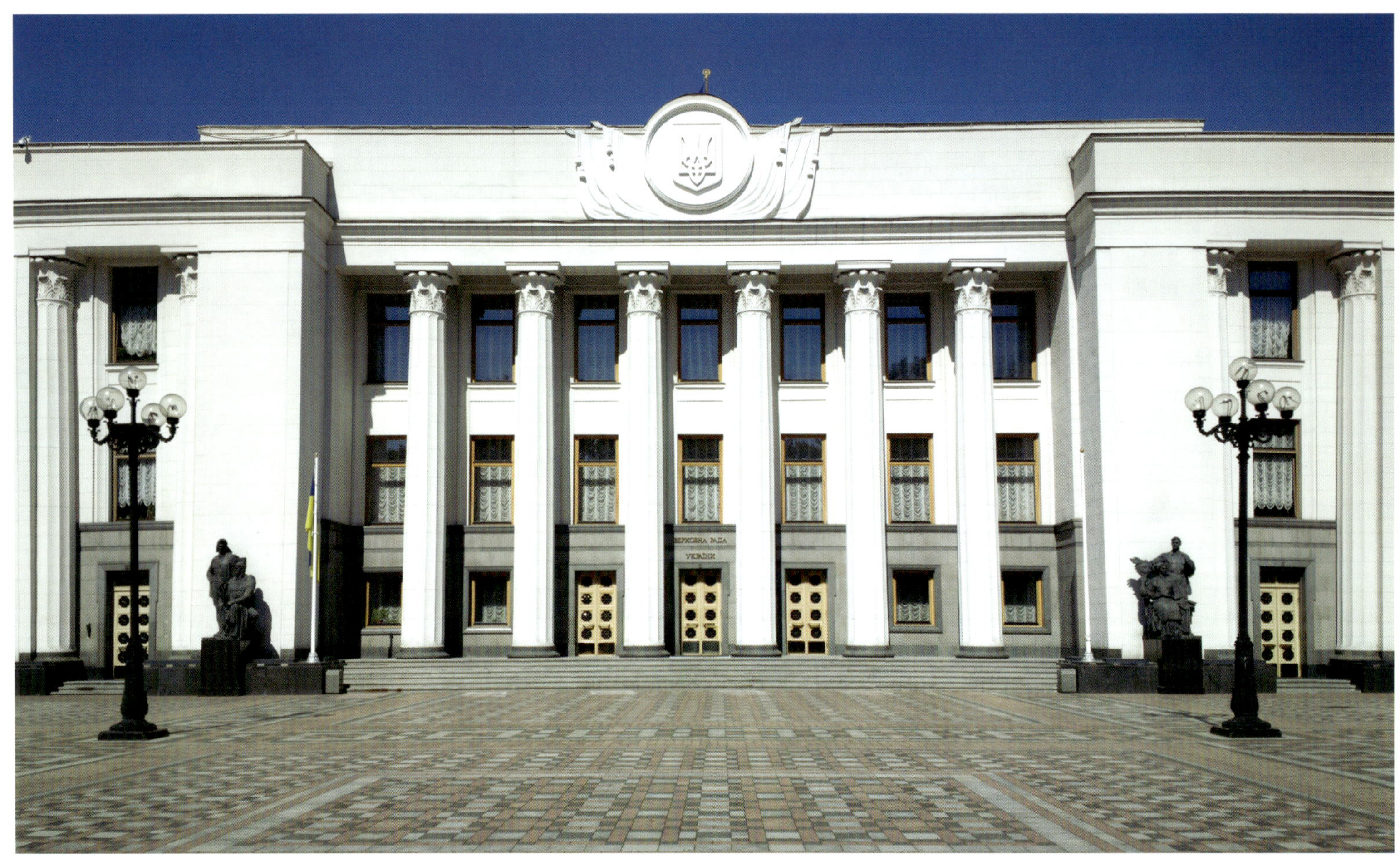

The Verkhovna Rada of Ukraine, 2013.
Photograph courtesy of iStock.

excursion outside the borders of the Soviet Union, and they spent their first day outside their country in Bloomington, Indiana."[3] He remembers the Ukrainian delegates' first exposure to life in the USA: "We took them to Gray Brothers Cafeteria, and we walked in, and they were just stunned . . . they just heaped their plates. They said, 'Can you tell us who is permitted to eat here?' That's how sealed off they were about anything in the West."[4]

After a week in Indiana, the group traveled to Washington, DC, where they met government officials, including former Senate Majority Leader Robert Dole, US Supreme Court Justice Sandra Day O'Connor, Senator Richard Lugar, and Representative Lee Hamilton. Although in 1991, the Communists still dominated the Republic of Ukraine and several of the delegates held high positions in the party, by the end of that first visit, all the delegates publicly expressed their expectation that Ukraine would become independent. Two years later, a third delegation returned to SPEA to discuss Ukraine's formal emergence into democracy and a market economy.

During that first historic conference on the US system of governance, the desire for a Ukraine independent of the Soviet Union was first stated on US soil—a bold statement before the fall of the Soviet Union. No one, except perhaps the Ukrainians themselves, could have guessed that in 1993, a third delegation would return to SPEA to discuss the developments of a free and independent state's steps toward democracy and a market economy. At a conference in November 1993 titled "The Role of the Legislative Branch in American Rule of Law," participants spent two weeks discussing specific issues arising from rebuilding government institutions, forming intergovernmental relations, and developing a new constitution in Ukraine. Charles Wise was, of course, a principal figure in each of these three conferences sponsored by the United States Information Agency, Indiana University, and the US Ukraine Foundation. Wise commented on the difficulties facing the Ukrainian parliament, a legislative body with 450 representatives: "They

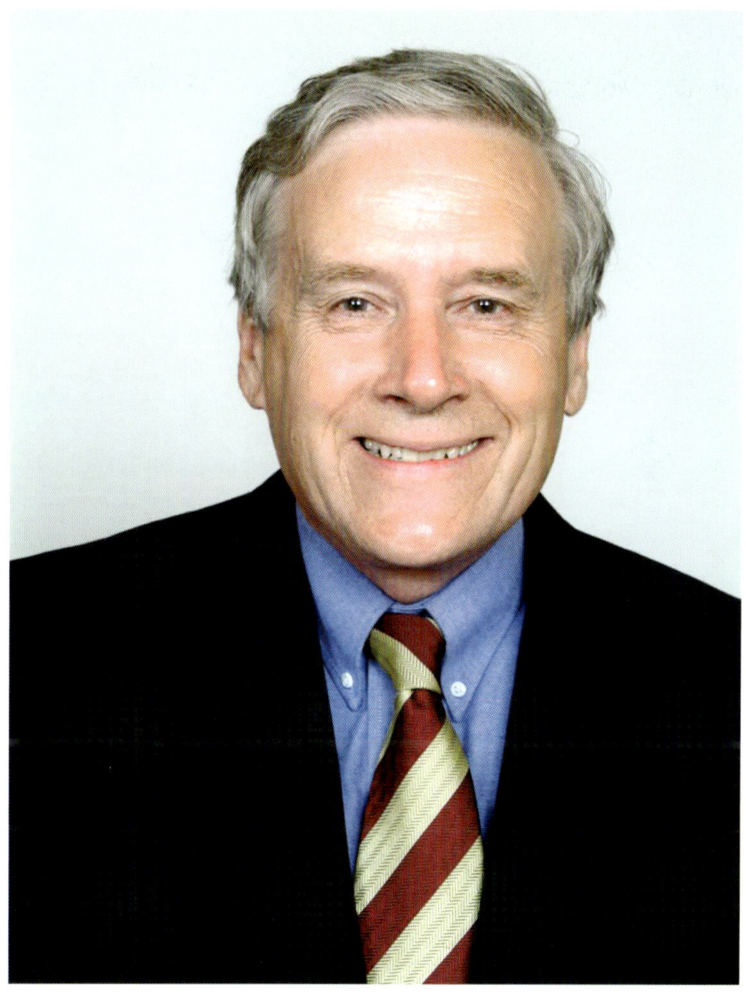

Charles Wise, professor emeritus, School of Public and Environmental Affairs, and former director of the Parliamentary Development Project for Ukraine. *Photograph courtesy of Indiana University.*

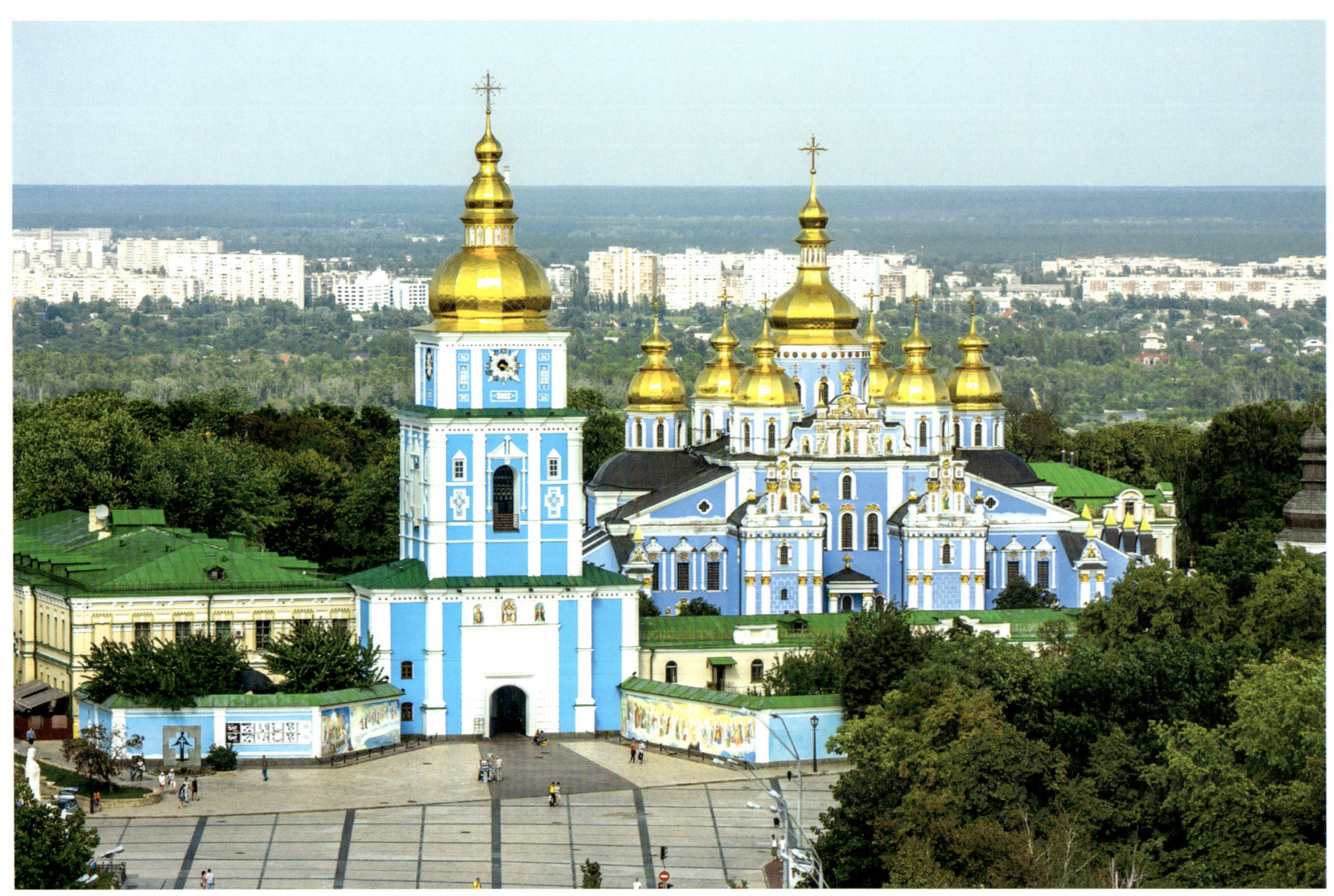

St. Michael's Monastery in Kiev, 2016. Established in 1713, the original cathedral was demolished by the Soviet authorities in the 1930s, but was reconstructed and opened in 1999 following Ukrainian independence in 1991.

Photograph courtesy of iStock.

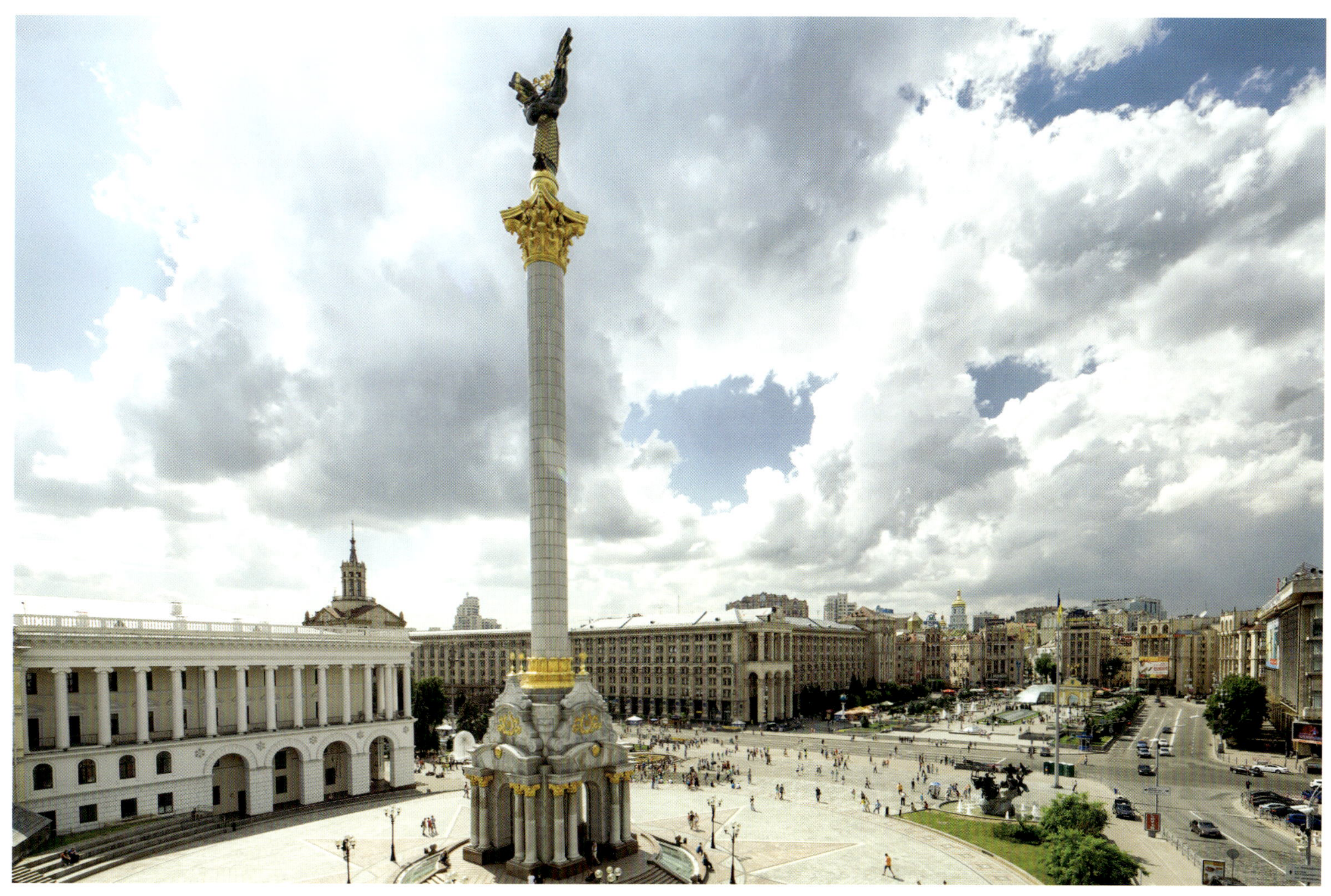

Maidan Nezalezhnosti, one of the main squares in Kiev, Ukraine, 2014.

Photograph courtesy of iStock.

are building all the democratic institutions that go into having a legal government. The legislature is also trying to help establish a court system and bureaucracy operating according to the rule of law, written law. In Ukraine's previous history, you didn't have a government or a society that operated on law. It operated on the whims of those in power. So their populace has no experience with this."[5] Wise added that laws were being passed, but there was difficulty with the executive branch actually implementing the laws to govern effectively. "They have to explain to the people how law will benefit them and then show how it does benefit them," Wise said.[6]

With offices in Bloomington and Kiev, the PDP was officially launched to help strengthen five key areas: legislative and executive relations, legislative committee structures and operations, legislative process, budget and appropriations activities, and representation and citizen relations.

During the November conference, Serhiy Dorohuntsov, chair of the Commission of the Environment, noted that parliament had already enacted more than one hundred new laws. Colleague Serhiy Sobolev added that nearly eight hundred amendments to these laws were on the books after just eight sessions of the existing parliament. "Perhaps everything in our legislation might not seem to be in harmony because of the wide scope of work that we have to do," Dorohuntsov commented. "The fate of our parliament has been that we have to start from square one with everything."[7]

A copy of the October 1993 draft of the Ukrainian constitution was presented to the Indiana University library as a gift from the delegation. Vladislav Nossov, a member of the parliamentary committee on legislation and legality, apologized for not having time to print the document in English. He said that the draft showed a tendency toward a presidential parliamentary republic, whereas the parliament previously had envisioned a presidential republic.[8]

Ellie Valentine, former associate director of IU's Russian and East European Institute, joined the project in 1994, served as the Parliamentary Development Project's (PDP's) field coordinator in Kiev, and remained there for almost seven years. She recalls the happenings in Kiev:

> The highlight of my work with the parliament had to be the constitutional debate. It was very dramatic—it was going on for over a week, they had a Council of Europe deadline to meet, they were meeting late into the night and on the final night, they were meeting all night. I can remember that we had been sitting in the gallery with colleagues from the US Ukraine Foundation. We had been sitting in the balcony until about nine p.m., watching and listening to the debate, and finally we said, "Okay, this is going to go on until tomorrow," so we left and went to our respective homes. In those days, the radios were hardwired—in the Soviet system, there was a radio in every home, and it wasn't something you could turn on or off, only down. I went to bed with that radio on low, and the thing that woke me up was the speaker saying, "Okay, so now we will have the last article before we have a vote," and it was about six o'clock in the morning, and I called a colleague who said, "We have to get down there—this is incredible!" And so we did; we made it over to the parliament. It was maybe ten o'clock in the morning when they had the final discussion on Article Ten; the president showed up, they had the final vote, and they passed the constitution. It was incredible! And to know that even in a very miniscule way, perhaps, our efforts had some impact on that was tremendous.[9]

While the group was in the United States, it met with a number of SPEA's adjunct and full-time faculty; speakers included adjunct faculty members Judge John Baker and David Allen, then Indianapolis mayor Stephen Goldsmith, and IU president emeritus John Ryan. While in Washington, DC, the parliamentarians sat in on the House of Representatives' debate on the NAFTA vote and received briefings on such topics as the legislative process, congressional oversight and investigations, lobbying Congress, and executive branch advocacy before Congress.

By April 1994, a grant from the United States Agency for International Development (USAID), plus support from Indiana University and the US Ukraine Foundation, allowed Wise to establish the Parliamentary Development Project for Ukraine.

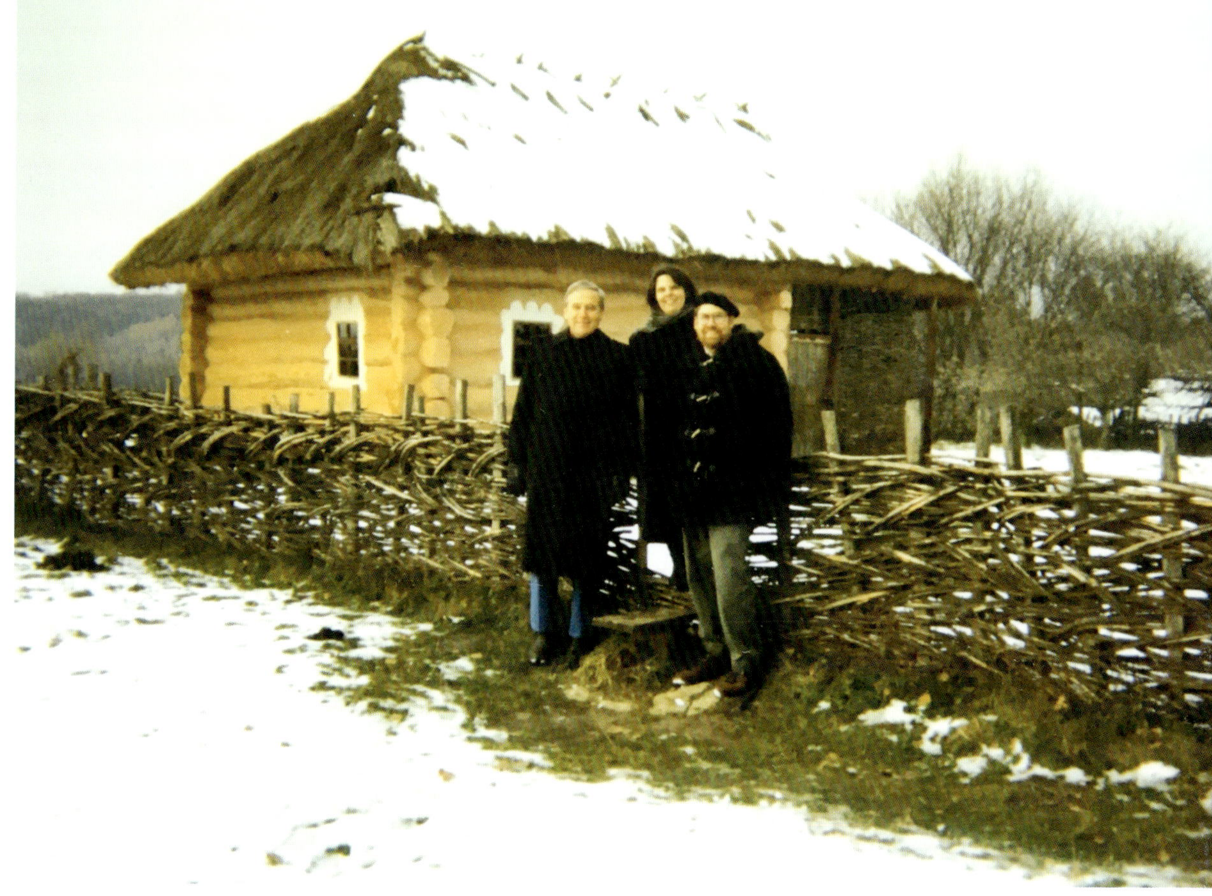

School of Public and Environmental Affairs faculty member Robert Agranoff (*right*), Charles Wise (*left*), and Parliamentary Development Project for Ukraine program field coordinator Ellie Valentine (*center*) in Ukraine. *Photograph courtesy of Charles Wise.*

With offices in Bloomington and Kiev, the PDP was officially launched to help strengthen five key areas: legislative and executive relations, legislative committee structures and operations, legislative process, budget and appropriations activities, and representation and citizen relations. Ukraine was, in essence, re-creating its constitution and transferring many of the powers from the president to the parliament. Human rights, trade laws, monetary policy, judicial powers, local government structure—all these basics of democracy were on the new administration's agenda. Another incentive for democratization at the time was possible admission to the European Union. In announcing the award, Senator Lugar said that "countries that are seeking to develop a more representative form of government deserve our support. Indiana University has the ability, the talent, and the track record to help Ukraine with this process. I am pleased an Indiana institution can assist with this important international work."[10]

Ellie Valentine comments on her duties in Kiev:

> One of my memories: I had not had any international development experience before. I had done academic exchanges, but those are very different from international development. When I showed up in Kiev, I had this blank slate, and part of what worked so well was that we didn't have this cookie-cutter notion of what needed to be done. It was very much a partnership—it was a partnership of IU with USAID, with the Ukraine Foundation, and, most importantly, with the parliament. Our biggest challenge in those days was actually the staff of parliament, not the elected members. The elected members recognized how they wanted to move forward and that they had a reform agenda. I think the staff was very hesitant because they were all formal central party staff, and they were very protective and dismissive of the notion that they didn't know what they were doing or how to serve the members. That was really our biggest challenge in those days—bringing key staff on board and helping them realize that we weren't a threat—that we were a resource. That was what ultimately led to our success.[11]

The PDP employed six Ukrainians as executive directors, including Svetlana Svetova, a graduate of SPEA's master of public affairs program. SPEA professors who worked with the PDP at that time included Larry Schroeder and Robert Agranoff. Agranoff added another dimension to the goals of the project: "One of the things we really worked hard on in the group was to instill in the parliamentarians and their staff, was that institutions matter. You have to believe, right or wrong, the parliament is the chief decision-making body in terms of the law, and the law is important. One of the things I always tried to get across to them is that yes, politics exist, but it isn't all politics—law is important as well."[12] Agranoff's expertise was also valuable because of his perspective on local institutions. "It was a country where it was highly suited for federalization and because there were certain things that were central, and maintained as central—education was a good example—but there were also things that were very local—economic development, certain aspects of taxes."[13]

In 2003, SPEA was awarded a new five-year, $4.9 million contract by USAID to strengthen democratic government in Ukraine. The grant enabled Wise and a development team to build on the work that they had done with the Ukrainian parliament over the past nine years. In September 2005, the PDP received a $500,000 cooperative agreement from USAID to facilitate further legislative reform in Ukraine and to supplement the $4.9 million award made in 2003.

In recognizing the award, Senator Lugar concluded that "Extraordinary events have occurred in Ukraine over this past year. A free press has revolted against government intimidation and reasserted itself. An emerging middle class has found its political footing. A new generation has embraced democracy and openness. A society has rebelled against the illegal activities of its government. It is in our interest to recognize and protect these advances in Ukraine."[14]

The future of democracy in Ukraine, and possibly Ukraine's position as an independent country, were at stake, according Wise: "Some years ago, Zbigniew Brzezinksi said that without

Democracy comes at a price. Most citizens under Soviet rule didn't know the perils of poverty—hunger, disease, homelessness, prostitution—until the collapse of communism.

—Charles Wise

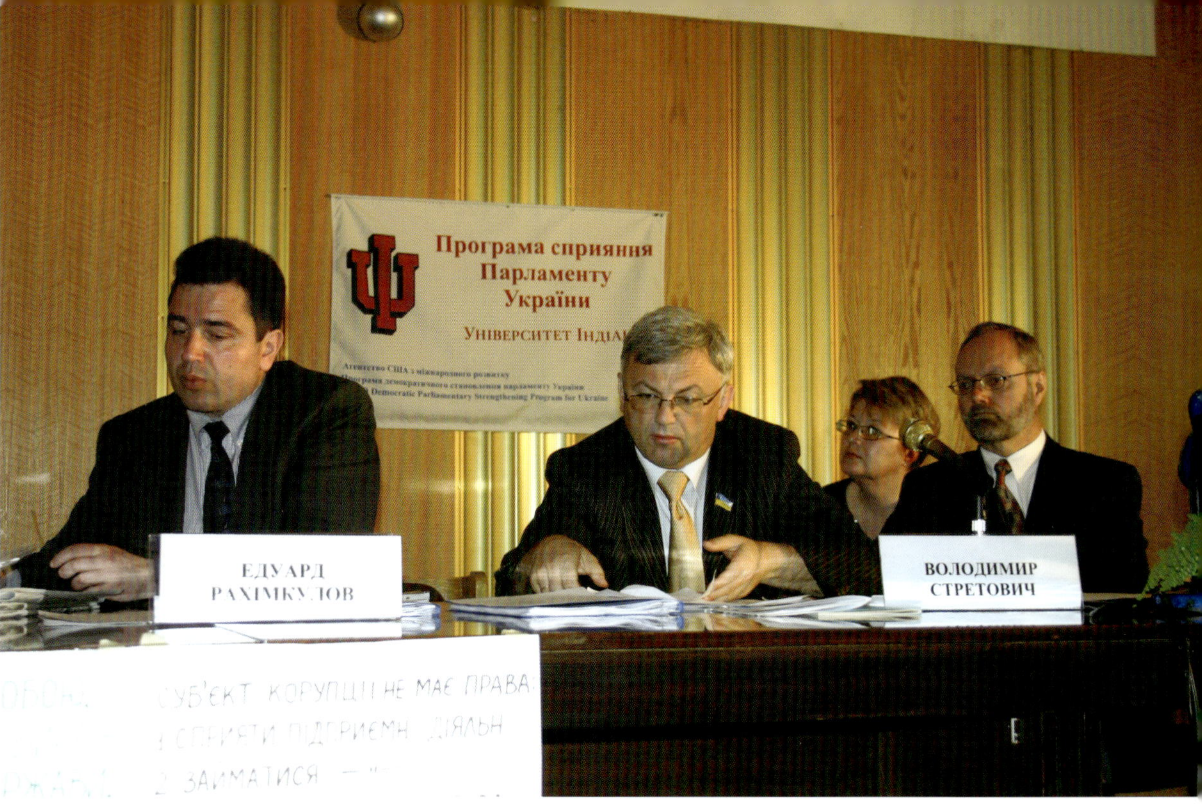

Parliamentary Development Project (PDP) associate director Edward Rakhimkulov, chair of the Committee on Fighting Organized Crime and Corruption Volodymyr Stretovych, and PDP chief of party Fred Bradley, at regional anticorruption hearings held by the Committee on Fighting Organized Crime and Corruption in Kherson, 2005.
Photograph courtesy of Ellie Valentine.

Ukraine, it would be impossible to reconstitute anything like the former Soviet Union, but with Ukraine, it would be entirely possible. Ukraine had both material and symbolic importance within the collection of states comprising the former Soviet Union. Besides Russia, by population, Ukraine is the largest republic of the former Soviet Union and is the most culturally and ethnically aligned with Russia. Without Ukraine, you simply cannot have a unified bloc of nations that means anything strategically."[15]

The year 2004 was a time of dramatic political changes in Ukraine. Leonid Kuchma had been in power for ten years, and his regime was seen as corrupt. There were two candidates in the election for his successor—Viktor Yushchenko and Viktor Yanukovych—but there was widespread belief that the election had been rigged in favor of Yanukovych and that there was intimidation at the polls. What was known as the Orange Revolution resulted in strikes, civil disobedience, and protests. In December 2004, the supreme court ruled that the election was invalid and that a new election, monitored by international observers, should take place. There was a clear majority for Yushchenko in this election.

In 2013, President Yanukovych decided not to sign a free trade agreement with the European Union. For many Ukrainians, particularly those in the west of the country, this meant that Ukraine was moving away from Europe and the protection of the North Atlantic Treaty Organization. In February 2014, amid unrest and student protests in Kiev and other parts of the country, demands were made for reform and new leadership. Some protesters were shot and killed during the protests, and under these conditions, Yanukovych was forced to resign. In March 2014, Russia intervened militarily in Crimea, which it subsequently annexed. It also began to actively support pro-Russian groups in the east of the country that resulted in Ukraine becoming enmeshed in a civil war. Agranoff recalls the sentiment expressed to him by so many Ukrainians during his visits to the country:

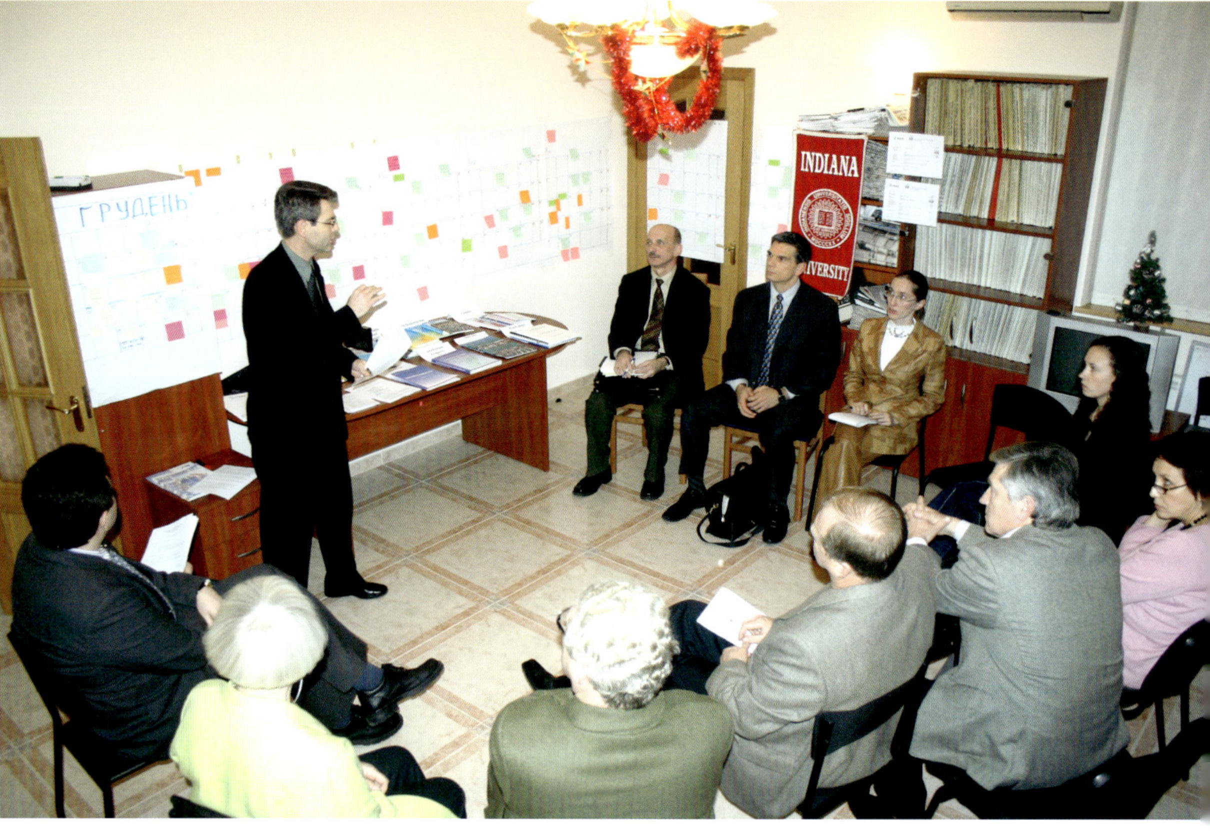

> "We don't want to be Russian—this is our country." The Ukrainians had great pride that we worked with the parliamentarians and their independence at that time, and they were very concerned about too much Russian influence. They made it very clear at the beginning that we were not supposed to introduce any data or anything that had to do with Russian practices—nothing at all. And that was a time before Putin. They made that very clear. Sometimes, it may have been lost in translation, but if there was resistance, the preface was, "We're a free people—we will do what we decide to do." I can't tell you how many times I heard that kind of thing—"We are free people, and we will decide what we want. We're very interested in what you tell us about practices in other countries, but we will decide." It was a time when they really had a lot of pride in being free from the Russians.[16]

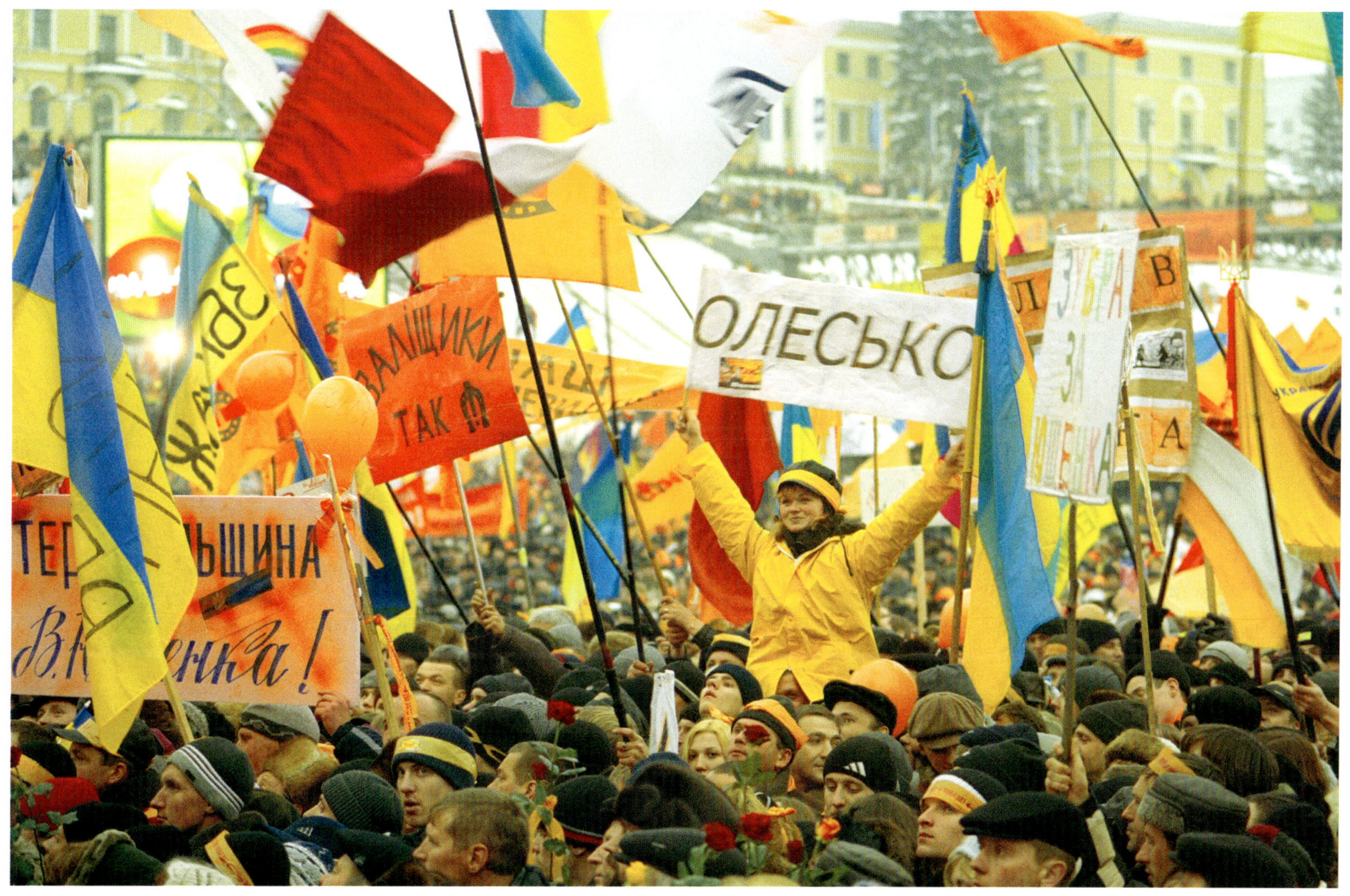

Facing, Bohdan Radejko (*standing*), Parliamentary Development Project (PDP) chief of party and PDP Ukrainian staff present the work plan to United States Agency for International Development mission director Earl Gast (*middle right*) and USAID senior democracy officer Oleksandr Piskun (*right*), 2007. *Photograph courtesy of Ellie Valentine.*

Protesters in Kiev's Independence Square.
Photograph by Igor Kostin/Corbis via Getty Images.

Given these tragic events of the recent Russian military intervention in Ukraine, was the IU involvement of any value? At one point, Wise had emphasized that the PDP was not trying to lead other countries into duplicating America's brand of democracy. He commented:

> Different cultures will perform better under their own tailored form of democratic institutions . . . our approach in Ukraine is that we provide options. If we get a particular committee in the parliament working on, say, military justice, we might show them eight or nine different alternatives currently in use by other countries. It's not up to us to say which alternative is best for them, but to expose them to the range of possibilities so there can be a democratic debate over which alternative is best for them. We don't have a stake in which model they choose, as long as they are choosing among democratic models.[17]

Wise was clearly aware of the risks and pitfalls involved.

> But democracy comes at a price. Most citizens under Soviet rule didn't know the perils of poverty—hunger, disease, homelessness, prostitution—until the collapse of communism. You have to understand that in Eastern Europe and the former Soviet Union, there were three mega-transformations under way at once. They were transforming their government, their economy, and their civil society. That's a magnitude of change across countries that the world has never seen before. They don't have a blueprint for that kind of massive change. But there's no way any given country would say, "Let's put the brakes on this and wait so we can plan everything out first." It's true that there was an expectation that if they adopted democracy, they would immediately get Western prosperity, and when they didn't, sizable segments of society were disappointed. But those expectations were never realistic.[18]

Because of the PDP, political procedures, structures, and ideas were expressed and perhaps became part of the prevailing political culture. The intervention of Russia and President Putin's fear that Ukraine would become part of the North Atlantic Treaty Organization could not have been anticipated.

12 | INDIANA UNIVERSITY *in* Kyrgyzstan

It is the first and only institution of higher education in the region that operates according to the American model with a credit-hour system, an American-style curriculum, and a commitment to academic integrity and honesty.

—Patrick O'Meara

AFTER THE FALL OF THE SOVIET UNION, THE REPUBLIC OF Kyrgyzstan came into being in 1991. This relatively small country of over five million people—bordered by Kazakhstan to the north, Uzbekistan to the west, Tajikistan to the southwest, and China to the east—was one of the poorest countries in Central Asia.

The American University Kyrgyzstan (AUK), was established in 1997 in the country's capital city, Bishkek, with support from the US government and philanthropist George Soros's Open Society Institute. AUK used American approaches to teaching and research.[1] Indiana University's Patrick O'Meara noted, "It is the first and only institution of higher education in the region that operates according to the American model with a credit-hour system, an American-style curriculum, and a commitment to academic integrity and honesty."[2]

Housed in a building that once was the home of the Communist Party of Kyrgyzstan, the institution grew rapidly from about forty students when it started to more than one thousand students in 2001. AUK's administration was headed by Provost Camilla Sharshekeeva, a Kyrgz, and by Martha Merrill, an American scholar who was vice president for academic affairs.[3]

In 1999, Charles Reafsnyder approached the dean of international programs, Patrick O'Meara, with the idea of submitting a proposal to United States

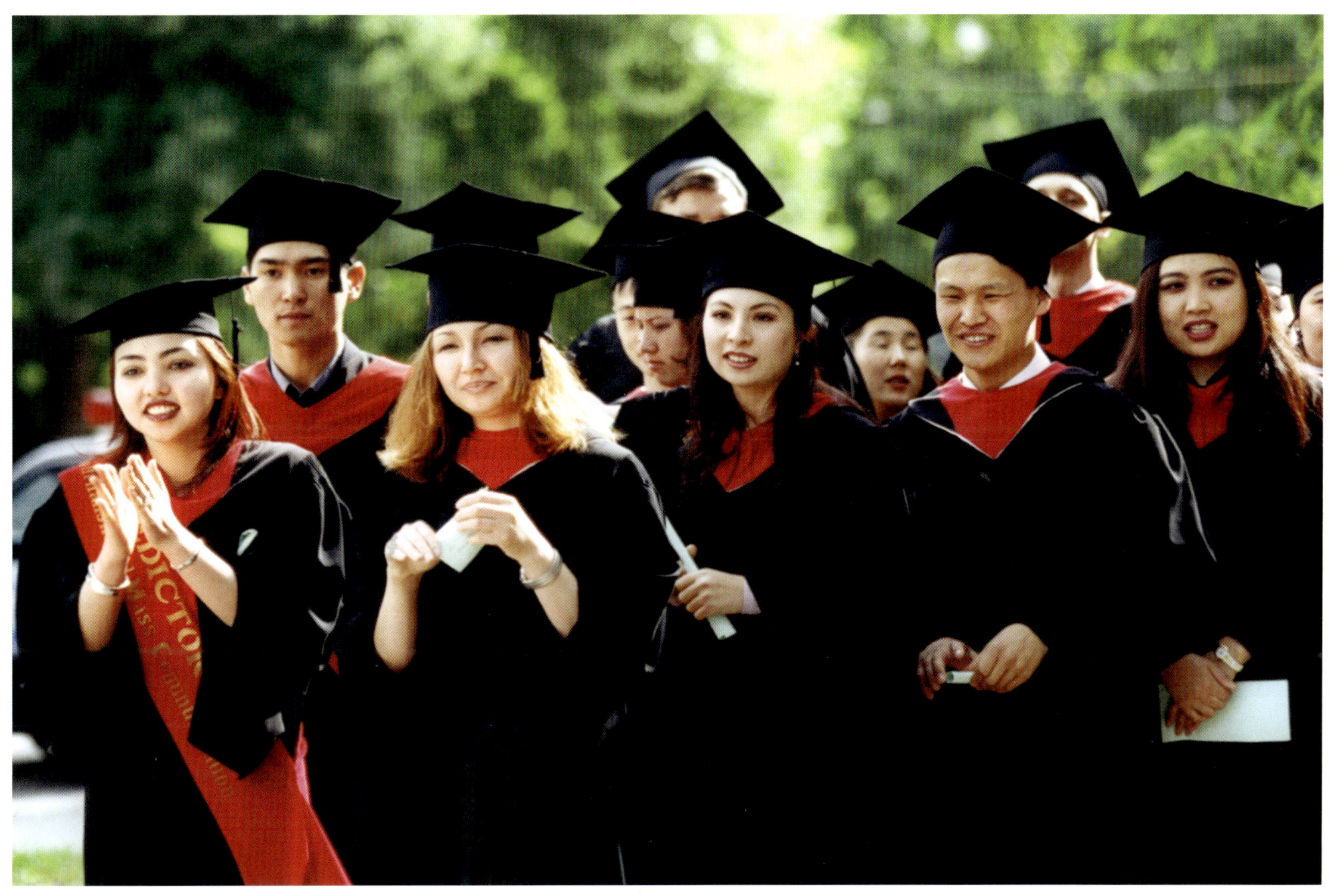

Graduating students at the American University of Central Asia in Bishkek.

Photograph courtesy of Charles Reafsnyder.

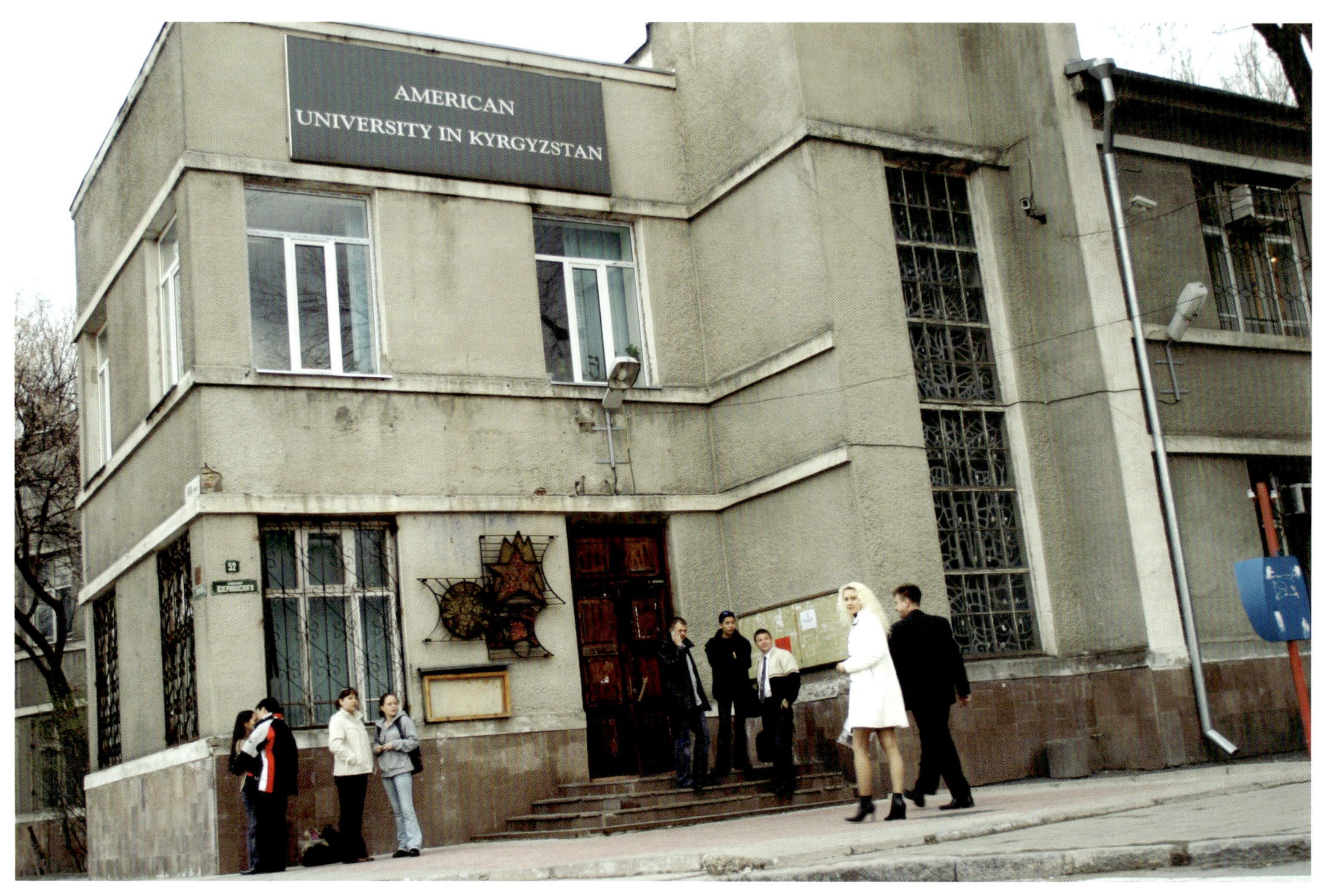

Entrance of the American University in Bishek, Kyrgyzstan, March 2005.
Photograph by Yoray Liberman/Getty Images.

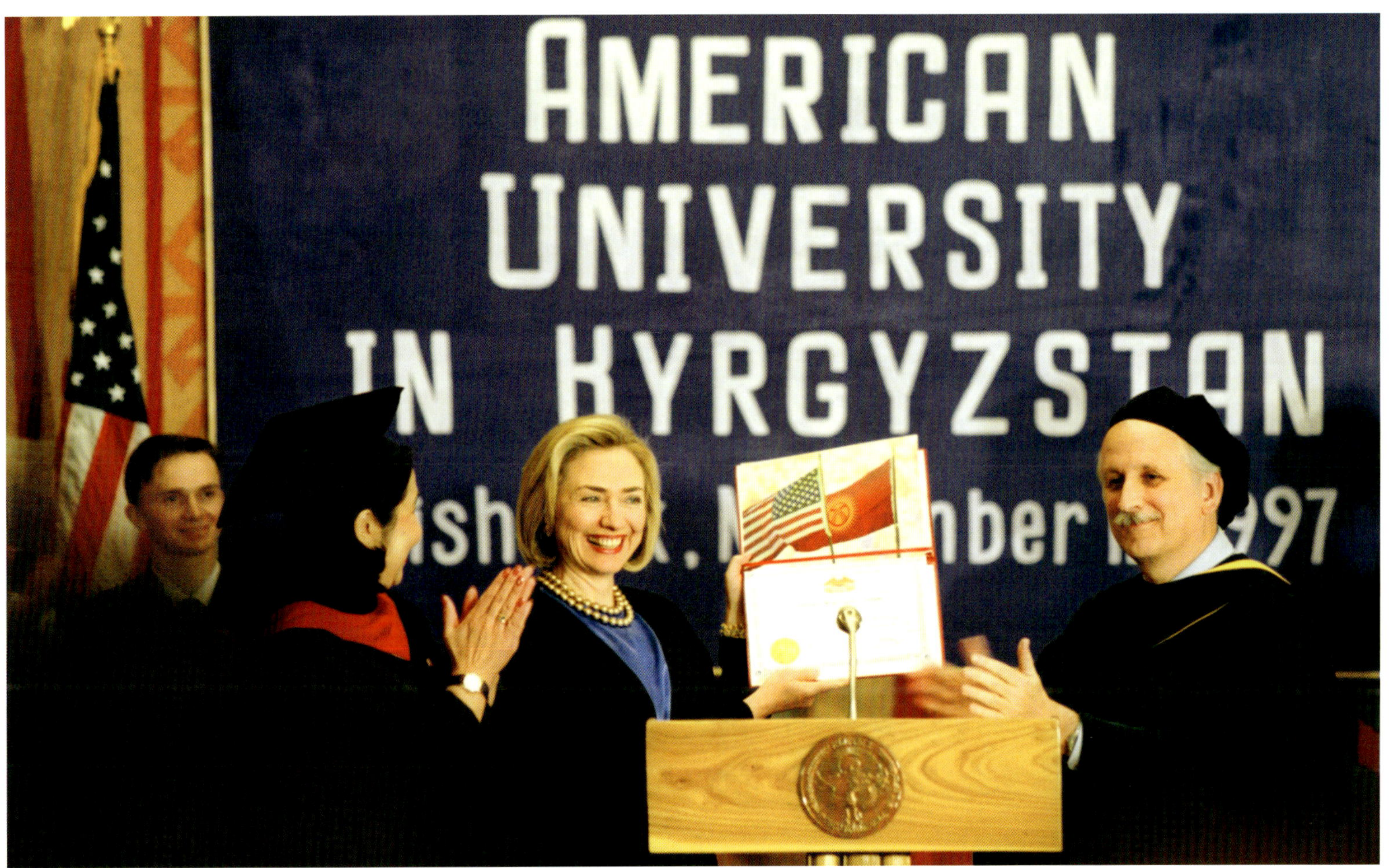

Then first lady Hillary Clinton receives an honorary degree from the newly opened American University in Kyrgyzstan during a tour through Central Asia, November 1997. *Photograph by David Hume Kennerly/Getty Images.*

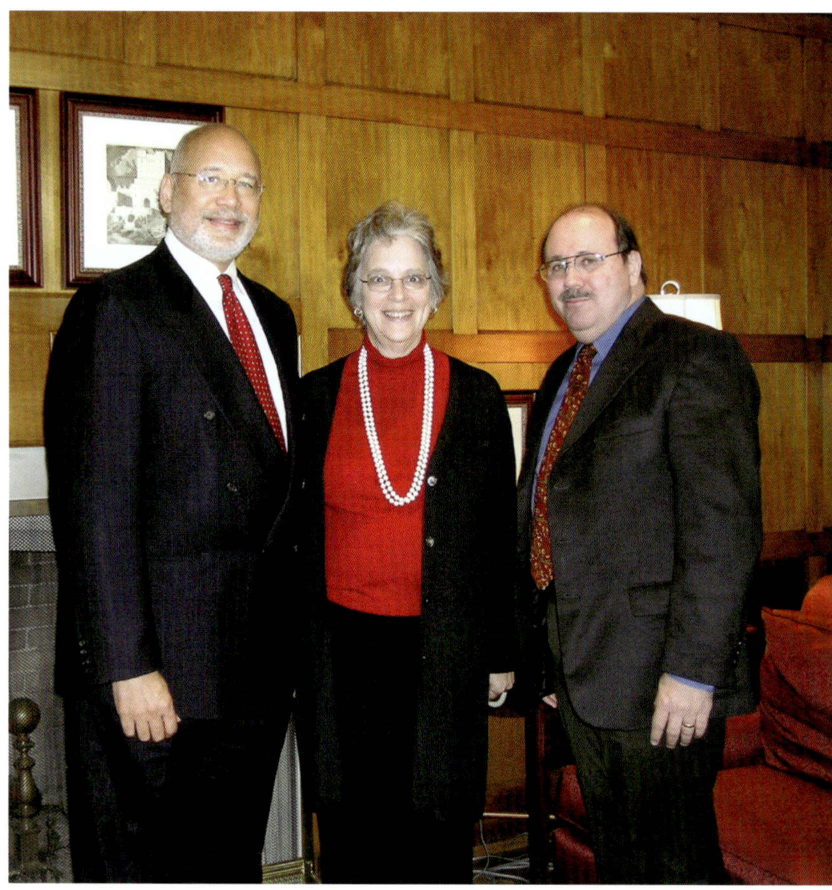

Indiana University president Adam W. Herbert (*left*), AUCA president Ellen Hurwitz (*center*), and Charles Reafsnyder (*right*), 2005.
Photograph courtesy of Roxana Newman.

Facing, Indiana University faculty member Anne Pyburn (*right*) in Chap, Kyrgyzstan, with Mrs. Abdykeev (*left*), a local artisan who made the rug in the photo using the wool of her sheep and local dyes, 2006.
Photograph courtesy of Anne Pyburn.

Agency for International Development (USAID) to support the activities of AUK. In preparation for the proposal, Reafsnyder visited Bishkek in early February 1999, where he met with Merrill, Sharshekeeva, acting president John Clark, and faculty members and students. He also talked with officials at USAID in Bishkek.

Indiana University had a long-standing interest in the region; the Title VI–supported Inner Asian and Uralic National Resource Center was known for its instruction, research, and outreach activities on Central Eurasia, including Kyrgyzstan.

Indiana University had a long-standing interest in the region; the Title VI–supported Inner Asian and Uralic National Resource Center (IAUNRC) was known for its instruction, research, and outreach activities on Central Eurasia, including Kyrgyzstan. In partnership with the Department of Central Eurasian Studies, the IAUNRC offered courses in such fields as anthropology, business, comparative literature, history, political science, and religious studies. IU's Summer Workshop in Slavic, East European, and Central Asian Languages (SWSEEL) listed courses in Azeri, Kazakh, Kyrgyz, Turkmen, and Uzbek. Indiana University Bloomington's deep commitment to teaching and research on Central Asia proved to be invaluable in preparing the grant application. IU faculty members and students would benefit from the expanded involvement in Kyrgyzstan.

The goals of the IU project included enabling AUK faculty, many of whom had been trained in the Soviet higher education system, to gain exposure to how the social sciences were

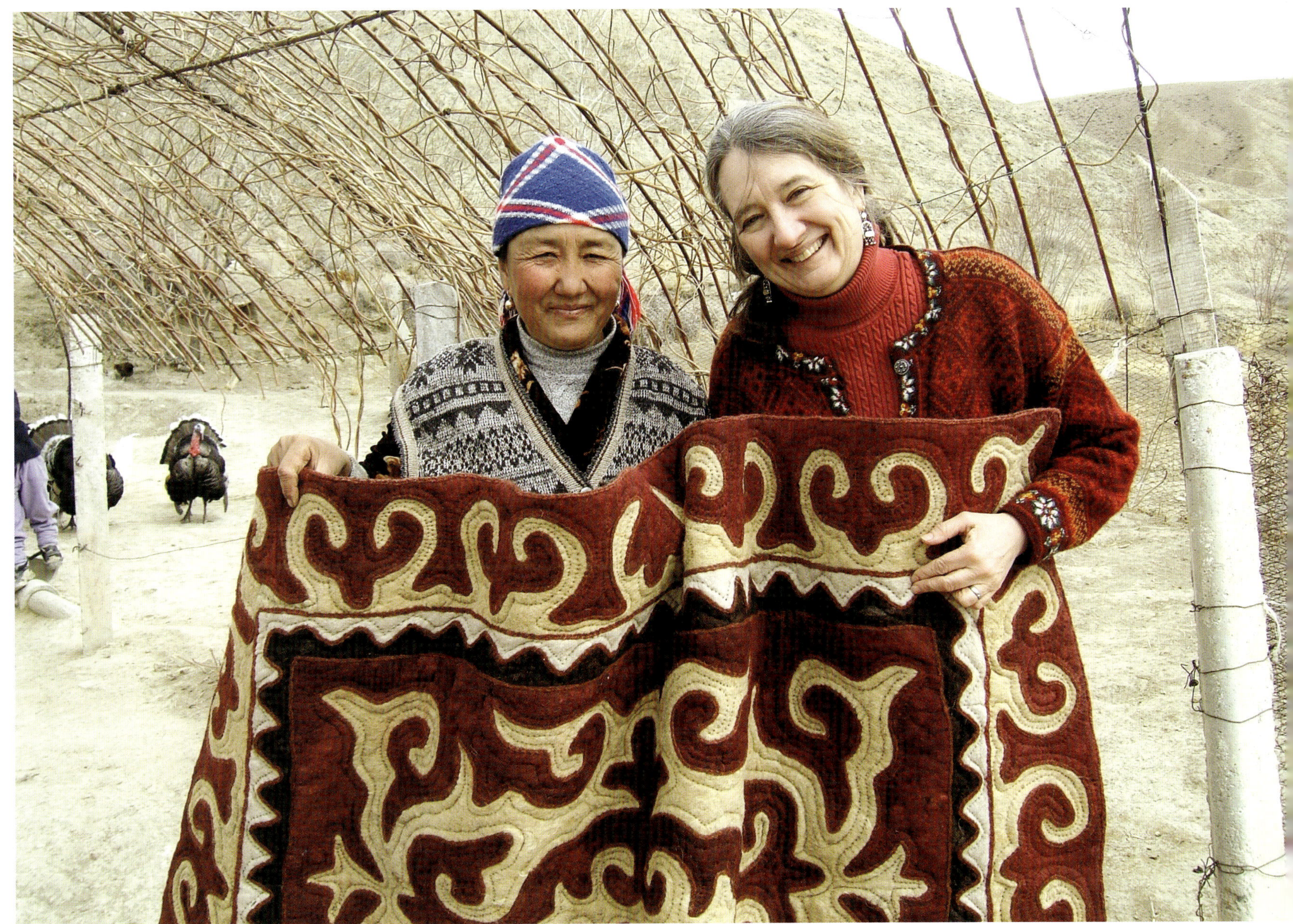

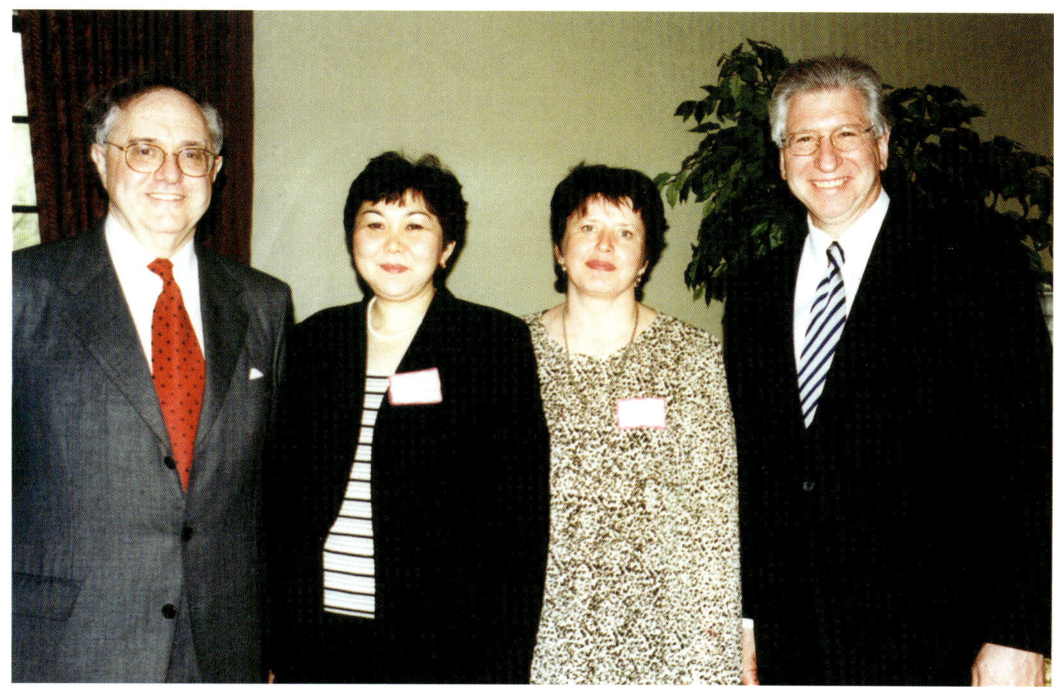

Visiting American University Kyrgyzstan (AUK) faculty and administrators at a reception hosted by Indiana University president Myles Brand (*right*), April 2001. *Left to right:* dean for international programs Patrick O'Meara, Nurila Sharshekeeva of the Program of British-American Studies, and Natalia Slastnikova, assistant to the president of AUK. Not shown is a third visitor, Galina Bityukova of the International Relations Program. The visitors spent part or all of the spring semester at Indiana University Bloomington under the IUB-AUK exchange project on faculty development and administrative training. Slastnikova spent time with various administrators at IUB, Indiana University–Purdue University Indianapolis, and DePauw University, while Sharshekeeva and Bityukova worked on curriculum development in their respective fields. *Photograph courtesy of Roxana Newman.*

studied and taught in the United States. The program included visits by IU faculty to assist with course and curriculum development in targeted disciplines; expansion and development of AUK library collections and access to electronic sources of information; and four-month internships for AUK administrators to learn about higher education in the United States. To meet all these objectives, Indiana University worked with some of the colleges and universities that were part of the Indiana Consortium for International Programs (ICIP).[4]

Special assistance was also provided by Counterpart International, a nonprofit organization with experience managing civic, social, and economic development projects. Previously, with USAID funding, Counterpart International had provided training and other programs in Kyrgyzstan for local nongovernmental organizations. Counterpart International contracted with IU and ICIP to provide logistical support through its Bishkek Office for housing, travel arrangements, airport greetings, communications, and receiving large shipments of books and other items.[5]

In 2002, because of AUK's expanding mission, its trustees decided to rename it the American University of Central Asia (AUCA) to attract students from adjacent countries.[6] IU provided opportunities in the United States for AUCA, including visits and training programs. For example, two staff members from AUCA received LLM degrees from Indiana

University–Purdue University Indianapolis (IUPUI) in May 2005, after which they returned to AUCA, where they taught in the law department. MBA and MA degrees from Ball State University and IU were awarded to three students in May 2006. They returned to teach American studies and business. Kubatbek Tabaldyeva, a senior professor of anthropology, came to IU in January 2005. IU faculty member Anne Pyburn asked Tabaldyeva to accompany her to an archaeological site in Belize. This special opportunity for the visiting Kyrgyz scholar led Pyburn to archaeological work in Kyrgyzstan. Natalia Slastnikova, director of development at AUCA, spent six weeks at Indiana University and two weeks at DePaul University. She met staff members from the Indiana University Foundation and reviewed the relevance of fund-raising and development activities at US universities to determine their relevance to AUCA and its cultural and economic environment. A number of MA, MBA, and LLM candidates were selected and subsequently came to the United States to study.

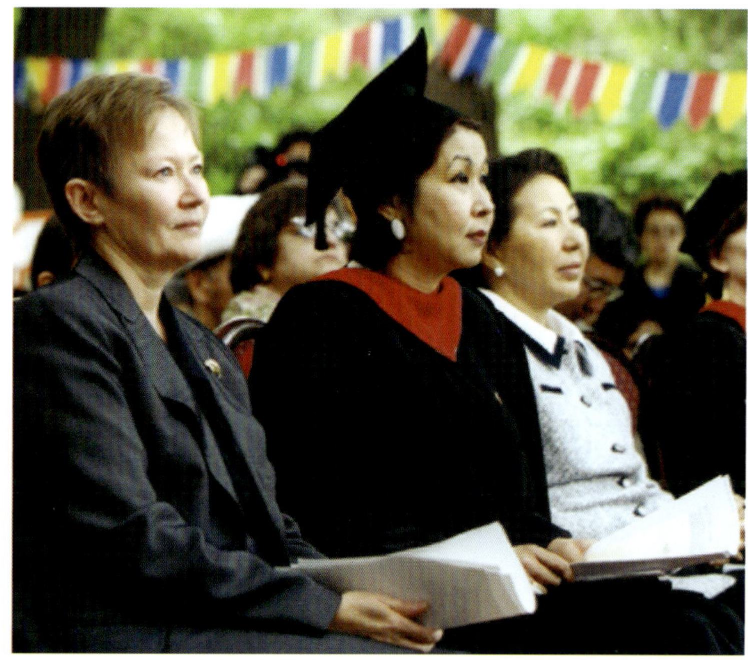

American University Kyrgyzstan provost Camilla Sharshekeeva (*center*) at graduation in Bishkek. *Photograph courtesy of Charles Reafsnyder.*

In turn, Indiana faculty members visited and worked at AUCA. Roy Shin, a professor at the IU School of Public and Environmental Affairs, joined Charles Reafsnyder and Shawn Reynolds on their fall 2003 trip to AUCA. While there, Shin reviewed the potential for the introduction of a public administration program at AUCA and interviewed junior faculty who wanted to come to IU to complete degrees. In November 2004, Shin and Astrid Merget, then dean of the School of Public and Environmental Affairs, followed up with a twelve-day visit to AUCA. They were able to initiate planning for a public administrative grant funded by USAID. Claire King, director of Indiana University Community Outreach and Partnership in Service Learning, spent three weeks at AUCA in 2004–2005, where she presented workshops on introducing an interdisciplinary service-learning approach to courses. Chris J. Foley, director of international admissions and chief of operations for undergraduate admissions, traveled to AUCA in September 2005 for two weeks to review its admissions and financial aid practices. Retired registrar of IUPUI, Mark Grove, and his wife, Mary, focused on academic policies, procedures, the AUCA's registrar's office, and general data issues. Mary

The assistance of IU and of partner ICIP institutions came at a time when AUCA was moving in new directions and consolidating its programs and operations.

Grove, who had also worked for IUPUI before her retirement, concentrated on both internal and external communication. Randall Powell, retired director of the Business Placement Office in IU's Kelley School of Business, was invited by AUCA to assess the career development needs of AUCA students.

During the grant period, an important development occurred. Columbia University's Ellen Hurwitz, former president of New England College in Henniker, New Hampshire, formerly of Albright College in Reading, Pennsylvania, was selected as the new president of AUCA. Reafsnyder was a member of the search committee that selected Hurwitz. Before assuming the presidency at AUCA, Hurwitz spent several days on the IU Bloomington campus, where she met with administrators and faculty and with the AUCA junior faculty enrolled in coursework at IU Bloomington, IUPUI, and Ball State University. Hurwitz reflects on the experience: "I centered my presidency on the mission of a liberal arts education. When I got there, the focus on the liberal arts was not entirely clear and sharp. There was more of a preprofessional emphasis. The faculty was more interested in its own scholarship and in the Soviet style than they were in the articulation of an appropriate liberal arts vision for that university."[7]

In addition, Hurwitz wanted to move AUCA in an interdisciplinary direction. "There was not that comfort with interdisciplinarity and exploration and risk taking in the pursuit of ideas that I was trying to foster."

For Hurwitz, AUCA had become an institution with a significant influence in Kyrgyzstan: "I see the definite impact of the university on a new cadre of professionals and intellectuals in Kyrgyzstan, so in that sense, it's really fulfilling its mission."[8]

IU continued to have a role for many years through the AUCA Endowment, which the IU Foundation had agreed to manage on its behalf. Reafsnyder played a key role in establishing the $15 million endowment for AUCA; $5 million came from the Open Society Institute and $10 million from USAID. The endowment replaced funding that AUCA had received from the Open Society Institute and USAID and was to be used to underwrite some of its operating expenses. Emita Hill, a former IU Kokomo chancellor and a trustee of AUCA notes that "It's been a very, very beneficial partnership. This is probably the most positive thing to have happened in the last several years. With this endowment, they have at least a very clear idea of what the base is, and if they're able to raise additional funds, they can do bigger and better things."[9]

The assistance of IU and of partner ICIP institutions came at a time when AUCA was moving in new directions and consolidating its programs and operations. Goals of strict admission criteria, the appointment of strong faculty members, and the overall absence of corruption were enhanced by the relationship. Charles Reafsnyder and his colleagues at the Center for International Education and Development Assistance also assisted in the early stages of planning and funding for the construction of a new campus for AUCA.

13 | INDIANA UNIVERSITY *in* Macedonia

After the breakup of Yugoslavia in the early 1990s, the Balkans experienced war, chaos, and civil unrest. Once again, Indiana University had an opportunity to become involved in development activities that would transform lives in a part of the world where there was a need for reconciliation.

AFTER THE BREAKUP OF YUGOSLAVIA IN THE EARLY 1990S, THE Balkans experienced war, chaos, and civil unrest. Once again, Indiana University had an opportunity to become involved in development activities that would transform lives in a part of the world where there was a need for reconciliation.

Beginning in 2001, Charles Reafsnyder, director of the Center for International Education and Development Assistance and associate dean in the Office of International Programs, began to explore an important initiative in the Republic of Macedonia. This was an opportunity to build on IU's long interest in the Balkans. For example, IU history professor Charles Jelavich focused throughout his career on modern nationalism in the Balkan Peninsula, and his wife, Barbara Jelavich, was a distinguished specialist on Balkan history. Slavic language department faculty member Henry Cooper's research and teaching dealt with south Slavic languages and literatures, especially Slovene and Croatian. Indiana University's role in the establishment of South East European University (SEEU) and a potential ongoing relationship with this newly founded university would enable IU to be of service in a part of the world that had been bitterly divided and, at the same time, to provide new opportunities and interests for the faculty.

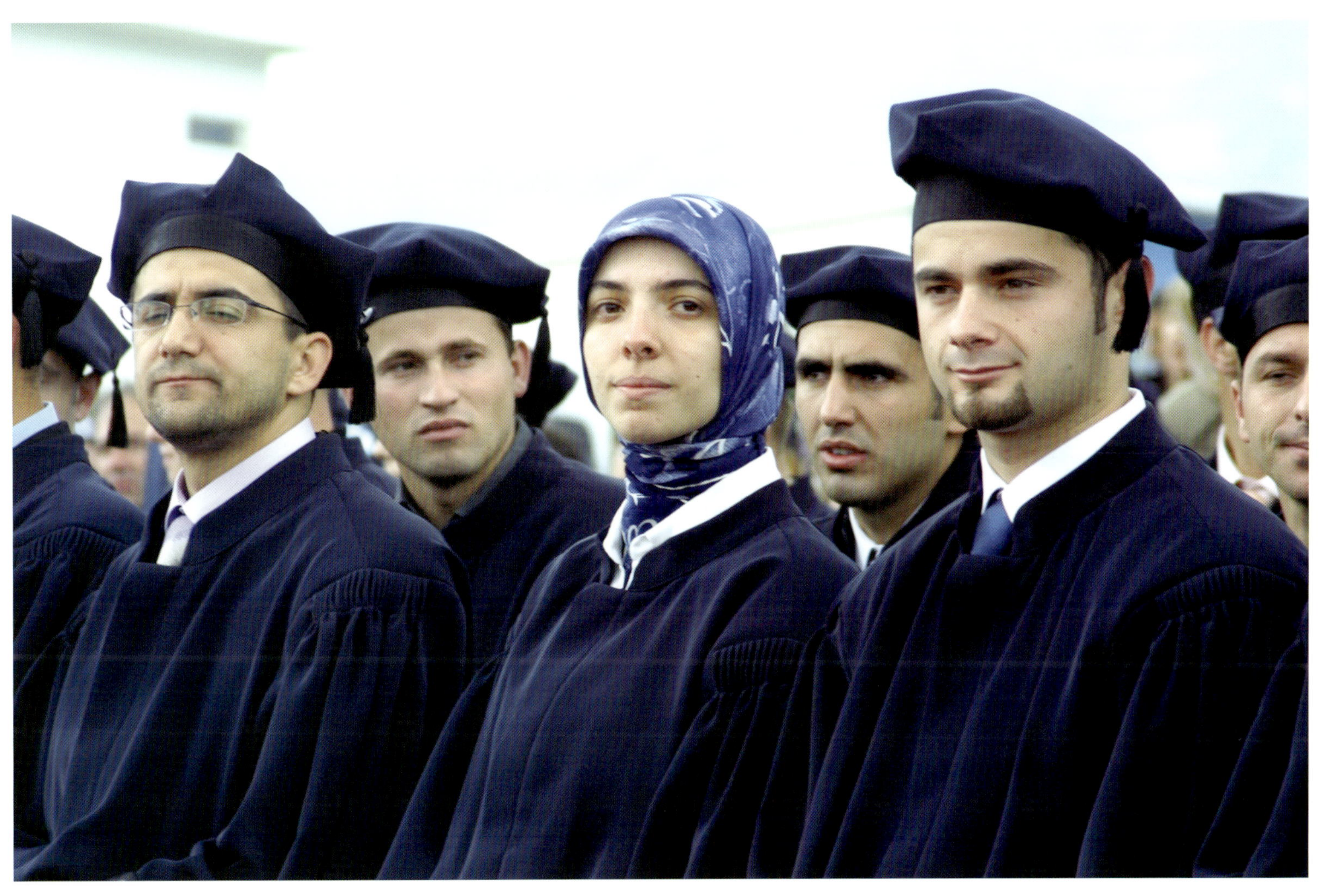

Members of the first graduating class at South East European University, spring 2004. *Photograph courtesy of South East European University.*

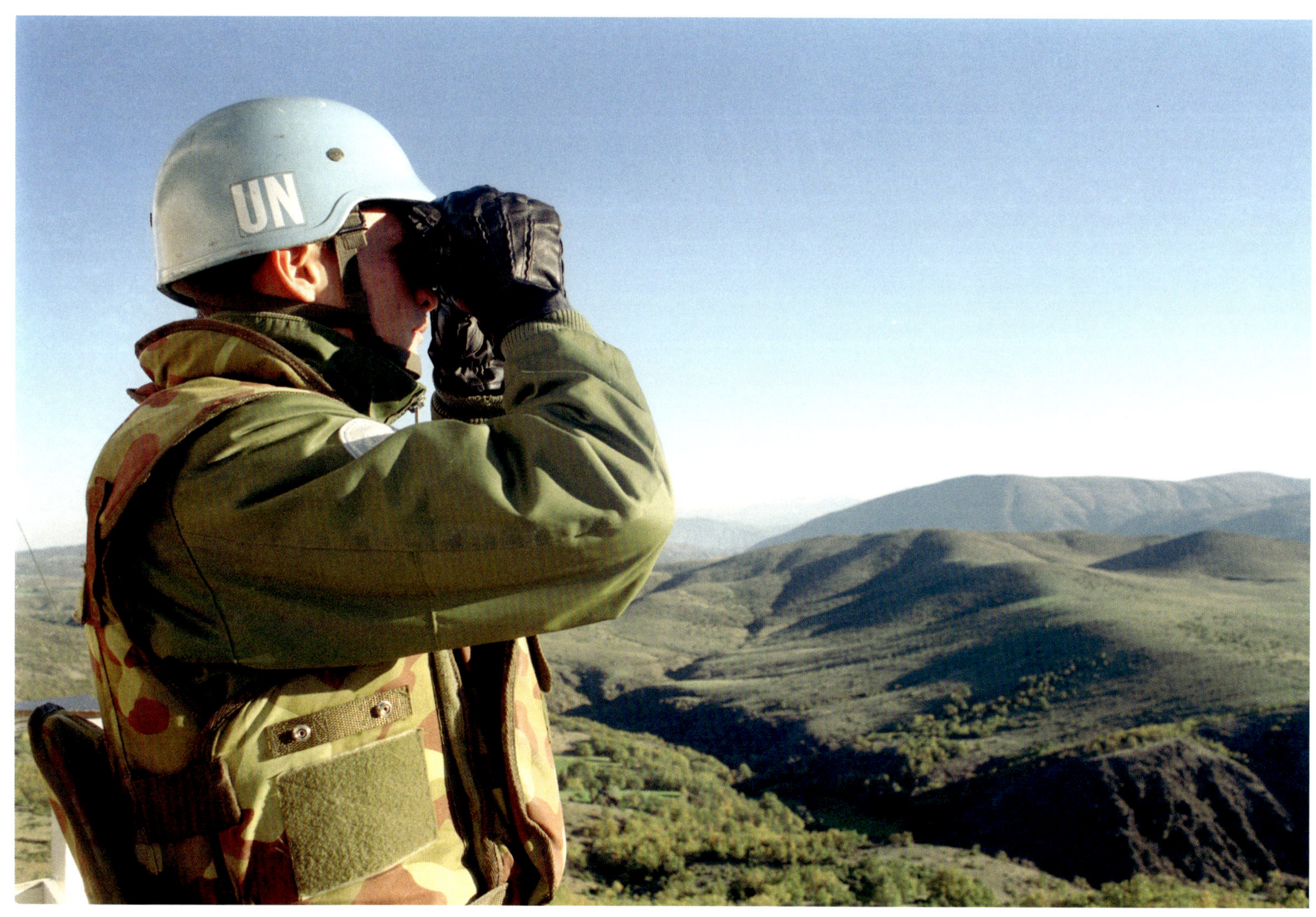

A United Nations Preventative Deployment Force peacekeeper monitors the border of the former Yugoslav Republic of Macedonia, October 1998.
UN Photo/Igor Vasilev.

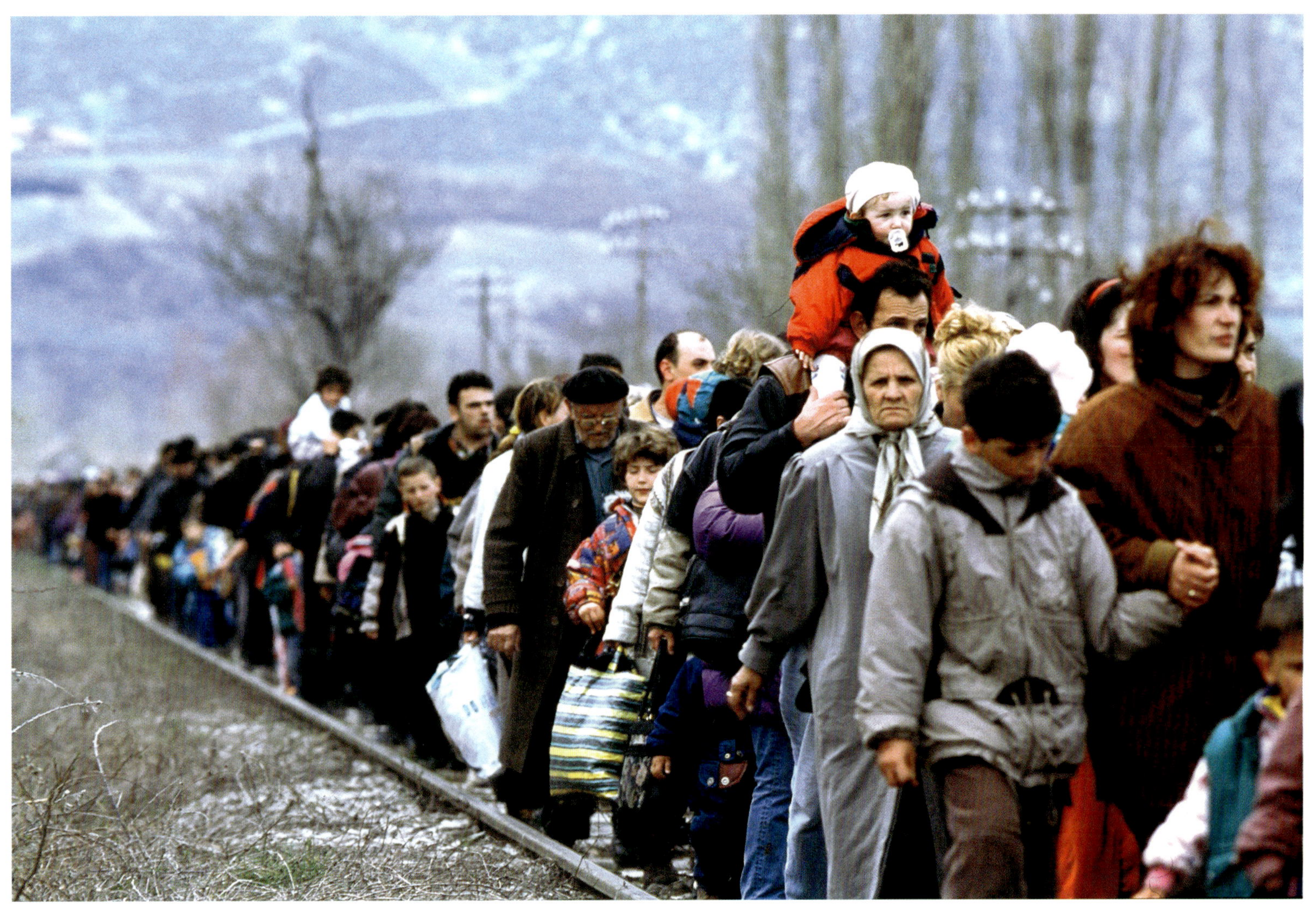

Kosovar refugees flee their homeland, March 1999.
UN Photo/UNHCR/R LeMoyne.

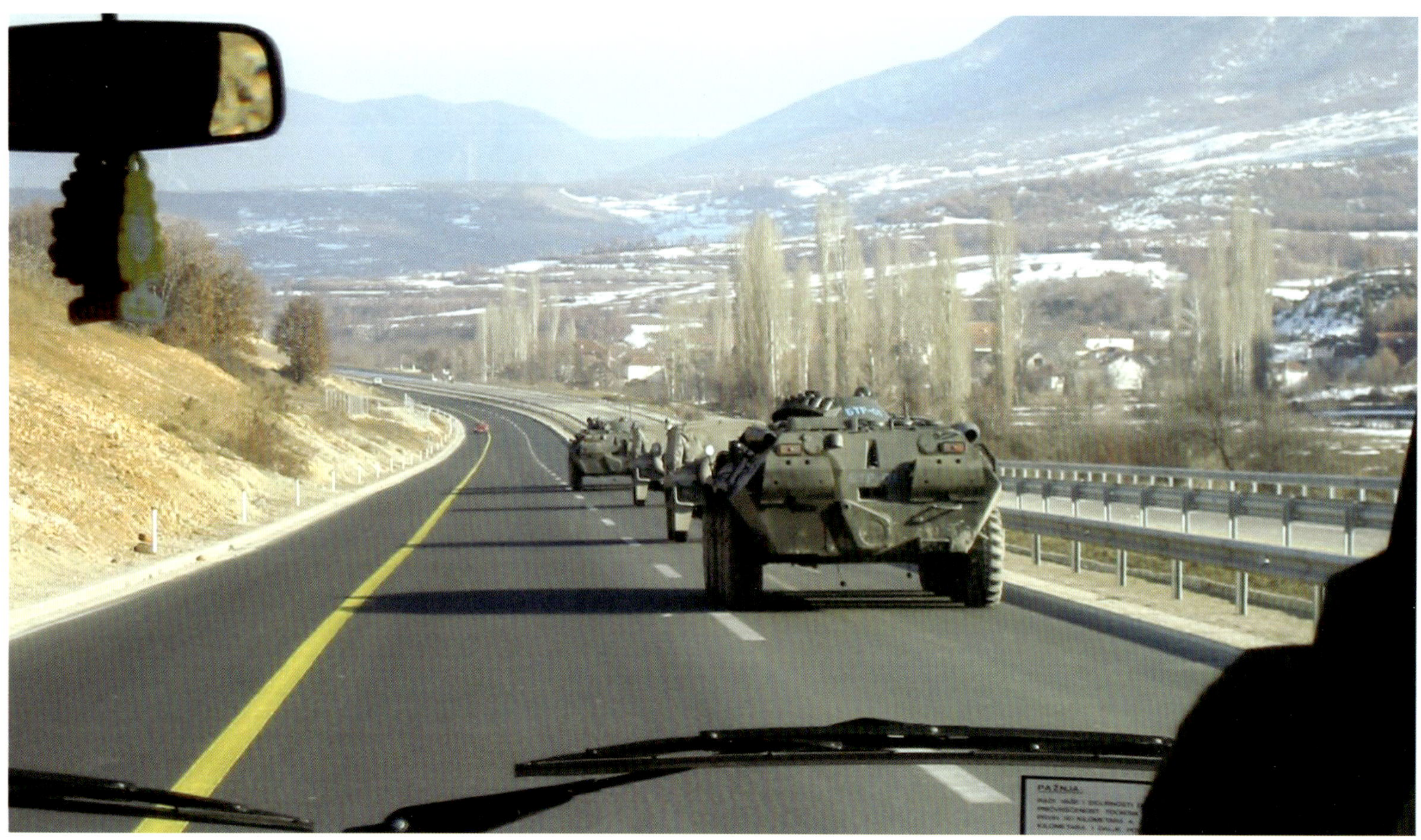

Military tanks on the road in northern Macedonia, 2001/2002.
Photograph courtesy of Robert Downey.

Unlike many of its neighboring countries, Macedonia did not have a civil war after it separated from Yugoslavia. However, it did experience interethnic tensions that escalated into a near yearlong armed conflict between Macedonians and ethnic Albanians.

The Ohrid Agreement, a peace deal signed by the government of Macedonia and ethnic Albanian representatives in

August 2001, opened the way for improving the rights of ethnic Albanians and included promises to support their higher education. Although the population of the country was primarily ethnic Macedonian, there were a number of towns—mostly in the western part of the country—where the majority of the population was Albanian. Out of a total population of almost two million, about one-third were Albanian. In addition to the Albanian population, large numbers of ethnic Albanian refugees from Bosnia, Serbia, and Kosovo sought refuge from civil wars and ethnic cleansing and settled in underdeveloped Albanian towns in Macedonia.

At that time, Macedonia had two public universities, where all courses were taught in Macedonian. Most Albanians had inadequate language skills in Macedonian and lacked the necessary elementary and secondary school background to succeed in these universities. Before 2001, only 56 percent of Albanian-speaking secondary school graduates applied for admission to these universities, while 94 percent of the Macedonian-speaking majority did so. Ultimately, because only a small percentage of ethnic Albanians were admitted, there was increasing Albanian discontent.[1] Marcin *Czapliński*, a senior assistant to the high commissioner on national minorities with the Organization for Security and Co-operation in Europe (OSCE), wrote: "One of the most serious issues affecting inter-ethnic relations was the problem of access of minorities to higher education in their mother tongue and the question of an Albanian language university. The significance of this issue does not lie merely in its symbolism."[2]

The state's response to the Albanian complaints was to introduce a quota system at the existing universities for them,

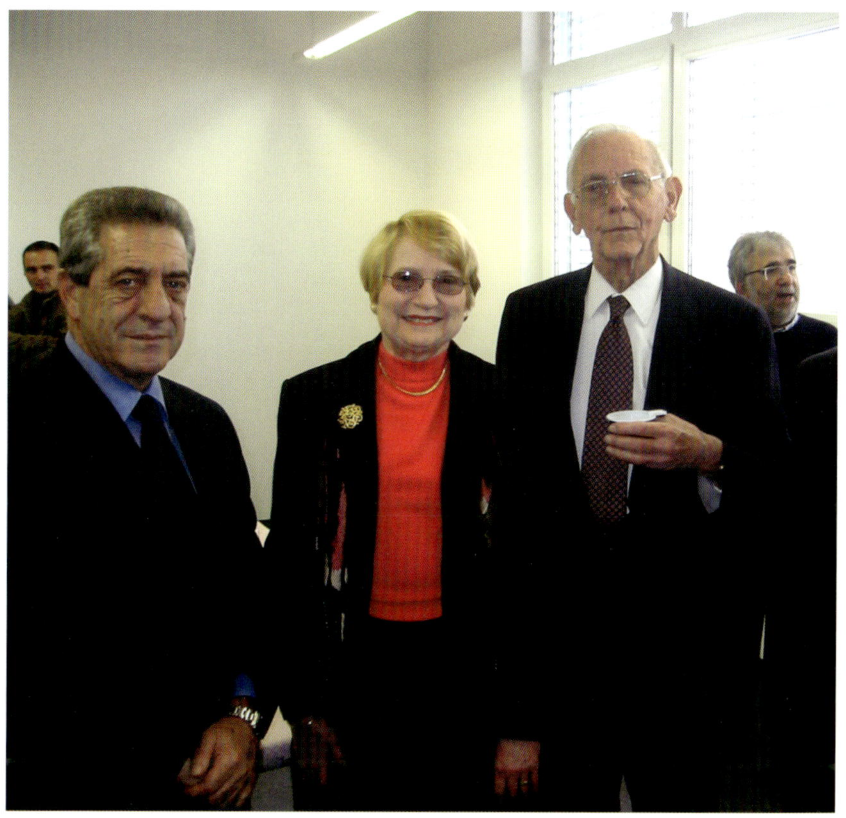

On the South East European University (SEEU) campus, in Tetovo *left to right:* SEEU founding rector Alajdin Abazi, Indiana University dean of faculty Moya Andrews, Organization for Security and Co-operation in Europe high commissioner on national minorities Max van der Stoel, and SEEU faculty member and program evaluator Michel Bourse (*right*). *Photograph courtesy of IU International magazine.*

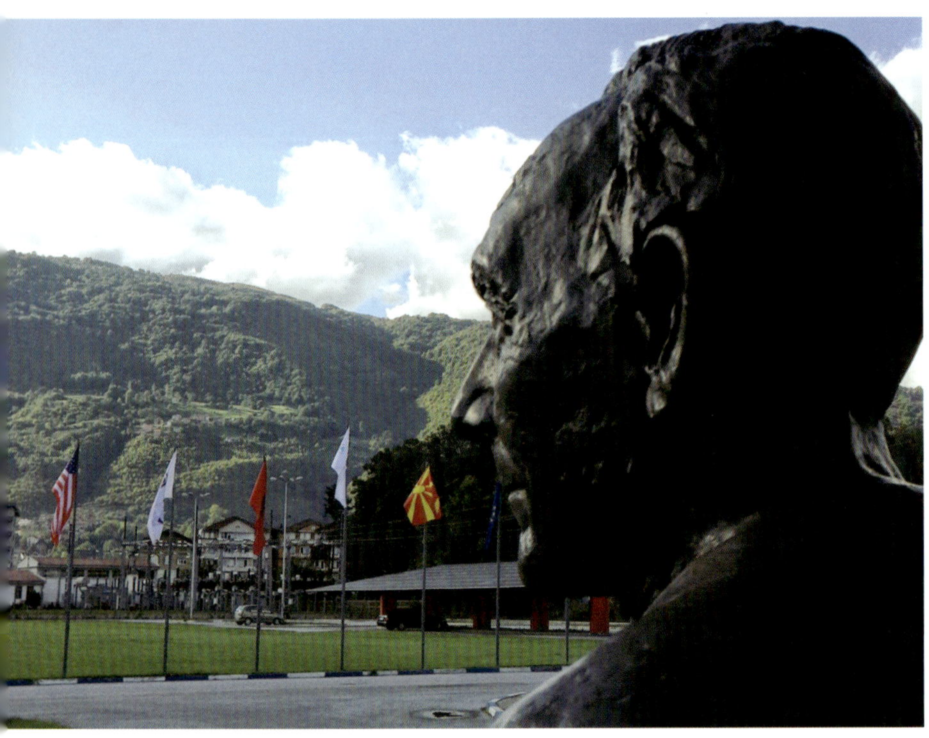

A bust of Organization for Security and Co-operation in Europe high commissioner on national minorities Max van der Stoel on the South East European University campus in Tetovo, September 2014.
Photograph courtesy of Leah Peck.

but the courses were still taught only in Macedonian. Charles Reafsnyder reflects on this period: "I do not exactly know when the conflict started, but the breakup of Yugoslavia was a precursor to SEEU."[3]

The high commissioner on national minorities with the OSCE, Max van der Stoel, who had been foreign minister of the Netherlands on two occasions, put forward a proposal in which Albanians would be allowed to attend private universities that did not receive state support. According to Paul Foster, who would become the provost of SEEU: "Van der Stoel started to work on some of the Macedonian issues in 1994, at the same time some local and international nongovernmental organizations were also working on them. The original idea was to start a new university for pedagogy only, to train a new generation of Albanian teachers . . . and work to develop the country that way. Max had a different idea. He saw it in Tetovo, not Skopje, based on more than just pedagogy, and geared more toward creating a new generation of Albanian elites."[4]

After discussions, the United States and OSCE member countries decided that it would be a good idea to establish a new university. SEEU was planned to be open to all and to offer courses taught according to the standards of the Bologna Process—a series of agreements between European countries designed to ensure comparability in the standards and quality of higher-education qualifications.

The new university was also to have a high-quality infrastructure and flexible use of languages—whether Albanian, Macedonian, or English. SEEU was perceived not only as a great experiment in resolving an old Balkan quarrel but also as a vehicle for introducing new ideas and methods of higher education. It was planned—initially, at least—to operate under Macedonian law as a private university.[5]

Although SEEU was a new institution, the problem it sought to address was a universal one: how to ensure access to quality higher education for underrepresented groups in society. SEEU was established to help redress this in the context of a multiethnic setting. Dennis Farrington, SEEU board president, wrote: "If it works in Macedonia, it can work elsewhere. SEEU is a model for other countries with similar problems."[6]

Once there was agreement that SEEU would be established, the process moved along rapidly. The European Union contributed a matching amount, and the Dutch and French governments gave substantial financial support. The French government provided funding for scholarships and for visiting French university faculty and instructors. A small part of the US commitment was set aside to help establish academic programs, to develop the curriculum, and for collaboration with universities. For the United States Agency for International Development (USAID), the major objectives of the university were to establish quality academic programs based on international standards in pedagogy and curriculum and to increase access to higher education for the Albanian minority.[7]

In many ways, Indiana University's involvement in the process was serendipitous. Reafsnyder had heard about a possible USAID request for proposal (RFP) from a colleague at the University of Louisville who had been a USAID consultant and from an IU alumnus who worked at the agency. In addition, Congressman Frank McCloskey, a representative of Indiana's ninth district, was closely involved with the Dayton Accords and was a prime mover in drafting, negotiating, and implementing them.[8] Reafsnyder reflects on how this put IU in an advantageous position: "It was rare to have a year's advance notice that an RFP was forthcoming."[9]

Indiana University's proposal for the SEEU project was submitted, and there was a quick turnaround. USAID knew that the peace process was moving to a resolution, and it wanted swift action to establish the new university. By the time the grant was awarded to IU, US State Department travel warnings were in effect, and US citizens were not allowed to travel from Skopje to Tetovo because the road between the two cities was not considered safe. Reafsnyder describes the prevailing political context: "The cease-fire line was said to literally run right through the campus in Tetovo—on one side, the ethnic Albanian part and on the other side, the ethnic Macedonian part; the site of the campus was right on the line."[10]

The insurgency in Macedonia was still going on at that point, and there was not yet a cease-fire. Of course, IU would not become directly involved while the conflict was ongoing. However, USAID wanted the project to start the moment the conflict ended. Before IU officially received the USAID contract, David Jones, a staff member at the IU School of Public and Environmental Affairs, agreed to go to Macedonia to review the prevailing conditions and to establish contact with people at SEEU. He met with the newly appointed rector of the university, Alajdin Abazi, and Abazi's administrative team. They all expressed interest in working with IU. Abazi, a former dean at the University of Pristina in Kosovo, was a native of Tetovo and a well-known scholar. Paul Foster remembers Abazi as "the type of person the university needed to attract and compete against this radical Albanian vision

Although SEEU was a new institution, the problem it sought to address was a universal one: how to ensure access to quality higher education for underrepresented groups in society.

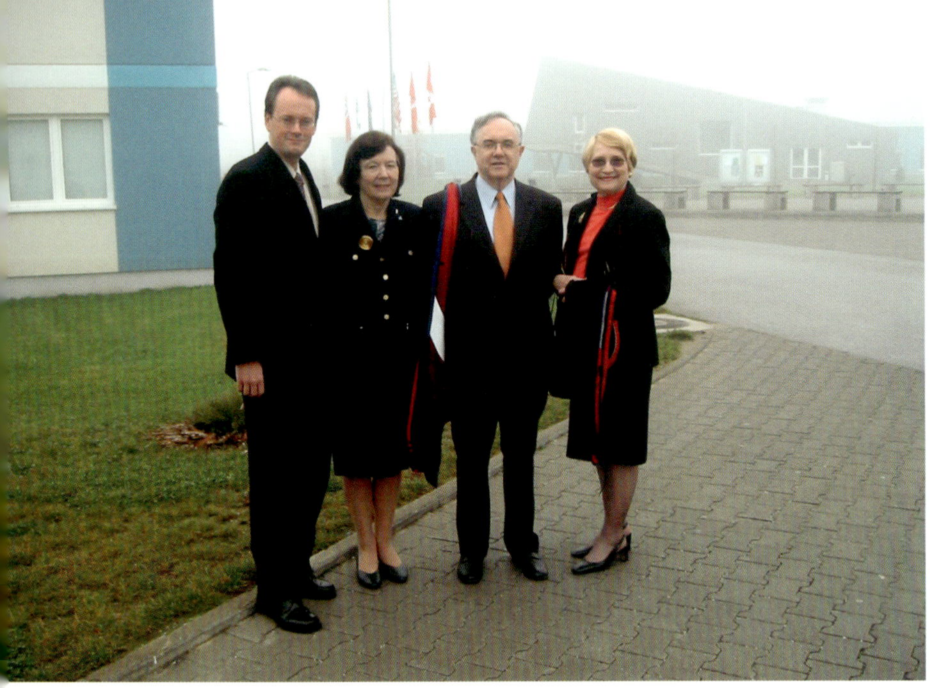

On the SEEU campus in Tetovo, *left to right:* United States Agency for International Development chief of party and later South East European University provost Paul Foster, Indiana University Kokomo chancellor Emita Hill, Indiana University dean for international programs Patrick O'Meara, and Indiana University dean of faculty Moya Andrews. *Photograph courtesy of IU International magazine.*

of separation. People respected him. They believed in him. He was able to recruit students. Having him was absolutely a deciding factor."[11]

On this preliminary visit, Jones had established good connections with the SEEU community in Tetovo, and Reafsnyder then began communicating with Rector Abazi and his team. Reafsnyder vividly remembers the next step—a crucial one: the identification of a chief of party. The person in this role would be central to the success of this project. Reafsnyder remembers:

> Once the RFP came out, we realized we were going to have to identify someone with good credentials to be chief of party. I contacted Henry Cooper, who said, "You should call Paul Foster," who was in Macedonia; Paul's wife had taught Macedonian at the IU Summer Language Institute. I took his advice immediately, which was a good thing, because the next day Paul had a call from Arizona State University, which was also going to apply for funding. They also wanted him as their chief of party, and after some more discussion, he decided that he knew IU better than he did Arizona State and joined our proposal.[12]

Foster recounts the conversation he had when Reafsnyder made the call to ask whether he would join IU's proposal: "I assumed the country was going to go up in flames. There had already been armed conflict, refugees, and atrocities. That's when Charlie [Reafsnyder] called me, saying, 'We're considering this new university project in Tetovo.' I said, 'Tetovo? Tetovo is on fire!' This was right after September 11, so it was a different world. I wasn't too interested in going back, but it was a compelling option. It wasn't too long after that Charlie called me and said I was to be there around October 1.[13]

In September 2001, USAID officially awarded a grant for the United States–Macedonia Linkage Program. IU and the Indiana Consortium for International Programs (ICIP), a group of Indiana-based universities and colleges, received the three-year USAID award to assist in SEEU's development. Foster, by now the chief of party, made a brief visit to SEEU to assess the initial needs of the campus and participate in a major press conference. At this press conference, Ambassador van der Stoel introduced IU and ICIP as major academic partners for SEEU. In June 2001, van der Stoel had already begun working with the European community to plan the construction of the new campus, and he had asked the May Group to prepare "a descriptive and financial business plan, including detailed analysis of academic, legal, institutional and financial arrangements."[14]

Paul Foster recalls: "The project was managed by the May Group in Switzerland, who were business consultants. They were in a bit over their heads, but they were good to work with. They hired a lot of people very quickly. Max van der Stoel brought together a board of directors for the university—prominent European educators, lawyers, and public policy individuals. Max basically set up shop at OSCE."[15]

The May Group facilitated the building of the campus using prefabricated and modular units. SEEU opened with thirty buildings providing forty-two classrooms, two lecture halls, two computing centers, two dormitories, and a library. A state-of-the-art language center, a large lecture hall, three classrooms, and two additional dormitories were added in 2001 and 2002. Referring to the contributions of the May Group and IU, Rector Abazi commented: "I used to say that we had hardware from Austria, but our software was from Indiana University!"[16]

By November 12, 2001, Foster and three full-time instructors were permanently on-site in Tetovo, assisting in the opening of the university. A fourth full-time instructor arrived later that month. All the IU people were provided with apartments in Skopje, because they were not permitted to stay overnight in Tetovo due to continuing security concerns. IU hired a car and driver to take them to campus in Tetovo every day. Even though there was a cease-fire, some radical armed rebel groups did not want to recognize it. It was safe to travel during the day but not at night. Reafsnyder describes the assignments of the newly hired personnel: "Their task was to assemble an ESL staff—local people to work in the center and to begin the training program. There was a faculty member from another university moonlighting at SEEU to develop the English language program. He was a very old-style language professor who believed that the way to learn was only through grammar."[17]

In its early days, SEEU experienced instances of continued civil unrest in Tetovo. From December 2001 through April 2002, on three separate occasions, mortars and armor-piercing shells from an automatic weapon and a grenade damaged SEEU campus buildings and grounds.[18] On two other occasions, protesters seeking to publicize their grievances to the Macedonian government blocked the road between Tetovo and Skopje for about seven hours.

Although these incidents were unsettling, SEEU faculty, staff, and students as well as five United States–Macedonia Linkage Program staff members from IU remained undeterred in their determination to continue the university's work.[19] The university was officially launched on November 20, 2001. Almost all the speakers at the launch event stressed the multilingual and multicultural approach of the SEEU to teaching and studying, emphasizing that a new chapter was open in the education of Macedonia's youth.[20] Patrick O'Meara describes traveling to Macedonia with Michael McRobbie for the ceremony to open the SEEU campus:

Michael McRobbie and I flew on a chartered airplane from Zurich to Skopje. After a nine-hour flight, we were glad to see Charles Reafsnyder waiting for us at the terminal. The next day, we traveled by road to Tetovo. The ceremony was able to take place because a truce had been declared for the day.

—Patrick O'Meara

"Michael McRobbie and I flew on a chartered airplane from Zurich to Skopje. After a nine-hour flight, we were glad to see Charles Reafsnyder waiting for us at the terminal. The next day, we traveled by road to Tetovo. The ceremony was able to take place because a truce had been declared for the day. While we enjoyed toasting the new university with champagne with dignitaries, Albanian and Macedonian forces could be seen in the distance on either side of the campus."[21]

In addition to Reafsnyder, the Center for International Education and Development Assistance staff included Associate Director Shawn Reynolds, Kay Ikranagara, and Pance Surkov—all of whom played significant roles in the administration of the project. Patrick O'Meara and Judy Rice, assistant dean for finance and administration, participated in the management of the project. On a day-to-day basis, counterparts in Tetovo were SEEU rector Alajdin Abazi, Dennis Farrington, and Secretary-General Xhevair Memedi. Michel Bourse, dean of the SEEU communications department, was also a major contributor to the development of SEEU's academic programs.[22]

Four ICIP institutions made significant contributions to SEEU: Indiana University–Purdue University Indianapolis, Ball State University, Butler University, and Indiana University Southeast. The IUPUI faculties of computer science and of communication contributed to their counterpart programs at SEEU. The chairs of these departments—Mathew Palakal and John Parrish-Sprowl, respectively—were deeply involved in the project and encouraged members of their faculties to participate. Gabrielle Goodwin and Robert Downey, now faculty members at Indiana University Bloomington School of Law, were involved in the early planning and implementation of SEEU. Before students were admitted, Goodwin and her colleagues set up the English language program, trained faculty, and prepared for the students' arrival.[23]

Downey established the computer literacy curriculum so that when the students arrived, they could be immediately introduced to using computers. There are photographs of the computer rooms soon after the project started, showing an empty room except for one person sitting at a terminal with fifty unused terminals around him.[24] Several months later, the room was packed with students using the computers. Rector Abazi reflected on this period: "There were a number of professors who came for teaching, helping, from Indiana University, and that was the best time of the university. Everything was new. We started distance education . . . plus the Career Center, the Business Center . . . we had an antenna here for a computer network for a satellite . . . it was very important to build a good IT network."[25]

The initial USAID three-year grant was extended for two additional years to permit degree students supported by the project to complete their studies in the United States. In 2005, IU received a $1.8 million grant from USAID/Macedonia to continue working with SEEU through the Higher Education Linkage Program. The partnership developed between

Indiana University and USAID/Macedonia was central to the awarding of the new grant, which allowed IU to continue developing active teaching approaches, student-centered instruction, and problem-solving assignments and case studies that involved faculty and students in collaborative learning.[26]

Several graduate students and potential SEEU administrators from Macedonia traveled to Indiana for short-term training or to pursue graduate degrees. SEEU implemented many modern practices, and instruction was in Albanian, Macedonian, and English, which fostered a multicultural, multilingual environment.[27] For Rector Abazi, overseas training was an important component: "It was a modern way to start a university, and I started to send young people abroad for other education, and that was possible with this Indiana University, this capacity building. A good part of them went to Indiana University in different fields, and although they went to other universities, most went to IU."[28]

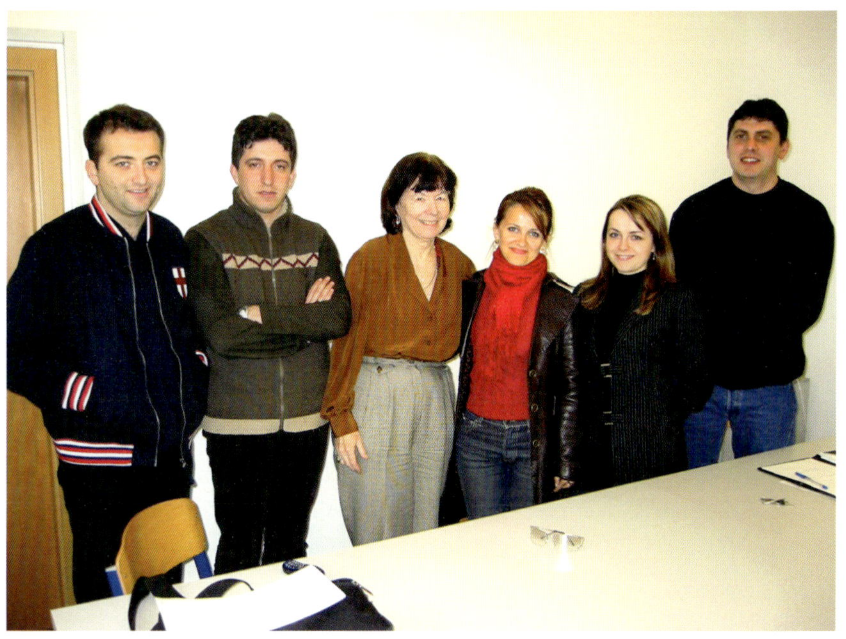

Indiana University Kokomo chancellor and then South East European University (SEEU) board member Emita Hill (*center*), flanked by SEEU staff and IU graduates Memet Memehti (*left*) and Linda Ziberi (*right*). *Photograph courtesy of Robert Downey.*

SEEU soon began to meet many of the criteria set out at its founding, including helping Macedonian democracy and its future development needs and preparing its graduates for employment. The impact of SEEU went well beyond the university itself. The growth in enrollment at SEEU produced an increase in the numbers of ethnic Albanians in higher education in Macedonia. The student enrollment grew from 910 in the 2001–2002 school year to over 5,300 in the 2006–2007 academic year. Of these, about 80 percent were ethnic Albanian, and the remaining students were primarily ethnic Macedonian.

SEEU provided a secure place for young ethnic Albanian and ethnic Macedonians to interact, learn about one another, form friendships, and forge partnerships to foster better communication between the two groups. Finally, approaches to education that were new to Macedonia were introduced. *Czapliński reflects on the importance of the endeavor:* "The founding of the South East European University was, first of all, aimed at preventing conflict and further escalation of inter-ethnic tensions as well as increasing the number of Albanians pursuing higher education. However, it also had

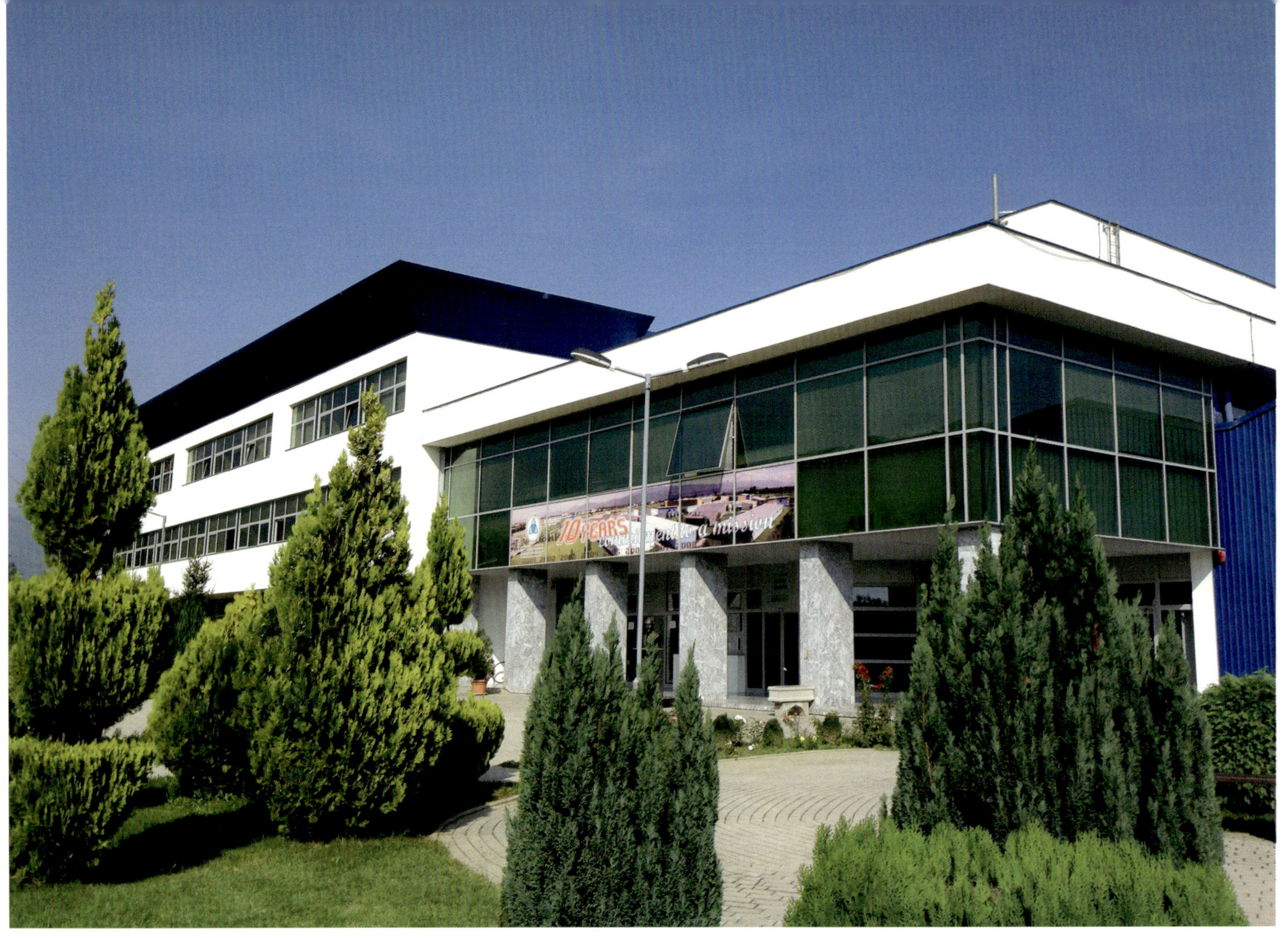

The rectory on the South East European University campus in Tetovo, September 2014. *Photograph courtesy of Leah Peck.*

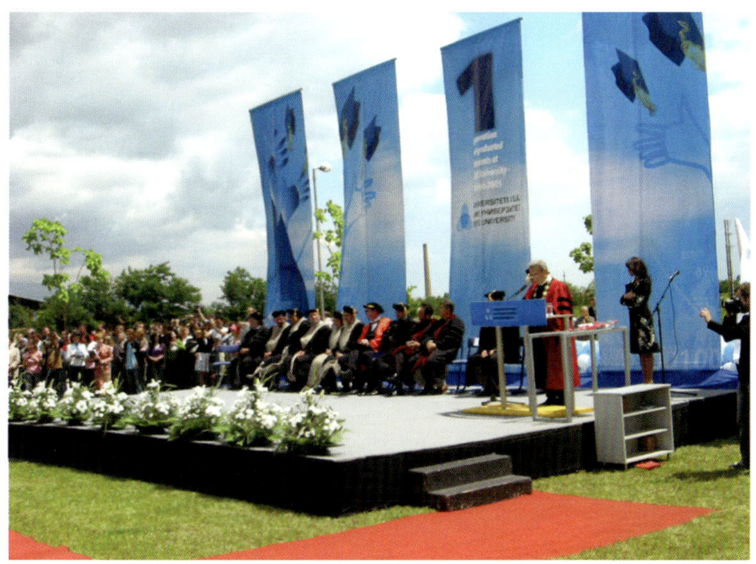

South East European University rector Alajdin Abazi speaks at SEEU's first commencement ceremony in spring 2004. *Photograph courtesy of South East European University.*

other goals, including the educational dimension—preparing young educated people being ready for the challenges of the future. It could be argued that SEEU had a significant impact on the whole educational environment in the country, initiating healthy competition and contributing to ongoing quality improvements at the existing state universities."[29]

Indiana University played an active and creative role in the early years of SEEU. At the same time, IU faculty members who participated in the project benefited personally and professionally from their time in Macedonia. Over the five years of the grant period, several IU faculty members from different campuses went to SEEU, where they were involved in training programs, taught courses, or conducted research. IU School of Education professor Terrence (Terry) Mason, for example, was very interested in the issue of conflict. While in Macedonia, he taught a multicultural course in which he emphasized the value and integrity of various cultural backgrounds. Those attending the course developed an interactive and collaborative pedagogy for students in schools in different parts of the country.

Indiana University played an active and creative role in the early years of SEEU. At the same time, IU faculty members who participated in the project benefited personally and professionally from their time in Macedonia.

Mason's course was one of the ways he promoted a method for reconciliation and the development of social cohesion within the schools. He maintained that the students could be focal points for these activities—a concept that was totally foreign to Macedonian education at the time: "People did not recognize that schools were places where kids could come together from different backgrounds, have interaction around these things, and that they could then have an effect on society."[30] Mason received a grant for the IU School of Education for a two-way undergraduate exchange program between education students at IU and SEEU.

When asked about their time at SEEU, Robert Downey and Gabrielle Goodwin summed up their experience in a positive way. Downey notes that "it had a tremendous impact on us as individuals, and I think the fact that we are both at IU now . . . we had a very positive experience through the process. We

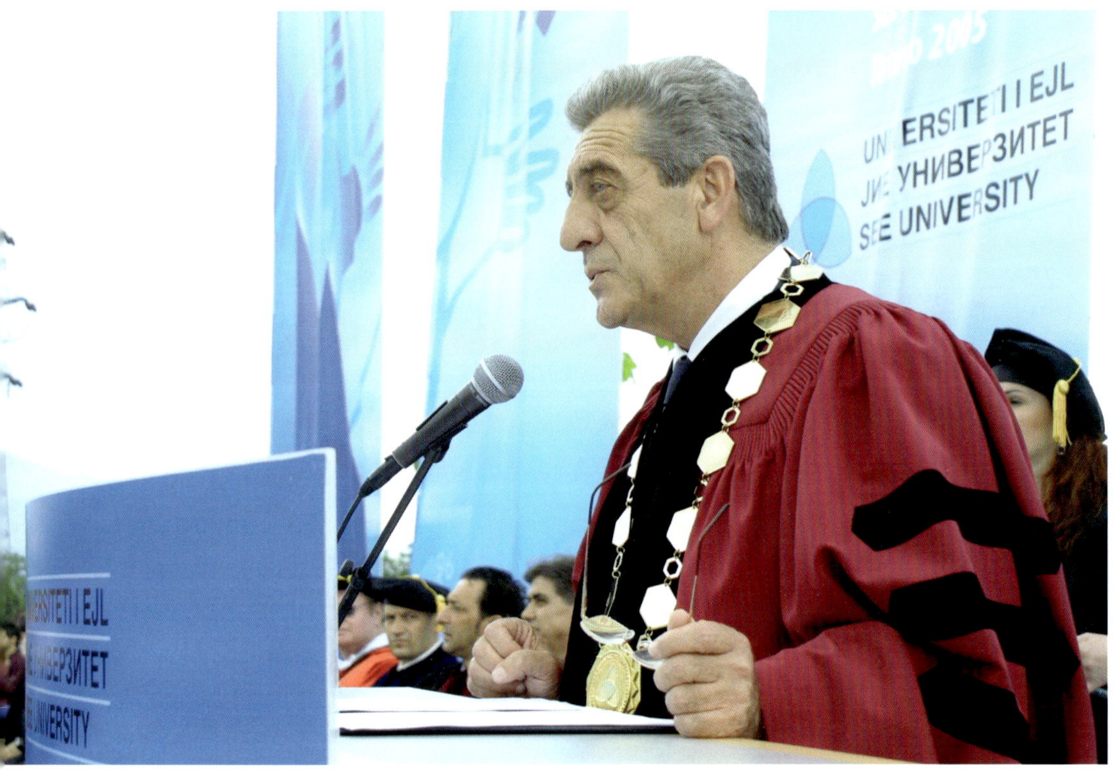

South East European University rector Alajdin Abazi speaks at SEEU's first commencement ceremony in spring 2004. *Photograph courtesy of South East European University.*

came out with a very positive view of IU and wanting to be associated with the institution long term."[31]

IUPUI School of Law faculty member Edward Queen taught a course at SEEU, and Jerry Wheat from Indiana University Southwest taught business courses. Mathew Palakal, from IUPUI's computer science department, played a formative role in implementing distance education courses for computer center instructors. John Parrish-Sprowl from communications at IUPUI also went to Macedonia on several different occasions. After performing an important role in the early stages of the IU relationship with SEEU, David Jones, who by this time had moved to international development at IUPUI, continued to be involved in the project, developing curriculum for undergraduate public administration courses. Robert Goehlert, subject and area specialist librarian at IU Libraries, recommended how the library at SEEU should be set up and how acquisitions should be done, and he helped select the head librarian.[32]

SEEU's tangible accomplishments helped heal some of the wounds of Macedonia's civil conflict in 2000 and 2001 by bringing ethnic Albanians and Macedonians together within the safety of a higher-education learning environment. SEEU attracted quality students because it was ranked as one of the best institutions in the country. It also subsequently established a branch campus in Skopje, with a graduate MIS program run by faculty who had studied at IU.[33]

Once SEEU was well established and growing, IU had achieved its major purpose with the USAID grant project. SEEU had moved to self-sustained growth by 2006. At that point, IU and SEEU proceeded to a different level of collegial and mutual cooperation and friendship. The achievement of SEEU is summed up by Czapliński: "The outcome of internal and external evaluations and prestige of the Institution inside and outside the region, it could be concluded that the SEE University is a success story."[34] IU continued its relationship with SEEU through the IU Foundation, which invested and assisted with its endowment.

IU president Michael McRobbie traveled to Macedonia in November 2011 to celebrate SEEU's ten-year anniversary. While there, he signed a renewed agreement of friendship and cooperation and received an honorary doctorate. In a speech he gave during the honorary degree ceremony, McRobbie remarked, "It has been our privilege at Indiana University to be one of SEEU's major partners in institutional development, and it has been a partnership of great and enduring benefit for both of our universities. Both of our institutions bring great strengths to this endeavor—the flexibility and energy of youth and the strength and experience rooted in traditions. Both of our institutions have gained from this exchange."[35]

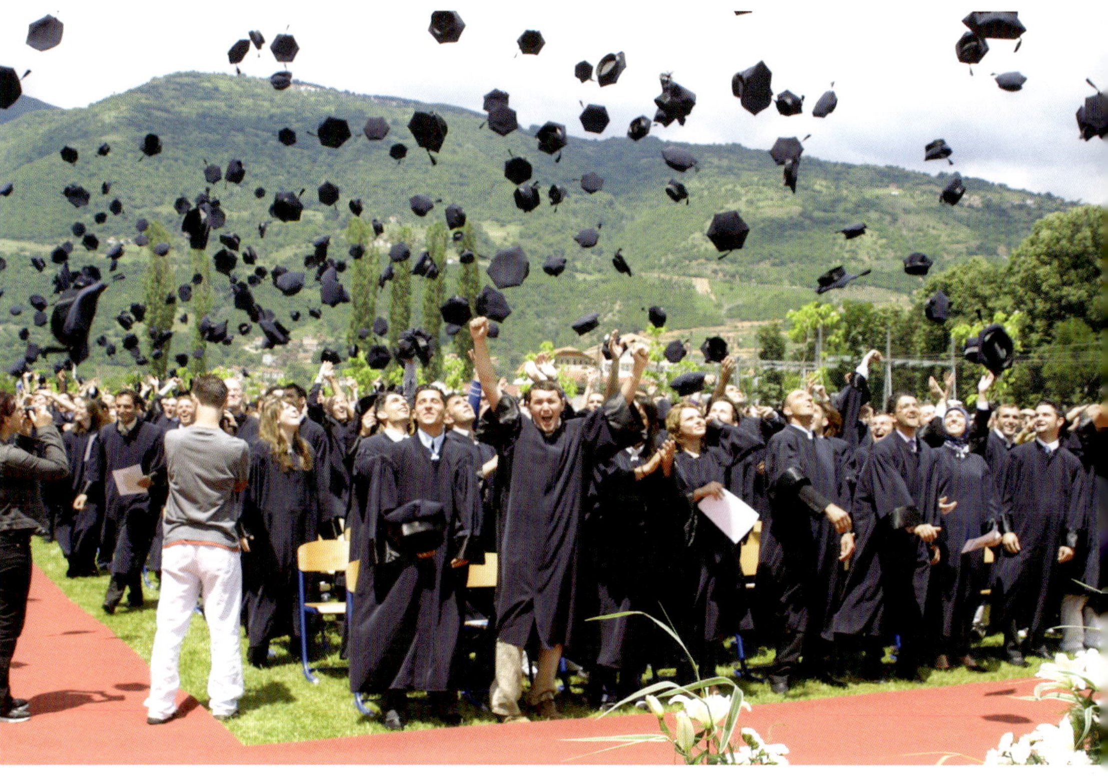

Members of the first graduating class of South East European University celebrate at the commencement ceremony, spring 2004. *Photograph courtesy of South East European University.*

14 | INDIANA UNIVERSITY *in* Namibia

THE NATION OF NAMIBIA, ONCE KNOWN AS SOUTH WEST AFRICA, came into being in 1990. Until the end of World War I, it had been a German colony. As part of the peace settlement in 1919, South Africa was given a mandate to govern the territory but not full control over it. In 1973, the United Nations recognized the liberation movement South West Africa People's Organization as the representative of the people of the country. After a protracted guerrilla war against South Africa, the new nation of Namibia received international recognition. The country, rich in gold, diamonds, and base minerals, had one of the smallest populations of all the countries on the African continent.

In the fall of 2002, only twelve years after independence was achieved, the IU Center for International Education and Development Assistance (CIEDA) received a partnership grant from the US State Department's Bureau of Educational and Cultural Affairs to advise and assist the University of Namibia (UNAM) as it established a regional campus in Oshakati, in the underdeveloped north of the country. UNAM was particularly interested in IU's experiences in administering such a structure. Indiana University East (IUE) in Richmond was chosen to partner with UNAM's Northern Campus (NC) in Oshakati because of the range of its experiences as a regional campus. Charles Reafsnyder and Patrick O'Meara, dean of the Office of International Programs,

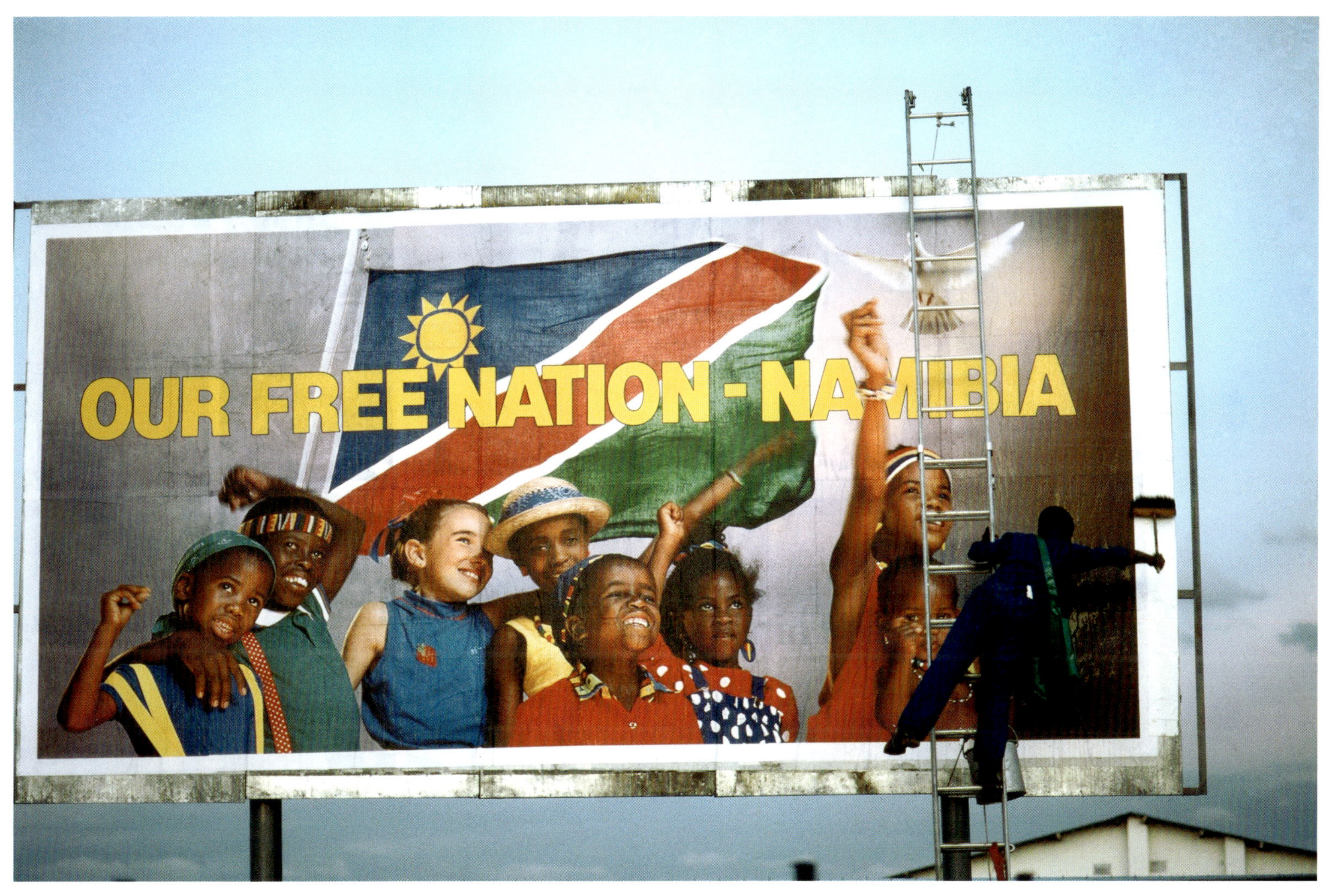

A worker puts up a billboard near Windhoek, Namibia, March 1990. *UN Photo/John Isaac.*

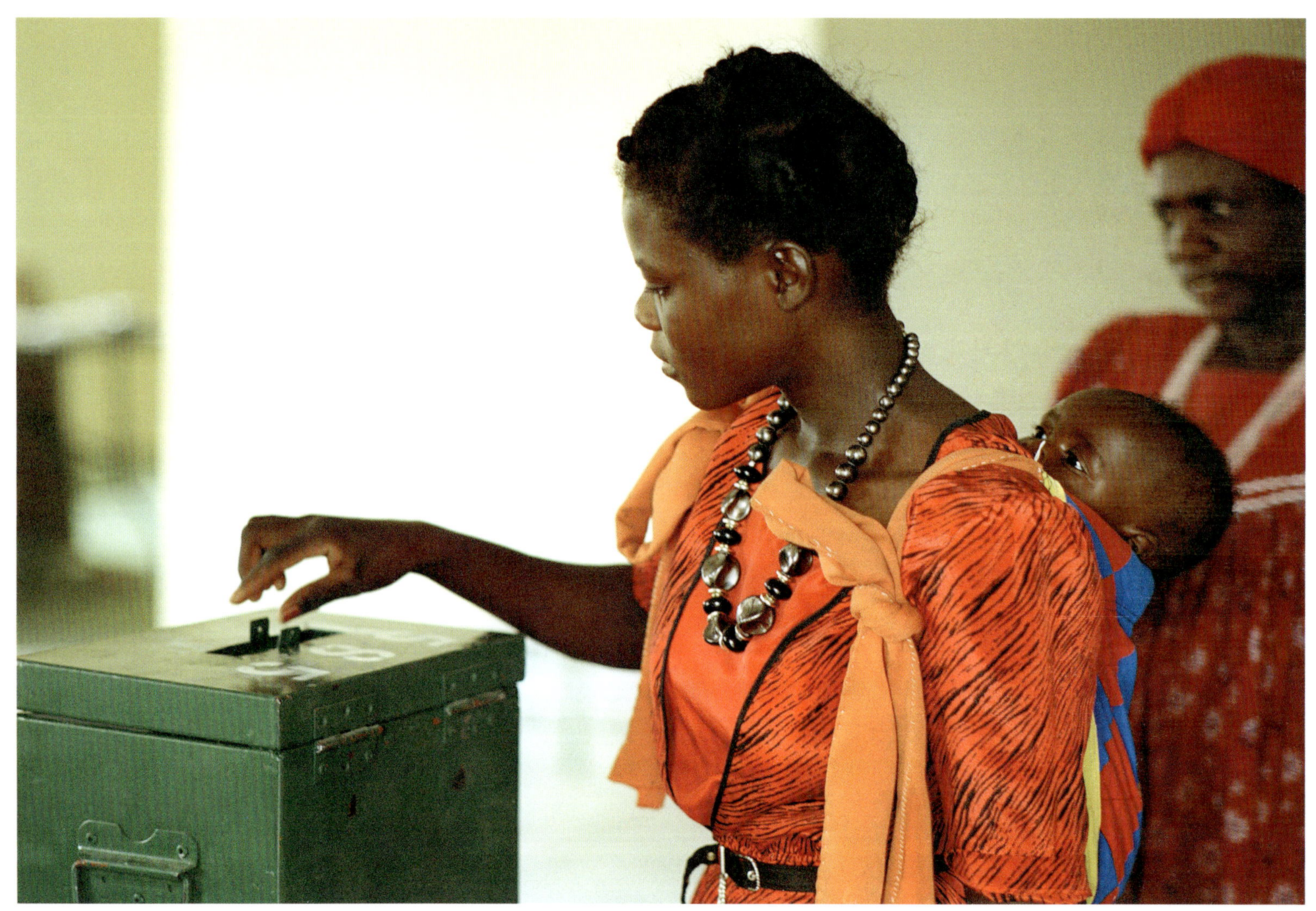

A voter casts her ballot at the polling station, Odangwa, Namibia, November 1989.
UN Photo/Milton Grant.

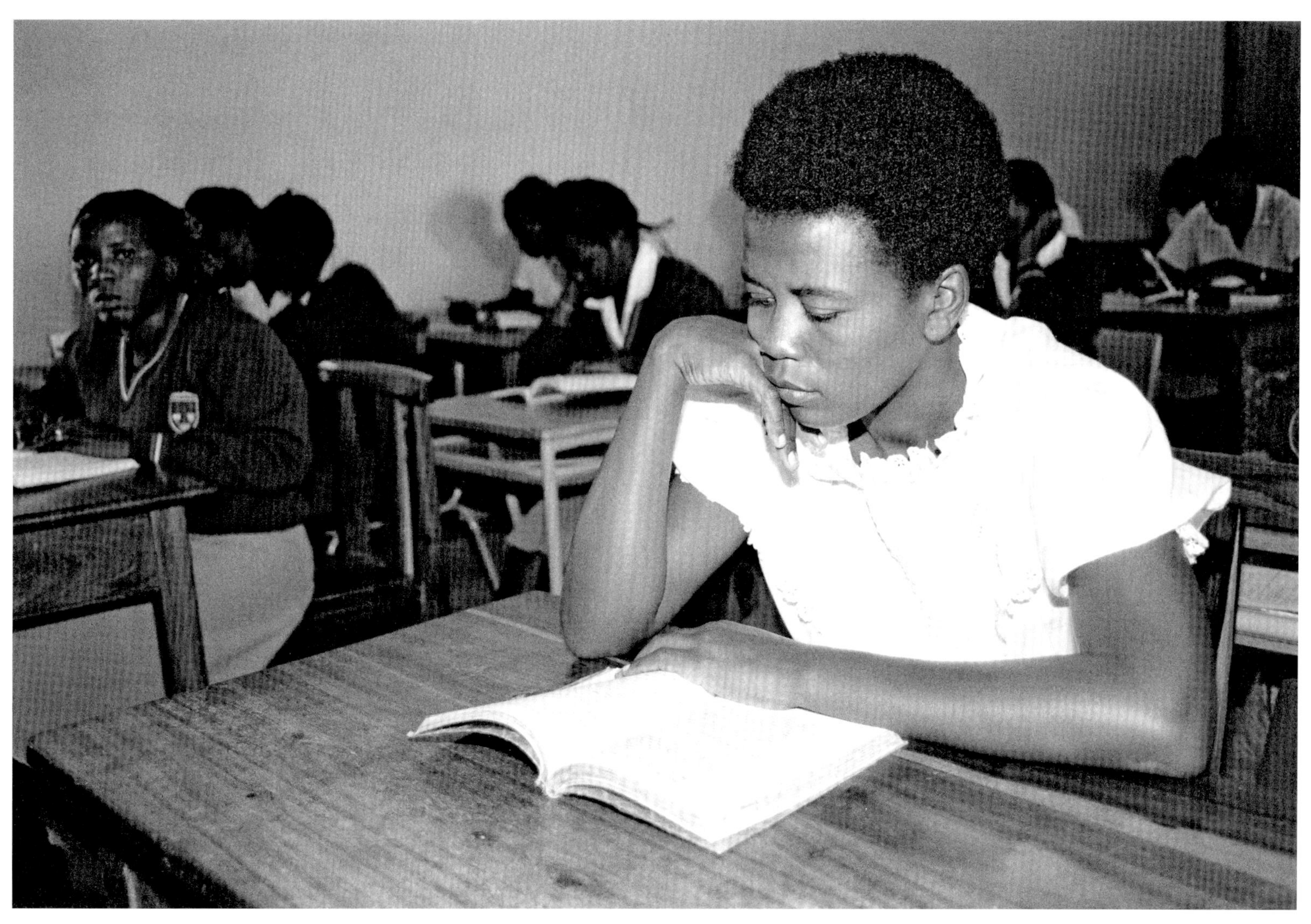

A student attends a class in Oshakati, Namibia, March 1990.
UN Photo/John Isaac.

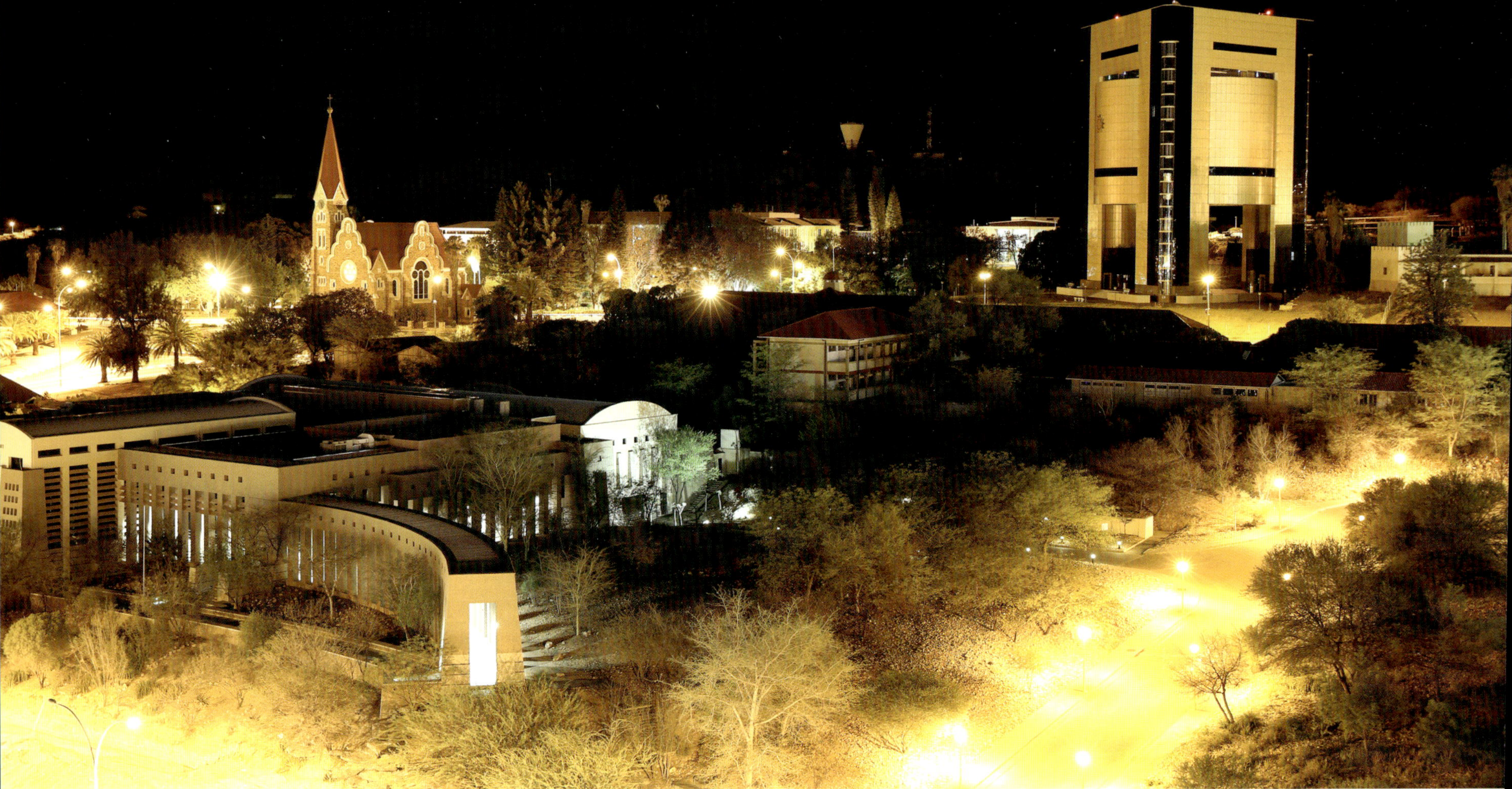

Independence Memorial Museum, Supreme Court, and Christuskirche, Windhoek, Namibia, November 2013.
Photograph courtesy of iStock.

decided that it would be valuable to directly involve an IU regional campus as part of the grant. The mandate of the Oshakati campus was to increase access to higher education in that part of the country and to include the local community in economic development. At the time, courses were delivered from Namibia's capital, Windhoek, by interactive video. The Northern Campus was supported by the Ford Foundation as well as from nonprofit development organizations. The IU partnership assisted with training for managerial and administrative personnel, especially in advancing an understanding of how financial, material, and technological resources could be managed. There were twenty short-term administrator and faculty visits between the Northern Campus and Indiana University East over the two-year period; in addition, administrators and faculty also spent time at the IU Bloomington campus and at the main campuses of the University of Namibia in Windhoek. In the fall of 2002, the first Northern Campus administrator, Paulina Ungwanga, visited the IUE campus to discuss issues in regional campus administration. IUE chancellor David Fulton commented on Ungwanga's visit: "In essence, we wanted to show Paulina how IU East works since we share a mission very similar to the Northern Campus in Namibia."[1]

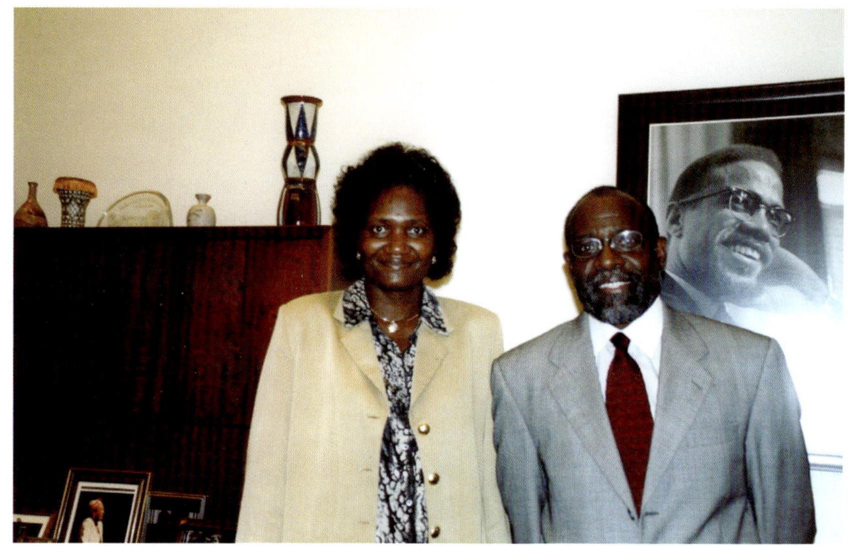

Itah Kandjii Murangi (*left*), director of the University of Namibia's International Relations and Programs Office, visits Charlie Nelms (*right*), Indiana University vice president for student development and diversity, September 2003. *Photograph courtesy of IU International magazine/ Roxana Newman.*

Ungwanga's visit to IUE was followed by a visit from Lazarus Hangula, vice chancellor of the University of Namibia. Hangula traveled to both Richmond and Bloomington. Chancellor Fulton and Suzi Shapiro, director of IUE's Teaching and Learning Center, subsequently went to Namibia, where they held discussions on university administration, technology, and distance education teaching at the Windhoek and Oshakati campuses. Namibians Carin Slabbert, registrar for the Center for Distance Education, and Alois Feldersbacher, assistant registrar, came to Indiana to discuss registration issues that arise between main and regional campuses, with special regard to distance education. Other consultants from IU included Jeremy Dunning of the School of Continuing Studies, Dwight Burlingame of the Center on Philanthropy, and Karen Hallett of the School of Education's Office of Instructional Consulting.

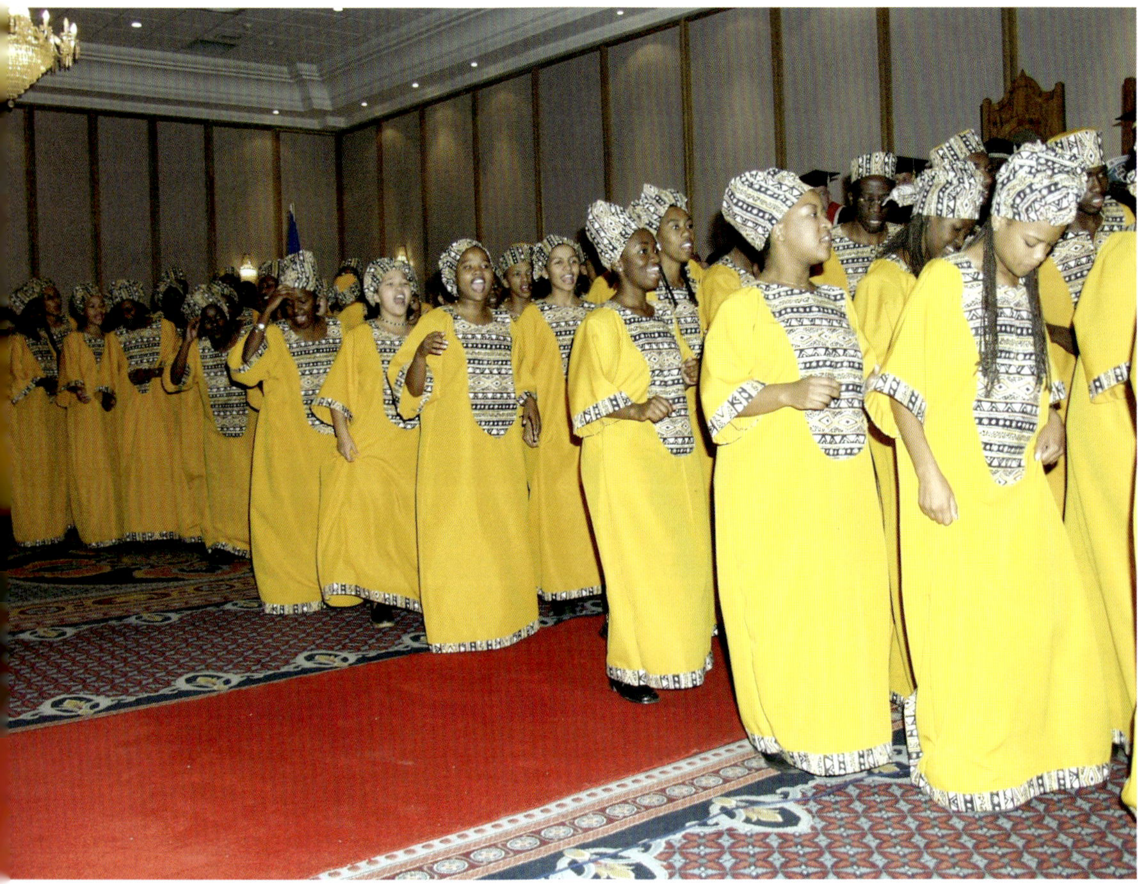

The University of Namibia choir performs a musical drama at the Neal-Marshall Black Culture Center, September 2004.
Photograph courtesy of IU International magazine/Roxana Newman.

An additional component of the relationship was a shipment to the new library of the Northern Campus in Oshakati of four hundred books on nursing, engineering, and children's literature sent by IUE's Teaching and Learning Center.

In May 2003, UNAM hosted an important southern Africa regional conference titled "Universities and Communities Engaged in Development." The conference was attended by Charlie Nelms, IU vice president for student development and diversity; Patrick O'Meara, dean for International Programs; and Shawn Reynolds, CIEDA associate director.

Reviewing the relationship, Itah Kandjii Murangi, director of the University of Namibia's International Relations and Programs, noted that, while UNAM had benefited from past linkages with both US and European universities, these had been more academically focused; she welcomed "the cross-fertilization that is occurring in the IU East–NC partnership concerning both academic and administrative components."[2] Chancellor David Fulton noted that: "The benefit of the partnership for IUE has been a unique opportunity to internationalize its administrators by giving them hands-on experience in a developing country . . . a wonderful opportunity for IU East to address issues of diversity and internationalism from a unique perspective."[3]

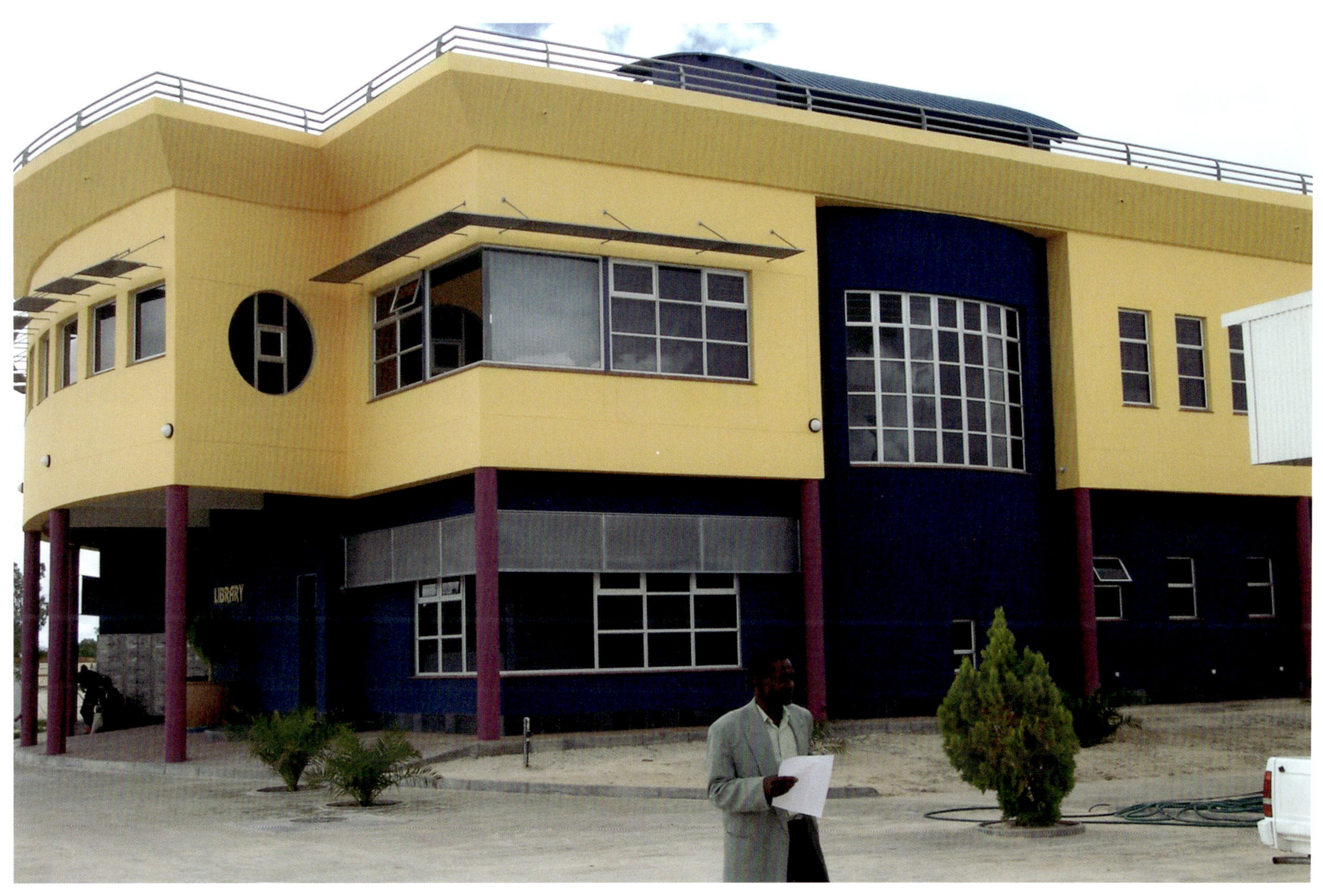

The new library at the Northern Campus, Oshakati, Namibia, 2004.
Photograph courtesy of IU International magazine/Roxana Newman.

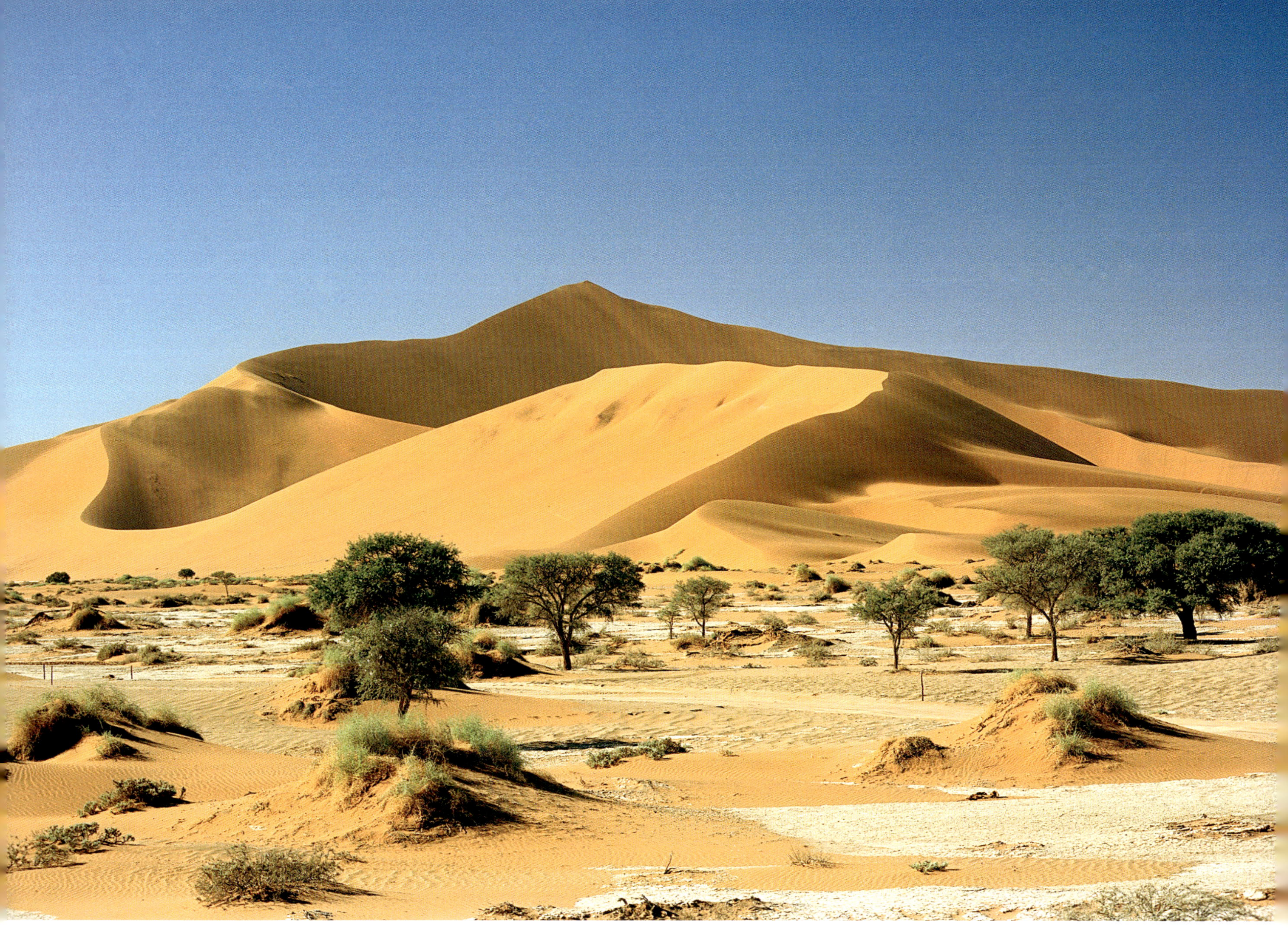

An added dimension to the engagement with Namibia was a 2003 visit by the University of Namibia Choir. The choir performed, conducted workshops and interviews, and met musicians and students on the IU Bloomington and IU East campuses. The UNAM Choir's visit to IU Bloomington included a public performance at the Grand Hall of the Neal-Marshall Black Culture Center, where they also met informally with Wells Scholars Honors College undergraduates. They held joint classes with the International Vocal Ensemble taught by Mary Goetze of the School of Music and the African American Choral Ensemble directed by James Mumford of the African American Arts Institute. Mumford was interested to see the differences in how Africans performed African American gospel songs. The choir spent its last full day in Indiana at IU East and offered an evening concert at the Mt. Olive Baptist Church in Richmond. Tim Williams, director of the Office of Multicultural Affairs, which sponsored the event, said, "This is just an example of the international reach of Indiana University, and it is an honor for IU East to assist in hosting our talented visitors from Namibia."[4]

Facing, Sand dunes near Sousevlei, Namibia, March 1990. *UN Photo/John Isaac.*

The IU Center for International Education and Development Assistance received a partnership grant from the US State Department's Bureau of Educational and Cultural Affairs to advise and assist the University of Namibia as it established a regional campus in Oshakati, in the underdeveloped north of the country.

15 | INDIANA UNIVERSITY *in* Liberia

Indiana University has had a long relationship with the West African country of Liberia, dating back to 1930, when anthropology professor George Herzog did fieldwork there.

Facing, Students check their exam scores on the University of Liberia campus in Monrovia, 2008. *Photograph courtesy of IU International magazine/Verlon Stone.*

INDIANA UNIVERSITY HAS HAD A LONG RELATIONSHIP WITH THE West African country of Liberia, dating back to 1930, when anthropology professor George Herzog did fieldwork there. In the 1960s, political science professor J. Gus Liebenow (who founded the African Studies Program at Indiana University in the early 1960s) pioneered political studies in Liberia. On his retirement in 1990, Liebenow received the first Lifetime Achievement Award of the Liberian Studies Association, a group of scholars from around the world. Liebenow's books *Liberia: The Evolution of Privilege* (1969) and *Liberia: The Quest for Democracy* (1987) are classics in the field. IU faculty and research scholars—including Ruth Stone, folklore; Verlon Stone, Liberian Collections; and Claude Clegg, history—worked in Liberia at various times and published many books and articles. David and Susan Williams, of the Maurer School of Law, had both been actively engaged in legal reform initiatives in Liberia beginning in 2005. Amos Sawyer, the former president of the Liberia Interim Government of National Unity, was for many years a research scholar and associate director at Indiana University's Workshop in Political Theory and Policy Analysis. Sawyer was also chair of the Liberian Government Reform Commission and split time between that assignment and his responsibilities at IU.

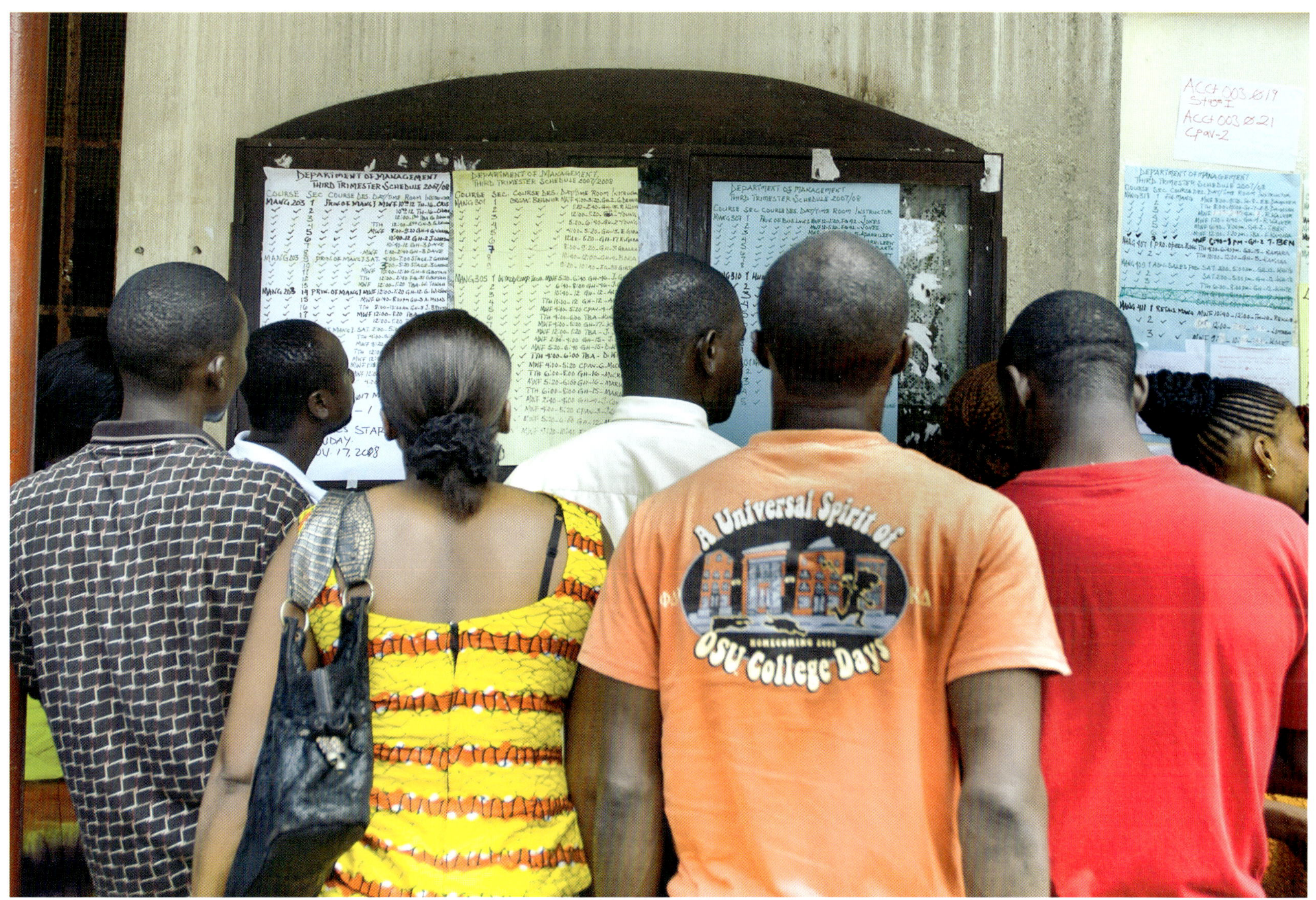
DEPARTMENT OF MANAGEMENT
THIRD TRIMESTER SCHEDULE 2007/08
DEPARTMENT OF MANAGEMENT
THIRD TRIMESTER SCHEDULE 2007/08
DEPARTMENT OF MANAGEMENT
THIRD TRIMESTER SCHEDULE 2007/08
A Universal Spirit of
OSU College Days

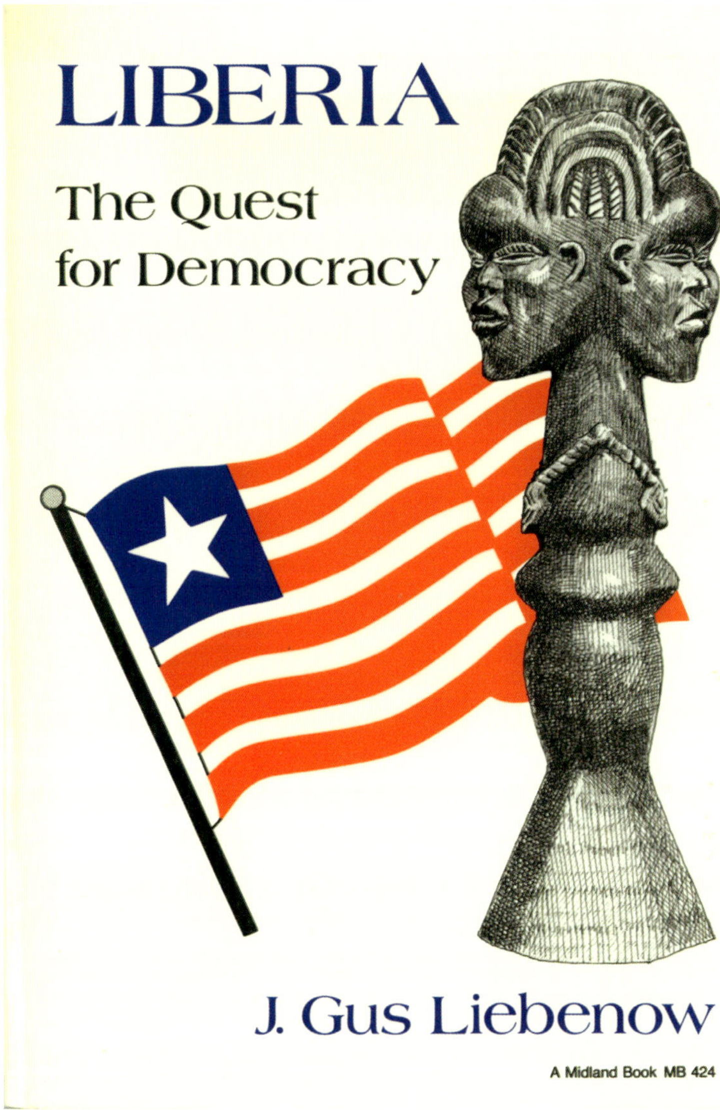

J. Gus Liebenow's *Liberia: The Quest for Democracy*, published in 1987. *Photograph courtesy of Indiana University Press.*

Al-Hassan Conteh, then president of the University of Liberia, and Sedia Massaquoi-Bangoura, the senior program coordinator of the University of Liberia, visited IU Bloomington in April 2005 to make the case for Indiana University to assist in the rebuilding the University of Liberia. This resulted in the signing of an Agreement of Friendship and Cooperation between the presidents of the two universities.[1]

In May 2008, Indiana University awarded an honorary doctorate to President Ellen Johnson Sirleaf in recognition of her contributions to African democracy and development. In October of that year, she was awarded the Nobel Peace Prize. Sirleaf's visit, and her presentations at several public events, galvanized interest in assisting Liberia's development among a broad array of faculty, staff, and trustees of Indiana University. Accompanying Sirleaf on the visit was Emmet Dennis of Rutgers University, who was chair of the University of Liberia's board of trustees. In meetings involving Sirleaf, IU president Michael McRobbie and other senior faculty and administrators pledged to expand its program of assistance to the University of Liberia.[2]

When Indiana University expressed interest in working with the university, the country was emerging from nearly two decades of civil conflict from 1989 to 2003 that killed an estimated 270,000 and displaced hundreds of thousands more of its citizens. During the long period of civil conflict, Liberian standards of health and well-being had declined dramatically. Liberia's infant and under-five mortality rates were among the highest in the world.[3]

In November 2008, Indiana University provided funding for a needs assessment visit to the University of Liberia by

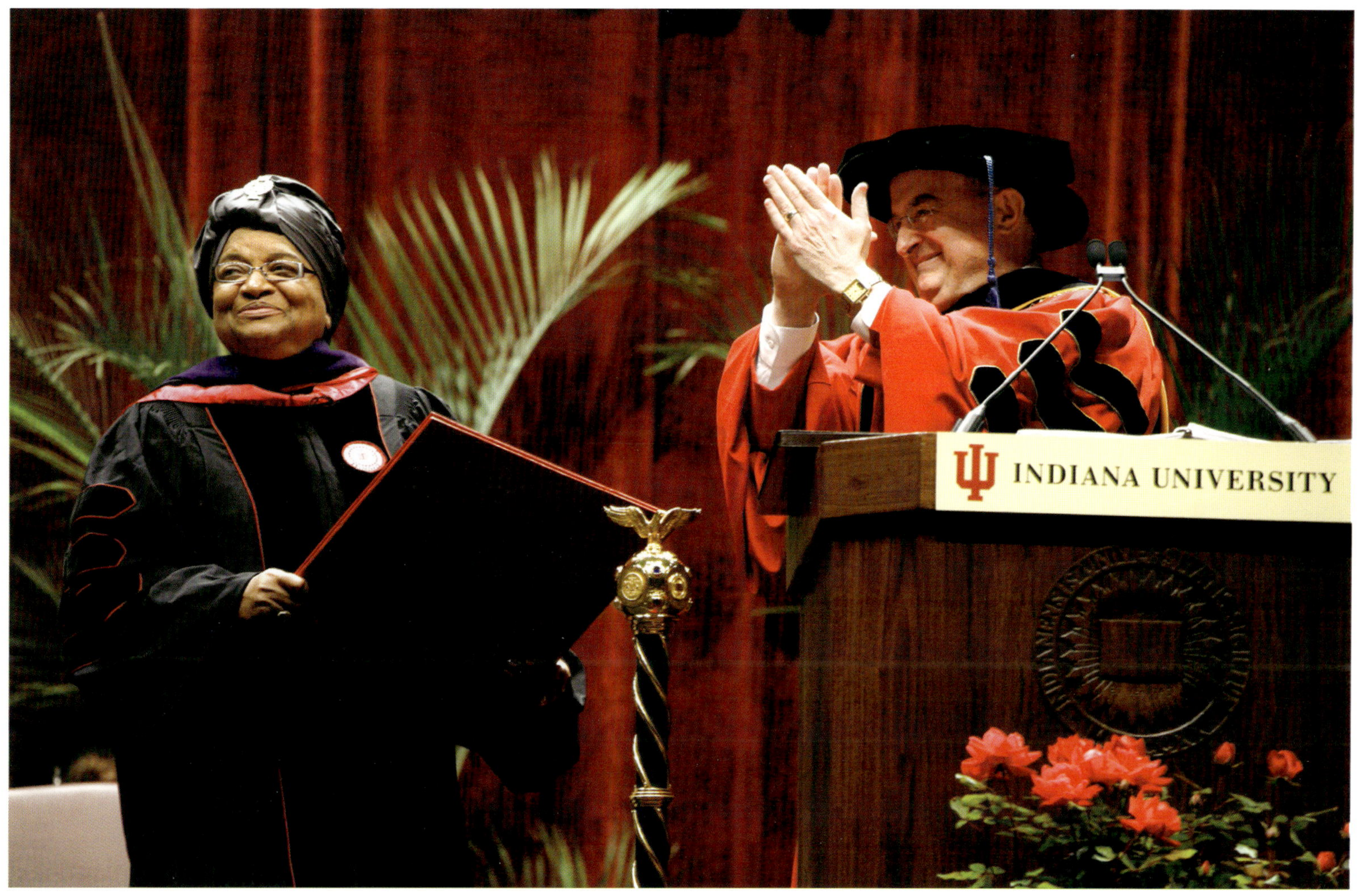

Indiana University president Michael McRobbie leads applause for Liberian president Ellen Johnson Sirleaf at the May 2008 commencement. Sirleaf was the first woman elected president of Liberia—and, in fact, the first woman president of any country in Africa. She received an honorary degree in recognition of her efforts to promote peace, justice, and democracy. The honor also reflects the close relationship between Liberia and IU. *Photograph courtesy of Indiana University.*

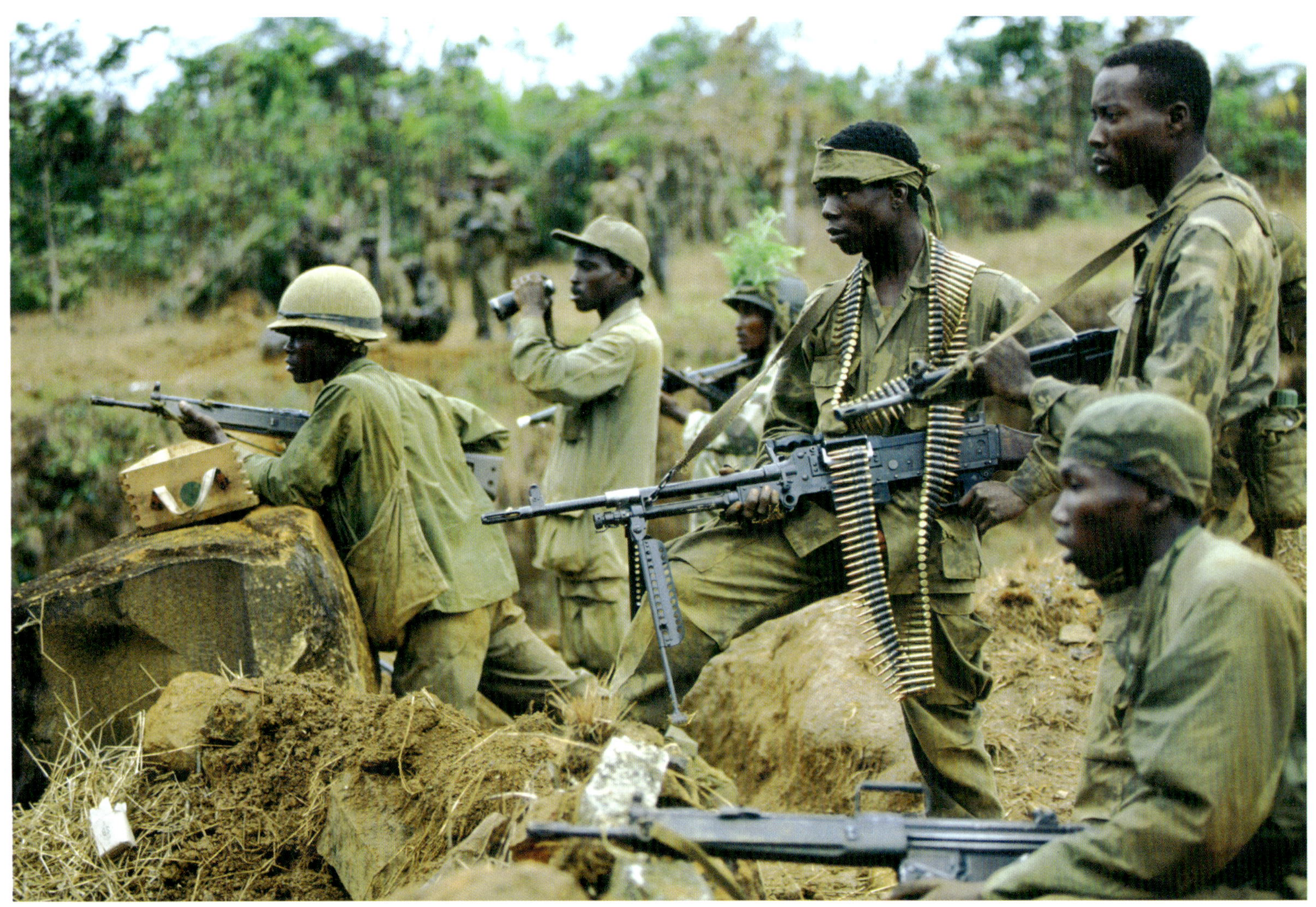

The Armed Forces of Liberia, the national army under the Samuel Doe regime, during the Liberian Civil War, Schieffelin, Liberia, November 1992. *Photograph by Patrick Robert/Sygma via Getty Images.*

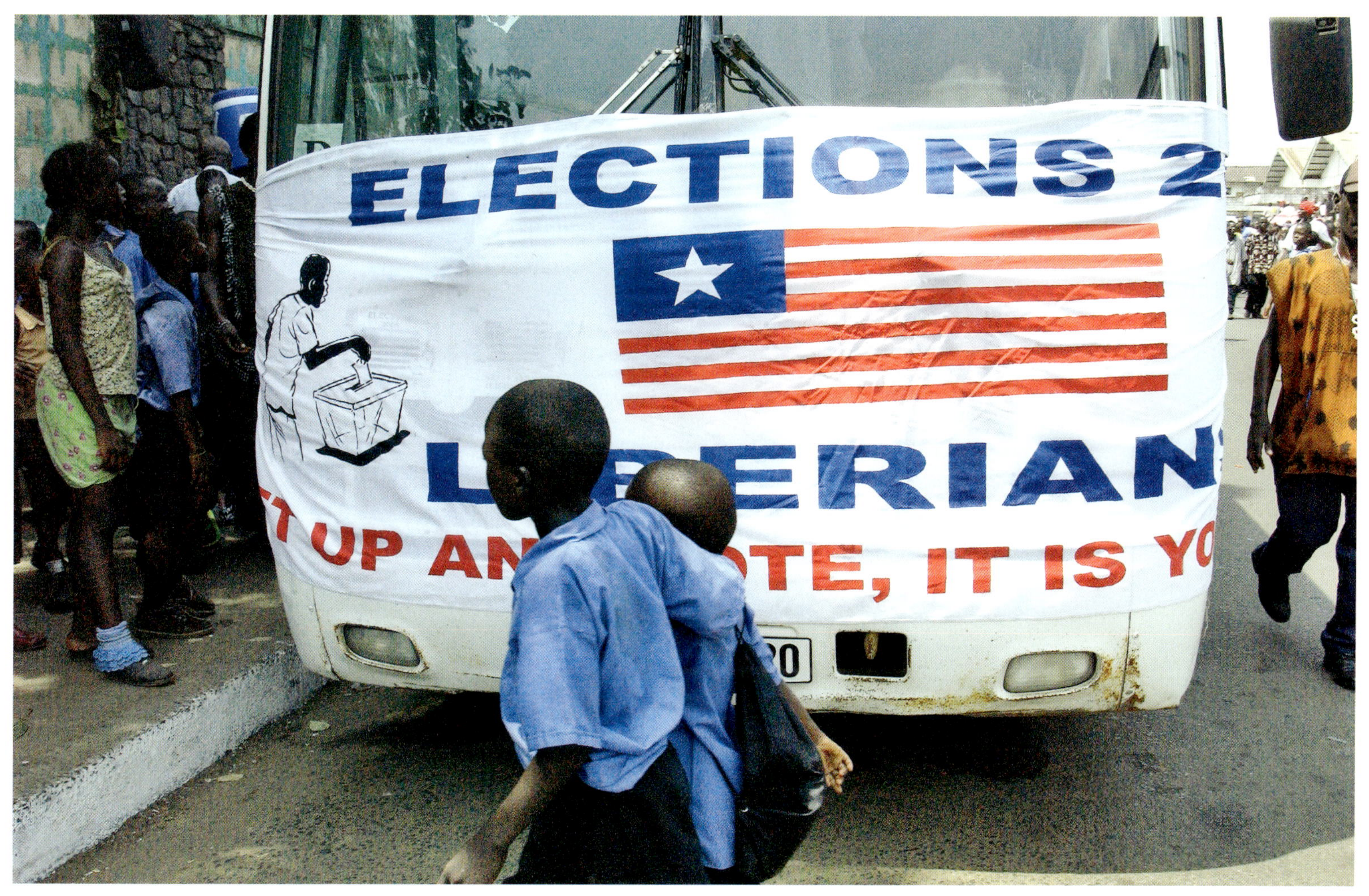

A United Nations Mission in Liberia Public Affairs Community Outreach sensitization campaign designed to create public awareness of the October 2005 elections in Monrovia, Liberia, February 2005. *UN Photo/Eric Kanalstein.*

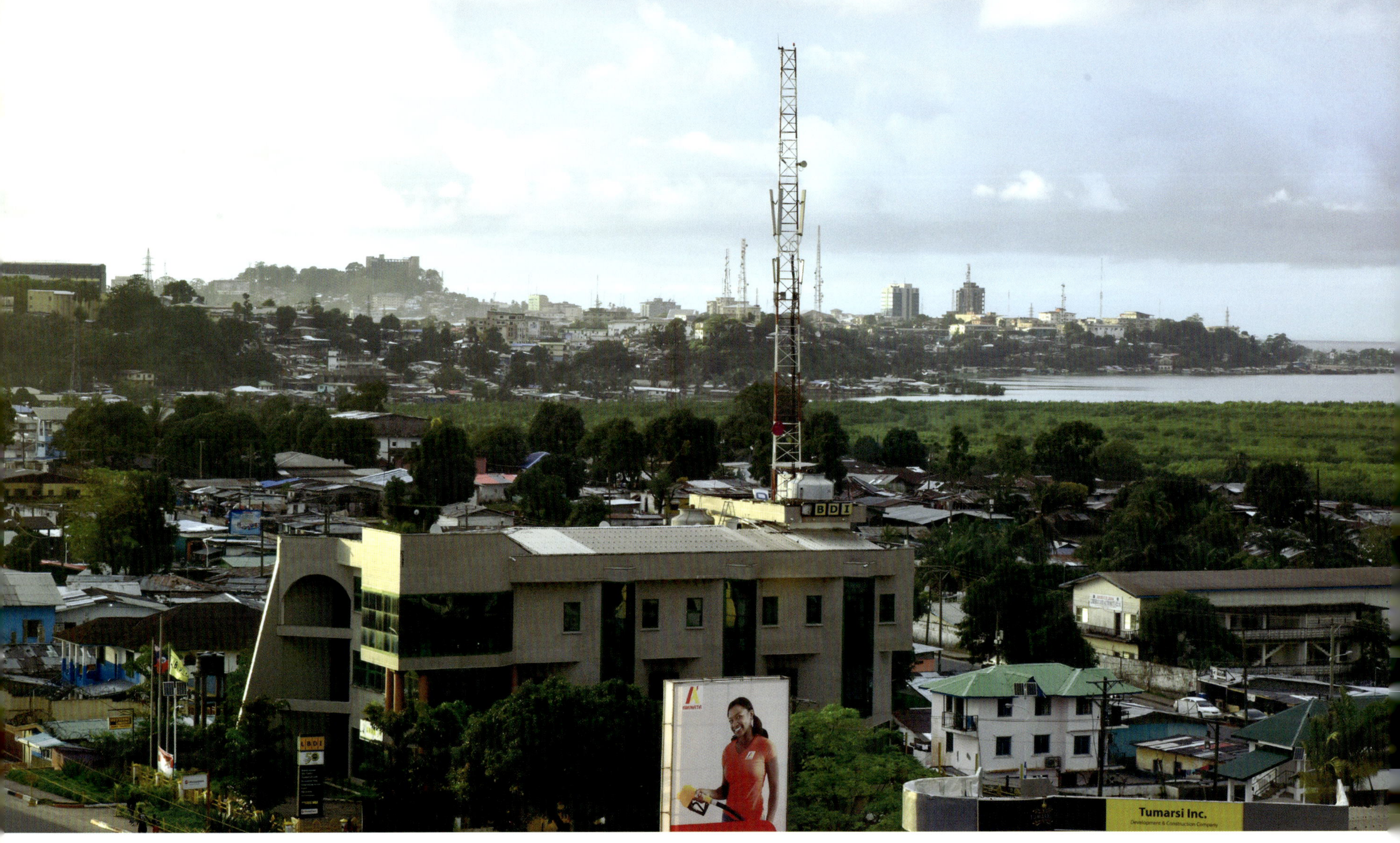

Monrovia, Liberia, October 2017.
Photograph courtesy of ISSOUF SANOGO/AFP/Getty Images.ç

Facing, Aerial view of Monrovia from a helicopter of the United Nations Mission in Liberia, December 2008.
UN Photo/Christopher Herwig.

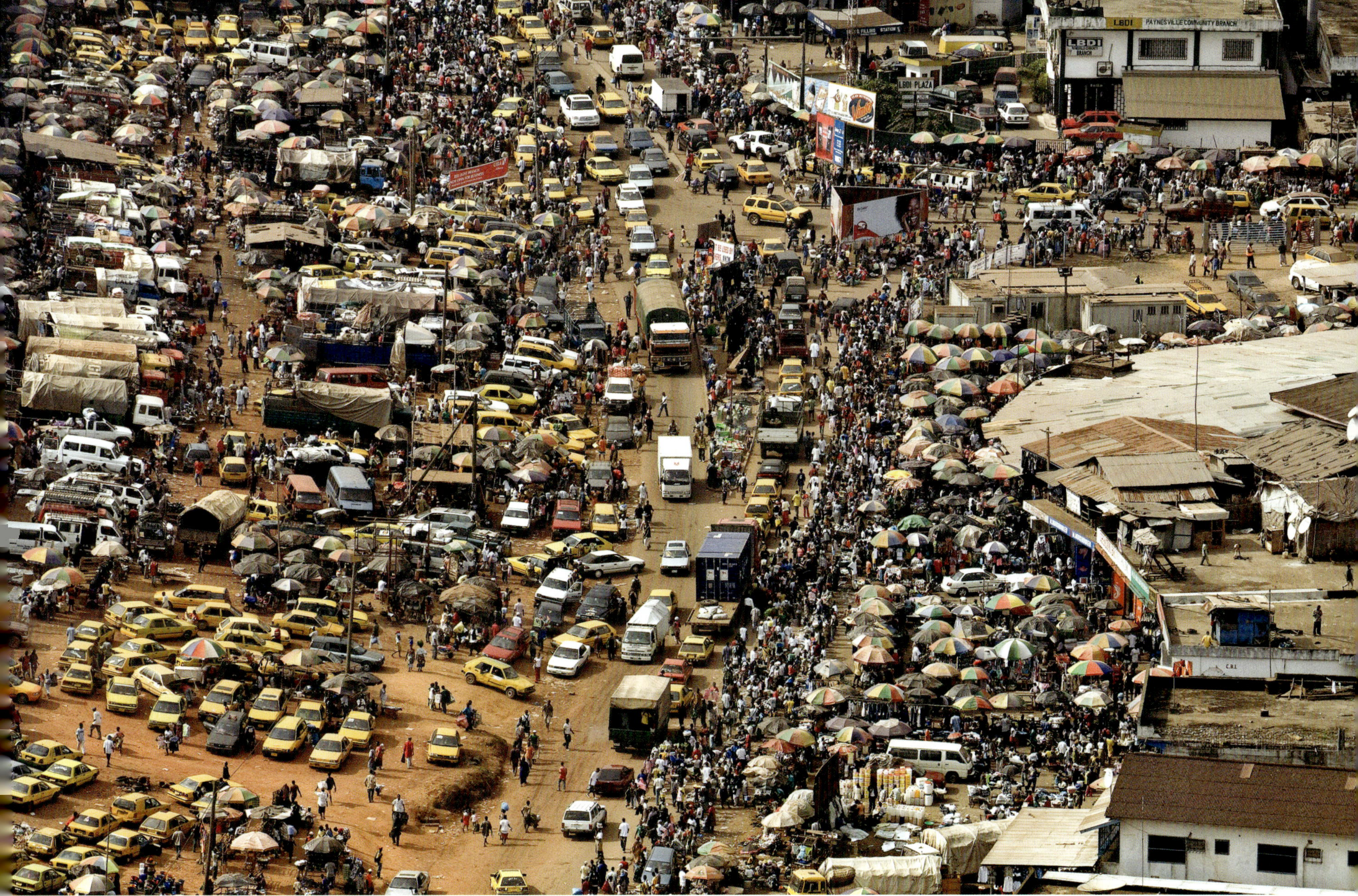
LBDI
PAYNESVILLE COMMUNITY BRANCH
LBDI
BRANCH
LBDI PLAZA
Vimto

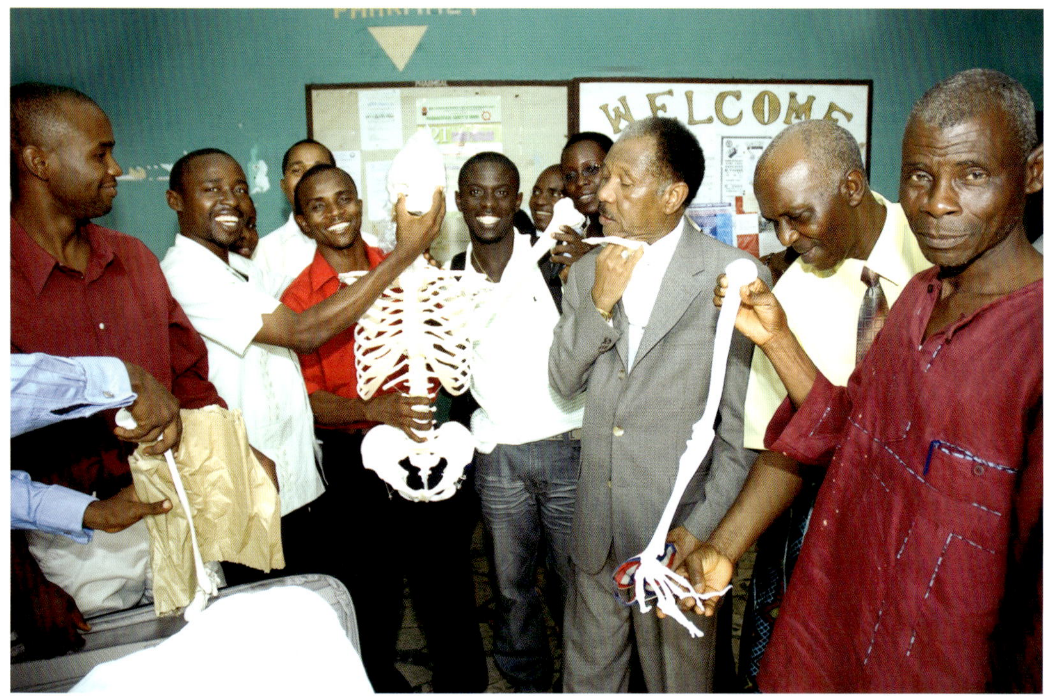

Emmet Dennis (*third from right*), Indiana University alumnus, and president of the University of Liberia, presents a plastic human skeleton to the University of Liberia College of Medicine. *Photograph courtesy of IU International magazine/Charles Reafsnyder.*

In 2004, in a country of little more than three million people, there was less than one health care worker per thousand people—only about 10 percent of the estimated need.

four Indiana University faculty and staff members. The team included Grover Browning, director of fiber optic network operations for University Information Technology Services; Charles Reafsnyder; Verlon Stone; and James Wimbush, dean of the Graduate School and professor of business administration.[4]

In 2008, the government of Liberia, in conjunction with the International Monetary Fund, developed an ambitious plan for rebuilding the country. The overall goal of the Liberia Poverty Reduction Strategy in health was to expand access to a basic package of health services that focused on six national health priorities: maternal and newborn care, child health, reproductive and adolescent health, communicable disease control (including HIV and AIDS), mental health, and emergency care. In addition, expanding access to disease prevention and control programs, such as antiretroviral therapy for the treatment of HIV infection and the treatment of tuberculosis, was a key goal.[5]

In 2004, in a country of little more than three million people, there was less than one health care worker per thousand people—only 10 ten percent of the estimated need.[6]

The shortage of health care workers totaled around eight thousand, which meant that a significant percentage of the population had limited access to health and social welfare services. After the war, several buildings at the University of Liberia, including its natural sciences building, were used to house refugees. In doing so, the buildings were stripped bare of resources, and there was an urgent need to renovate the facilities. Charles Reafsnyder commented that more than 80 percent of biology faculty at the University of Liberia lacked advanced degrees beyond the bachelor's degree. There was,

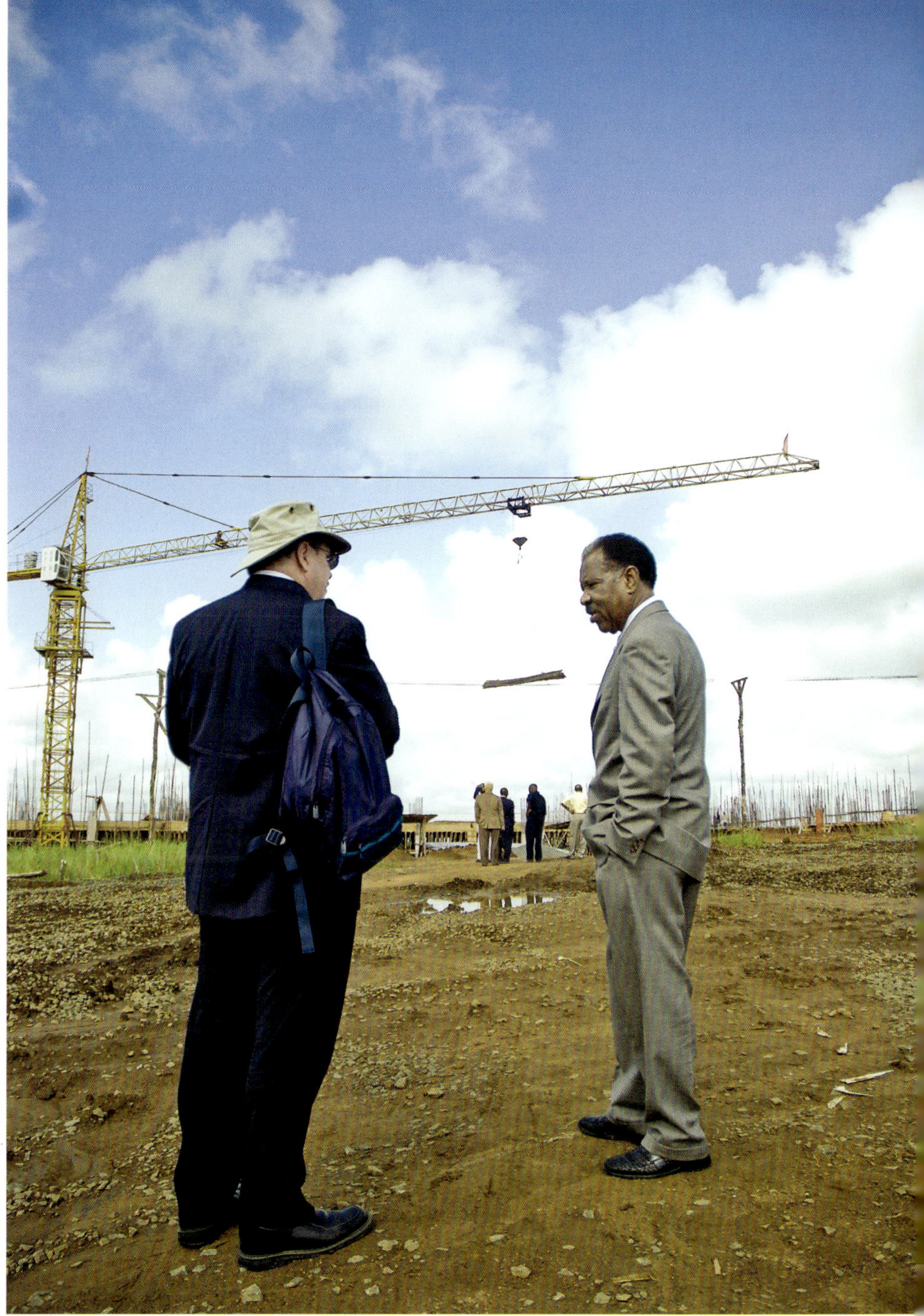

Charles Reafsnyder (*left*) and Emmet Dennis (*right*) in Monrovia, Liberia, 2008. *Photograph courtesy of IU International magazine/Verlon Stone.*

therefore, an urgent need to develop new human capacity for the country's health workforce.[7]

Recognizing the potential of African higher education to contribute to development, the United States Agency for International Development provided support for planning grants for partnerships between US institutions of higher education and their counterparts in sub-Saharan Africa. Thirty-three US institutions were selected from among three hundred applicants. The subsequent applications resulting from these planning grants were subjected to rigorous review by a panel of experts convened by Higher Education for Development, a nongovernmental organization. The partnership between the University of Liberia, Indiana University, and the University of Massachusetts Medical School was one of eleven schools selected by the United States Agency for International Development for funding. These universities thus put into place a $2.7 million project that addressed a national shortage of health care workers. As part of the grant, the Center for Excellence in Health and Life Sciences was founded at the University of Liberia and began to develop new academic and research programs in public health and nurse-midwifery and preclinical training in medicine and pharmacology.[8]

"Indiana University and the University of Liberia produced well-outlined, comprehensive project objectives to improve Liberia's healthcare education," said Higher Education for Development deputy executive director Jeanne-Marie Duval. "Their work to develop new undergraduate courses in health

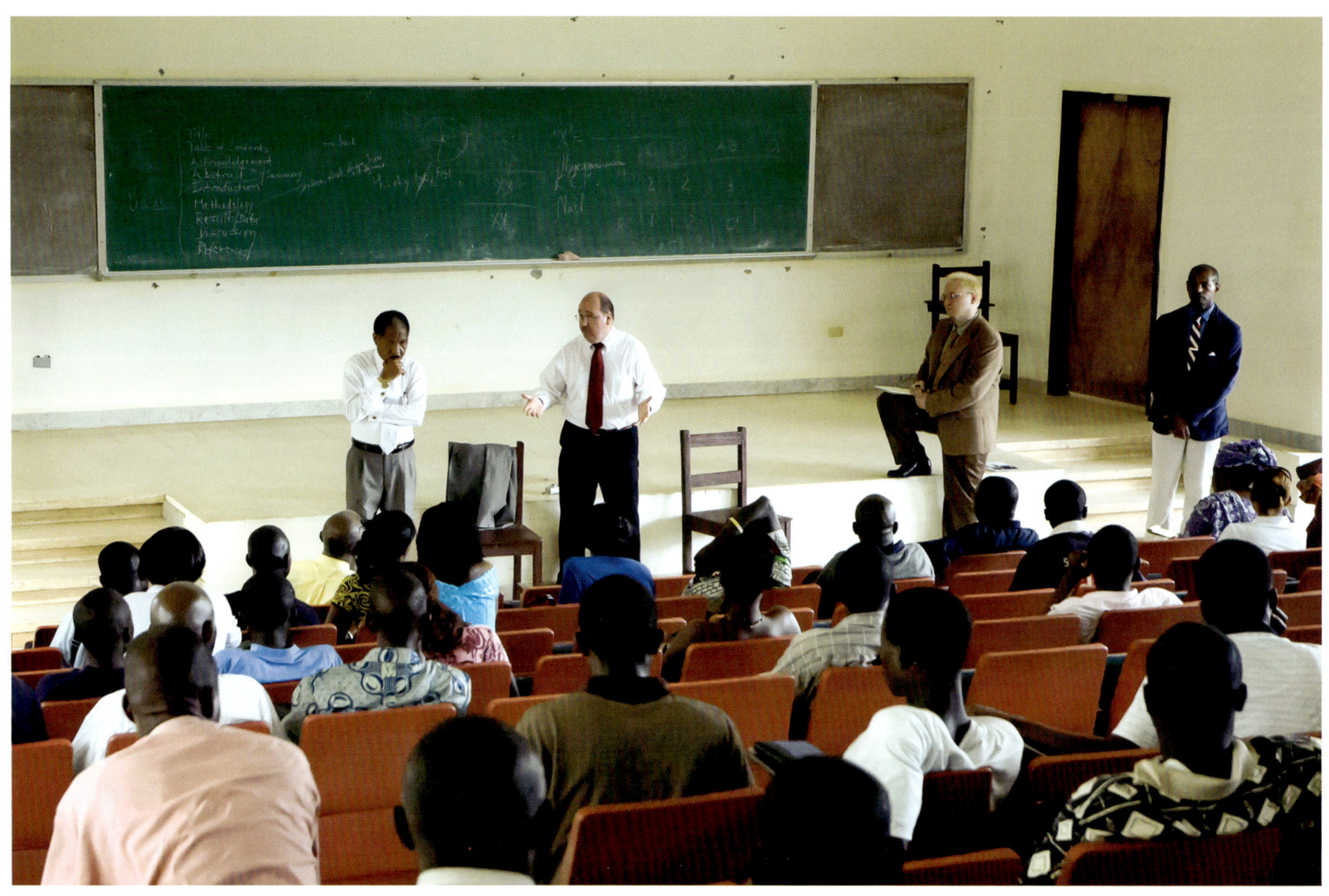

Emmet Dennis (*standing, left*) and Charles Reafsnyder (*standing, center*) lead a discussion of ways to improve the university experience and listen to student suggestions of priorities for the future.

Photograph courtesy of IU International magazine/Verlon Stone.

and life sciences will contribute to Liberia's important rebuilding efforts. These talented partners are prepared to train faculty and students, enhance educational institutions, and support healthier communities."[9]

Emmet Dennis, who had become president of the University of Liberia in 2008, provided leadership for the Liberian side of the partnership. IU was the lead institution for the project, which was managed by its Center for International Education and Development Assistance, directed by Charles Reafsnyder. Key actors at the University of Massachusetts Medical School were Katherine Luzuriaga, associate provost, and Donna Gallagher, codirector of Global Health.[10]

IU President Michael McRobbie commented on the grant: "Liberia is emerging from nearly two decades of civil conflict that not only killed 270,000 people but also ravaged the nation's standards for health and well-being. This project will help a nation already restoring standards of justice, equality and human rights to also rebuild its ability to care for the most basic medical needs of many of its citizens. Indiana University's lengthy and productive partnership with our friends and colleagues in Liberia now takes on even deeper meaning as we support an effort that will save lives."[11]

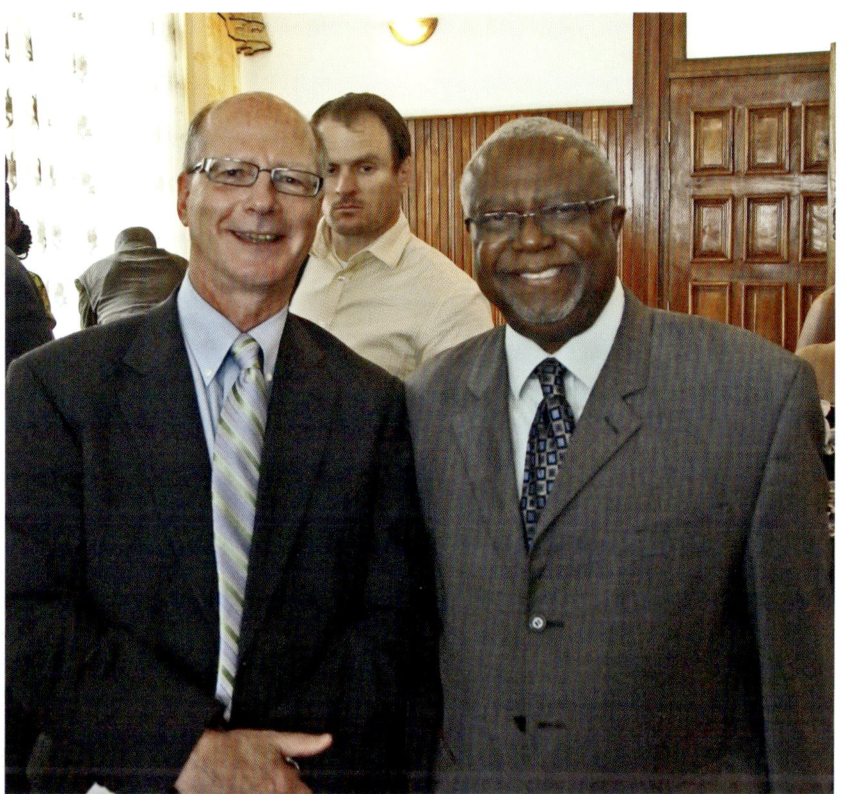

David Zaret, then vice president for international affairs (*left*) and Amos Sawyer (*right*), president of Liberia, 1990–1994. *Photograph courtesy of IU International magazine/Charles Reafsnyder.*

Dennis emphasized that what "this grant represents is a culmination of the excellence in the interaction that has occurred between the two American universities and the University of Liberia. This grant is substantial and will go a long way in terms of strengthening our life and health sciences, something that is indispensable to the health of the nation. It is a model of collaboration between institutions in the developed world and in the developing world. It's not often you find such models, and I think other institutions have a lot to learn from the model that has been established from this collaboration."[12]

In addition to the grant were other projects and activities in Liberia. In 2010, the administrator of the John F. Kennedy Medical Center asked the IU School of Nursing to assist in building nurse leadership; students pursuing the doctor

When we went to Liberia for the first time, the UN peacekeepers were still there. There were emplacements on corners with sandbags and big guns. In the capital city, the windows of most of the buildings were blown out, and there were bullet holes in the walls of the Supreme Court. The university, across the street from the presidential palace, had been completely destroyed . . . everything had been taken—no desks, no books, no anything. So that was the situation helping the faculty to feel like they had some hope, and they had some training to deal with the situation, and they could recommit to making this institution work again.

—Susan Williams

of nursing practice degree were provided with training on adolescent pregnancy, quality improvement, and strategic planning.[13]

Joining IU law faculty members on a visit to Liberia during the 2006–2007 academic year were Lauren Robel, then dean of the Maurer School of Law; David C. Williams, executive director of the Center for Constitutional Democracy and the John S. Hastings Professor of Law at the Maurer School of Law; and Susan H. Williams, Walter W. Foskett Professor of Law at the Maurer School of Law and director of the Center for Constitutional Democracy. Susan and David had been working with Amos Sawyer, who thought the center might be able to do productive work in Liberia. Ellen Sirleaf came to Indianapolis to give a talk when she was still a candidate for the presidency. David Williams spoke with Sirleaf about constitutional reform, and she said that she was very open to exploring this should she become president. Susan Williams sums up the interest of the center: "Liberia was of interest in a number of ways. Ellen Sirleaf was the first woman head of state elected in Africa, and part of why she was elected was the political mobilization of women in Liberia. At the same time, Liberia had a pretty low rate of political participation by women in their legislature, for example. So this opening on the gender front was relevant to me. In addition, Liberia had constitutional issues that both David and I were concerned with."[14]

David Williams and Susan Williams had worked with the Liberian government on constitutional reform since 2005. Their work included writing a treatise on the meaning of the Liberian constitution for use by lawyers and judges, drafting anticorruption statutes, and developing the process for constitutional reform. David and Susan Williams returned to Liberia in June 2008 for planning meetings, where he met with the chief justice and associate justices of the Supreme Court of Liberia, members of the national legislature, and the minister of justice. Subsequently, the center was asked to advise the Constitutional Review Committee of the Government of Liberia on amendments to the 1986 constitution. Susan Williams describes the experience:

> When we went to Liberia for the first time, the UN peacekeepers were still there. There were emplacements on corners with sandbags and big guns. In the capital city, the windows of most of the buildings were blown out, and there were bullet holes in the walls of the Supreme Court. The university, across the street from the presidential palace, had been completely destroyed . . . everything had been taken—no desks, no books, no anything.

> So that was the situation helping the faculty to feel like they had some hope, and they had some training to deal with the situation, and they could recommit to making this institution work again.[15]

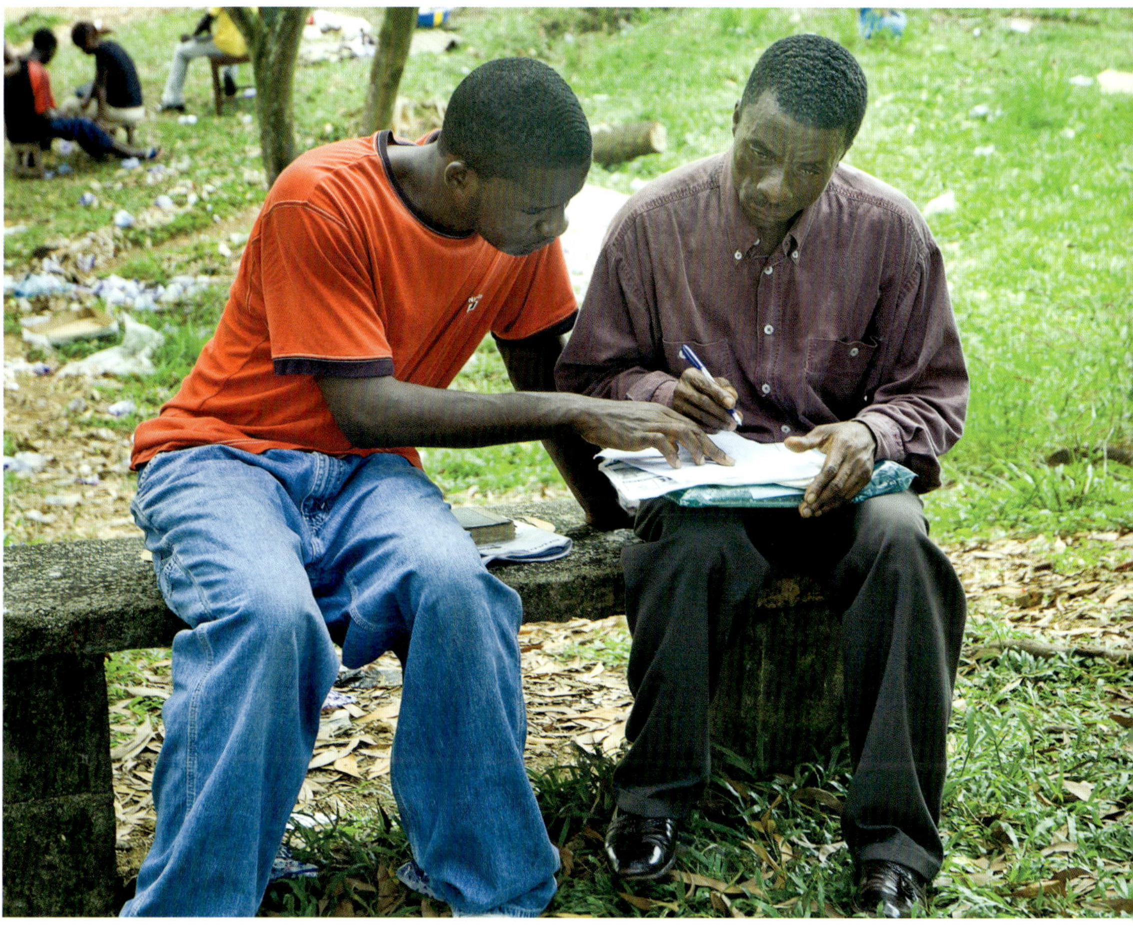

The center's advising included civic education about the existing constitution; public consultations to gather information about the needs and desires of the people; constitutional drafting to help the Constitutional Review Committee design amendments; and public education about the final proposed amendments. The public consultations were administered by teams of local experts who were trained by Susan Williams. The team developed guidelines for consultations with women, youth, and disabled and rural people who did not speak English.[16]

Another project, the Indiana University Liberian Collections, based in Bloomington, continued and flourished and filled an important need. This collaborative venture involved the Archives of Traditional Music as a key partner and was one of the largest collections of Liberian documents and published resources in the United States. The Liberian Collections included historical and ethnographic documents, newspapers, government publications, books, journals, dissertations, maps, slides, negatives, photographs, microfilms, audio- and videotapes, artifacts, and memorabilia. The IU Liberian Collections make

Students studying on the University of Liberia campus.
Photograph courtesy of IU International magazine/Verlon Stone.

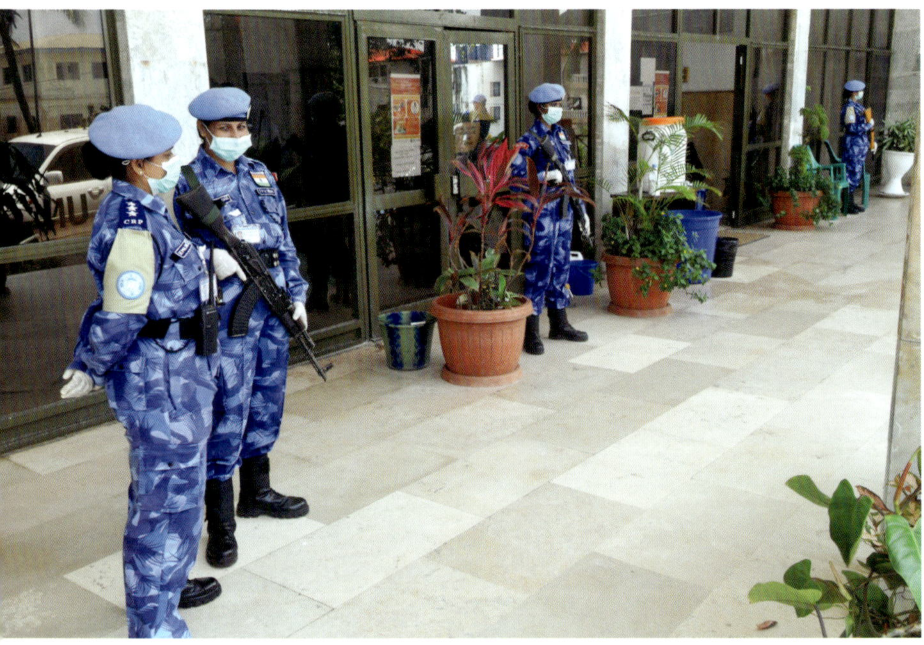

Peacekeepers with the United Nations Mission in Liberia wear protective masks while on duty at UN offices in the capital city of Monrovia, September 2014. *UN Photo/Andrey Tsarkov.*

available a comprehensive range of materials and information about Liberia for researchers, students, and teachers, with special emphasis on reaching Liberians in Liberia and in the diaspora. Among its activities are acquiring, assessing, preserving, inventorying, indexing, cataloging, organizing, describing, managing, and publicizing Liberia-related materials in all formats.

Early deposits of Liberian materials came from William Siegmann, an IU graduate; Jane Martin, an anthropologist; Jeanette Carter, a scholar; and religious leader John Gay and his wife, Judy. They created an informal but quickly growing collection. Initially, these donations were accepted in addition to the audio and video recordings that are the primary format of the Archive of Traditional Music collections. As these documents acquired a critical mass, the possibility arose of creating an independent repository of the materials on Liberia. Verlon Stone took the lead in further development of the project, including the rescue of important cultural, historical, and government documents in the aftermath of the bloody civil war. Many documents were lost because of the war, and the damaged buildings offered little protection from the tropical weather. However, due to the efforts of the IU Liberian Collections, many of these important documents were saved, photocopied, or scanned, preventing a significant part of the history of the country from being lost entirely.[17]

IU's contribution to health care began to set the country in a positive direction. Because of the Ebola outbreak, activities stopped or had to be reconfigured. The deadly outbreak of the virus was reported in Lofa and Nimba Counties in March 2014. In August of that year, President Sirleaf declared a national state of emergency. Hospitals were unable to cope with the number of cases, and infections and deaths increased. The country lacked the necessary protective gear for doctors and nurses. Some hospitals were abandoned, while those still functioning lacked rubber gloves, sanitizing supplies, and isolation wards. President Obama authorized the deployment of troops to Liberia and other countries to help West African nations cope with the epidemic by building Ebola treatment units and training local medical staff. Under these conditions, the Indiana University project had to be put on hold. Because travel to Liberia was not possible at this time, to maintain momentum on the projects, IU reconfigured its plans to maintain contact through online curriculum development and videoconferencing.

The ravages of war and of Ebola deeply damaged the morale of many Liberians and the country's fragile infrastructure. IU's contribution to health care was setting the country in an important direction until projects were curtailed because of the Ebola outbreak. Nonetheless, IU made important contributions to the health care, history, and constitutional future of Liberia.

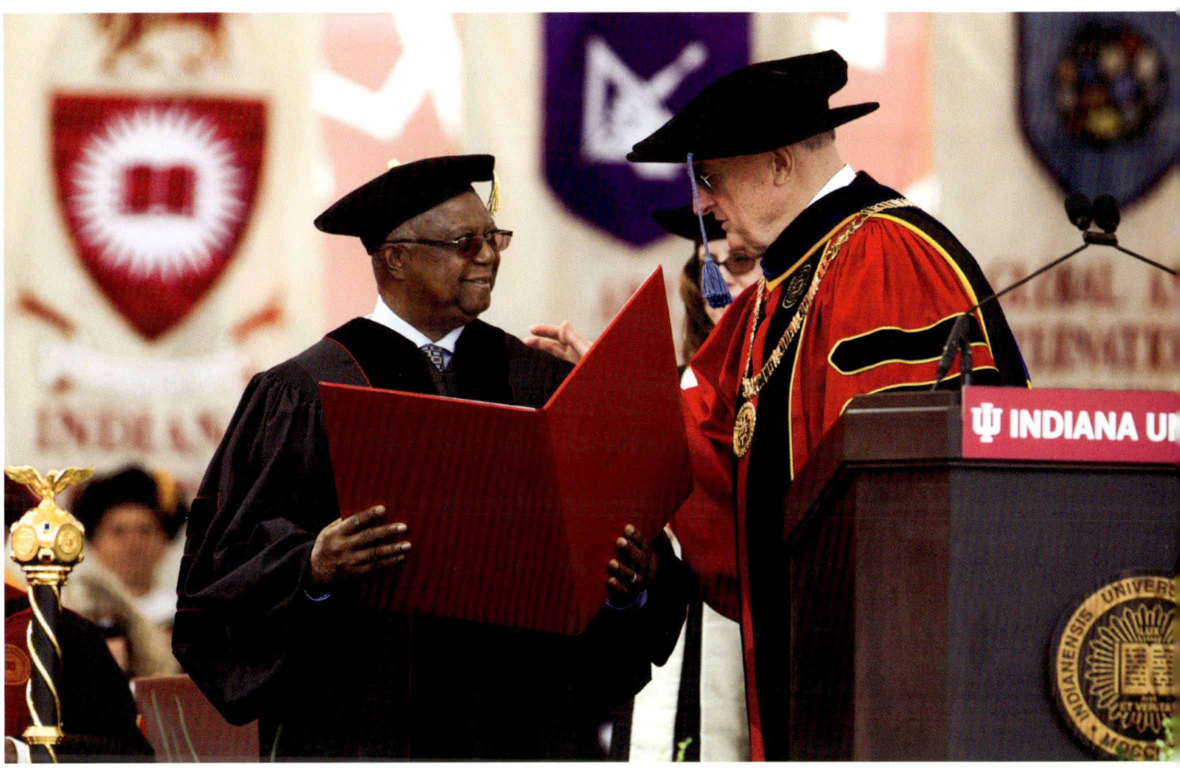

Indiana University president Michael McRobbie (*right*) presents Amos Sawyer with an honorary doctor of humane letters degree at the May 2018 graduation ceremony in Bloomington. *Photograph courtesy of Indiana University.*

IU's contribution to health care was setting the country in an important direction until projects were curtailed because of the Ebola outbreak. Nonetheless, IU made important contributions to the health care, history, and constitutional future of Liberia.

16 | INDIANA UNIVERSITY *in* Egypt

This LLM was fully an American degree aimed at graduates of the four-year bachelor of laws programs at the two Egyptian universities as well as practicing attorneys and judges in Egypt.

In January 2008, the Indiana University McKinney School of Law launched an American Bar Association–approved master's degree with a focus on international commercial law at two law schools in Egypt: the Faculty of Law at Alexandria University and the Faculty of Law at Cairo University.

Cairo University, a leading academic institution in the Middle East, was founded in 1908. Its graduates include former secretary-general of the United Nations Boutros Boutros-Ghali; a secretary-general of the Arab League, Arab presidents and heads of state, and former judges at the International Court of Justice. The Faculty of Law, one of Cairo University's oldest faculties, contains three main undergraduate sections: the Arabic Section has the majority of students; the English Section, which was the first department offering legal education in English in Egypt; and the French Section, which operates in association with the University of Paris I Pantheon Sorbonne. The Faculty of Law also offers a wide variety of postgraduate diplomas and certificates, along with the LLM (master of laws) degree and PhD degree.[1]

Alexandria University was originally a branch of Cairo University; however, in 1938, it was declared an independent university. The law school was the second school to be established at Alexandria University, with its first class graduating in 1941. It ranked as the second most important in the country, with graduates spread throughout the Muslim world, serving in all fields of legal practice

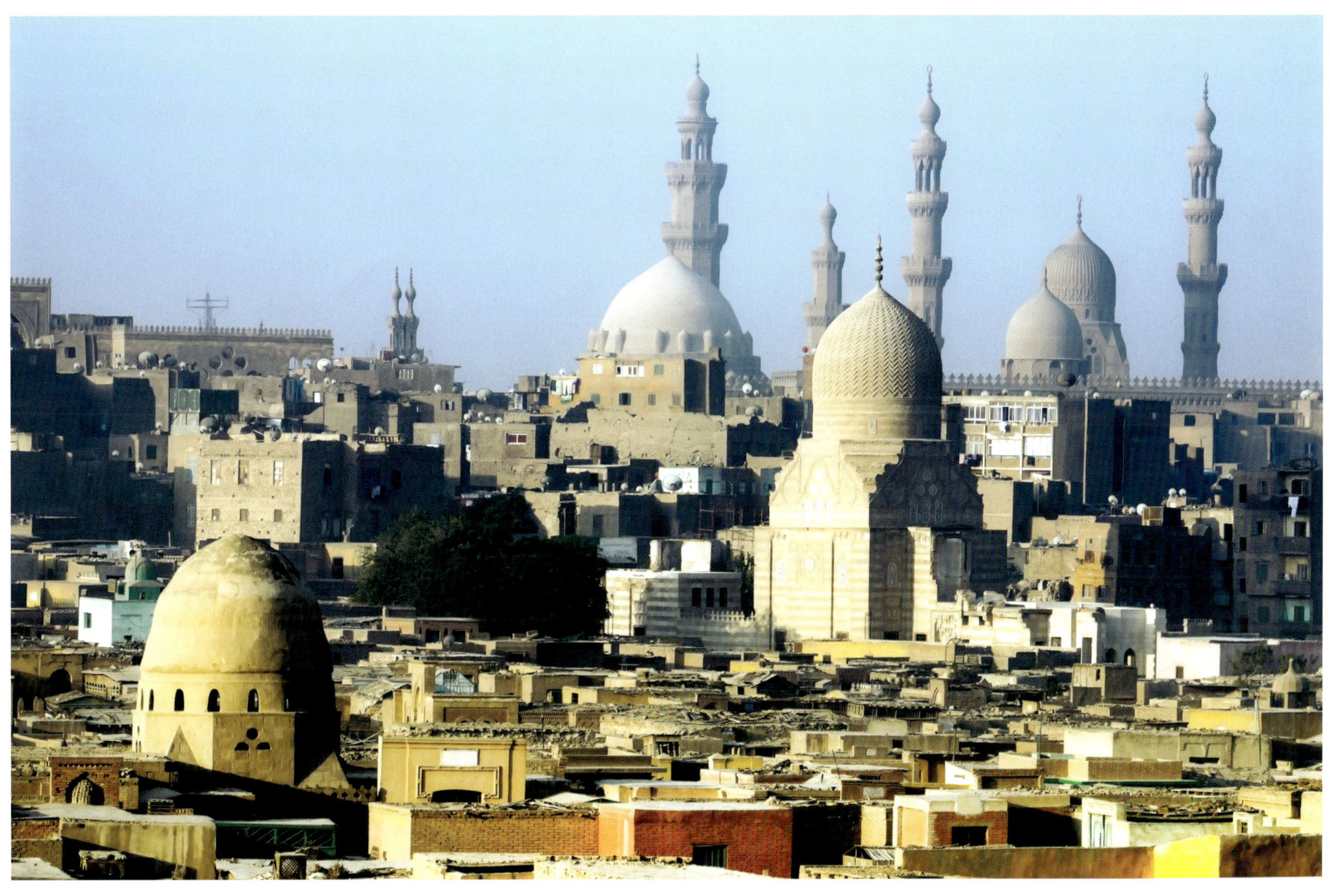

Cairo, Egypt, July 2011.
Photograph courtesy of iStock.

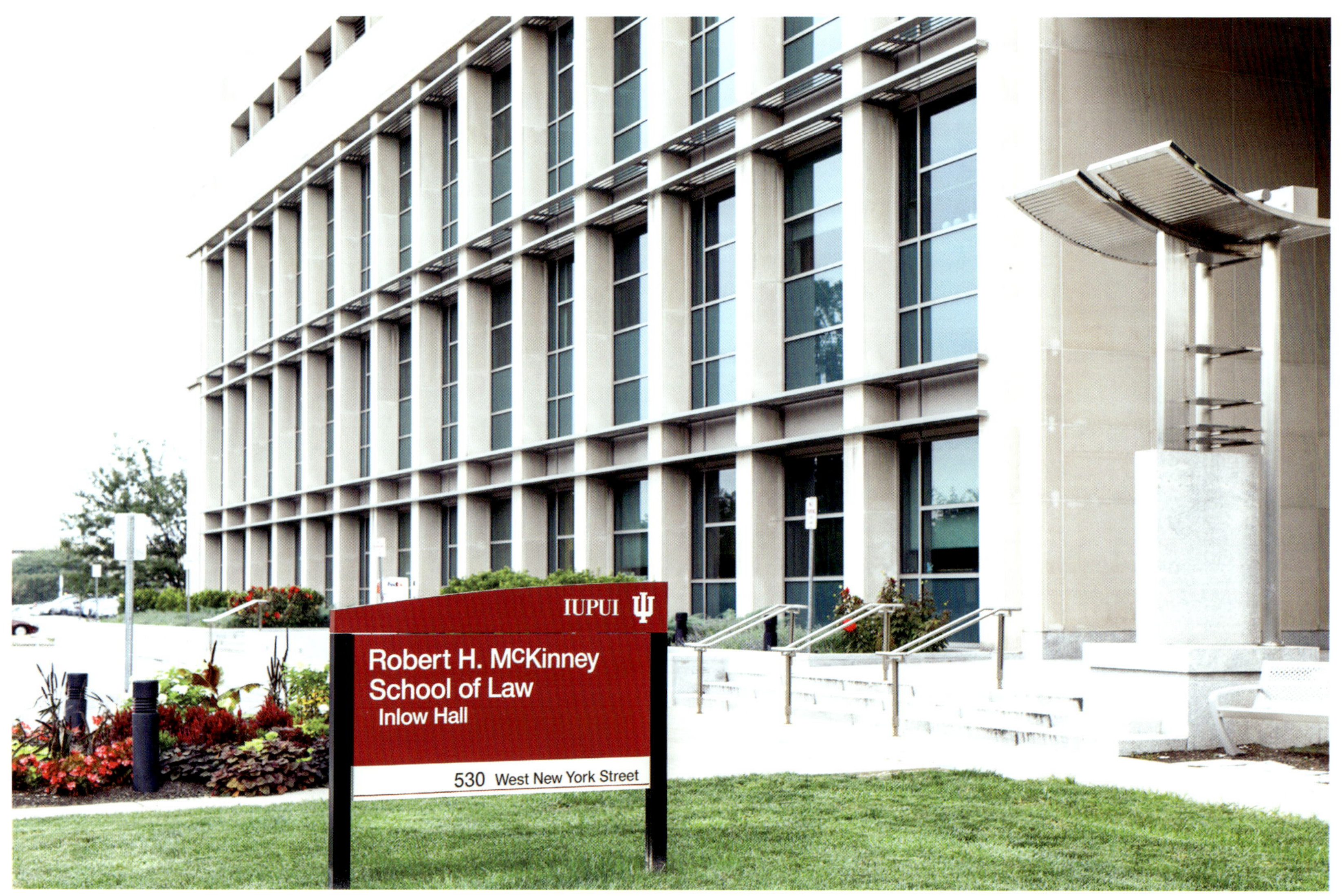

Robert H. McKinney School of Law at Indiana University–Purdue University Indianapolis.

Photograph courtesy of Indiana University.

and as leaders in their communities. Many faculty members held degrees from European or American universities. Faculty members have served as an essential force in bringing about some of the most important changes in society, not only in Egypt but throughout the Arab and Muslim worlds.

As part of an initiative to help Egypt modernize its economy and legal system, the United States Agency for International Development (USAID) awarded a three-year, $6.7 million grant to operate a master of laws program. The Indiana University–Purdue University Indianapolis (IUPUI) Robert P. McKinney School of Law submitted a competitive application; among the other finalists were Georgetown Law Center and the law school at the University of Washington.

Frank Emmert, program director and law professor, saw this as a groundbreaking collaboration between an American law school and two of the leading law schools in the Middle East. Emmert specialized in European Union law, comparative law, international business transactions, international commercial arbitration, international trade law, legal systems in transition, and world trade organization law. Emmert reflects on the process of securing the grant for the LLM program from USAID: "USAID sent people from Egypt—a group of academics and administrators—to IUPUI and to the University of Washington in Seattle. Then they invited everyone who was still in the running to Washington, DC, where we made a presentation at what they called a bidder's conference. They asked us, in front of everyone, to do both partnerships. No other university was willing to deliver a degree in Egypt. Other applicants wanted to bring people to the US, but the impact on the ground was limited".[2]

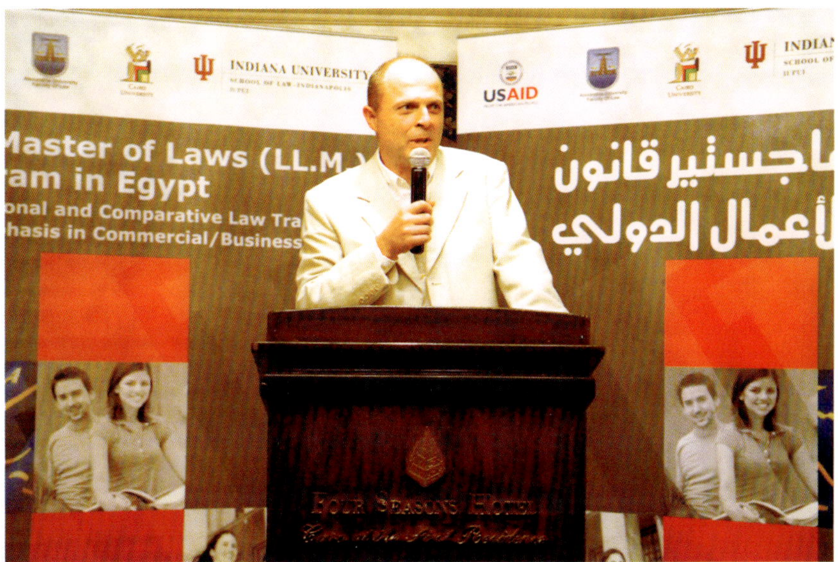

Indiana University–Purdue University Indianapolis McKinney School of Law professor and master of laws program director Frank Emmert in Cairo, 2010. *Photograph courtesy of Indiana University.*

This LLM was fully an American degree aimed at graduates of the four-year bachelor of laws programs at the two Egyptian universities as well as practicing attorneys and judges in Egypt. Emmert explains: "The students were essentially from three different backgrounds: one-third recent graduates, fresh out of law school basically, and in the market for a job; second, private-sector attorneys working for an international corporation or a law firm during the day and realizing they needed a degree like this to better serve their clients and employers; and the third, civil servants. In fact, these places were almost fought over and the institution that became the dominant

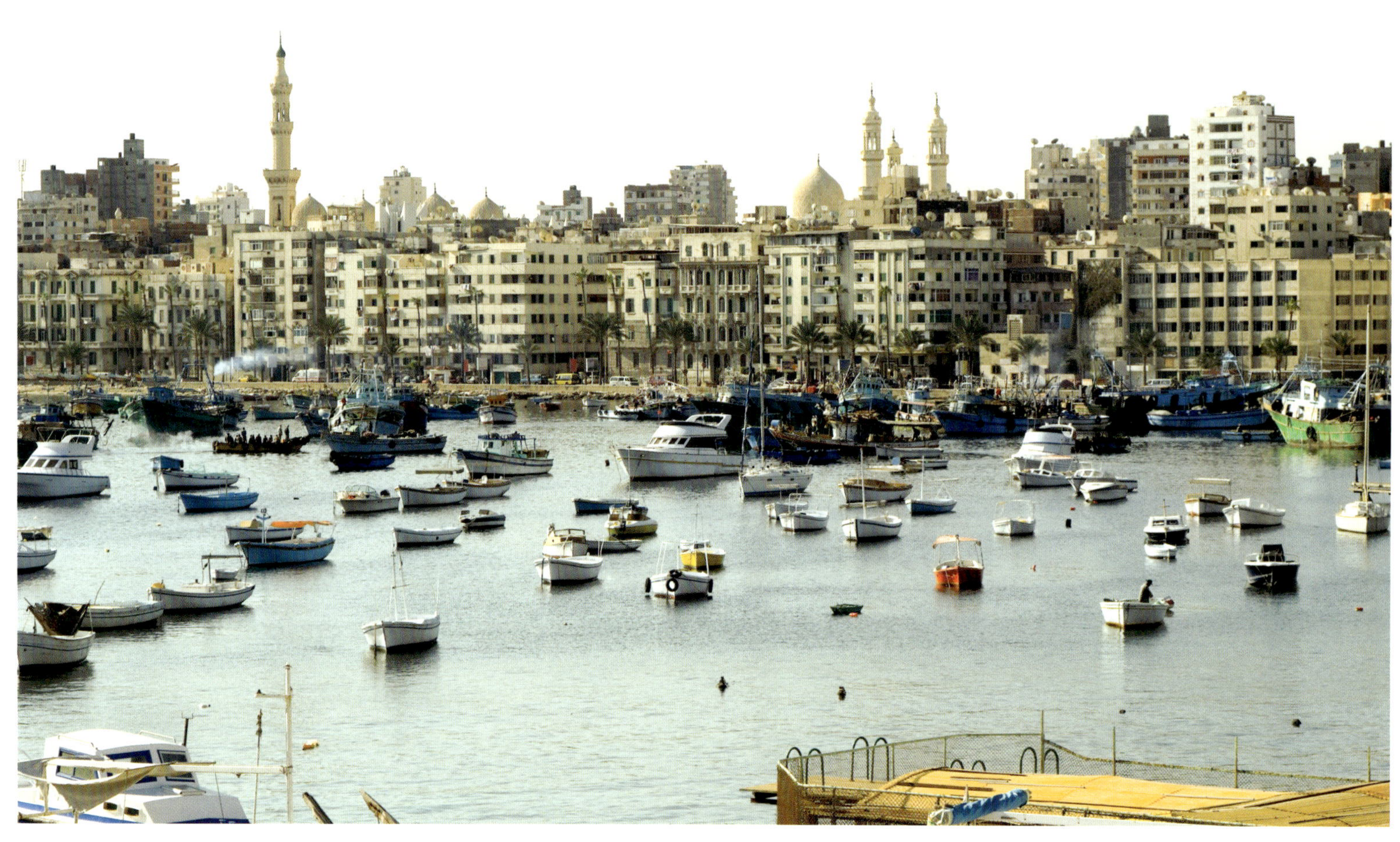

Port of Alexandria, Egypt, November 2012.
Photograph courtesy of iStock.

Graduates of the two law schools could handle local cases, but they could not deal with international trade and business transactions.

subscriber was the Council of State, the federal court system basically."[3]

Graduates of the two law schools could handle local cases, but they could not deal with international trade and business transactions. So Egyptian companies relied on foreign lawyers to do their international business, and foreign investors brought their own lawyers. The traditional approach had been to award Fulbright scholarships, and not all recipients necessarily returned to Egypt. There was an additional feature in the proposal that was important. Only a small number of women students would study abroad; typically, families were not happy for women to travel when they were not married. Furthermore, since most of the classes were in the evening, the degree programs were accessible to working professionals.

Emmert describes the ambitious goals for the project: "We wanted to work with four pillars: (1) institutional and facilities upgrade, (2) libraries, computer labs, and classrooms, (3) the delivery of the master's program, and (4) bringing students to IUPUI for doctoral studies, usually their junior faculty members basically. Their recruitment of faculty was from their top graduates in-house—the top eight or nine graduates out of a thousand people."[4]

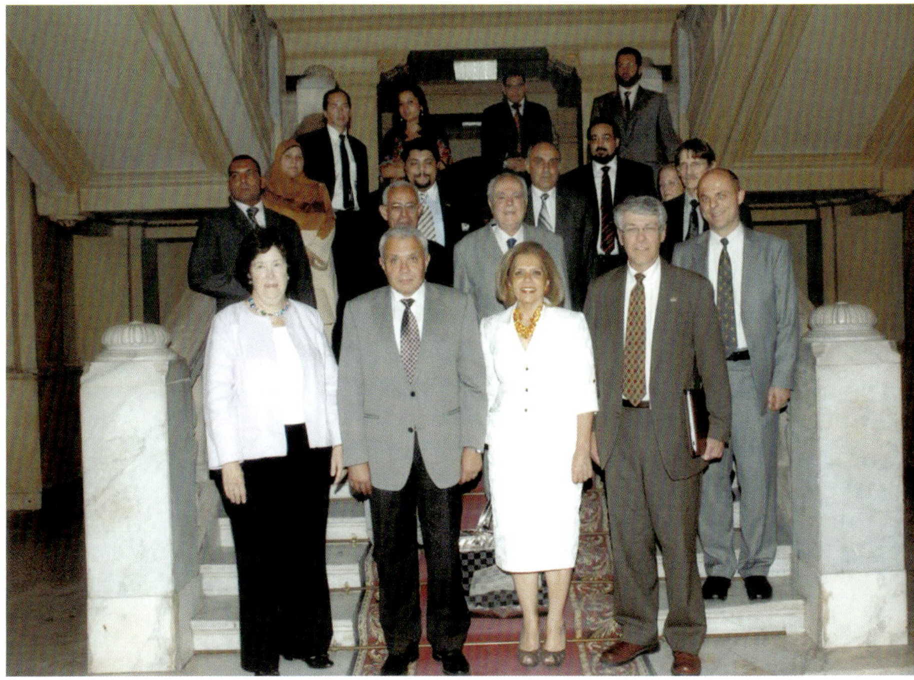

Master of laws faculty pose for a graduation celebration photo with US ambassador to Egypt Margaret Scobey (*left*), in Cairo, 2010. *Photograph courtesy of Indiana University.*

Implementing the program from scratch posed many challenges. The program coordinator, Sonja Rice, had the responsibility of working with architects and builders to prepare suitable space for the faculty and classes. She describes this daunting task:

> The contract was signed in May 2007 for both partnerships. We wanted initially to start in September, but the renovations weren't ready, the student recruitment wasn't—we wanted to be

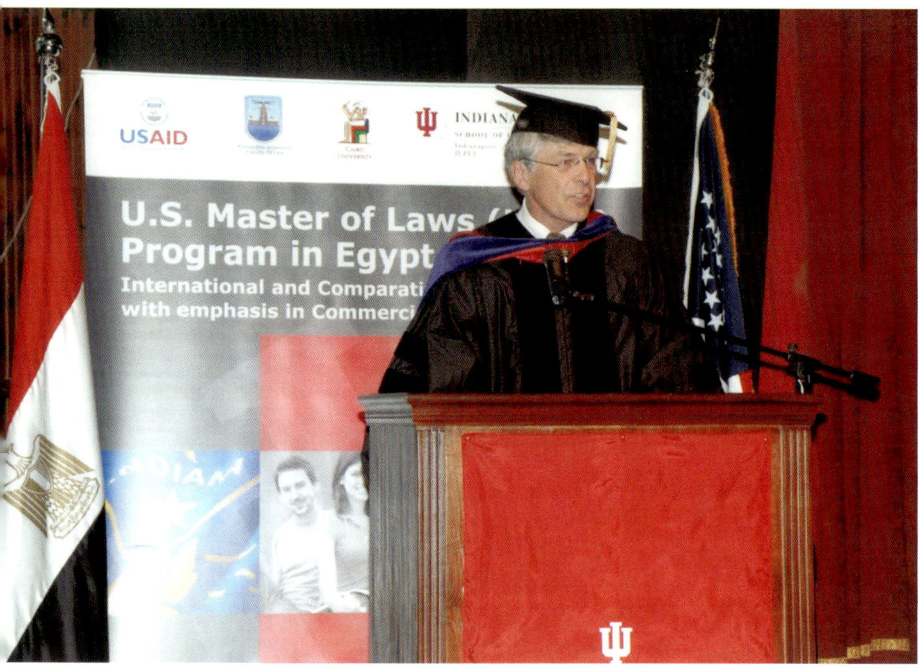

Indiana University–Purdue University Indianapolis McKinney School of Law dean Gary Roberts speaks at the master of laws graduation ceremony in Cairo, 2010. *Photograph courtesy of Indiana University.*

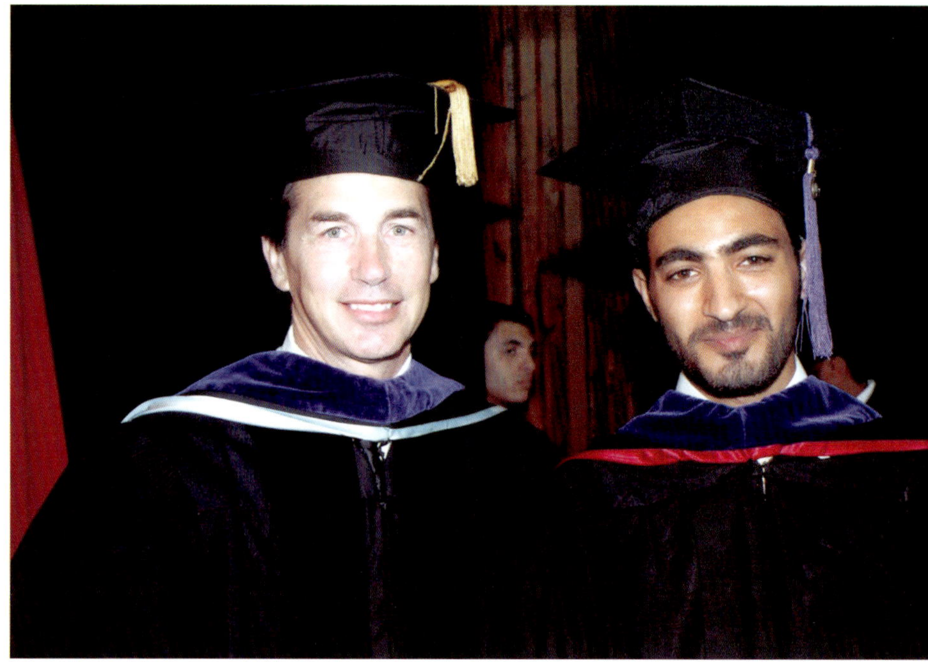

Indiana University–Purdue University Indianapolis McKinney School of Law professor James Nehf (*left*) and graduating student at graduation in Cairo, 2010. *Photograph courtesy of Indiana University.*

> in the academic year here, but then we decided instead of waiting a year, to start in January 2008. I was brought on in October of 2007, while I was waiting to see if I passed the bar, and I had already interviewed for the job. Right away, things started to get busy. We flew over to Egypt, and I went back for a month and stayed there to help with the process of getting our local offices set up. We actually hired local staff—Egyptian nationals to serve as on-site program managers—and staffs in Alexandria and Cairo.[5]

In addition to these logistical concerns, there was an urgent need to put into place academic procedures and policies. Rice explains: "We essentially became our own mini law school. We handled our own admissions, scholarships, matriculations; we shepherded everyone through the process that our registrar would normally handle; we set up all of the courses, and the dates, and the registering of the students. There were things that didn't fit nicely into IU, and we had to figure out how to make it work while still respecting the IU rules, regulations, and policies."[6]

There was also the major need to recruit qualified and available faculty. Emmert recalls: "We didn't have enough IU

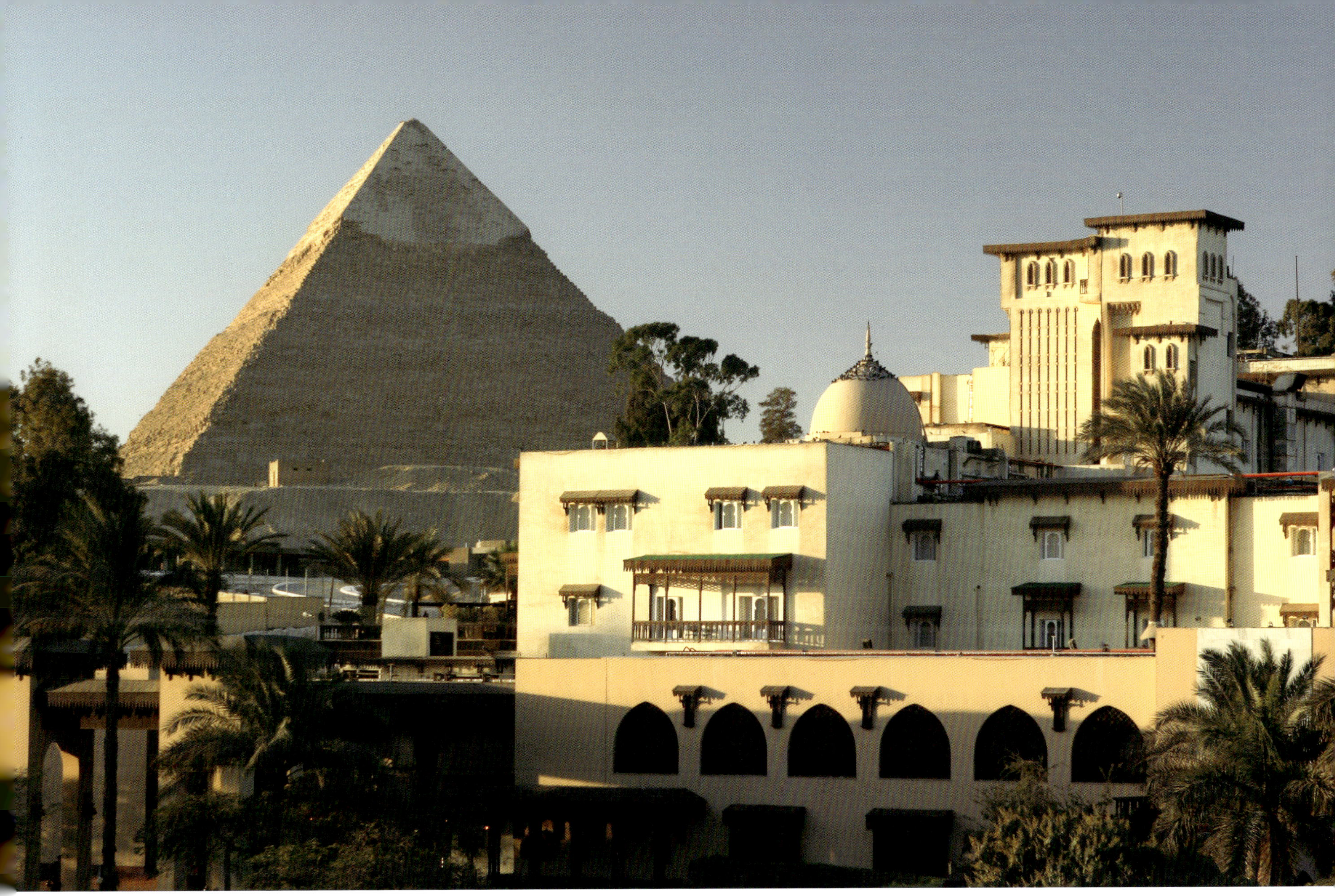

Cairo skyline with pyramids in the background.
Photograph courtesy of iStock.

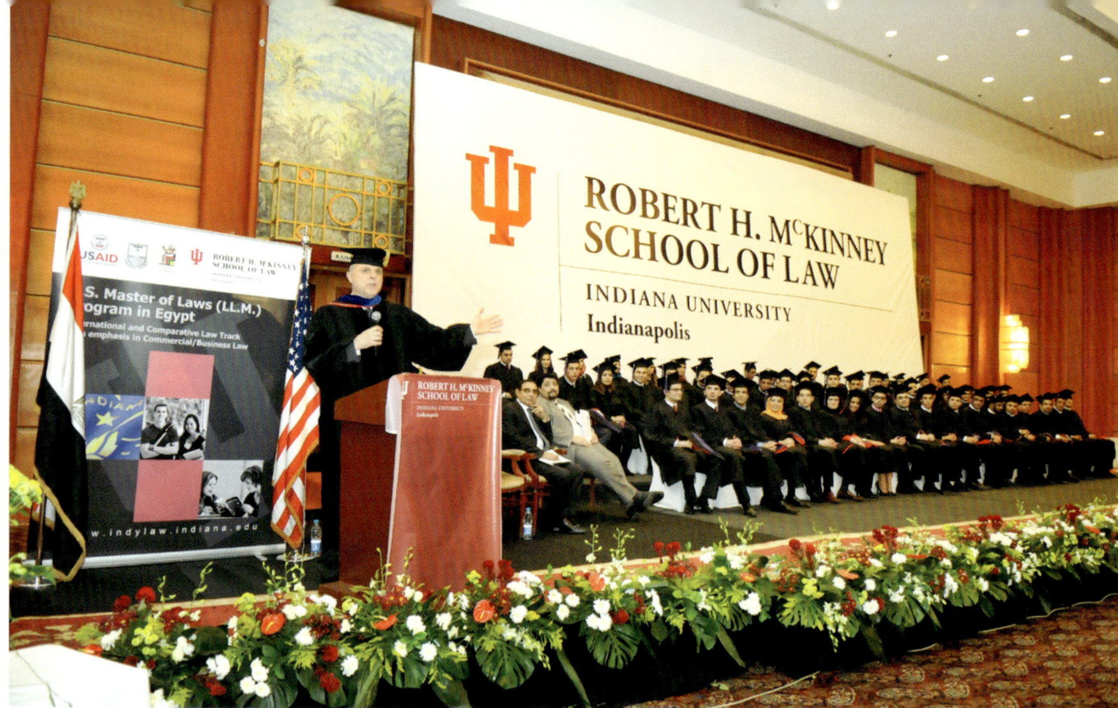

Master of laws program director and Indiana University–Purdue University Indianapolis McKinney School of Law professor Frank Emmert speaks at graduation, 2013.
Photograph courtesy of Indiana University.

faculty to staff two programs, so we started hiring adjuncts who taught at IUPUI before, and we also appointed a few additional adjuncts. We also hired a small number of Egyptian colleagues, for example Dr. Mohammed Abul-Wahab of Cairo University, an international arbitrator, with a doctorate from Manchester University."[7]

Special arrangements were necessary to enable IUPUI faculty and others to participate in the instructional program. Emmert explains the teaching schedule for participating law faculty: "The courses were designed to be delivered in block format, so people didn't have to spend a whole semester there, because it would have been very expensive to have five or six professors there for a whole semester. We sent people for two to three weeks to teach four nights a week, four hours a night, which was pretty intense for everyone. However, it was easier on our faculty—some of whom used spring break and maybe added another week."[8]

In addition to Frank Emmert, IUPUI faculty included Fran Quigley, who directed the Human Rights Clinic; James Neff, a specialist in contracts, consumer law, and commercial law; Swadesh Kalsi, an adjunct professor who taught international trade law; Judith Ford Anspach, who served as director of the Ruth Lilly Law Library and who dealt with technology resources for lawyers; and Victoria Woest, a legal scholar and legal history specialist.[9]

It is noteworthy that the courses at Cairo and Alexandria tended to be very large, sometimes with more than a thousand students. The IUPUI courses were small classes with close interactions between professors and students. Rice explains how the program grew: "We started out with thirty-two students in Cairo and nine in Alexandria in the first cohort, and we had designed the classrooms to host up to sixty-five students in each location, so there was a lot of unused opportunity there, but then it quickly filled up because word of mouth spread."[10]

By December 2013, when the grant came to an end, 235 of the 281 students enrolled had successfully completed the program. The McKinney School of Law had offered eighty-one classes and a number of workshops during the program. Legal textbooks or printed classroom materials were provided to the enrolled students.[11]

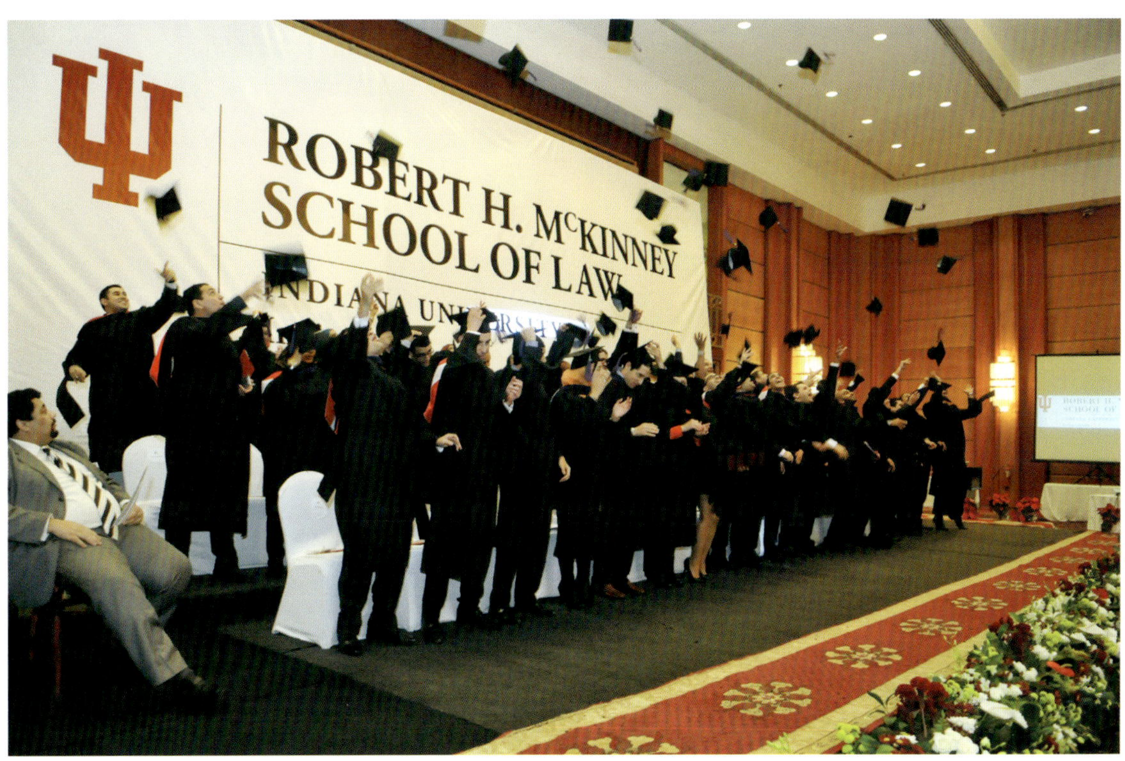

Master of laws students celebrate their graduation from the program, 2013. *Photograph courtesy of Indiana University.*

It was hoped that those who completed the degree would ultimately play a significant role in improving Egypt's economy and legal system and meet the country's need for lawyers who were qualified to handle international business transactions, modern corporate laws, and commercial transactions. This was not an exchange program; the law school offered classes taught by both American and Middle Eastern professors, culminating in a law degree from IUPUI. Students who applied in Egypt had to meet the same requirements as anyone who applied in Indianapolis. Students also had to be proficient in English, as would any other nonnative English speaker who would attend classes in Indianapolis. As Rice explains, "Once students graduate from this program, they get an IU School of Law–Indianapolis LLM degree that makes them eligible to sit for the bar exam wherever an IU School of Law–Indianapolis JD graduate is eligible to sit for the bar exam."[12]

By December 2013, when the grant came to an end, 235 of the 281 students enrolled had successfully completed the program.

17 | INDIANA UNIVERSITY *in* Indonesia

The United States was one of the first countries to establish diplomatic relations with the Republic of Indonesia following its independence from the Netherlands in 1949.

Facing, Herman B Wells (*in dark suit*) visits the Indiana University contract team in Jakarta, Indonesia, February 1960. To the right of Wells are Walter W. Mode and Owen J. Stine (*wearing glasses*). *IU Archives (P0029333).*

THE UNITED STATES WAS ONE OF THE FIRST COUNTRIES TO establish diplomatic relations with the Republic of Indonesia following its independence from the Netherlands in 1949. In a country with one of the world's highest populations and largest number of Muslims, Indonesia's efforts at democratization and reform increased its stability and security and strengthened US–Indonesia relations. Because of Indonesia's strategic position in the South China Sea, the nation had considerable regional and global significance.

Indiana University had a long history of working with universities in Indonesia, dating back to the late 1950s, when Herman B Wells visited the country. In 1959, a Public Administration Program in Indonesia was funded by a grant from the US Agency for International Development and coordinated by the Institute of Training for Public Service in the IU Bloomington Department of Government (renamed the Political Science Department in 1969). IU collaborated with the Indonesian government in setting up the National Institute of Administration in Jakarta. Walter W. Mode, a professor in the Department of Government, served as chief adviser, and Lynton K. Caldwell, a professor in the same department, was director of the project and served as campus coordinator. On the Bloomington campus, more than seventy Indonesians studied public administration and business; in Jakarta, modernizing office systems and procedures was one of the institute's primary purposes.[1]

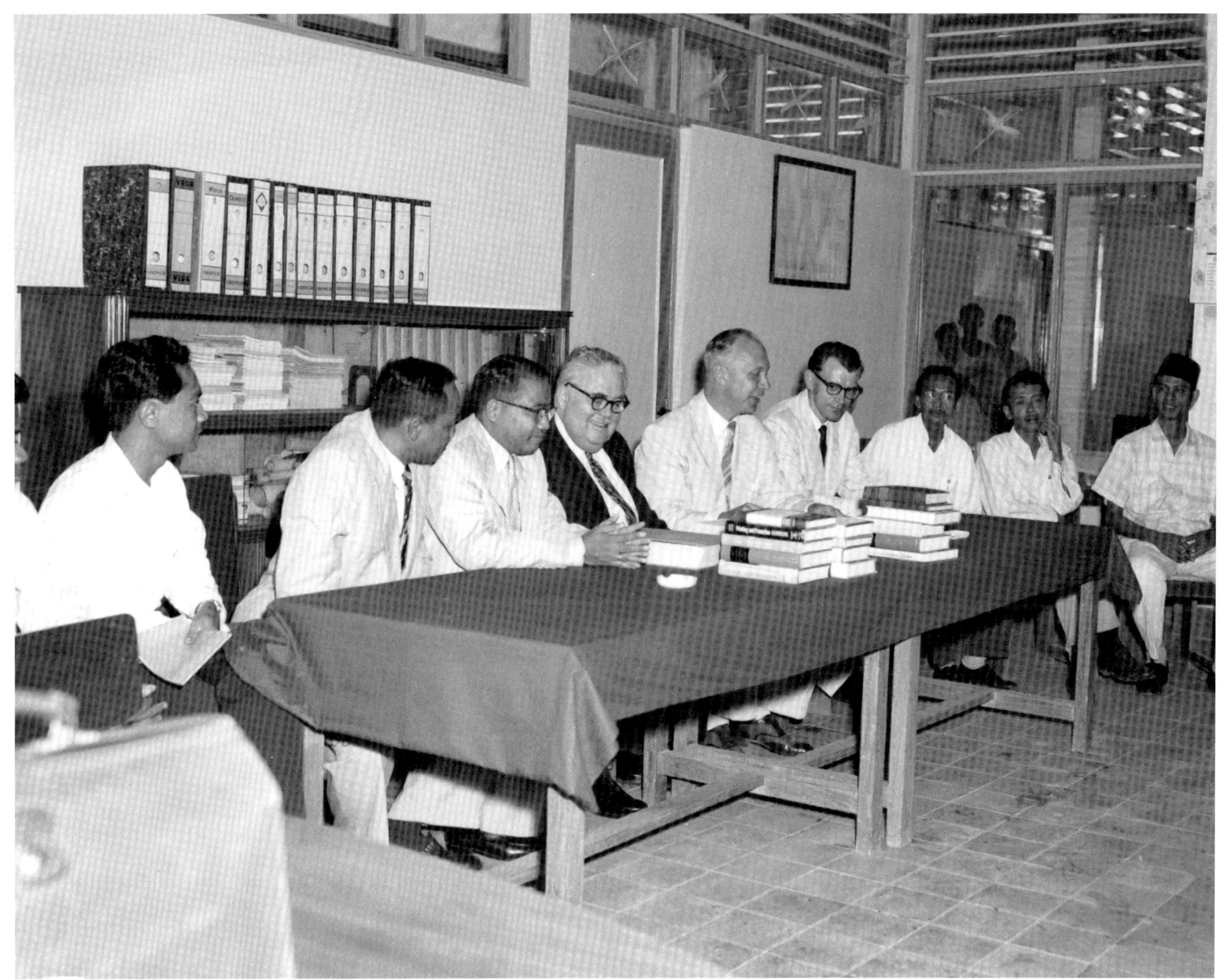

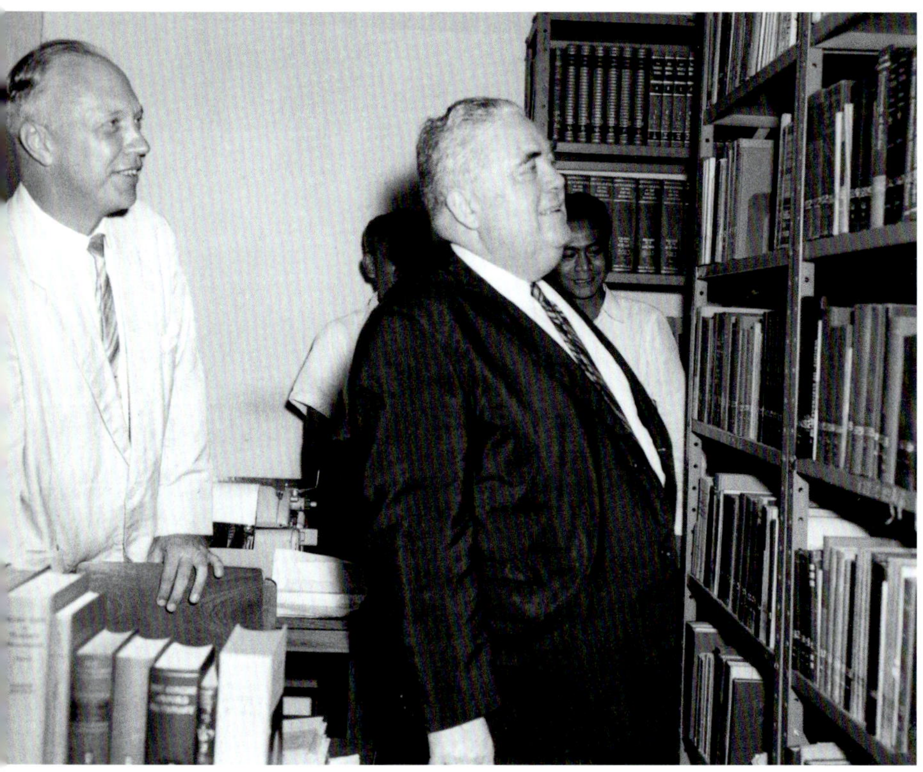

Walter Mode (*left*) and Herman Wells (*right*) look at books in Jakarta, Indonesia, February 1960. *IU Archives (P0029332).*

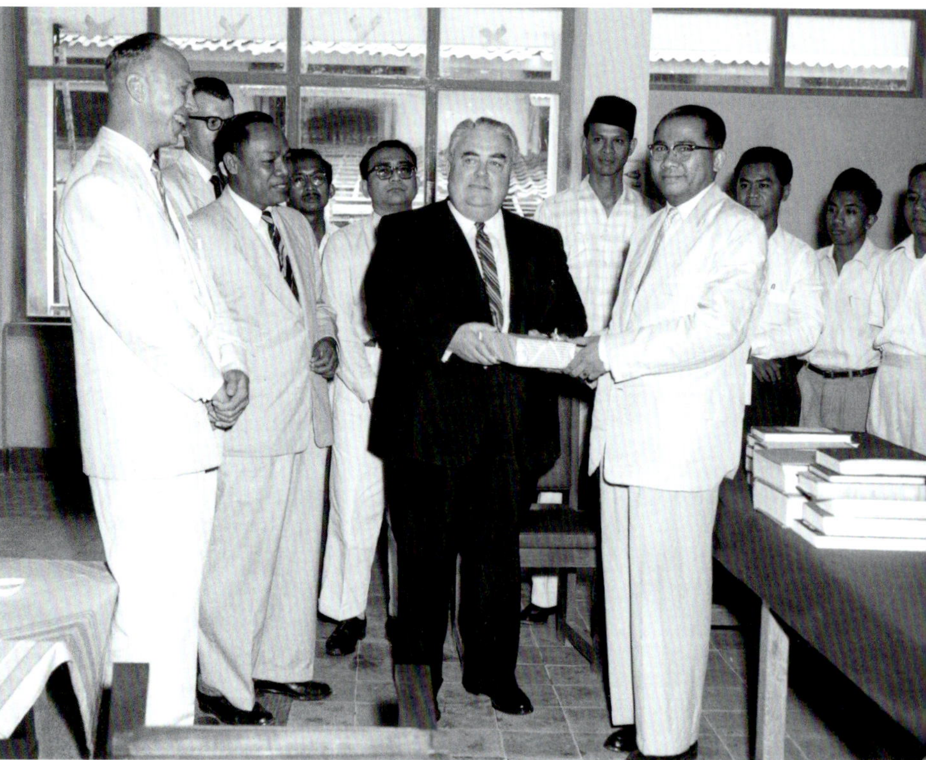

Herman Wells (*center*) presents library books to the Institute of Administration in Jakarta, Indonesia, February 1960. In a speech during the presentation, Wells remarked: "The library is the very heart of an educational project, and the development of a great and distinguished library in Administration is one of the important steps in providing assistance. It should become the working tool for students to use, as here they have the whole experience of the world at their fingertips. . . . I, on behalf of the Indiana University, present to you these books which are symbolic of the large number of volumes to follow." *IU Archives (P0055969).*

Indiana had a long history of working with universities in Indonesia, dating back to the late 1950s, when Herman B Wells visited the country.

In 2011, the Higher Education Leadership and Management project was funded by the United States Agency for International Development to provide technical assistance to Indonesian higher-education institutions.

Unfortunately, there were problems in administering the project. The National Institute of Administration had operated for eighteen months prior to the start of the relationship, and training programs, course content, curricula, and staffing were already in place. Thus, changing existing programs and the administrative structure was challenging. The 1963 final report concluded that it was difficult to measure specific achievements.[2]

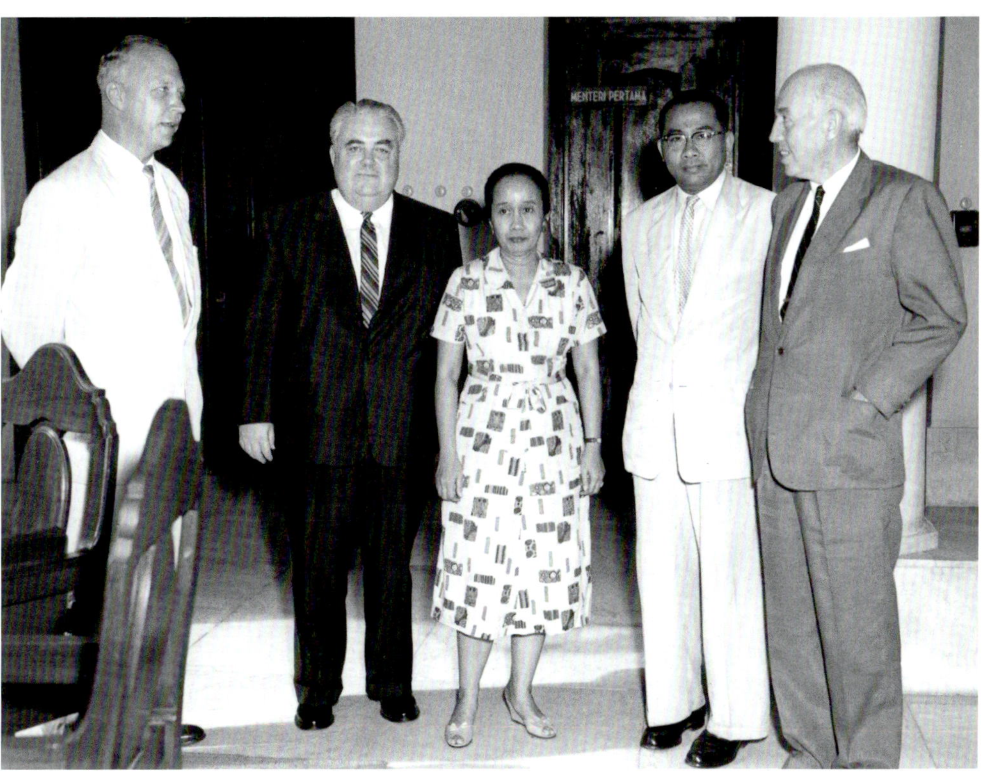

Herman Wells visits the Indiana University contract team in Jakarta, Indonesia, February 1960. *Left to right:* chief of party of the IU contract team Walter W. Mode, IU president Herman B Wells, director of the Office of the Prime Minister Maria Samtoso, director of the Institute of Administration Dr. Prajudi, and US ambassador Howard Jones. *IU Archives (P0055966).*

A major, and more successful, initiative started in 2011. The Higher Education Leadership and Management (HELM) project was funded by the United States Agency for International Development to provide technical assistance to Indonesian higher-education institutions; it focused on management, general administration and leadership, financial management, quality assurance, and collaboration.[3]

Overall funding for the HELM project was received by Chemonics, a Washington, DC–based organization that was founded in 1975 to work on issues of development, political instability, and health care.[4]

A part of HELM's funding was devoted to a postgraduate special initiative, and Indiana University, in an alliance with the University of Illinois and the Ohio State University, provided technical assistance for the development of four

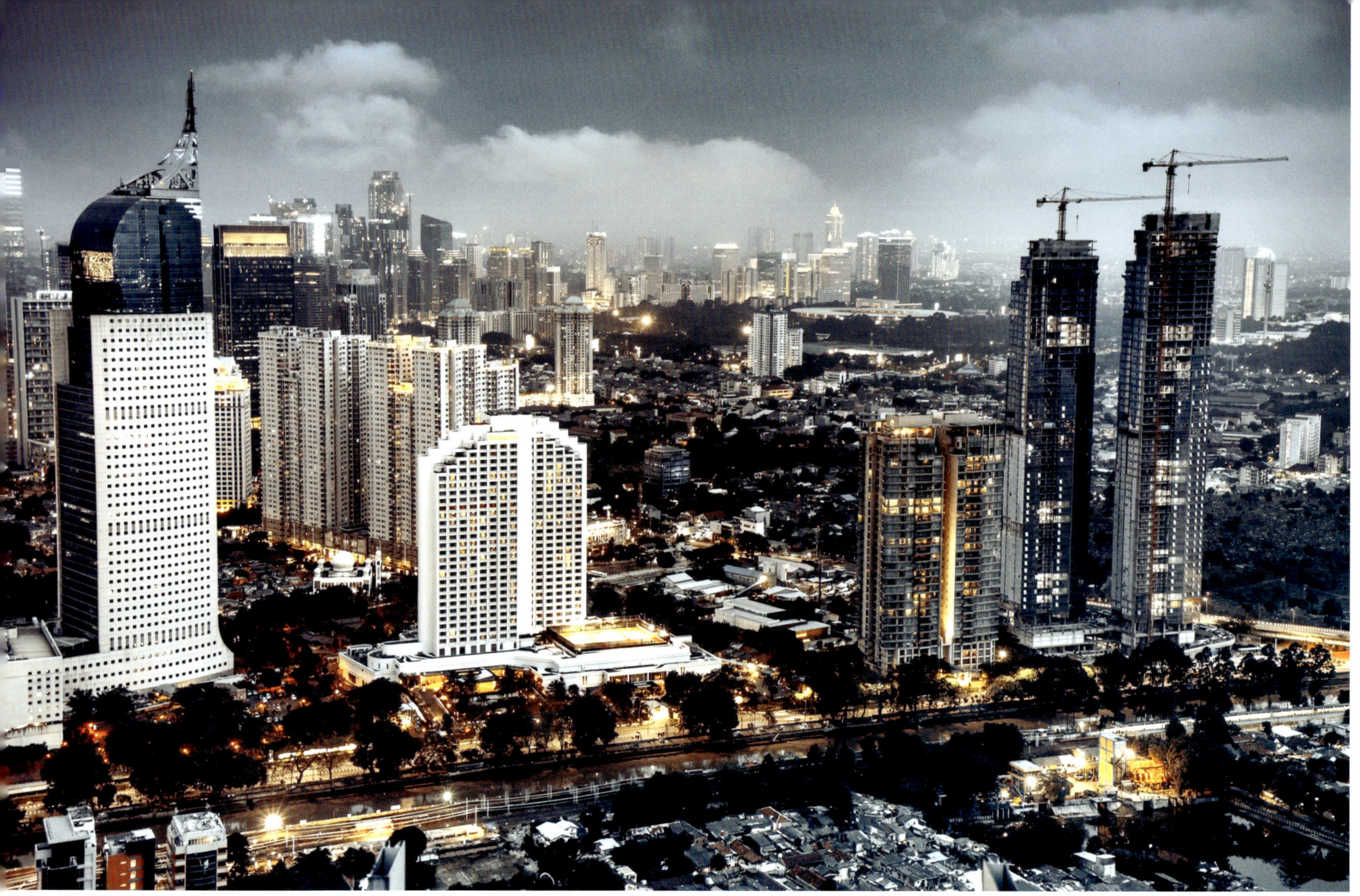

Jakarta, Indonesia, skyline, November 2016.
Photograph courtesy of iStock.v

graduate programs in the field of higher-education leadership and management at the Indonesia University of Education, Bogor Agricultural University, Gadjah Mada University, and Padang State University.[5]

IU had partnership agreements with these top-ranked universities and was eager to work with them to develop new opportunities. IU School of Education professor Margaret (Peg) Sutton played a key role in the project from the outset: "We were actually involved in the HELM project from the very beginning, and that made a difference. The project provided professional development and capacity building for fifteen universities, but we were contracted to create postgraduate programs in the field of higher education; none existed at the time."[6]

Sutton describes her deep interest in Asia and in Indonesia:

> In 1976, while I was a master's student in Vancouver at the University of British Columbia, I finished my thesis and went off to see the world. And when I did that, my destination was Indonesia; the culture appealed to me. I spent about four years in Asia before pursuing doctoral work in the field I'm in. At the point I did that—actually, when I started my doctoral studies, I had this fascination with Francophone West Africa, and I spoke some French. In my first year, I went to see my adviser, Hans Weiler, and said, "I would really like to do my dissertation research in West Africa," where he had also worked, and he said, "Why don't you start with a place you do know?" So Indonesia was the place, and I was very interested as an academic in how intellectual activities were influenced by local culture. So I did my dissertation research in Indonesia, and therefore, when I left academe to work in development, my connections within Indonesia already existed.[7]

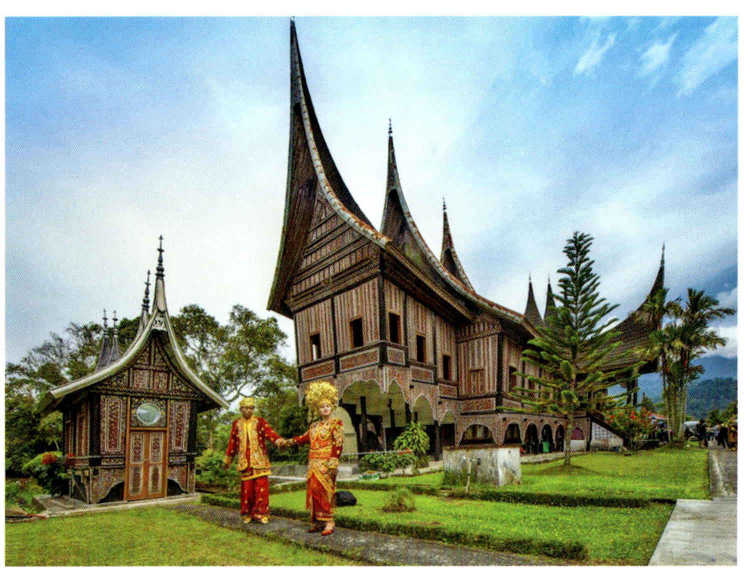

Traditional house in West Sumatra, Indonesia.
Photograph courtesy of Afriva Khaidir.

The HELM project's focus on teacher training, education administration, and management programs was important because, although the country had several programs in education management, almost all of them focused on primary and secondary education. The four universities had been identified by the Indonesian Ministry of Education Directorate General of Higher Education (DIKTI) for strengthening its postgraduate programs. The goal was to increase the understanding and application of effective university leadership, management, and decision making among university administrators. It also

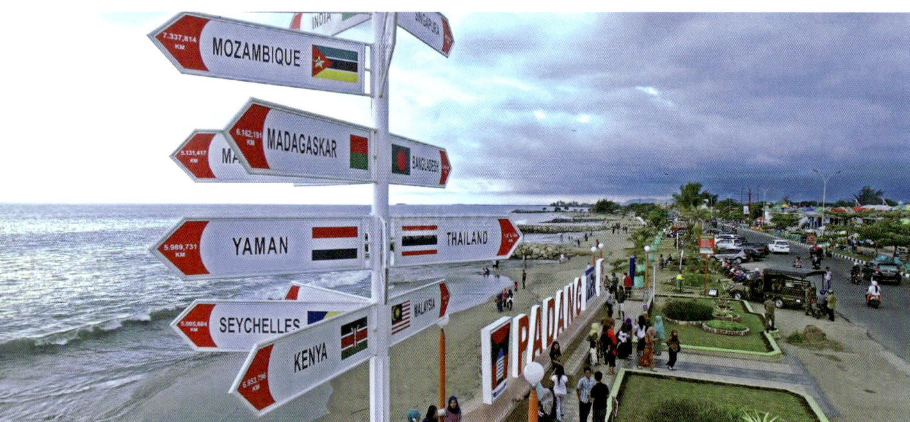

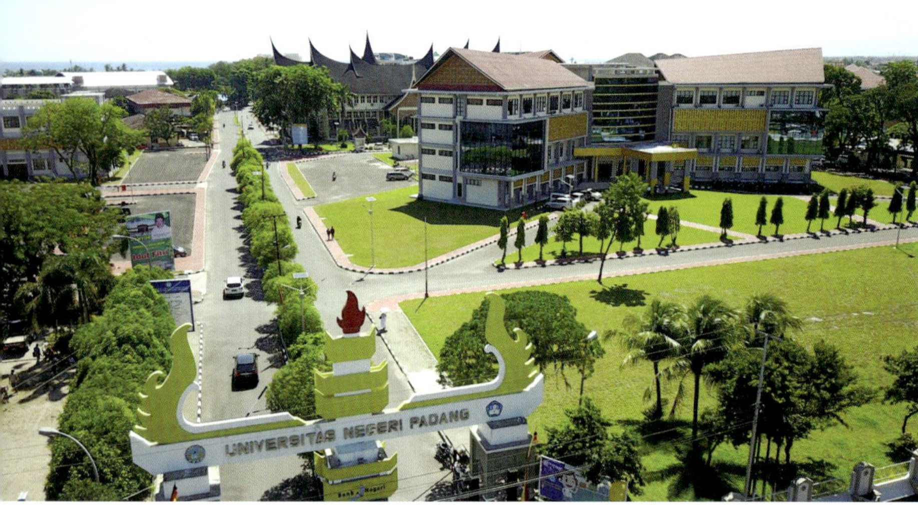

Top, The beach at Padang, Indonesia. *Photograph courtesy of Afriva Khaidir.*

Above, The grounds of Padang State University in West Sumatra, Indonesia. *Photograph courtesy of Afriva Khaidir.*

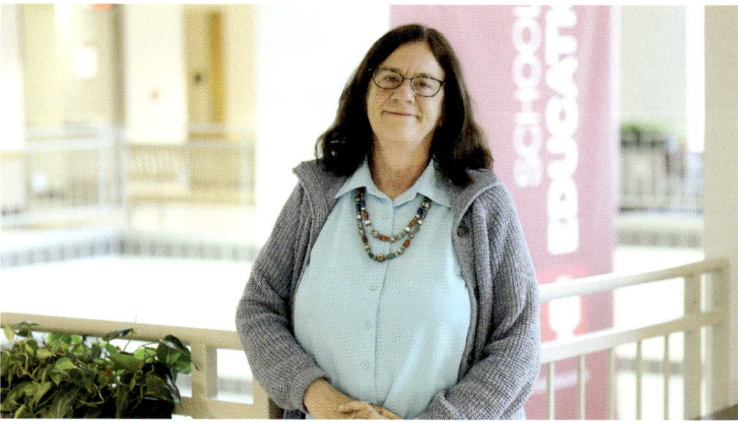

Indiana University faculty member Margaret (Peg) Sutton. *Photograph courtesy of Indiana University.*

set out to build capacity for applied research for DIKTI and the higher-education community on issues of faculty governance, financial management, quality assurance, and workforce development. The background report for the project outlined the opportunities and challenges facing implementation. In particular, the study found:

> a very weak scientific knowledge base on higher education in Indonesia. The team was unable to identify a single person holding a degree in the field of higher education, nor a single research center, journal or program focused on scholarly or scientific knowledge of Indonesian higher education. As a consequence, the higher education focused content of the programs is rather ad hoc, deriving from personal experience. Such information is valuable and, as courses are developed, becomes recorded as case study material. It is not, however, a substitute for knowledge of Indonesian higher education that is validated through careful forms of research.[8]

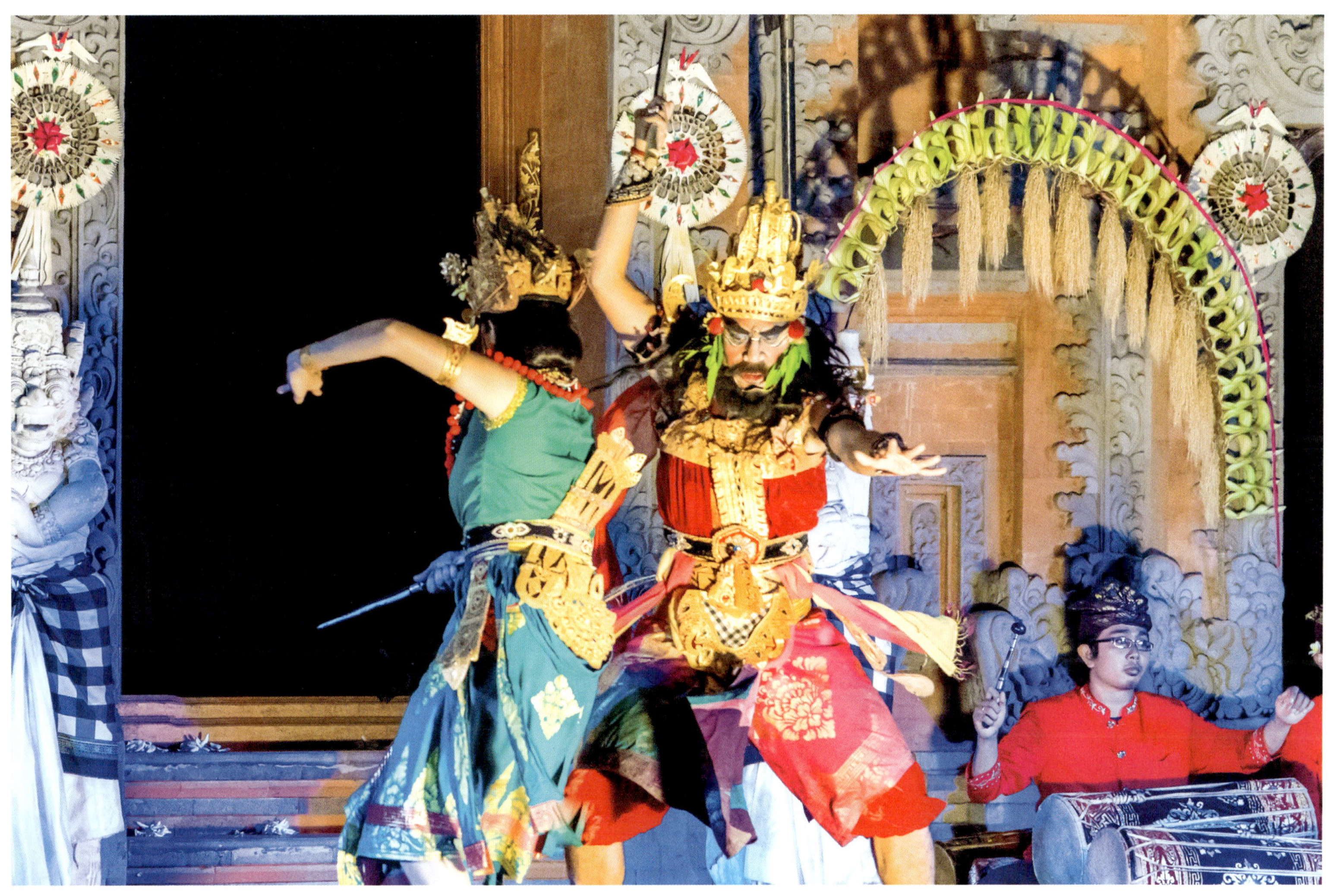

Traditional Balinese dancers performing Ramayana Ballet, a traditional Hindu story at Puri Saren Palace (or Ubud Royal Palace) in Ubud, Bali, Indonesia. May 2017.
Photograph courtesy of iStock.

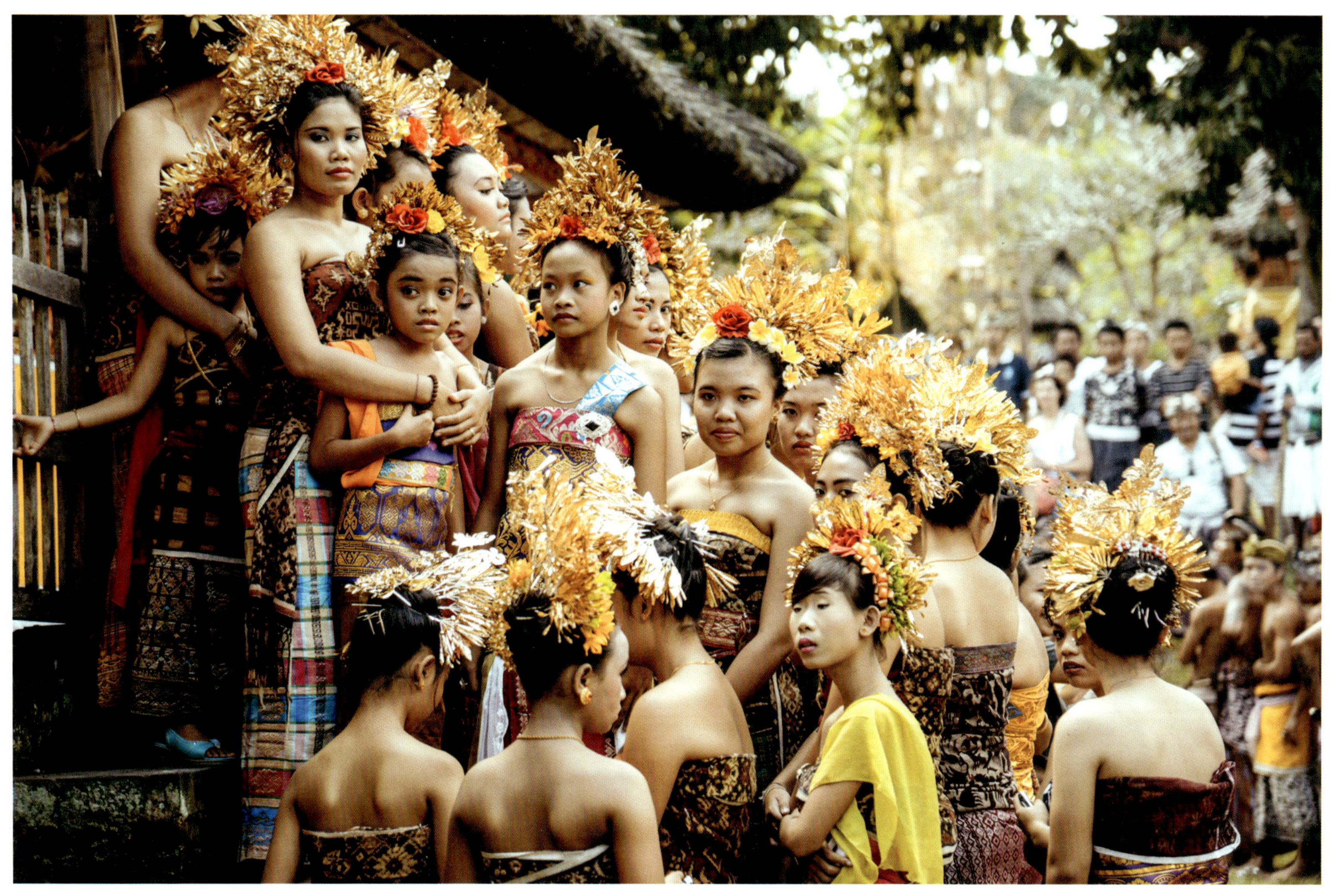

Dancers in traditional costumes dance in a street parade at an art and culture festival, Bali, Indonesia, July 2013.
Photograph courtesy of iStock.

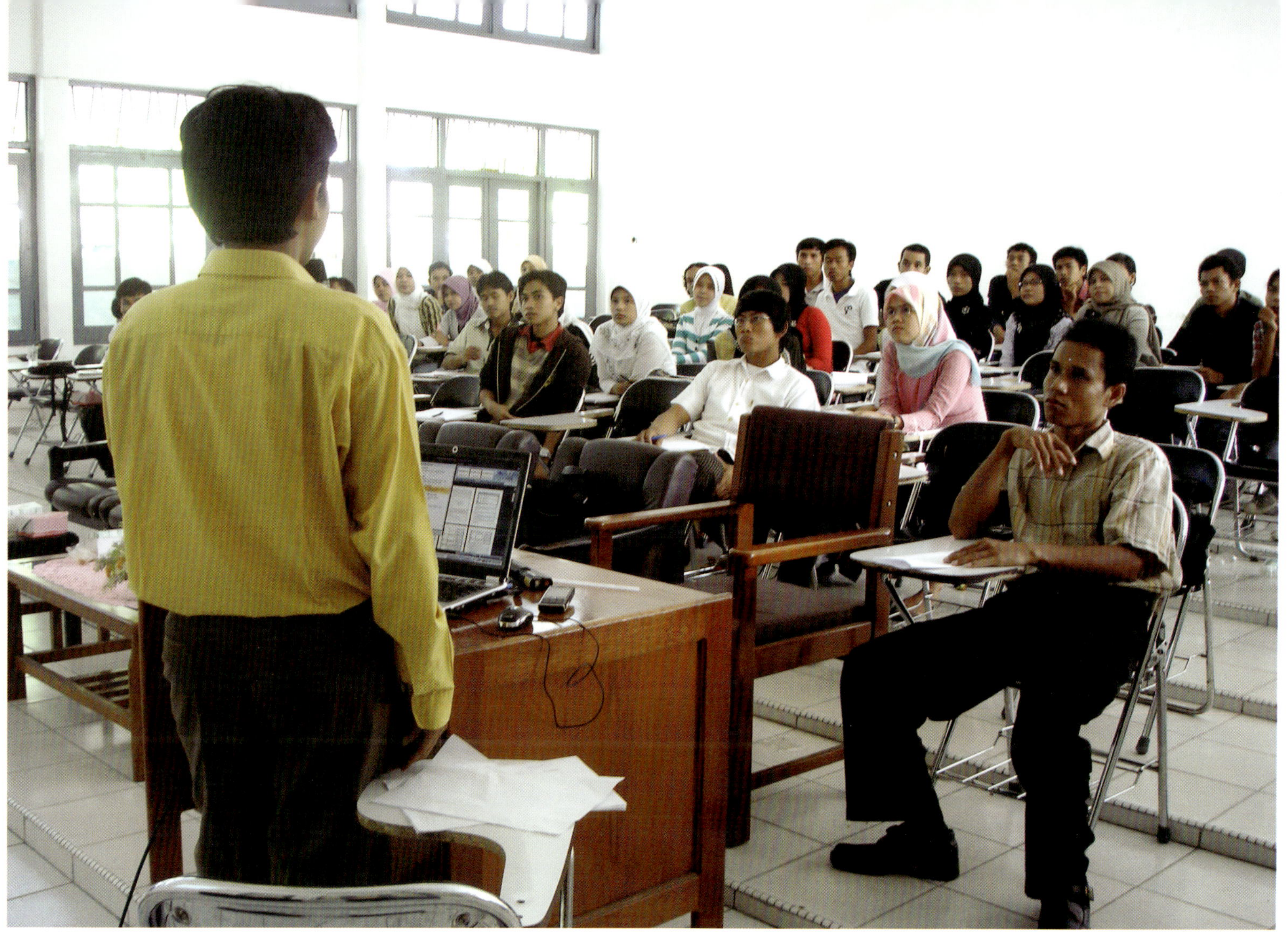

Inside a classroom at the Padang State University, West Sumatra, Indonesia.
Photograph courtesy of Afriva Khaidir.

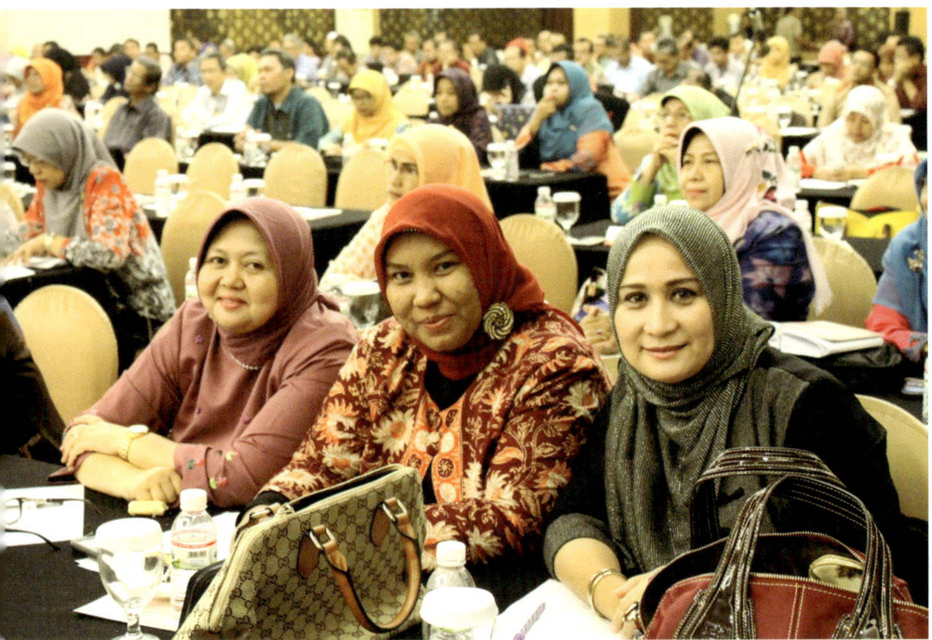

Lecturers at the Padang State University, West Sumatra, Indonesia. *Photograph courtesy of Afriva Khaidir.*

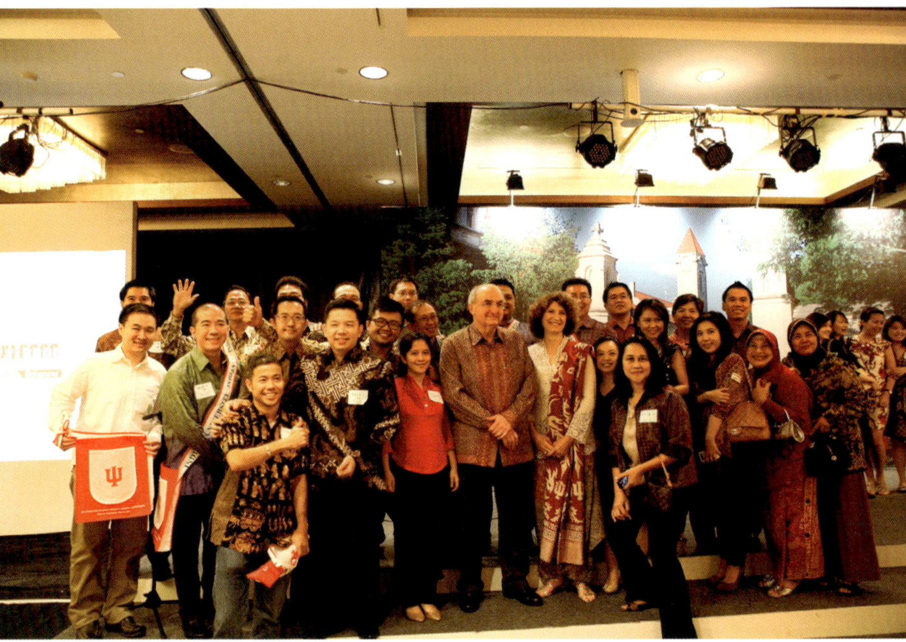

Indiana University president Michael McRobbie and first lady Laurie Burns McRobbie (*center*) with members of the Jakarta chapter of the IU Alumni Association, May 2012. *Photograph courtesy of Indiana University.*

Facing, Indiana University president Michael McRobbie (*left*) presents Henry Alex Tilaar with the Thomas Hart Benton Mural Medallion and certificate, May, 2012. The medal recognizes individuals who are shining examples of the values of IU and the universal academic community. Tilaar is a professor emeritus at State University of Jakarta and Universitas Indonesia and director of the Institution of Management. *Photograph courtesy of Indiana University.*

The study concluded that "there is a need for two forms of graduate level education for academic leadership: (1) degree programs for some, to establish a foundation for scientific study of Indonesian higher education, and (2) short-term leadership programs for teaching staff that are selected by peers into structural leadership positions."[9]

Kay Ikranagara, who had been on the staff of IU's Center for International Education and Development Assistance for several years, was working in Indonesia, where she played a

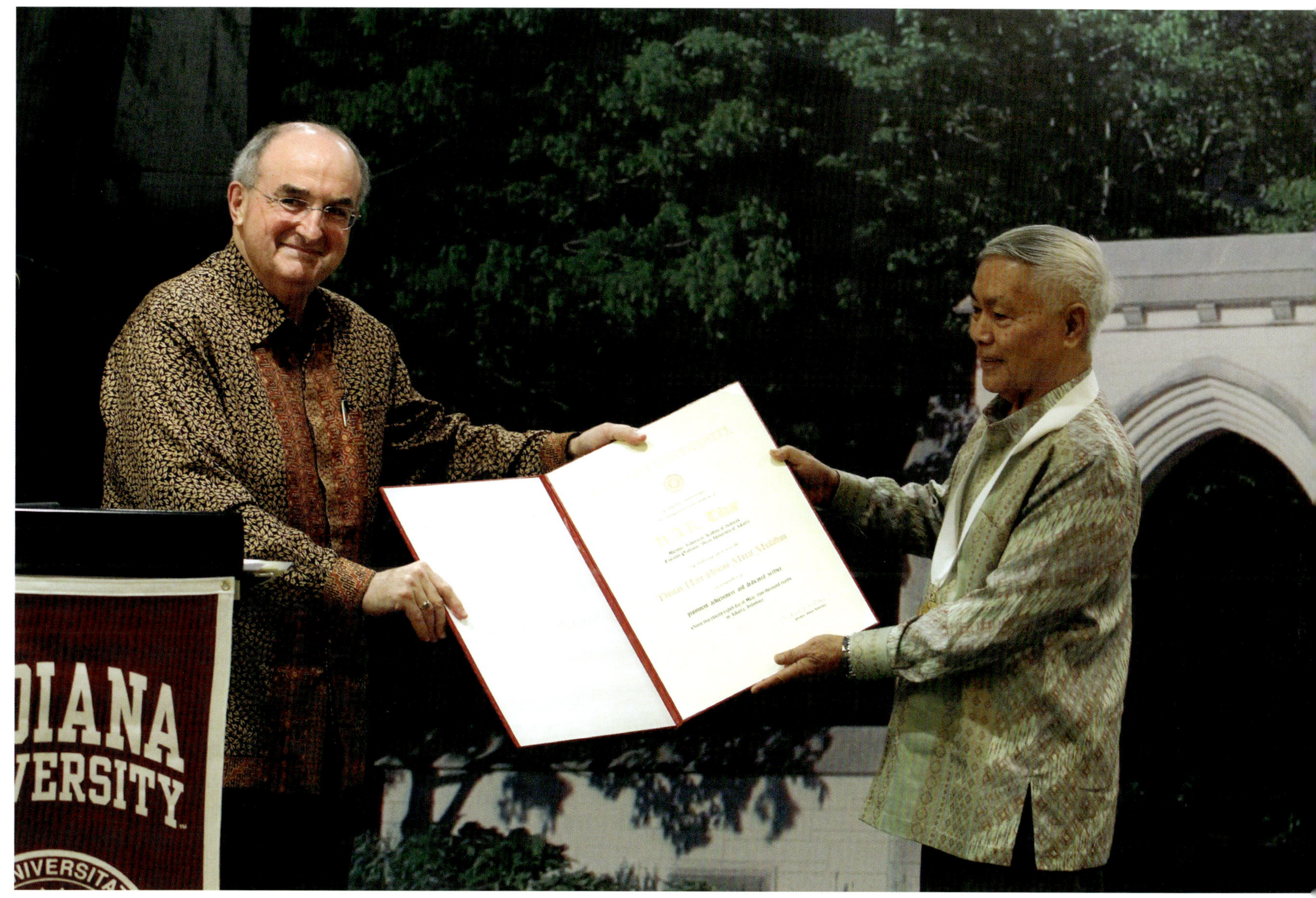
DIANA
VERSITY

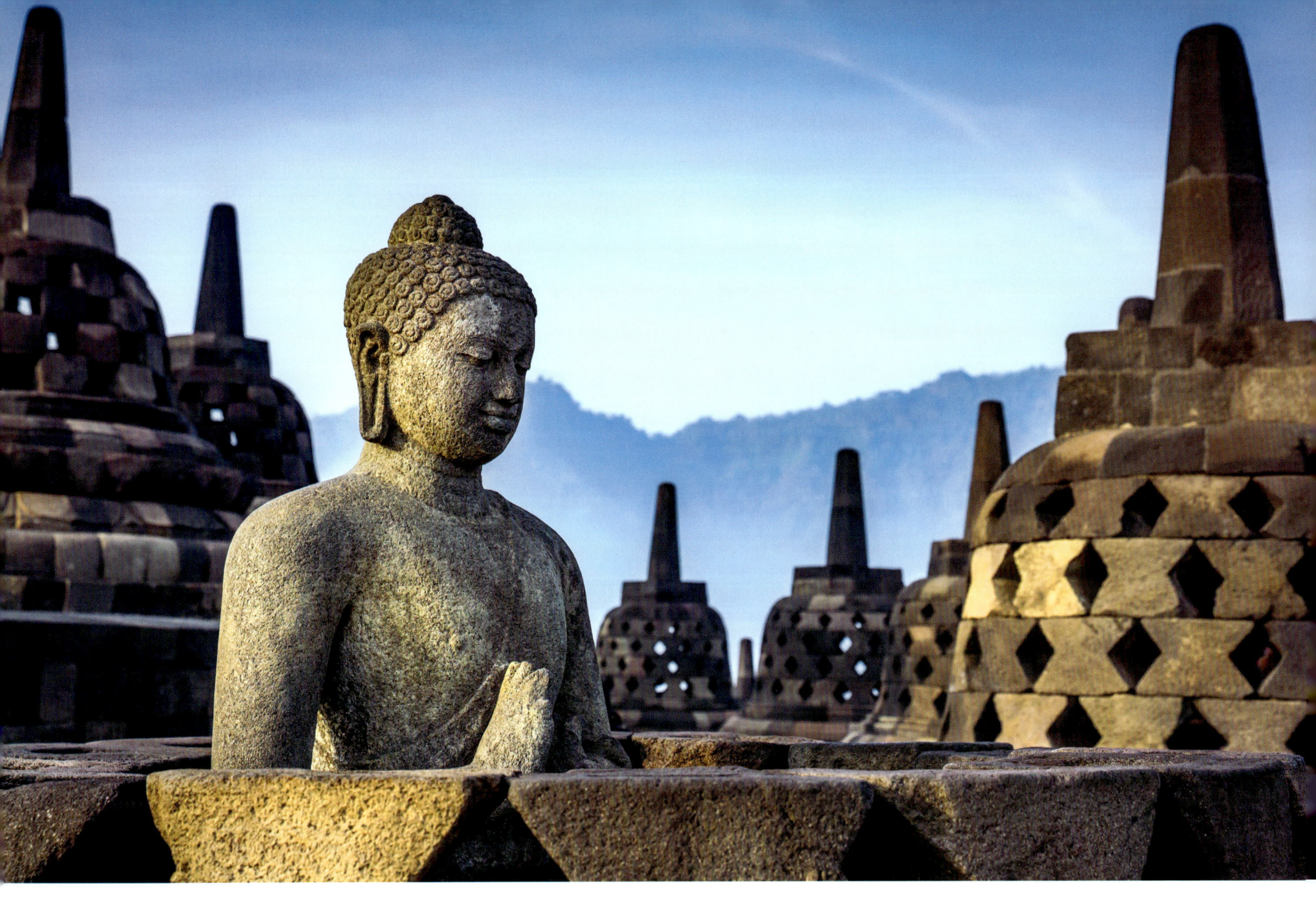

Buddha statue in Borobudur Temple, Java, Indonesia, August 2016.
Photograph courtesy of iStock.

key role in developing postgraduate programs in the field of higher education under the HELM project. She joined the staff of HELM when it started in 2012, and she made initial hiring recommendations and became a liaison with officials at the Ministry of Education. She alerted colleagues at IU about the forthcoming project and advised Charles Reafsnyder and others on whom to approach if there was interest in the idea.[10]

The HELM project was significant not only for the field of higher education. Sutton sums up its wider relevance: "When I was there on my sabbatical in the early 2000s, after democratization, it was stunning to see how vibrant this made the universities. So there was a bureaucracy, but Indonesia is a leader of reformist Islam. There were people who were concerned about the same things we're facing in higher education—bringing in marginalized student populations and operating at a high quality."[11]

Compared with IU's involvement in the 1960s, the HELM project was very successful and had a deep bilateral impact. In the end, according to Sutton, "The ways in which Indonesians were addressing issues taught us a great deal."[12]

In 2012, IU president Michael McRobbie signed the agreement formally instituting this partnership. It was the first time that an IU president had been to Indonesia since the visit of Herman Wells.[13]

In May 2015, McRobbie delivered the keynote address at the Symposium on Establishment of the Field of Higher Education Leadership and Management in Bogor, Indonesia. This symposium was held concurrently with a meeting of the Indonesian Council of State Rectors. The topic of McRobbie's speech was "Higher Education Leadership and Management: Leading for Change—Innovation and Research.[14] During this visit, McRobbie also participated in the IU Asia-Pacific Alumni Conference in Bali. At the reunion of nearly three hundred Asia-Pacific Indiana University alums, he recognized the active Indonesian chapter based in Jakarta and thanked it for organizing and hosting the reunion.

18 | INDIANA UNIVERSITY *in* South Sudan

At the time when Indiana University began activities in the South Sudan, the region had been engaged in wars with the larger country of Sudan for more than forty years.

Facing, Children of South Sudan practice a dance routine for the performance at the football match between South Sudan and Kenya during the independence celebrations of South Sudan, July 2011. *UN Photo/Paul Banks.*

At the time when Indiana University began activities in South Sudan, the region had been engaged in wars with the larger country of Sudan for more than forty years. The education system had been devastated, a majority of school-age children were not being educated, and very few women were literate. In 2012, the United States Agency for International Development sought to actively address these serious problems through the South Sudan Higher Education Initiative for Equity and Leadership Development.[1]

The overall award was made to the organization Higher Education for Development in partnership with Indiana University, Virginia Polytechnic Institute and State University, the University of Juba, Upper Nile University, and the South Sudan Ministry of Higher Education. Higher Education for Development managed such competitive projects in coordination with the American Council on Education, the American Association of Community Colleges, the American Association of State Colleges and Universities, the Association of American Universities, the Association of Public and Land-grant Universities, and the National Association of Independent Colleges and Universities. IU's role was to promote the empowerment of women in South Sudan by improving their access to secondary and higher education. Julia Duany, who was born in South Sudan, led the in-country administration of the project. Duany, her husband, Wal, and her family had fled to the United States when civil war

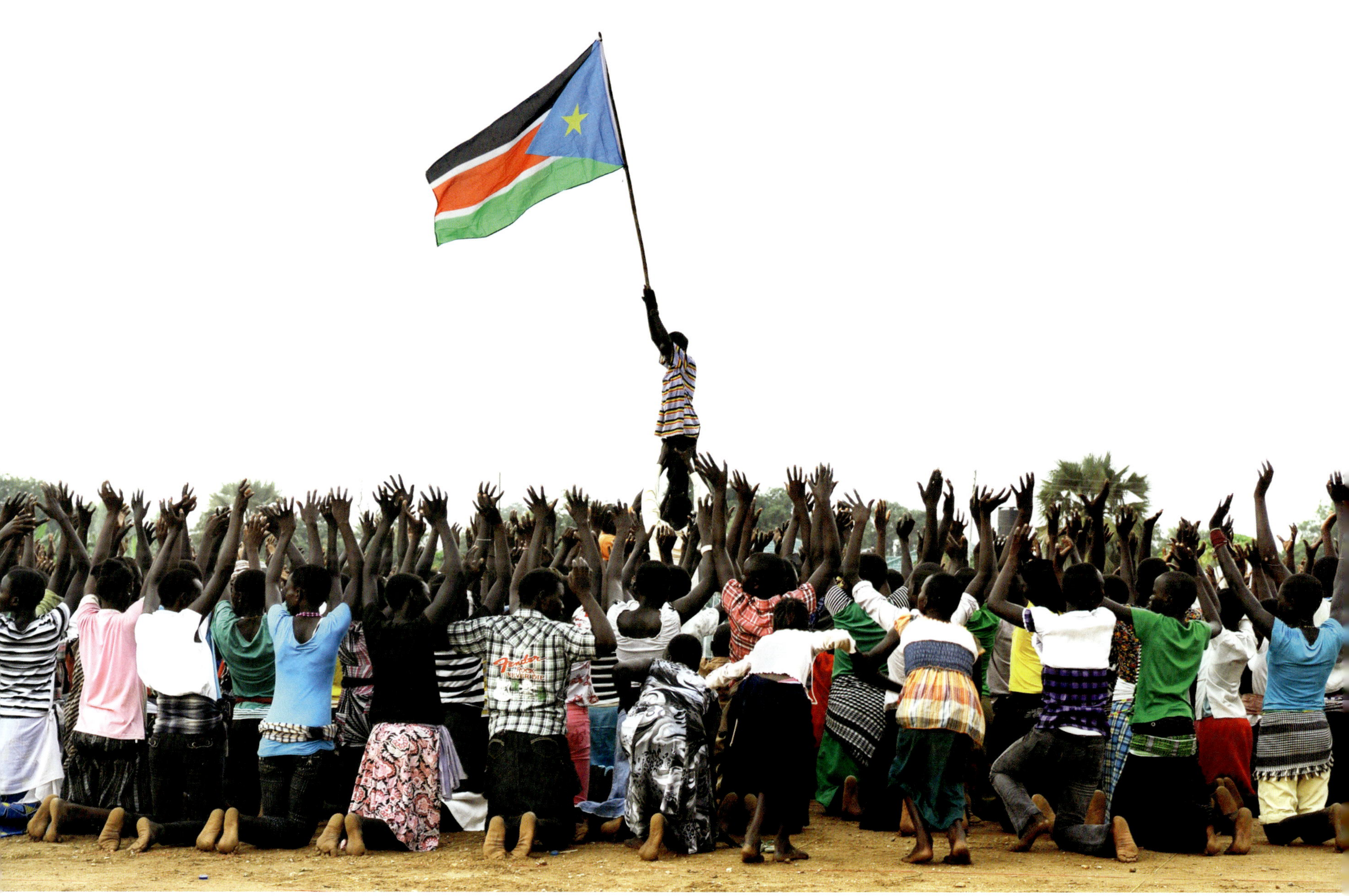

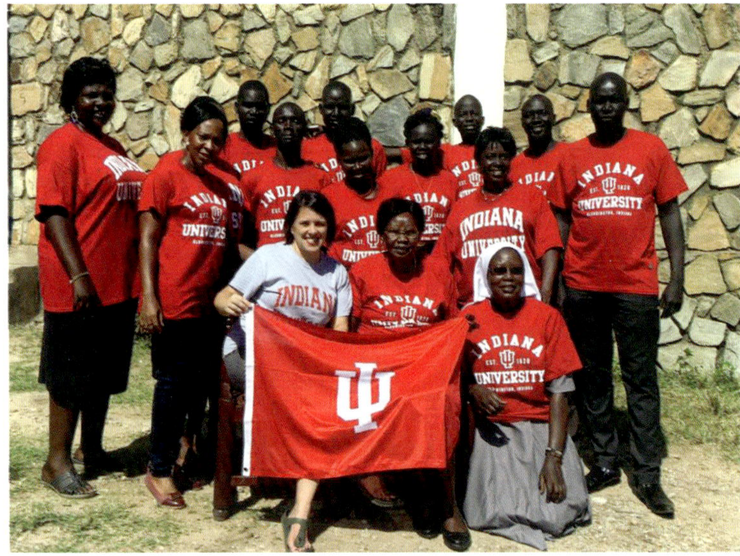

Center for International Education, Development, and Research South Sudan project manager Arlene Benitez (*front left*) and students in the USAID-funded program, 2017, Juba, South Sudan.
Photograph courtesy of Indiana University.

broke out in 1984. Subsequently, she earned her bachelor's, master's, and PhD degrees from the IU School of Education, and her husband completed a joint doctorate in the School of Public and Environmental Affairs and political science. After returning to South Sudan in 2006, Duany was appointed undersecretary for parliamentary affairs; her duties included finding ways to bring women into parliamentary leadership roles. Duany saw education as "the soul of whoever is going to become a leader; in this program, not only will we work with the universities, we will also work with the secondary schools and have programs that can enlighten young women and help them finish their education. They have to seek more capacity-building programs so that they can become leaders of tomorrow."[2]

In the United States, the project was administered through the Center for International Education, Development and Research (CIEDR) in the IU School of Education, which was directed by Terrence (Terry) Mason, professor of curriculum and instruction. CIEDR staff member Arlene Benitez, managed project operations. Initially, the project made good progress; however, intense new conflict in South Sudan in December 2012 made it impossible to fully implement the project.

As Mason explains, "With the conflict that broke out, it became evident that that plan was not going to come to fruition at all. I thought the project was over. I thought USAID would find other ways to spend that money and that we would not be able to continue."[3] However, Mason and his staff began considering other ways to reach the goals of the program. "We decided that if we can't go to South Sudan, South Sudan can come here."[4]

The project, originally designed to send IU faculty and others to South Sudan, shifted focus to become one that brought participants to the United States. Fourteen women, professionals in education, were selected to represent diverse geographic and ethnic areas of South Sudan. Before coming to IU at the beginning of the 2014–2015 academic year, the participants attended classes in Kampala, Uganda, to prepare for study in Bloomington. At IU, they completed master's degrees in education. Mason notes, "We were able to identify fourteen courageous and brilliant women from South Sudan who

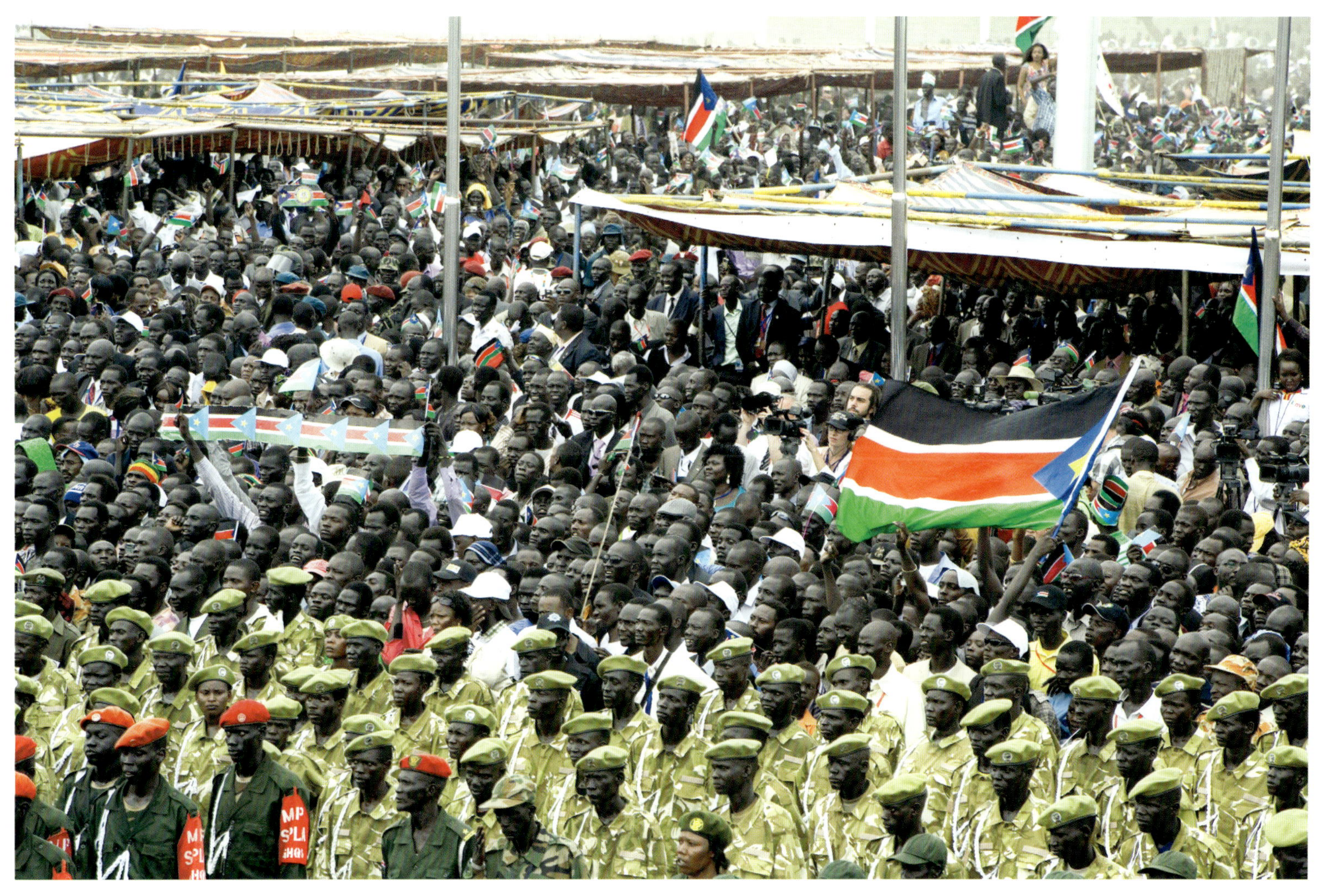

Independence ceremony, Republic of South Sudan, July 2011.
UN Photo/Eskinder Debebe.

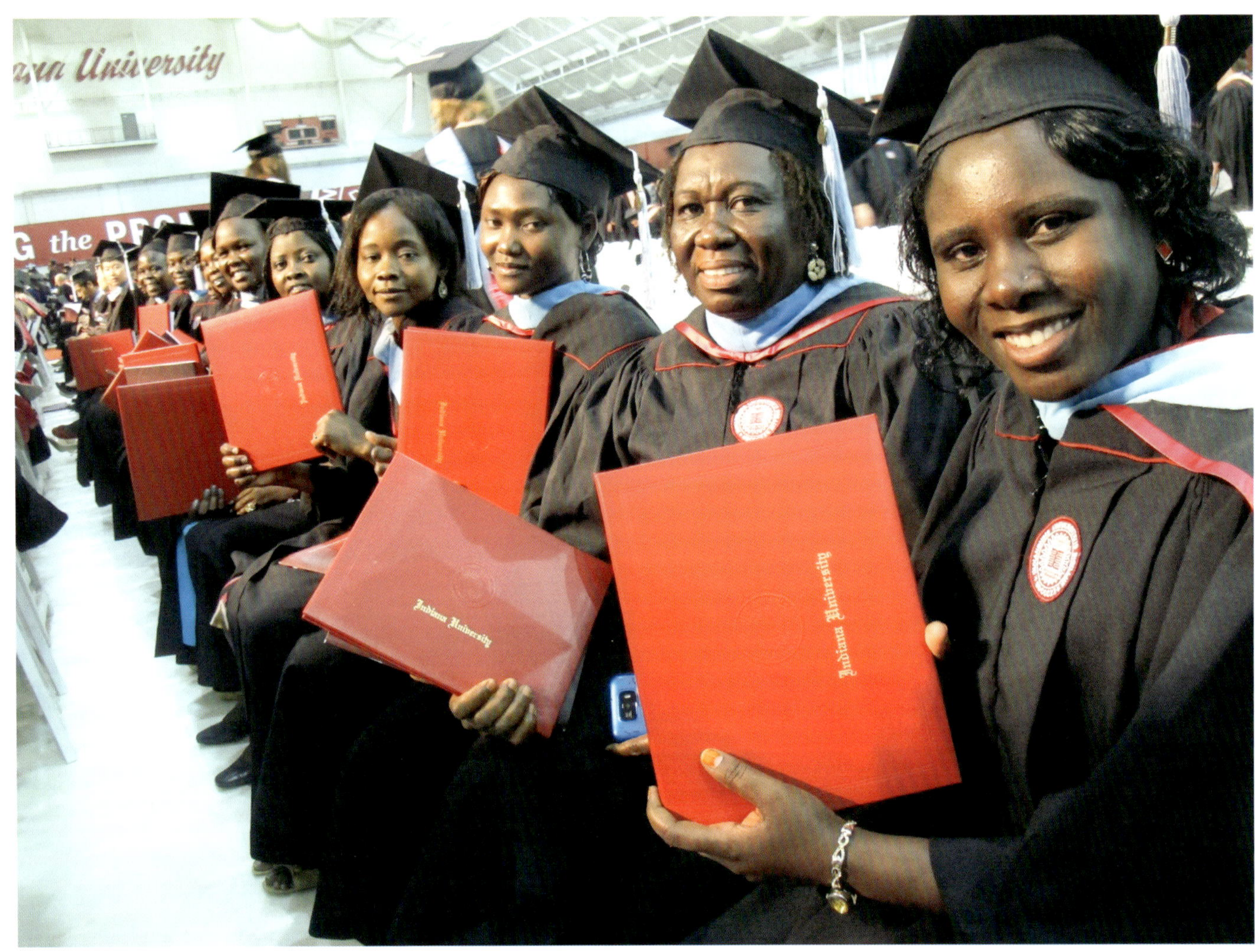

Graduates from South Sudan at commencement ceremony in Bloomington, Indiana, 2015.
Photograph courtesy of Indiana University.

Facing, People prepare plastic containers to collect water in a refugee camp, Juba, South Sudan, February 2012.
Photograph courtesy of iStock.

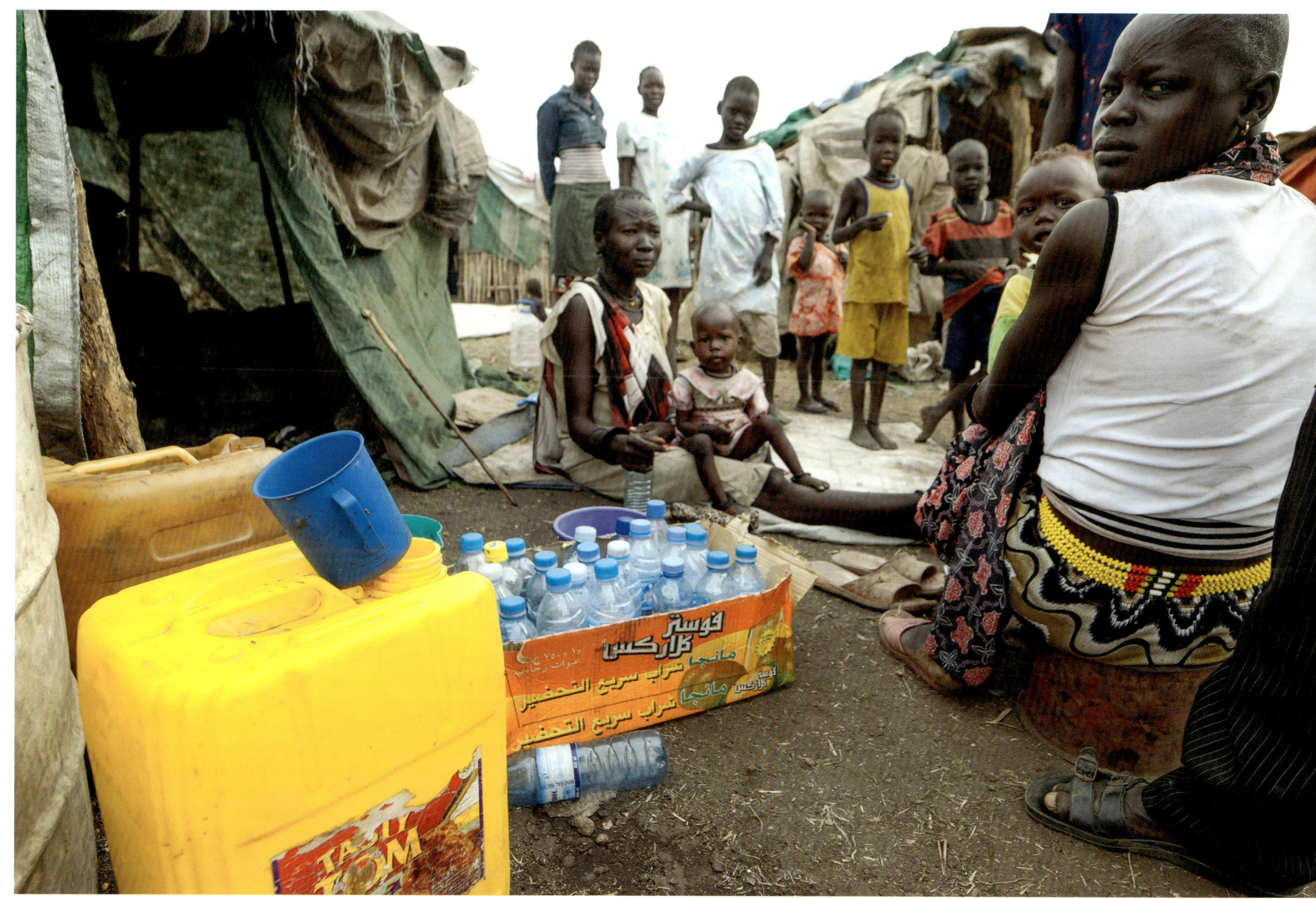
فوستر كلاركس
مانجا
شراب سريع التحضير
مانجا شراب سريع التحضير

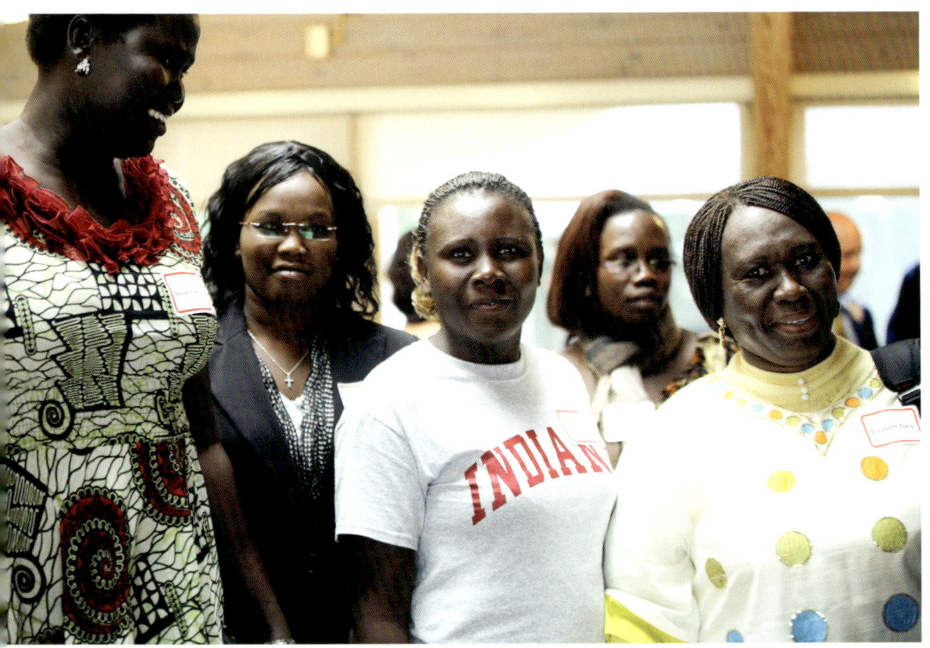

South Sudan scholars during a reception at Indiana University Bloomington. *Left to right:* Nyawir Mayen, Viola Abango, Akwero Obwoya, and Elizabeth Elario. All were seeking a master's in secondary education. *Photograph courtesy of Indiana University.*

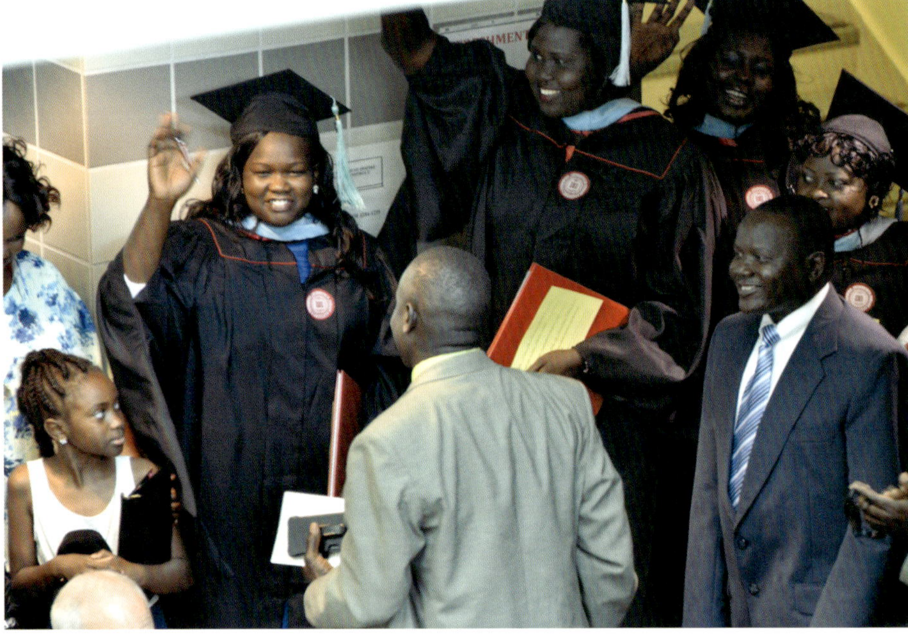

Members of the first graduating cohort celebrate at commencement, 2015, Bloomington, Indiana. *Photograph courtesy of Indiana University.*

qualified to come and study for a master's degree. They will go back and change the life of South Sudan."[5]

Another IU unit had also played an active role in South Sudan. The IU Center for Constitutional Democracy advised the South Sudan Ministry of Parliamentary Affairs during the country's transitional constitution drafting process and supported the government during next stage, the permanent constitution drafting process. Under the leadership of the executive director, David C. Williams (John S. Hastings Professor of Law and executive director of the center), and Susan H. Williams (Walter W. Foskett Professor and center director), the center had a reputation for activities in other parts of the world. The staff provided guidelines on how law contributed to democratic institutions, practices, and cultural evolution.

In summer 2011, center personnel traveled to South Sudan to advise the legislative committee overseeing the drafting

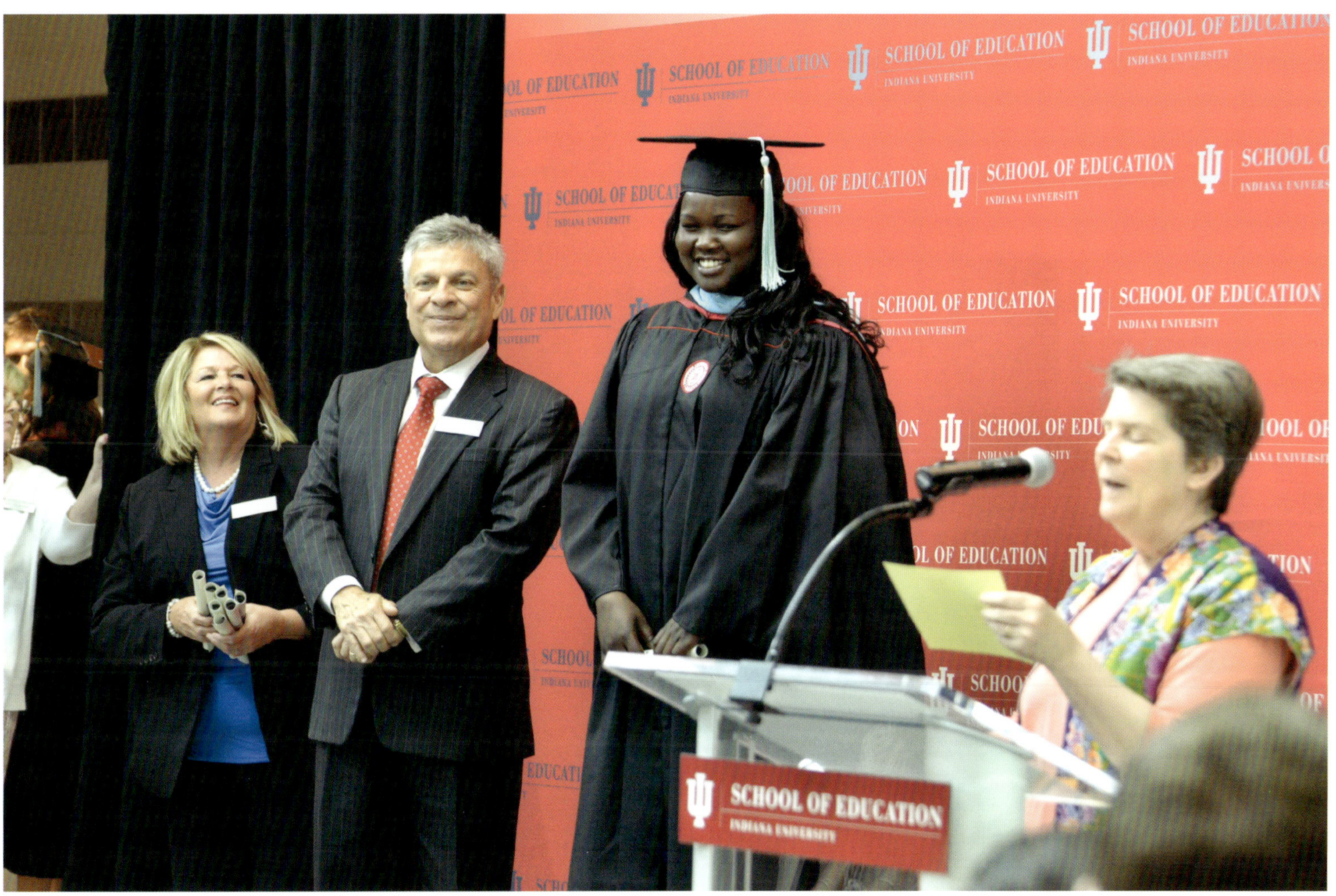

Elizabeth Boling (*right*), interim executive associate dean of the School of Education, announces graduate Viola Abango as then dean Gerardo Gonzalez looks on from the platform.

Photograph courtesy Indiana University.

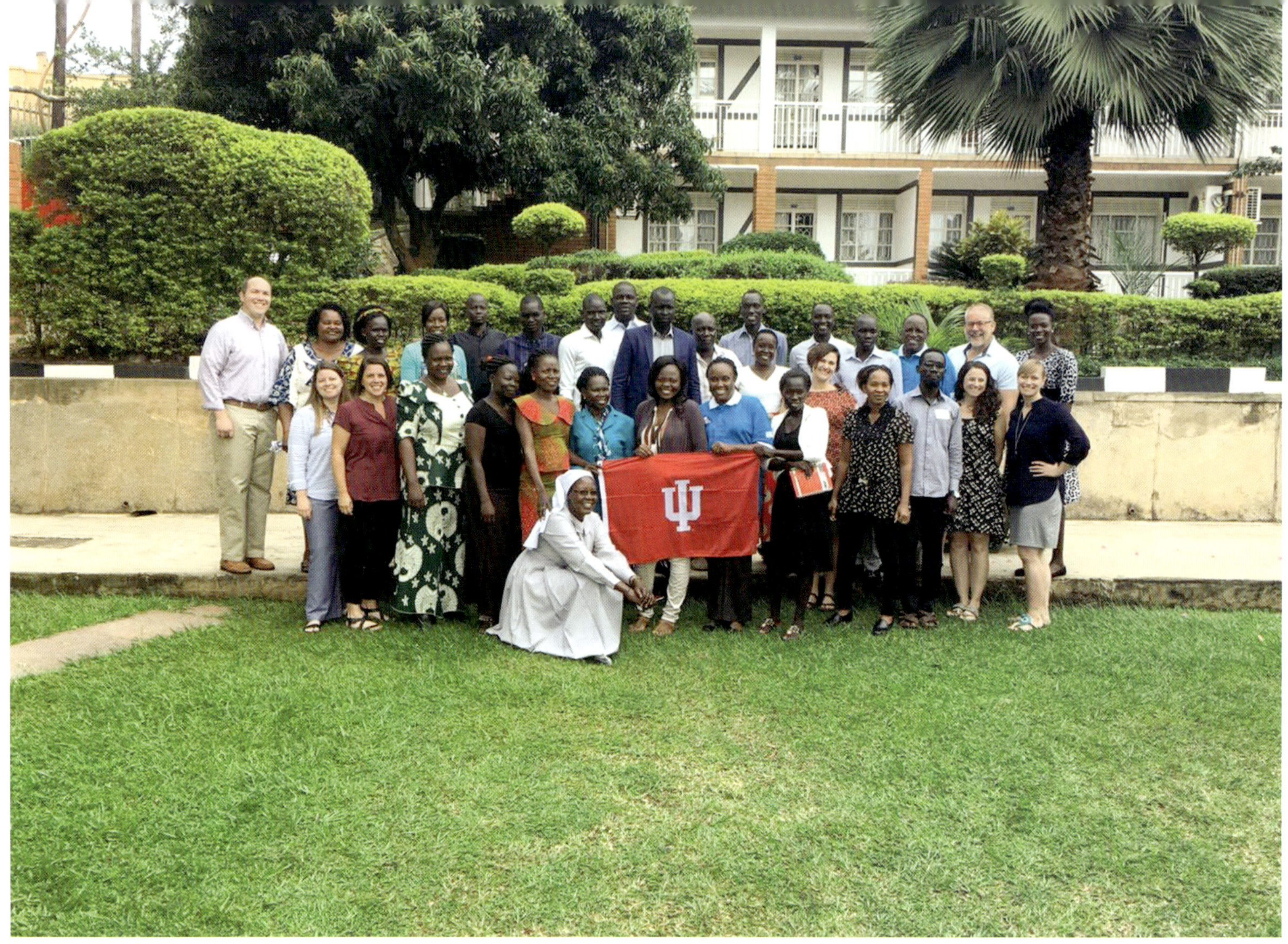

Students in the program and staff from Indiana University's Center for International Education, Development, and Research office in Uganda.
Photograph courtesy of Indiana University.

process for the transitional constitution. After meeting with various stakeholders, such as government officials and political party leaders, the center drafted a memorandum that provided comments on the transitional constitution, addressing issues related to the concentration of executive power. The memorandum was circulated to the Ministry of Parliamentary Affairs and to the leadership of the parliament. It also met with the speaker and legal counsel to discuss the issues raised in the memorandum.[6]

A Speakers' Forum convened in June 2011, bringing together members of state legislatures and the Ministry of Parliamentary Affairs at state level to discuss governance during the transitional period. Center personnel worked with the Directorate of Legislative Affairs to convene the forum and report on it and worked with individual state legislators as they were thinking through their recommendations for the transitional constitution. A final report of the forum's proceedings and recommendations was circulated to the state legislators and government officials in Juba.

We were able to identify fourteen courageous and brilliant women from South Sudan who qualified to come and study for a master's degree. They will go back and change the life of South Sudan.

—Terry Mason

The process for writing the permanent constitution formally began in January 2012. Center personnel were asked by the South Sudanese Ministry of Parliamentary Affairs to write a white paper on various constitutional aspects of governance after the transitional period in order to inform their decision making. In January 2014, in an attempt to prevent the fragile cease-fire from breaking and to take steps toward appeasing all of South Sudan's conflicting parties, the center was asked by a group of civil society organization leaders to produce a memo of guiding principles for the cease-fire and constitutional reform process. The memo was drafted in February 2014 and contains an explanation of the roots of the conflict, guidelines for the creation of an interim government, resource management in the interim period, and a description of the constitutional reform process during the interim period.

The center was also invited on several occasions to meet and work with women's organizations in South Sudan to help them advocate effectively for gender equity.[7]

19 | INDIANA UNIVERSITY *in* Palestine

In 2015, when world concern and interest was on Palestine, the US Department of State awarded Indiana University a grant to improve the lives of entrepreneurs and to support Palestinian economic development.

In 2015, when world concern and interest was on Palestine, the US Department of State awarded Indiana University a grant to improve the lives of entrepreneurs and to support Palestinian economic development. Under the Middle East Partnership Initiative, the three-year program to Indiana University and Bethlehem University, targeted Bethlehem, East Jerusalem, and the southern region of the West Bank. According to LaVonn Schlegel, executive director of the Institute for International Business at IU's Kelley School of Business, "The Palestinian Territories face continuing economic challenges arising from stagnation of economic growth as well as many political and governing restrictions that limit major new investments. Years of political instability have created a resilient and creative Palestinian community made up of well-educated young people who are increasingly turning to entrepreneurship to create their own job opportunities and stable employment."[1]

The goal for the Young Entrepreneurship Livelihood Program was to improve Palestinian economic development by helping young entrepreneurs build successful businesses. The grant provided consulting services to small businesses in Bethlehem and other cities in the southern region of the West Bank. With the advice of faculty from both universities, Kelley Direct Online MBA and Bethlehem University business students formed teams to help the

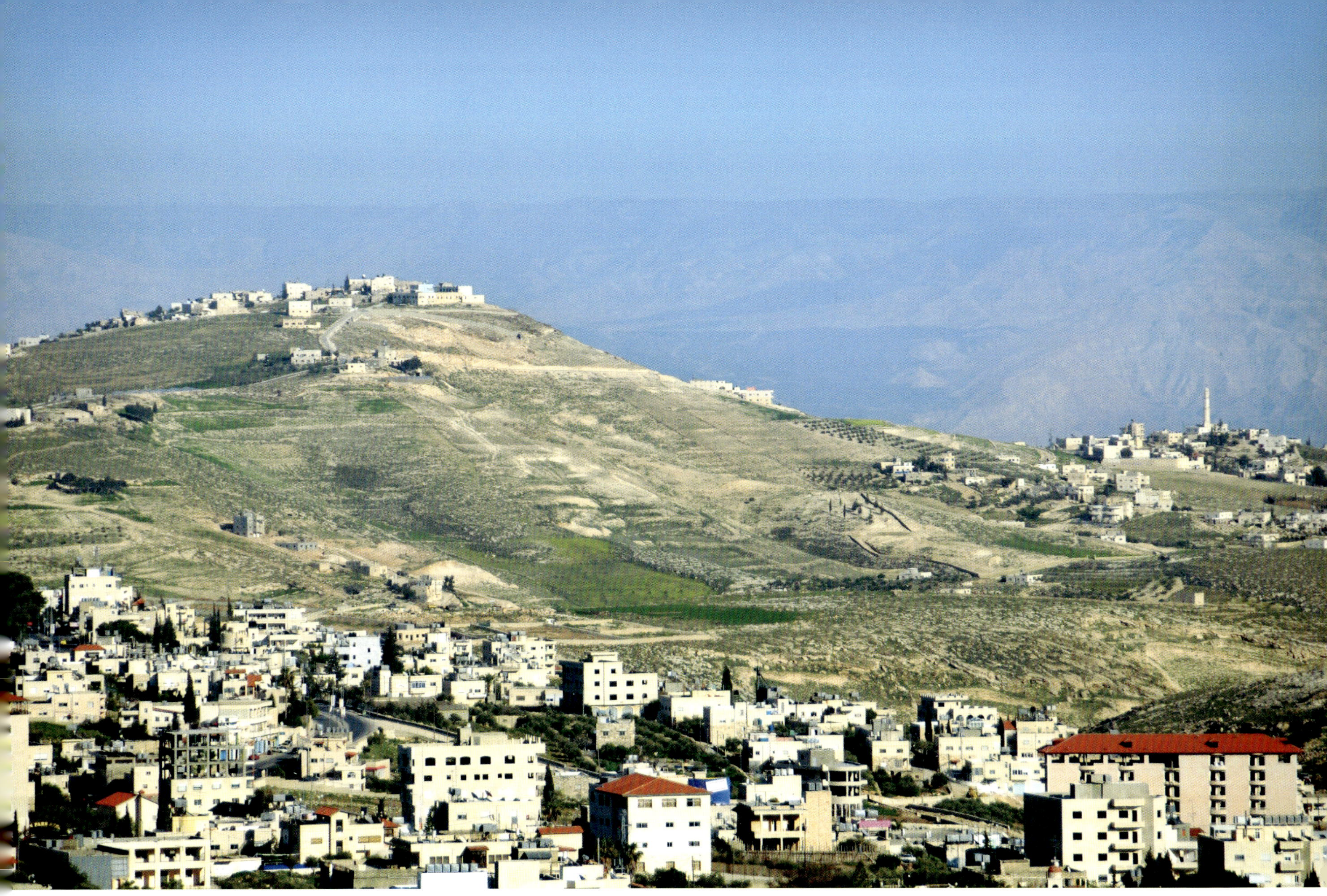

Facing, Bethlehem, West Bank.
Photograph courtesy of iStock.

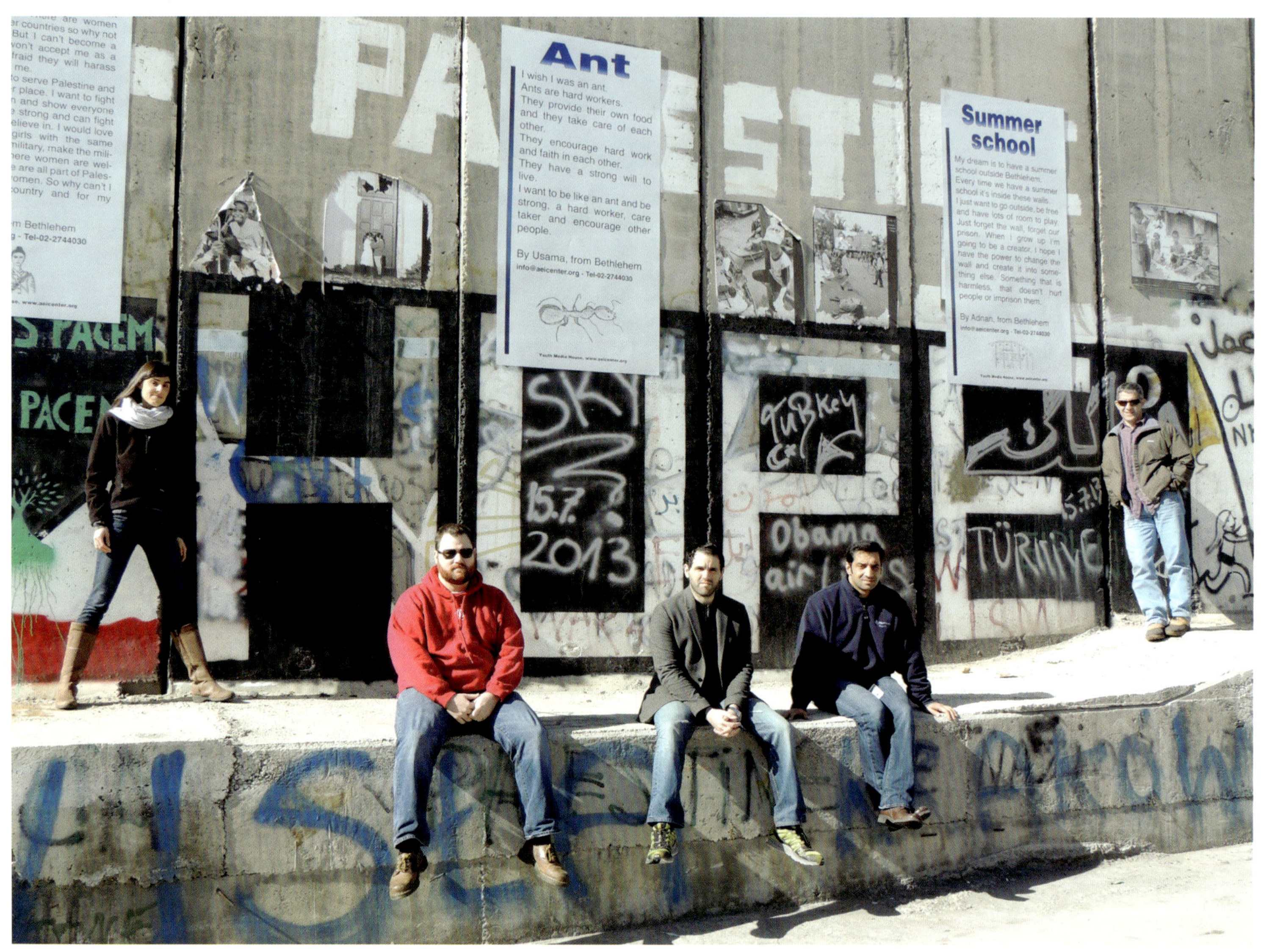

Participants in the Youth Entrepreneurship Livelihood Program project pose for a photo in front of the Israeli West Bank barrier.

Photograph courtesy of LaVonn Schlegel.

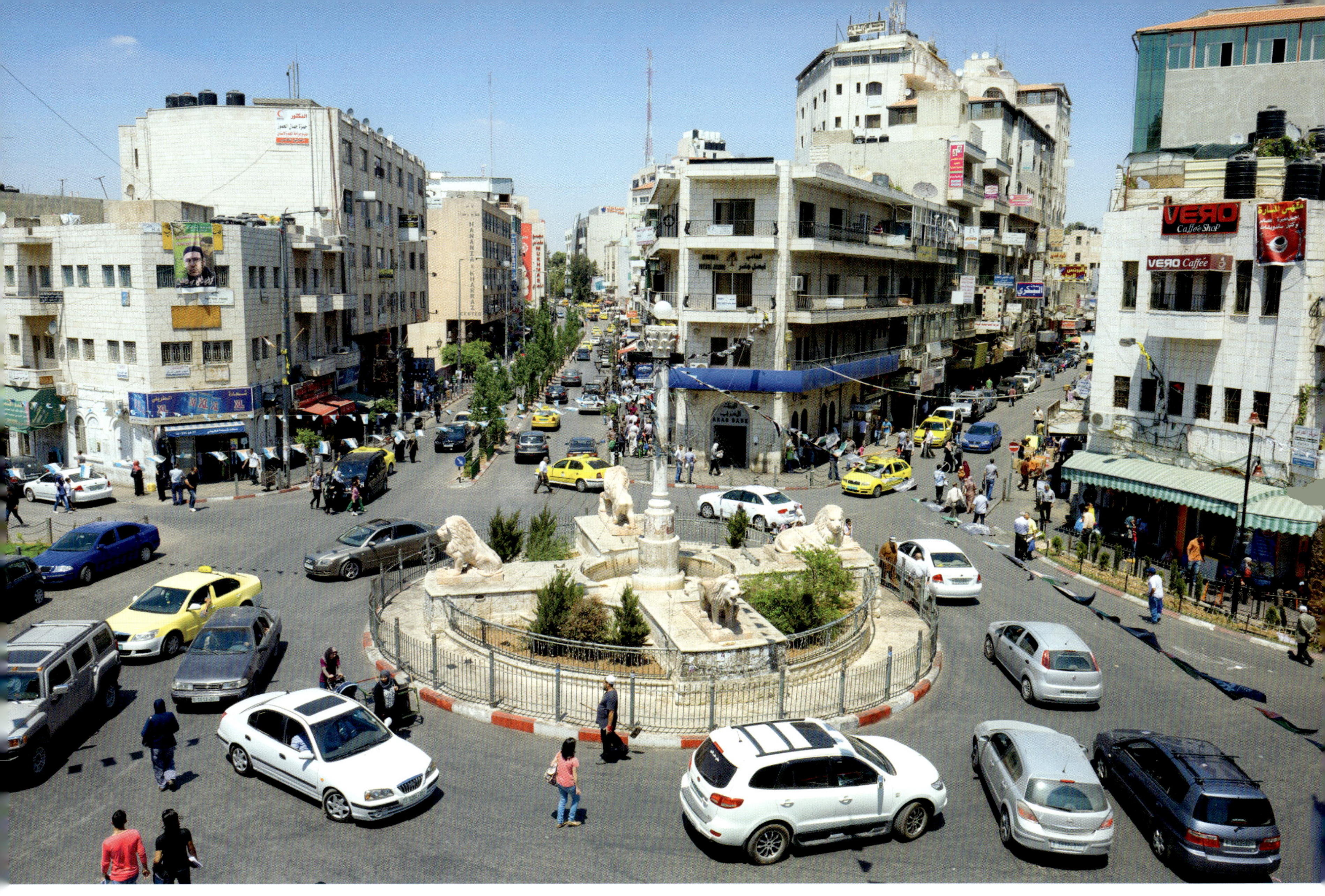

Traffic in downtown Ramallah, West Bank, Palestinian Territories, July 2013.
Photograph courtesy of iStock.

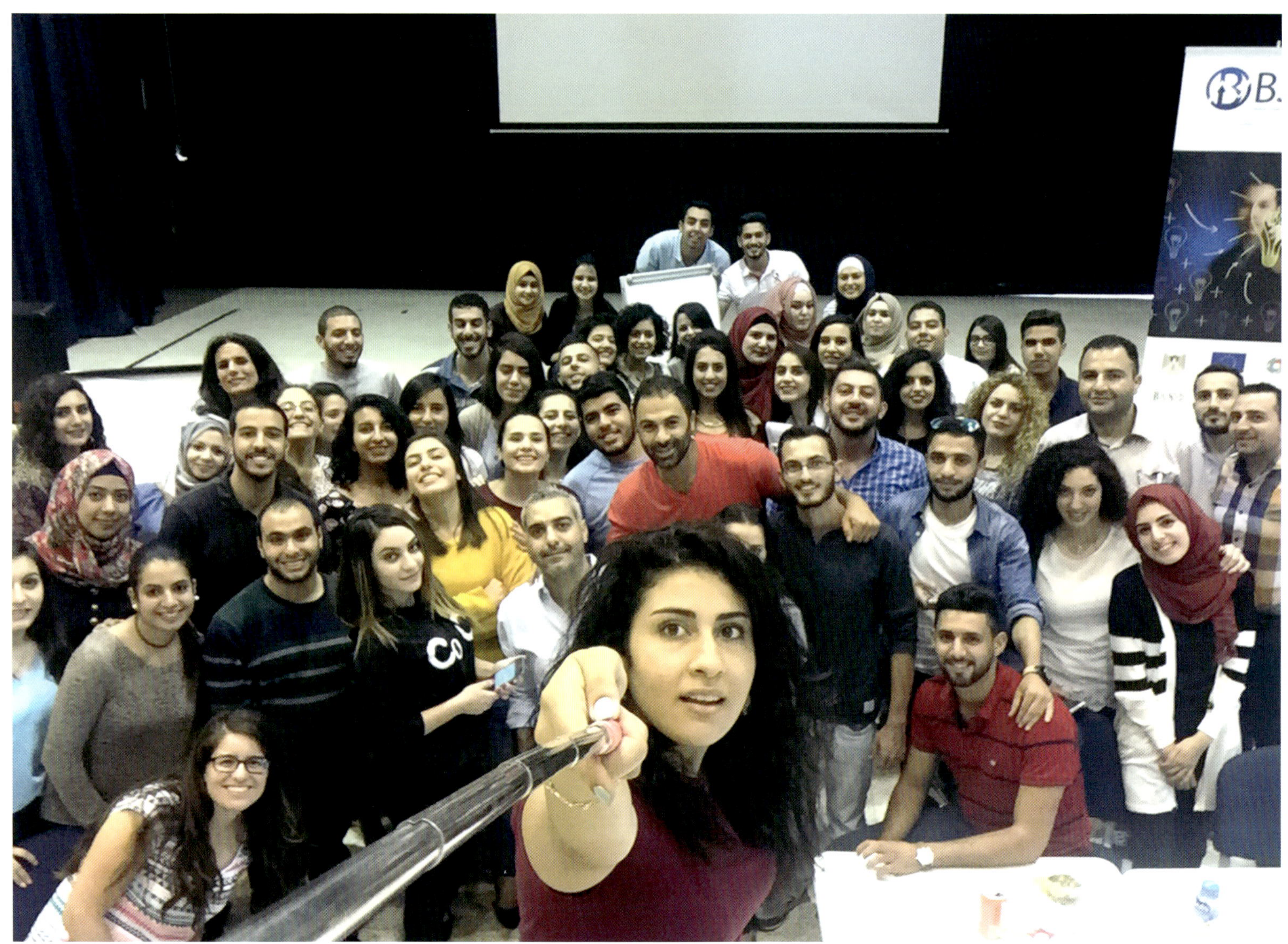

Students in the Building Entrepreneurship Excellence and Developing Economic Enterprises program pose for a group selfie.
Photograph courtesy of LaVonn Schlegel.

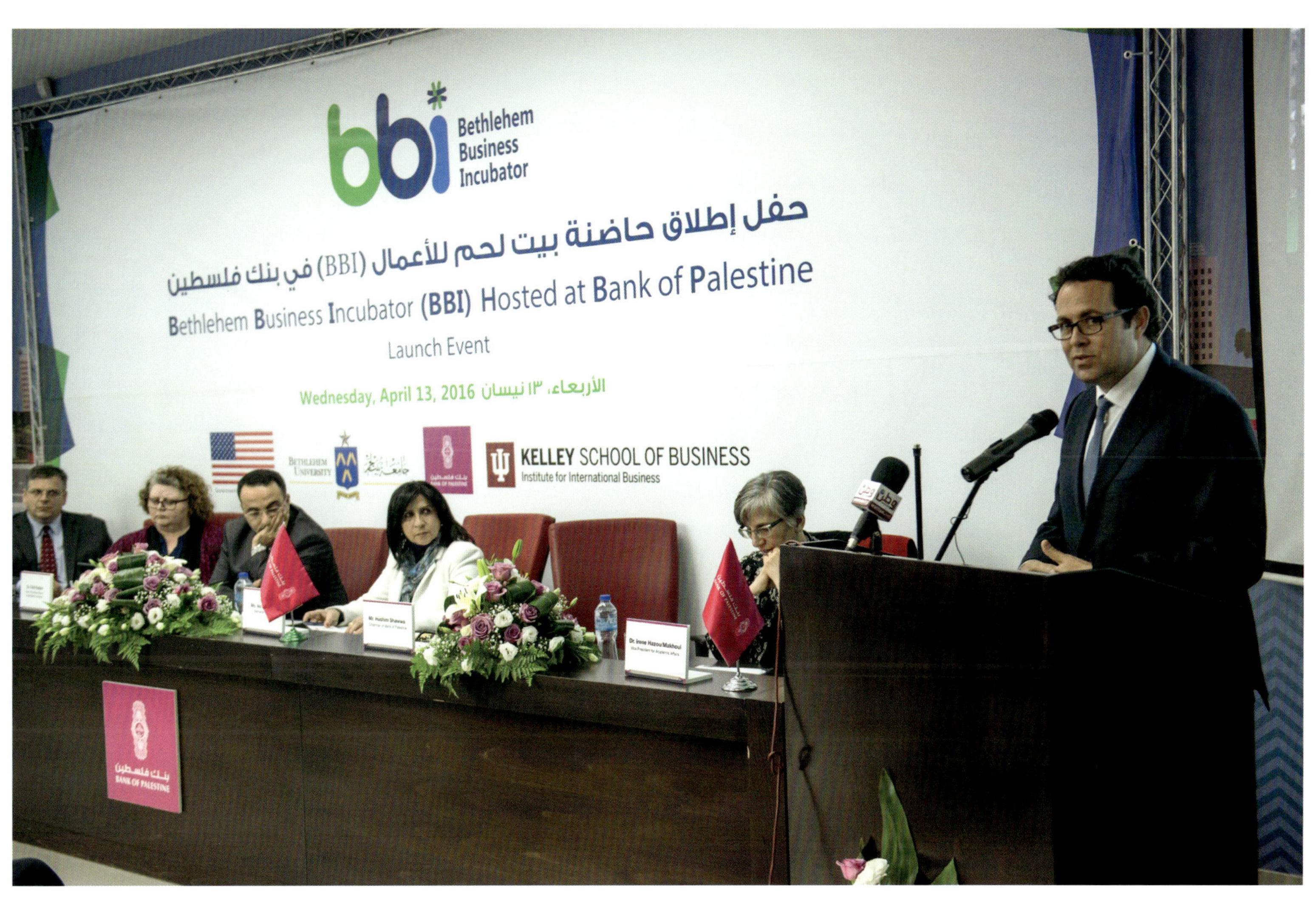

Bank of Palestine chairman Hashin Shawa addresses the audience at the Bethlehem Business Incubator launch ceremony on April 13, 2016.

Photograph courtesy of LaVonn Schlegel.

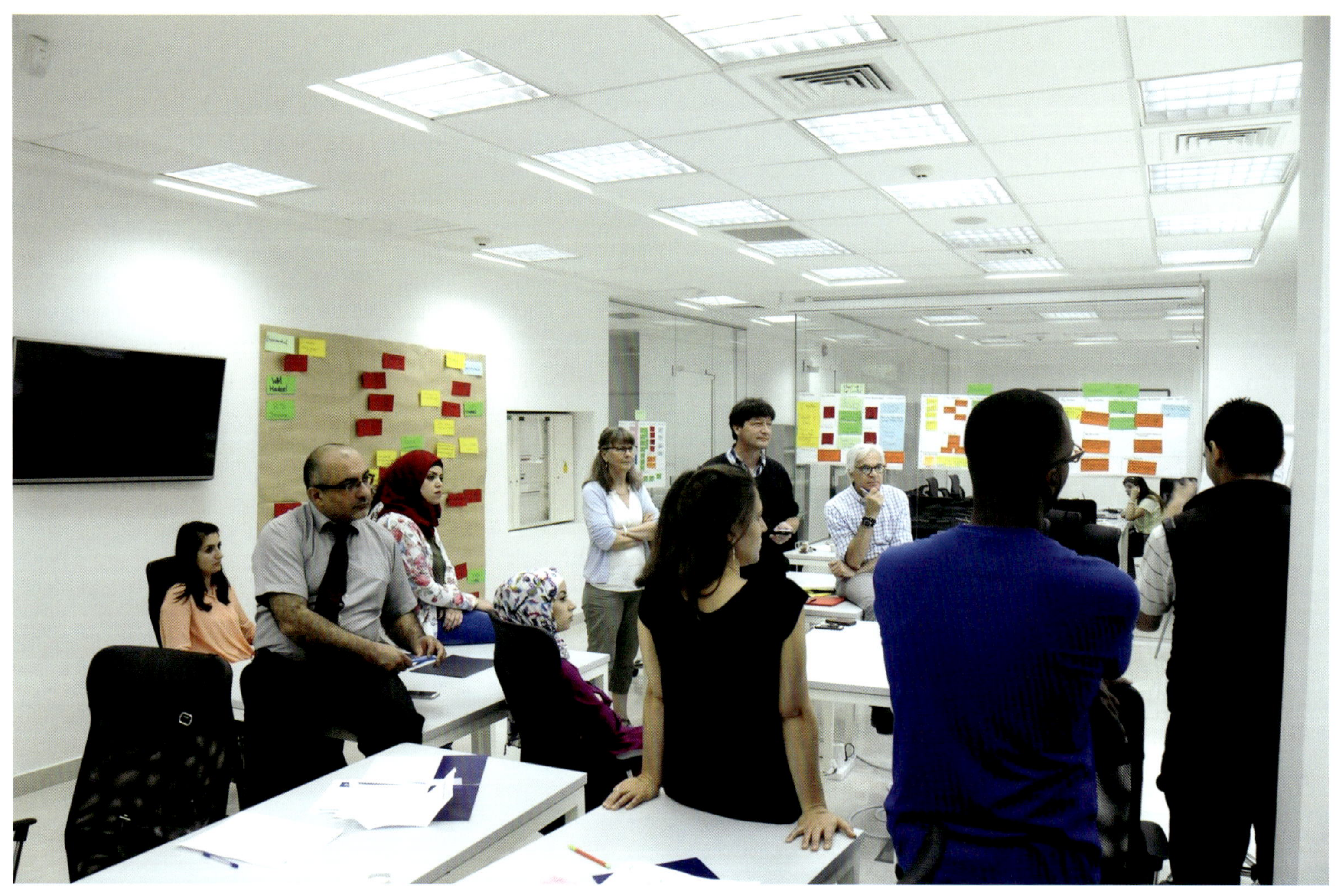

Training session at the Bethlehem Business Incubator.
Photograph courtesy of LaVonn Schlegel.

Palestinian entrepreneurs. The twelve businesses in Bethlehem, Hebron, and Ramallah included medical, ceramics, agriculture, and food and beverage enterprises. Toward the end of the consultation, the Kelley students traveled to Bethlehem for a weeklong visit to meet with team members there and with the clients.[2]

"This project builds a strong network with local Palestinian students to transfer knowledge and training of consulting methodology from Kelley School faculty and MBA students. While the project supports our culture of teamwork and our mission to be of service to others, it's also a transformative experience for our students," shared Idalene Kesner, dean of the Kelley School.[3]

Fadi Kattan, dean of the Bethlehem University School of Business Administration, noted that "the international consulting program would help to build the skills and abilities of his students, who would continue to play a key role in providing a support network for Palestinian firms. Involving undergraduate students in such an activity will be a great experience for them and might encourage some of the participants to start thinking of starting their own businesses as well."[4]

Richard Buangan, the United States Consul for Press and Cultural Affairs, commented on the project: "Everywhere in the world, the private sector—not the government—is the engine for economic growth. Building business and creating jobs means more people can live a dignified life. We are pleased that Indiana University's Kelley School of Business will play such an important role in doing this."[5]

A second project, Building Entrepreneurship Excellence and Developing Economic Enterprises, set out to support women and young entrepreneurs ages fifteen to twenty-eight by increasing their access to start-up resources and training. The Bethlehem Business Incubator, supported by the Bank of Palestine, offered training, workshops, mentorships, networking opportunities, internships, and follow-on investments to increase clients' chances of success after they left the Incubator.[6]

20 | INDIANA UNIVERSITY *in* Latin America and the Caribbean

Facing, Plaza de Armas, Lima, Peru, February 2011. Surrounding the plaza are the Government Palace, the Cathedral of Lima, the Archbishop's Palace of Lima, the Municipal Palace, and the Palace of the Union.

Photograph courtesy of iStock.

OVER THE YEARS, CENTRAL AND LATIN AMERICA WERE NOT AREAS where Indiana University projects thrived. The strength of different IU Language and Area centers and programs and the availability of outside contracts and grants resulted in significant activity in other parts of the world. Thus, the early activities documented in this chapter were limited in scope and effectiveness in this part of the world. With the presidency of Michael McRobbie, there was renewed interest in the region. The opening of an IU Gateway in Mexico in 2018 marked a major commitment for future opportunities, and his visits to Brazil and Argentina resulted in promising agreements for friendship and cooperation.

Peru

In 1964, the Ford Foundation awarded a grant for the improvement of administrative and operating procedures at the National University of San Marcos in Lima, Peru. Joseph A. Franklin, IU vice president and treasurer, administered the project. San Marcos had grown far beyond its capacity, placing enormous pressure on the facilities and faculty. The campus had been designed

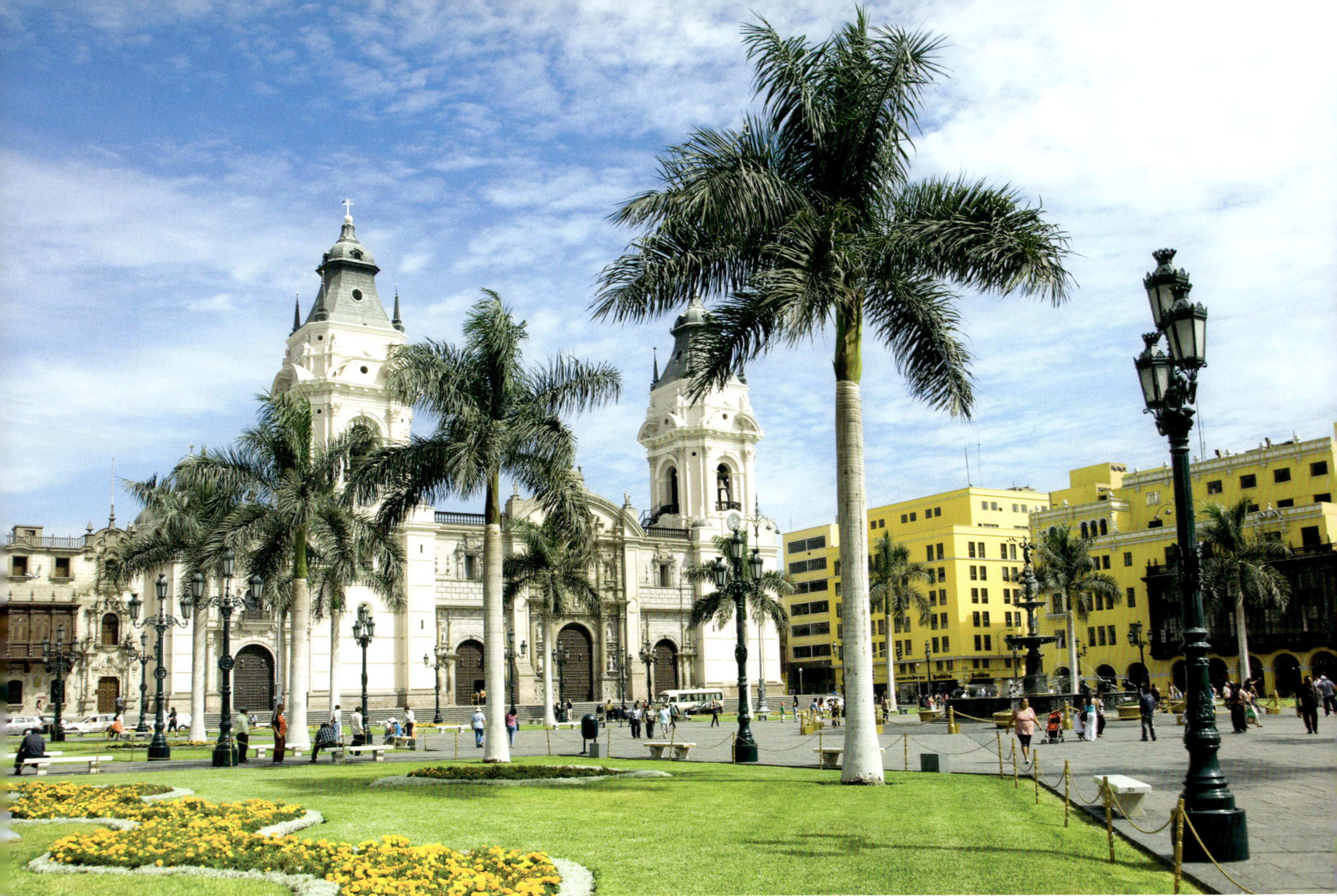

We are excited and honored to be forming this new partnership with the University of the West Indies and Indiana University, which will combine the energies of these institutions to address the challenge of creating new business opportunities in Barbados and its neighboring countries, especially for Caribbean young people.

—James Goggin

for about two thousand students, not the nearly fourteen thousand who were there at the time of IU's involvement.[1]

IU was expected to assist in improving records management, hiring procedures, budgeting, payroll, and physical plant. Indiana University faculty and administrators traveled to Peru to work with their counterparts to achieve these goals.[2]

In January 1969, the project was suspended because the rector had apparently lost interest in the project and stopped supporting it. However, another factor might have been a lack of awareness of cultural sensitivities. A memo in 1965 from the secretary of the Indiana University Board of Trustees Robert E. Burton to Franklin concludes that IU "representatives realized the need for balance between assisting the USM while still respecting their traditions. We can't solve all the political and economic problems, but our recommendations must be developed for Lima, Peru, and not Bloomington."[3]

Uruguay

In 1964, the School of Education implemented a two-year project sponsored by the United States Agency for International Development (USAID) to upgrade the mechanical and electronic engineering divisions of the Universidad del Trabajo in Montevideo, Uruguay.[4]

The main purpose of the project was to develop courses in the use of electronic and mechanical equipment, improve assembly line production, and upgrade facilities. H. Robert Kinker, IU professor of education, led the project, and David J. Hoffman, a lecturer in electronics, worked with faculty and administrators from the Universidad del Trabajo. Despite bureaucratic delays and other minor problems, achievements included an educational program in industrial electronics and an increase in student enrollment because of some of the innovations.[5]

Mexico

In February 2000, the IU School of Optometry opened a clinic in Guanajuato, Mexico, about 150 miles northwest of Mexico City. At the clinic, IU optometry students provided eye and vision care to patients for whom such care had been previously unavailable. Students from the school had been making Volunteer Optometric Services to Humanity trips to Guanajuato for several years before the clinic started.[6]

Discussions had taken place between IU faculty member Douglas Horner; IU optometry graduate Cynthia Foster; Carlos Perez Lopez, a medical director for the state of Guanajuato; and Anthony Gutierrez of the humanitarian organization I Care International. The clinic opened in the general hospital of Guanajuato, and IU students participated in twelve-week rotations there. In addition, donations of eyeglass frames,

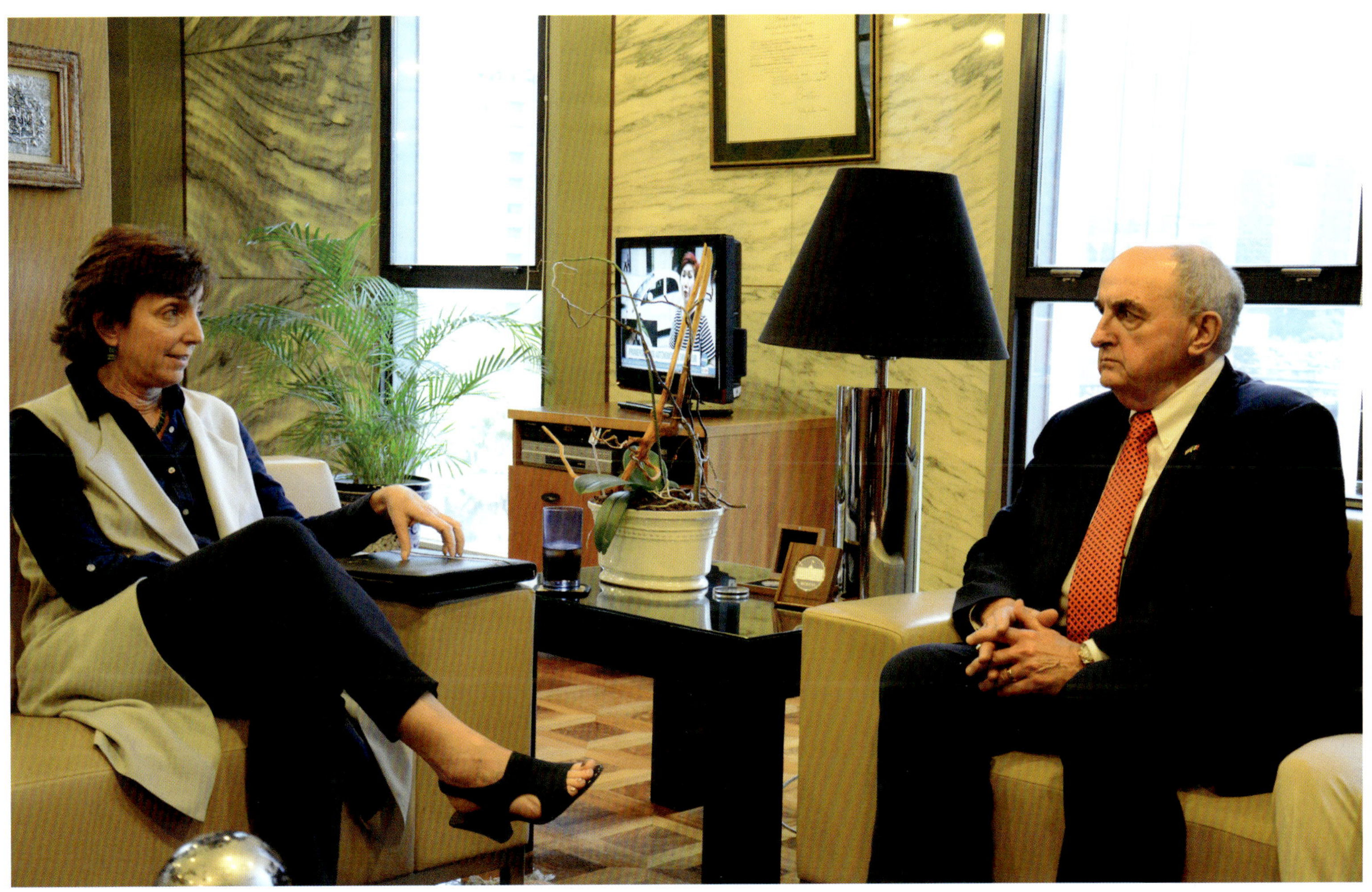

Indiana University president Michael McRobbie (*right*) meets with US ambassador to Mexico Roberta S. Haconson to discuss, among other subjects, IU's increased collaboration with National Autonomous University of Mexico. IU identified Mexico as one of thirty "priority" countries the university is seeking to enhance relations with as it carries out the mission of its international strategic plan, 2016.

Photograph courtesy of Indiana University.

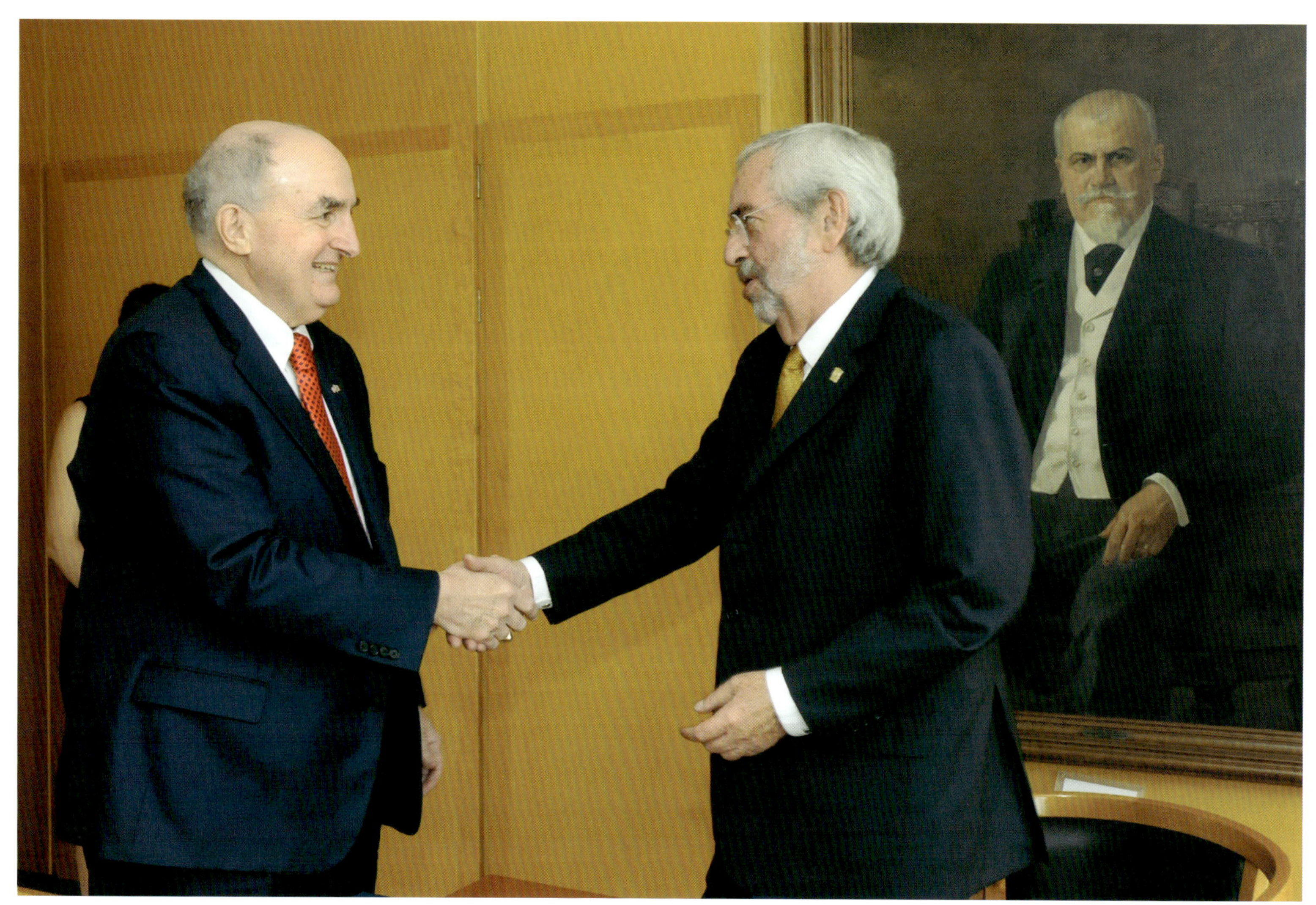

Indiana University president Michael McRobbie (*left*) meets with Enrique Graue Wiechers, president of the National Autonomous University of Mexico. During the meeting, the two leaders agreed to explore further areas of collaboration between their respective institutions, 2016.

Photograph courtesy of Indiana University.

lenses, and equipment were received over the years, and an ophthalmic laboratory was added.[7]

For many years, the Schools of Medicine, Nursing, Dentistry, and Social Work on the Indiana University–Purdue University Indianapolis campus operated public health services and education programs in the mountainous regions of Hidalgo. These short-term clinical activities were expanded by a more formal agreement with the Autonomous University of the State of Hidalgo, which included the liberal arts, engineering, and education. Many immigrants from the Hidalgo region were living in the Indianapolis area, which added significance to the connections.[8]

In September 2016, IU president Michael McRobbie and Enrique Graue Wiechers, president of the National Autonomous University of Mexico (UNAM), signed an agreement to explore further areas of collaboration between the two institutions. IU's relationship with UNAM dated back to 1999, when collaboration had begun between the UNAM and the Ostrom Workshop in Political Theory and Policy Analysis. The workshop had been founded in 1973 by Nobel Prize–winning economist and IU distinguished professor Elinor Ostrom.[9]

Barbados

In 2011, the Institute for International Business at Indiana University's Kelley School of Business was awarded a $1.35 million, three-year grant from the USAID and Higher Education for Development to help the Caribbean nation of Barbados encourage the creation of new companies. The Kelley School was chosen from among eight formal proposals. The Barbados JOBS (Job Opportunity for Business Start Up) initiative was a partnership between the Institute for International Business and the Cave Hill School of Business at the University of the West Indies.[10]

The purpose of the project was to provide critical entrepreneurship training to the Barbados region to help the area combat growing social and economic issues by increasing the skills needed to compete in a globalized market. In implementing the grant, the Kelley School and the Cave Hill School of Business collaborated on an entrepreneurship program in the Cave Hill MBA program, advised the school on establishing an entrepreneurship program, and prepared case studies relevant to Caribbean companies. IU faculty member Mark Long helped set up an incubator for start-up firms on the island.

Bruce Jaffee, IU professor of business economics and public policy and director of the Institute for International Business, saw the IU effort enabling Barbados "to be a leader in entrepreneurship in the next five to 10 years."[11]

Barbados faced two major challenges at the time: Its sugar-dependent economy was experiencing stiff competition from other countries, and tourism—another important source of revenue—was seeing losses due to fewer visitors to the island. The government, therefore, decided to explore alternative sources of revenue, including doubling of the number of annual business start-ups. Dan Smith, dean of the IU Kelley School of Business at the time, noted that the business school

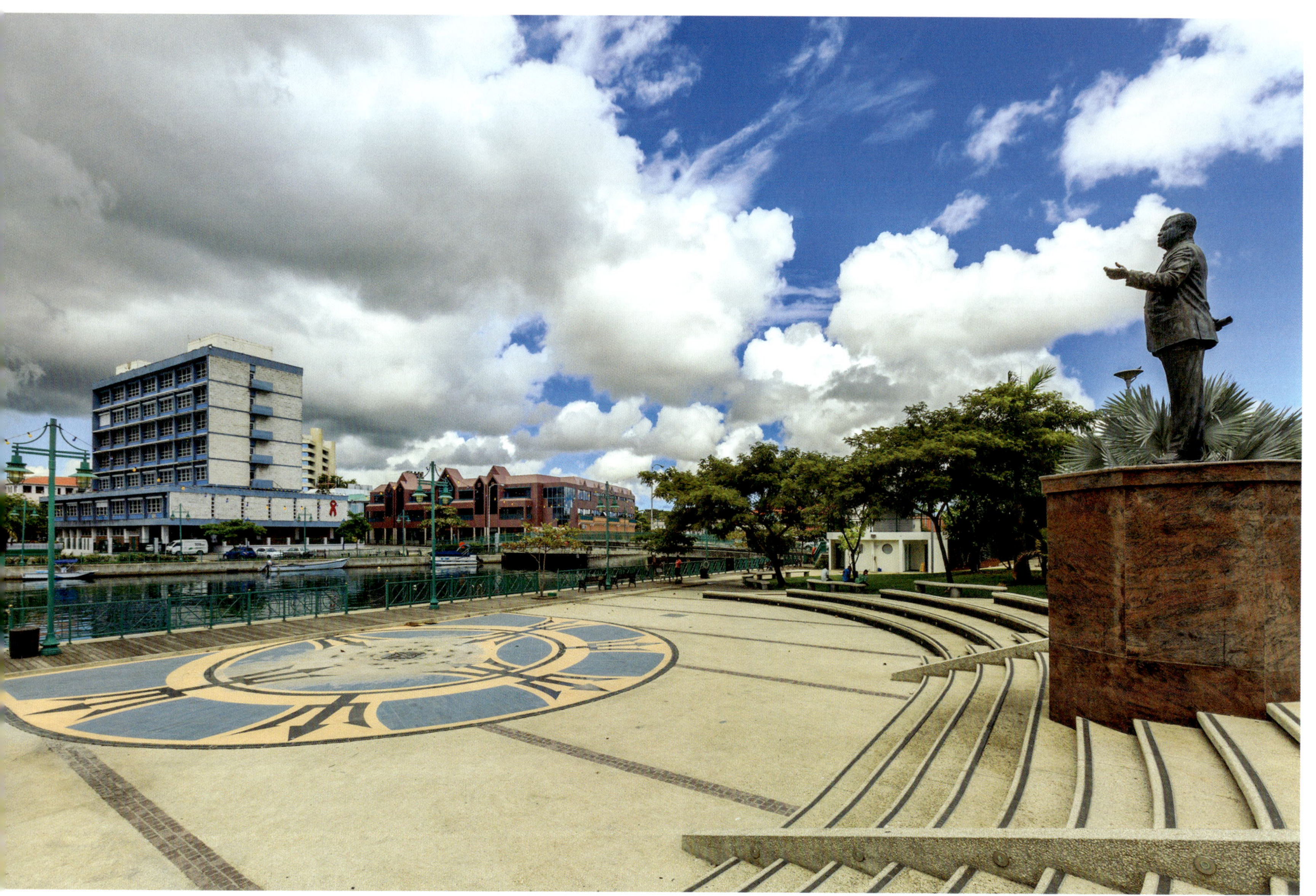

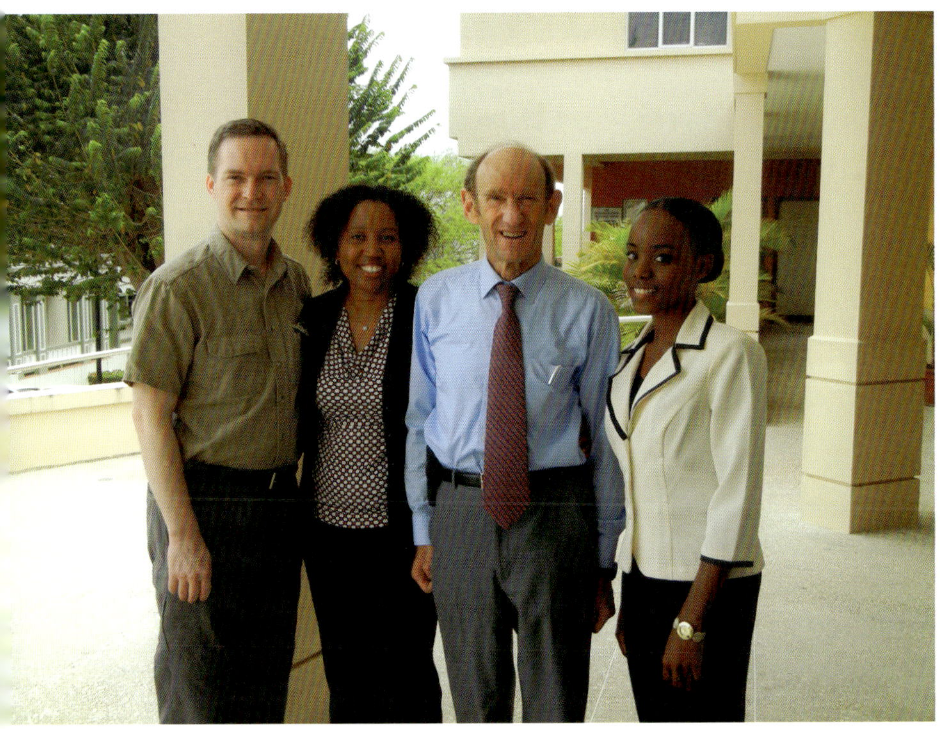

Kelley School of Business professor Bruce Jaffee (*second from left*) with participants and facilitators from the Train the Trainer Workshops. *Photograph courtesy of LaVonn Schlegel.*

Facing, Independence Square, Bridgetown, Barbados, November 2011. Visible from here are the parliament buildings, National Heroes Square, and the historic buildings of Bridgetown. *Photograph courtesy of iStock.*

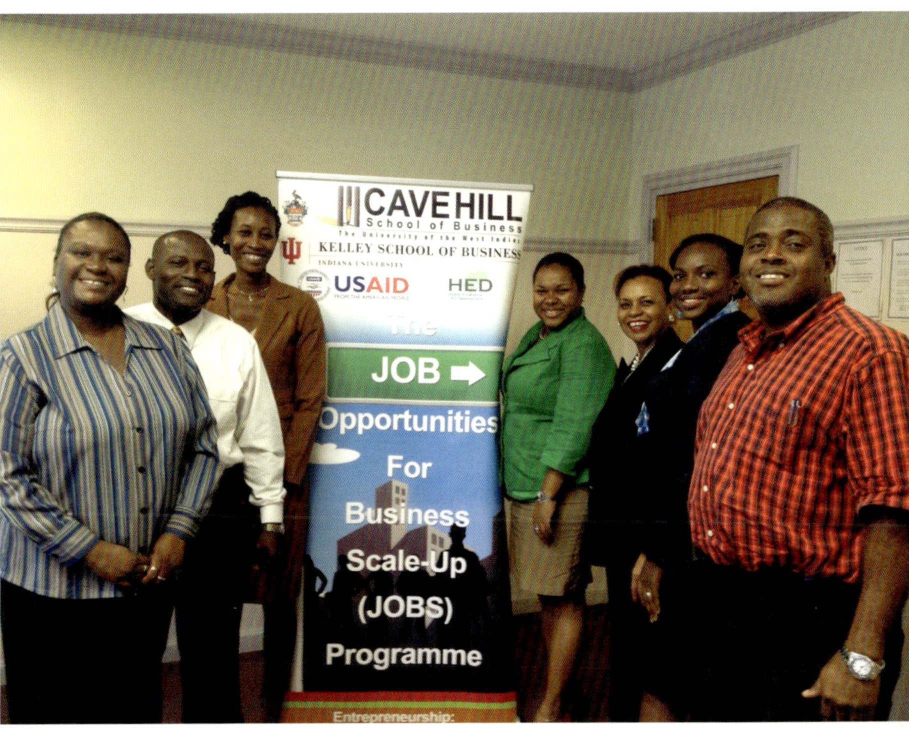

Participants at the Cave Hill School of Business at the Barbados JOBS (Job Opportunity for Business Start Up) Mentorship Symposium in Wanstead, Barbados, 2011. *Photograph courtesy of LaVonn Schlegel.*

had been extensively involved in similar social entrepreneurship projects around the world, including in East Europe and the Baltic Republics after the fall of communism.[12]

James Goggin, the USAID Barbados representative, commented on the project: "We are excited and honored to be forming this new partnership with the University of the West Indies and Indiana University, which will combine the energies of these institutions to address the challenge of creating new business opportunities in Barbados and its neighboring countries, especially for Caribbean young people."[13]

21 | INDIANA UNIVERSITY *in* Burma-Myanmar

In 1990, the US Congress established a program to prepare future leaders of a democratic Burma. In 1995, one of the outcomes was the Burmese Refugee Scholarship Program administered by Indiana University's Office of International Programs.

Facing, Yangon, Myanmar, January 2009. The Shwedagon Pagoda, the main city temple, is visible in the background. *Photograph courtesy of iStock.*

BURMA, NOW THE REPUBLIC OF MYANMAR, WAS RULED BY BRITAIN from 1824 until 1948, when it became an independent nation. The Japanese occupied Burma for a few years during World War II. After a coup d'état in 1962, the nation became a military dictatorship governed by a revolutionary council led by a general. During this era, which lasted until 1974, strict controls were imposed on the media, business, and freedom of expression. There was some opening up of the political process, but in 1989, martial law was declared. In 1990, the government held new elections in which Nobel Prize winner Aung San Suu Kyi's party, the National League for Democracy, won 392 out of a total 492 seats. However, the military refused to cede power and continued to rule until major reforms were made in March 2011.

In 1990, the US Congress established a program to prepare future leaders of a democratic Burma. In 1995, one of the outcomes was the Burmese Refugee Scholarship Program. It was administered by Indiana University's Office for International Programs through grants—first from the former US Information Agency and later through the US Department of State. Scholarships were awarded every year until 2014, and the funding made it possible for several hundred Burmese refugees from India and Thailand to come to the United States. They had fled their homeland for fear of imprisonment by Burma's ruling military junta because they had participated in prodemocracy movements.[1]

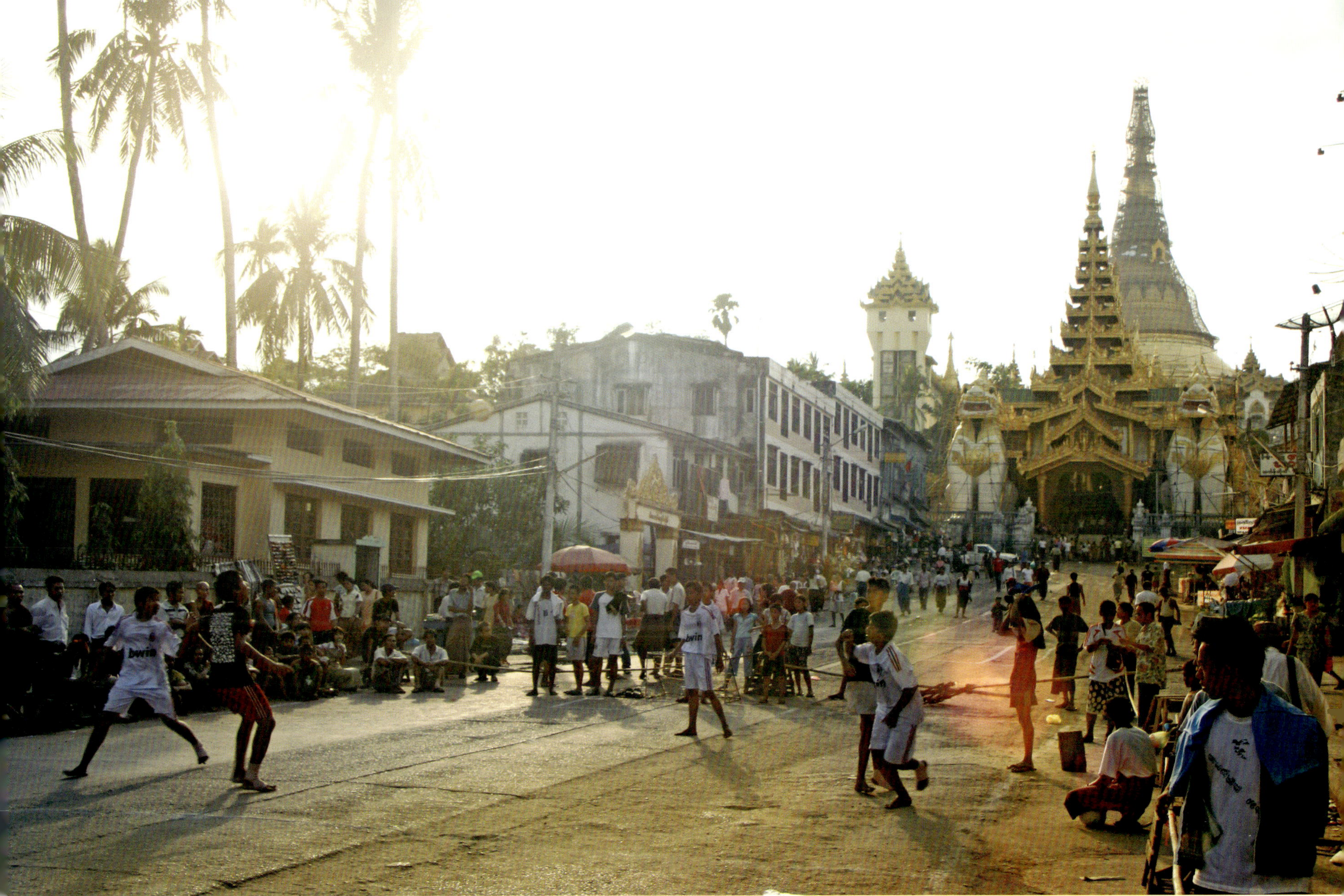
bwin
bwin

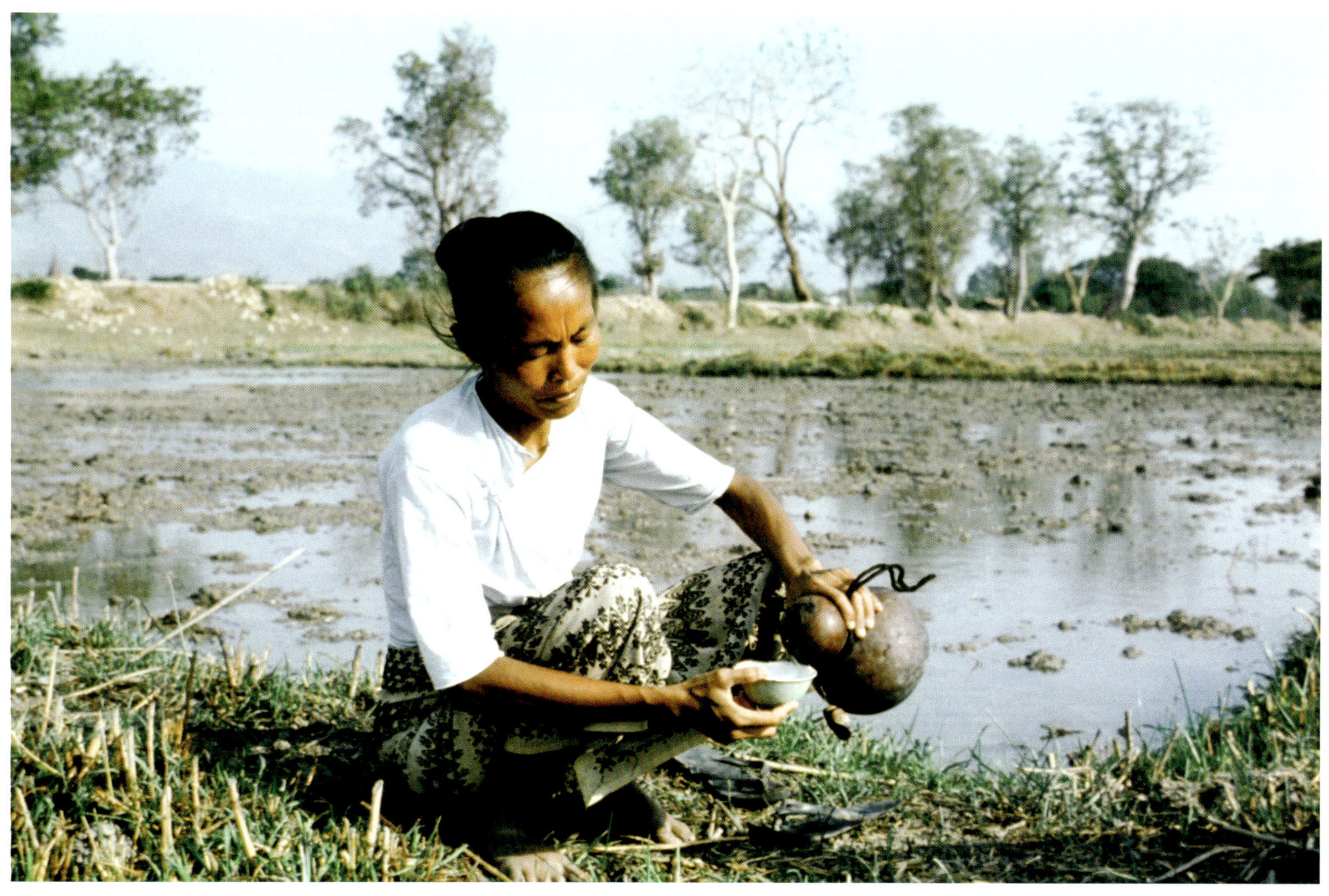

A woman takes a tea break in a rice field, Shan State, Myanmar (Burma), January 1976. *UN Photo/NJ.*

Facing, Yangon Institute of Economics undergraduate students, 2015. *Photograph courtesy of LaVonn Schlegel.*

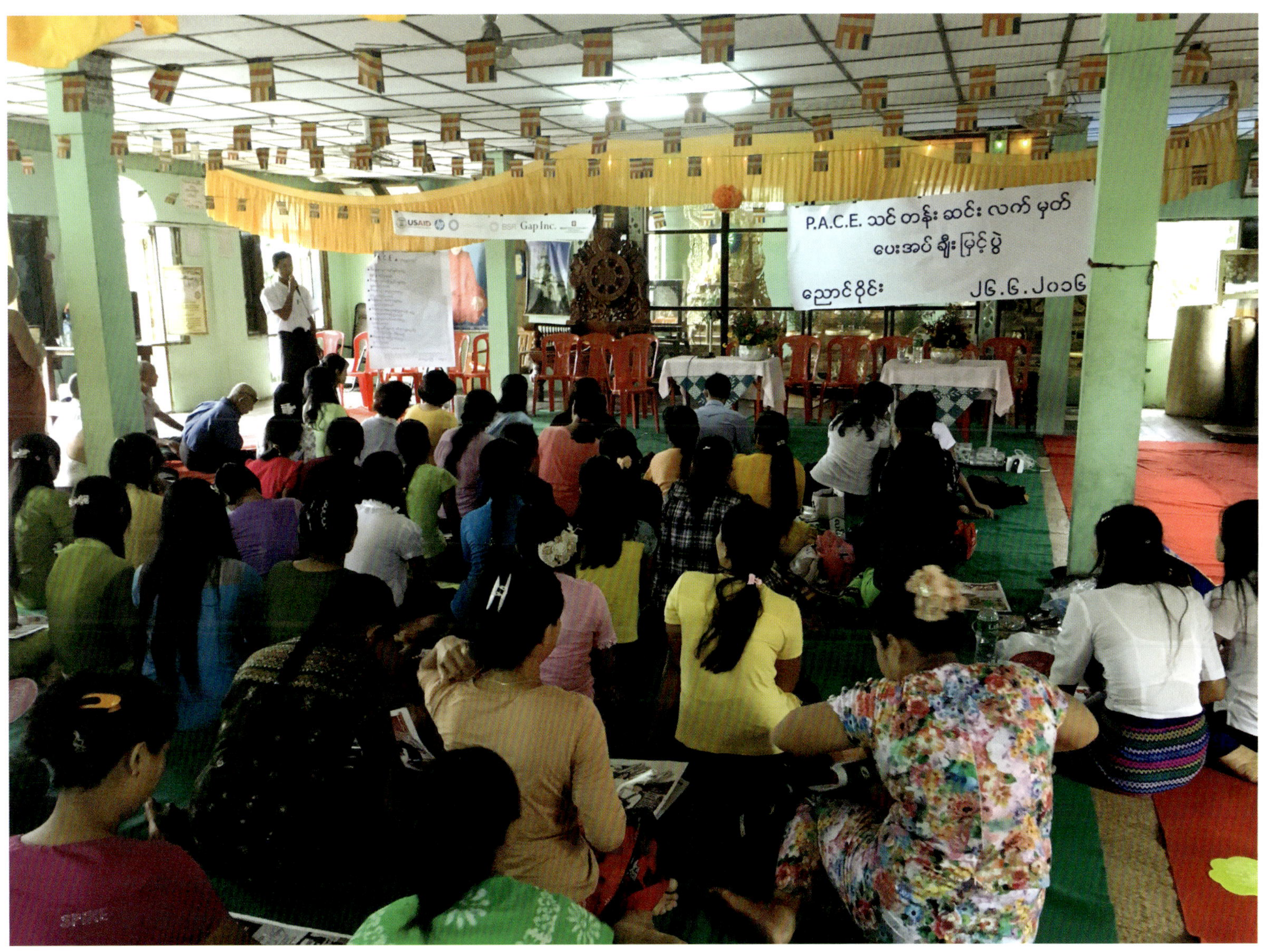
USAID
BSR Gap Inc.
P.A.C.E. သင်တန်းဆင်းလက်မှတ်
ပေးအပ်ချီးမြှင့်ပွဲ
ညောင်ဗိုင်း ၂၆.၆.၂၀၁၆

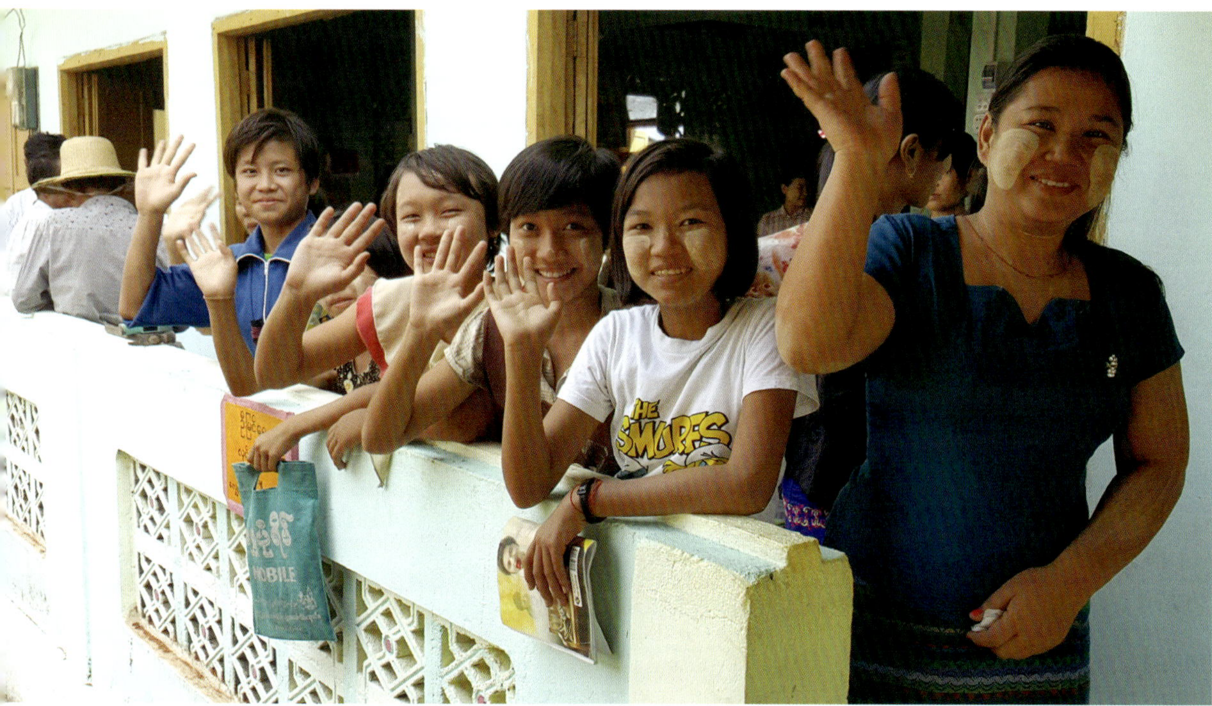

Yangon Institute of Economics students attending the Kelley School of Business Entrepreneurship Seminar breakout session, 2016.
Photograph courtesy of LaVonn Schlegel.

All of the scholarship recipients came to the IU Bloomington campus for preacademic orientation, English-language training, and they were then admitted to universities in different parts of the United States. The purpose of their participation was to prepare them for positions as community leaders when they returned home.

A short-term program in the spring of 2014 continued IU's contact with Burma. The US State Department Youth Leadership Program funded a program for twenty young Burmese to come to Bloomington for several weeks to learn more about the United States and improve their leadership skills. They visited the *Indiana Daily Student,* nonprofit organizations such as United Way and Goodwill, participated in discussions on human rights, and met with community and campus leaders.[2]

A major initiative with the Kelley School of Business followed. In 2014, because of improved relations, the first bilateral agreement between the United States and Myanmar was signed. The United States Agency for International Development awarded $1 million to IU's Kelley School for a Global Development Alliance project to extend the teaching and outreach capabilities of the Yangon Institute of Economics (YECO), the country's leading business school, and to help micro- to medium-sized business enterprises become more successful.[3]

Advancement and Development through Entrepreneurship Programs and Training (ADEPT) was the name of the first Global Development Alliance grant awarded to IU. Partners in the project were Hewlett-Packard, Business for Social Responsibility, and the Vietnam-based VinaCapital Foundation,

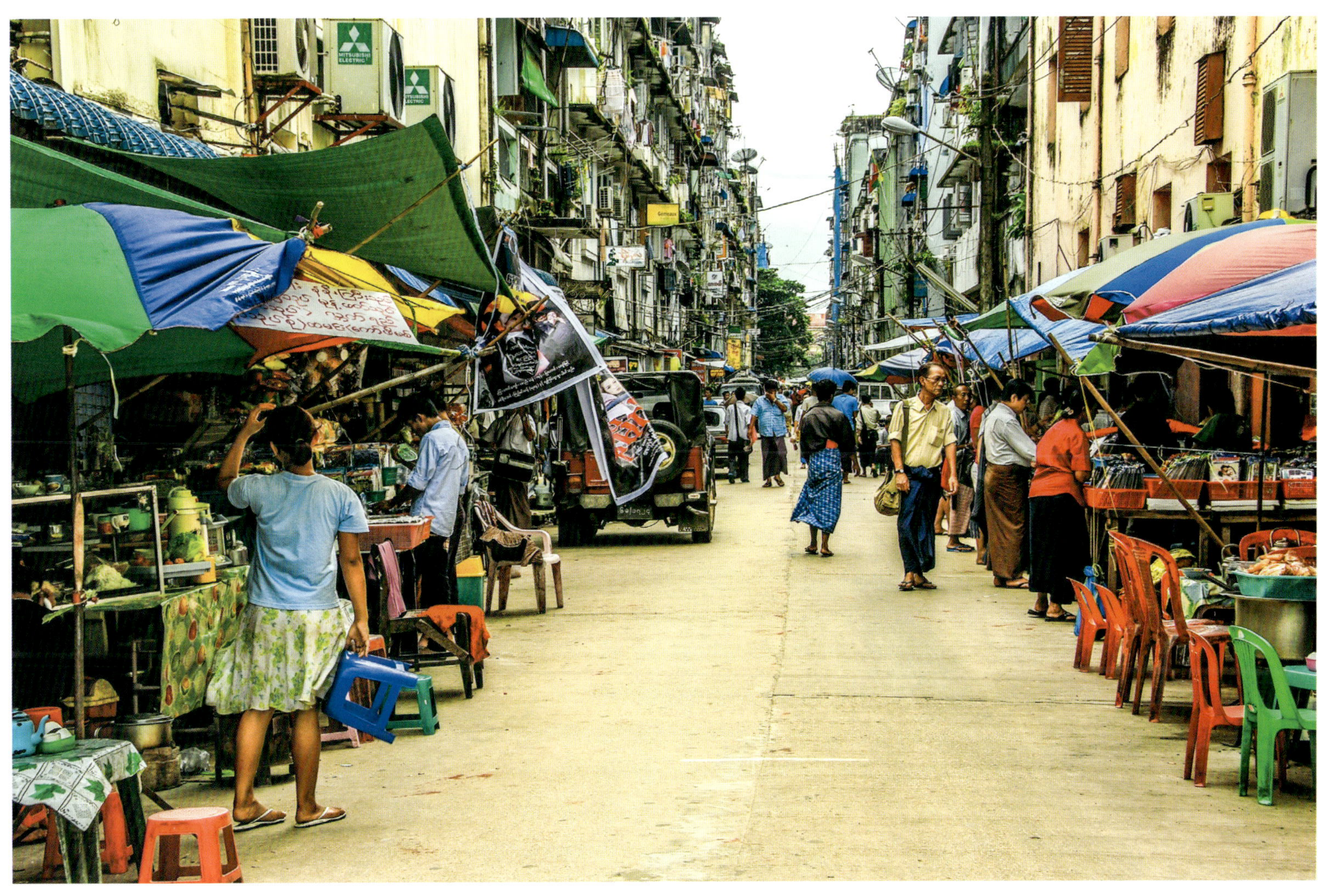

Downtown Yangon food stalls, August 2011.
Photograph courtesy of iStock.

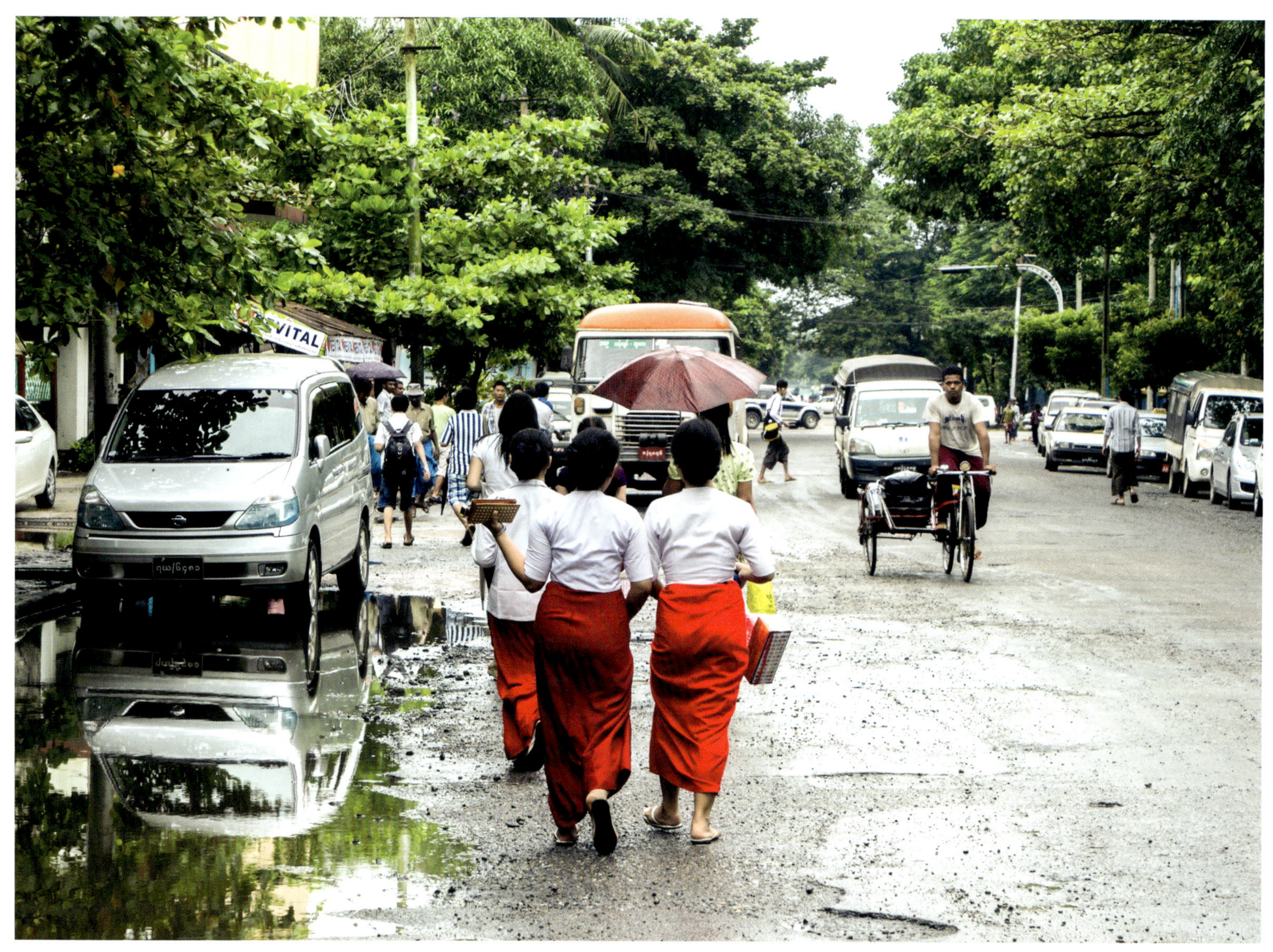

A street in Yangon, Myanmar, after a rain, August 2013.
Photograph courtesy of iStock.

all of which provided funds and assistance. The primary objectives were to increase the institutional effectiveness of the Yangon Institute and strengthen entrepreneurial activities for self-employed microentrepreneurs, small-business owners, and middle managers.[4] The existing situation was limiting growth and competitiveness among small- to medium-sized enterprises, which were 96 percent of the country's business activity. In addition, the Burmese government was eager to encourage foreign direct investments, particularly in information and communications technology, which is necessary to fuel social and economic development.

The Kelley School worked with YECO on degree programs, research capabilities, and setting up an Entrepreneurship Center of Excellence. YECO faculty visited Bloomington as well as other Kelley international partners such as Sungkyunkwan University in South Korea and Australia National University. The Kelley School's Institute for International Business implemented the grant. The principal investigators on the project were Ash Soni, executive associate dean for academic programs and Arcelor Mittal Faculty Fellow in the Kelley School. A special feature of the relationship was a contribution from Kelley faculty of a 2,000-volume teaching library that replaced the outdated YECO Management Studies Department library.[5]

Idalene Kesner, dean of the Kelley School of Business and the Frank P. Popoff Chair of Strategic Management, who traveled to Myanmar to teach one of the first workshops, saw IU's involvement as an important milestone. "We are thrilled to create a lasting legacy as we work to deepen and broaden the teaching and outreach capacities of the country's top business school, Yangon Institute of Economics. It is our hope to improve lives by working with the school to identify opportunities that will lead to economic development and a robust private sector."[6]

A major initiative with the Kelley School of Business followed. In 2014, because of improved relations, the first bilateral agreement between the United States and Myanmar was signed.

IU president Michael McRobbie commented on the wider implications of the relationship: "We are very pleased to be academically engaged again with Burma and also with the other major partners in this project, as Burma emerges and becomes further integrated into the rest of the global community. This grant is the latest example of Indiana University's decades-long engagement and commitment with many of the countries of Southeast Asia that form the Association of Southeast Asian Nations."[7]

The IU Center for Constitutional Democracy based in the IU School of Law, also played formative role in Myanmar The center operated under the leadership of executive director David C. Williams, John S. Hastings Professor of Law, and director Susan H. Williams, Walter W. Foskett Professor, both at the IU Mauer School of Law. The center became actively involved in the country's constitutional process, establishing special connections within the Burmese democracy movement; offering training in constitutionalism, democracy, and the rule of law to participants; and working with opposition parliamentarians. Many of the participants thought that the Burmese constitution that had been put in place during a brief parliamentary period did not sufficiently protect their interests.

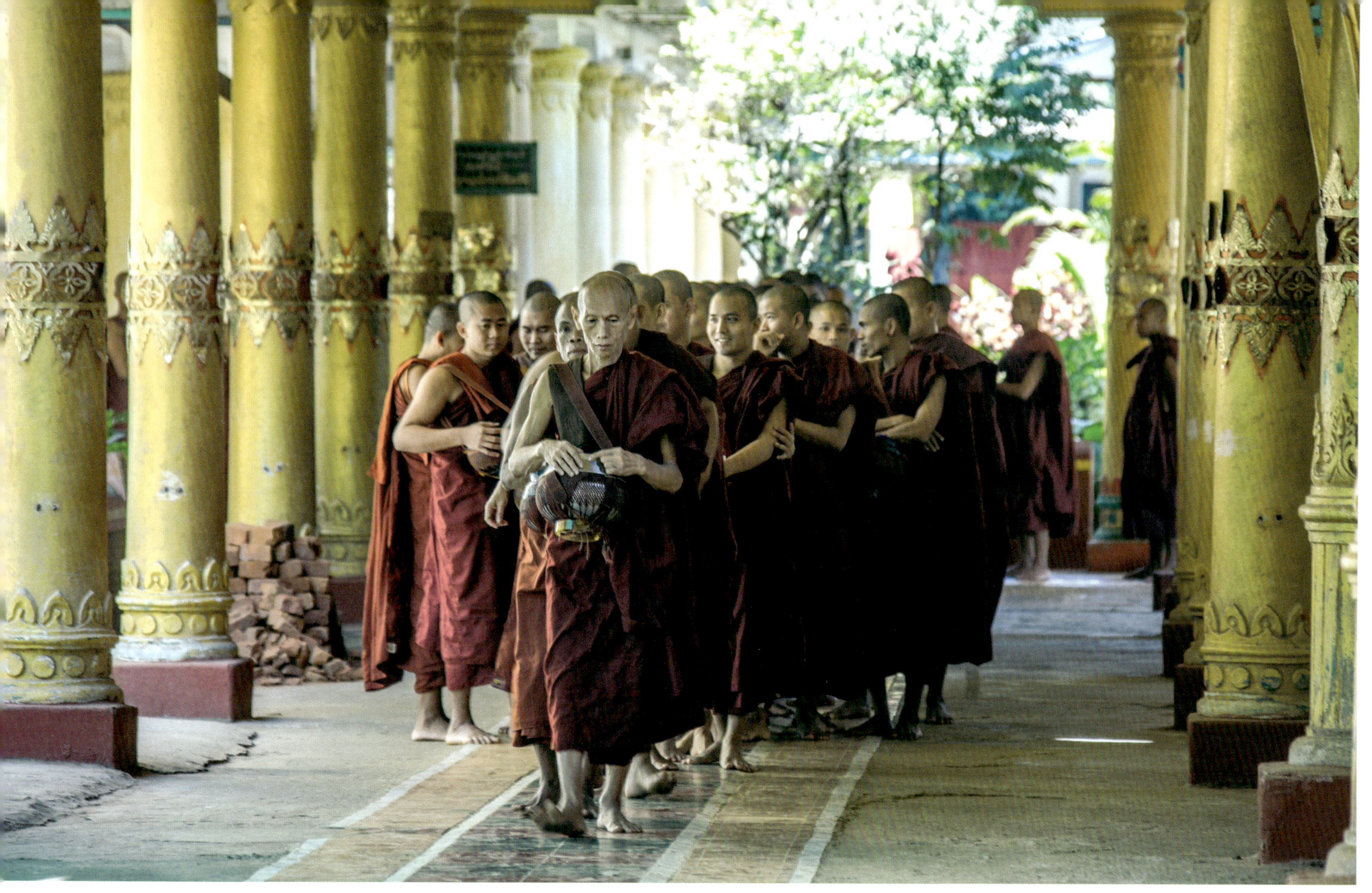

A group of monks sets out to collect alms at dawn from the Kyat Khat Wine Monastery in Bago near Yangon in Myanmar, January 2013.
Photograph courtesy of iStock.

David Williams comments on the early years of the center's activities:

> I was involved in Burma well before we ever went there, because I had a Burmese doctoral student who had been a revolutionary soldier and knew everybody in that power structure. He was writing his dissertation on federalism in Burma. A couple of years into that process, he asked me to meet with some Burmese people to talk about constitution reform.
>
> When we started, it was one of the worst dictatorships in the world. The military was in control, there was no prospect of reform, even with the central government, let alone constitutional reform. We went for five years under those conditions, two or three times a year; no one was paying attention to Burma at that point. There was no news from Burma. It wasn't until things started to change that people started paying attention, and they felt abandoned by the world, so the fact that we kept coming back, that we kept trying to do whatever we could do under those conditions created really strong bonds, and that's what is happening now.[8]

In the late 1990s and early 2000s, the ethnic armed leaders realized that they could not go on fighting forever, and, if change were to occur, they should be ready not just to ask for democracy but to know what kind of democracy; not just ask for federalism, but what kind of federalism. Hence, they began to look for academic experts to advise them.

Susan Williams saw their purpose in a broader context:

> Some of them still wanted independence, and writing a state constitution was the way of envisioning what they would want for themselves if they actually got their own state. There was money from the UN, from Norway, Scandinavian governments, to meet this need. We actually do believe we had an impact throughout the process. The first impact, the early stage, was to bring groups together so that they were all on the same page about what they wanted, and to help them see that federalism would work for them, and that they would not need separate independence. The second impact was just to help them cope at a time when the rest of the world was not paying attention to Burma. The third impact was the inclusion of women into the process; they would otherwise not have had a voice at the table.[9]

David Williams continues: "In terms of what we might have accomplished . . . they were really divided when we first came in, and that's in part because they were really thinking they were each going to be independent countries and so, frequently, they were actually fighting with each other. What we saw happening is that they came together to develop a shared constitution, and they came to realize that if that's the situation, they're all in it together."[10]

We actually do believe we had an impact throughout the process. The first impact, the early stage, was to bring groups together so that they were all on the same page about what they wanted, and to help them see that federalism would work for them, and that they would not need separate independence. The second impact was just to help them cope at a time when the rest of the world was not paying attention to Burma. The third impact was the inclusion of women into the process; they would otherwise not have had a voice at the table.

—Susan Williams

Long-standing discrimination against the Muslim Rohingya minority in Myanmar erupted into in increasing violence starting in 2017. Thousands died, and hundreds of thousands fled the country to seek asylum in Bangladesh. The government of the predominantly Buddhist country, which had never granted the Rohingya people citizenship, claimed that its action

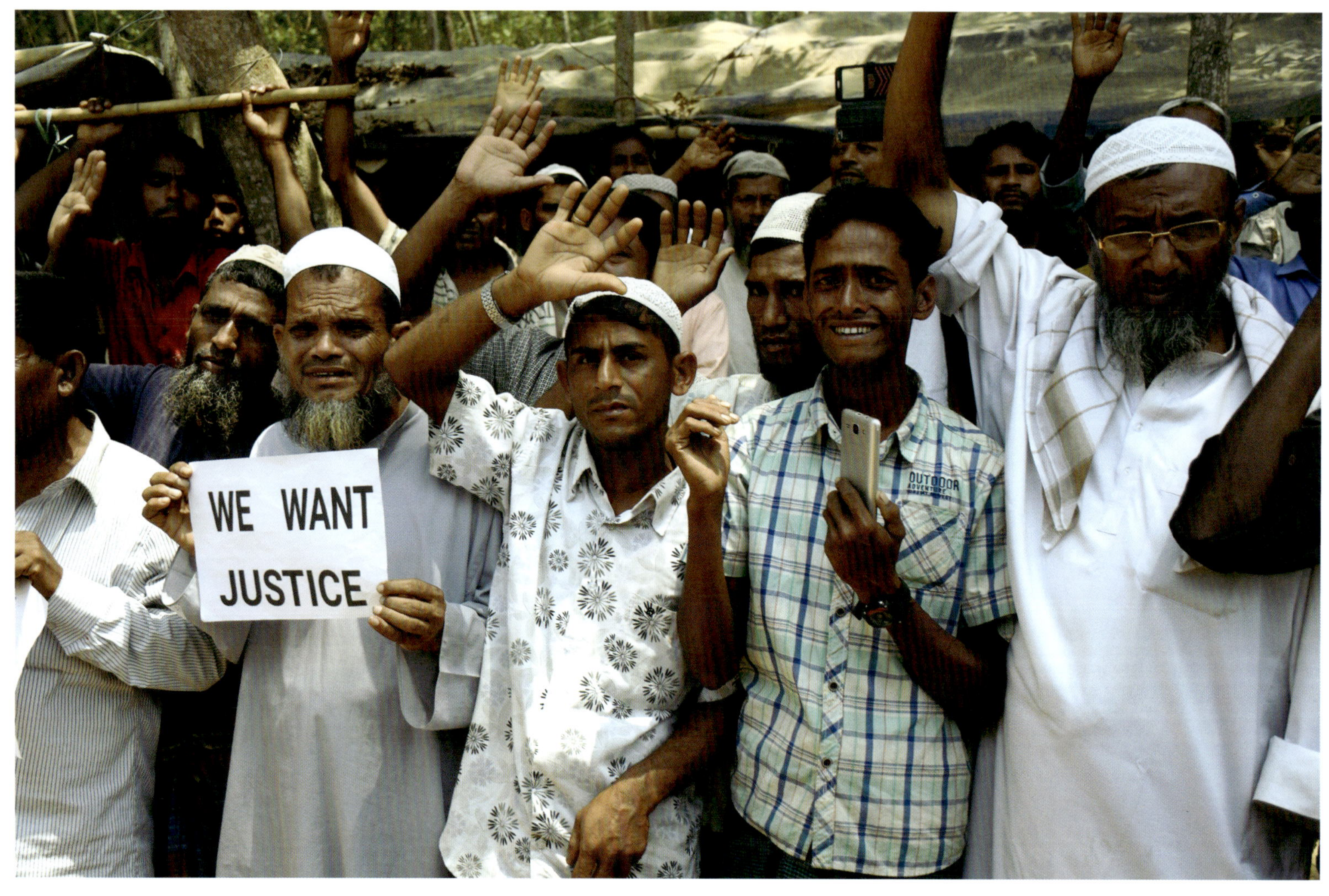

Rohingya refugees living in Cox's Bazar, Bangladesh, April 2018.
UN Photo/Caroline Gluck.

was necessary to reinstate order and sustain the country's fragile democracy. Nobel Prize winner Aung San Suu Kyi, in effect the country's political leader, said that there were no official attempts at ethnic cleansing and ignored international criticism of her assessment of the situation. Because of her many years in detention and her fight for democratic values, it was thought that she might have been more sympathetic to the plight of the Rohingyas.[11]

Lee Feinstein, founding dean of the Indiana University School of Global and International Studies, traveled to the region in the summer of 2018 on behalf of the Simon-Skjodt Center for the Prevention of Genocide, a program of the United States Holocaust Memorial Museum. He concluded that the Rohingya people of Myanmar remain in grave danger a year after government-instigated attacks that international observers have called ethnic cleansing or even genocide. In an opinion column in the *Washington Post* on August 24, 2018, Feinstein and *Cameron Hudson, senior strategic adviser at the museum,* presented their observations of the problem: "Despite their persecution, the Rohingya we met wanted to go home. But a safe and voluntary return is a dim prospect. It will require Myanmar, also known as Burma, to grant them protections they have long been denied: full and equal citizenship, official recognition of their ethnicity as Rohingya, plus accountability and justice for those responsible for atrocities."[12]

In terms of what we might have accomplished . . . they were really divided when we first came in, and that's in part because they were really thinking they were each going to be independent countries and so, frequently, they were actually fighting with each other. What we saw happening is that they came together to develop a shared constitution, and they came to realize that if that's the situation, they're all in it together.

—David Williams

22 | INDIANA UNIVERSITY Toward the Future

Facing, Indiana University India Gateway office in New Delhi.

Photograph courtesy of Indiana University.

Michael McRobbie's Presidency and the Future

From the outset of his presidency, Michael McRobbie made it clear that international and global scholarship and activities would be hallmarks of his presidency. His decision to travel around the world to meet with academic and political leaders began to pave the way for IU's future directions in a global context.

McRobbie's commitment to international engagement led him to countries in Africa, Asia, South America, and Europe to strengthen the university's global partnerships. He put forward an outline for such travel; he would go to parts of the world where IU had significant partnerships, or where new ones might be developed, preferably with top-tier universities. He also planned to recognize the special anniversaries of long-standing partners or events or connections that were of unique importance to IU. For example, in 2009, he attended the ceremony in Stockholm at which faculty member Elinor Ostrom received the Nobel Prize in Economics. His agenda also included attending alumni events in different countries, and he was an active participant in two major regional alumni reunions: the first in Seoul, Korea, in 2009 and an Asia-Pacific event in Bali, Indonesia, in 2016. McRobbie's first visit as president was to Asia, and during his presidency, he made frequent visits to countries such as China, India, Japan, Korea, Thailand, Malaysia, and Vietnam. He explained: "The extraordinary

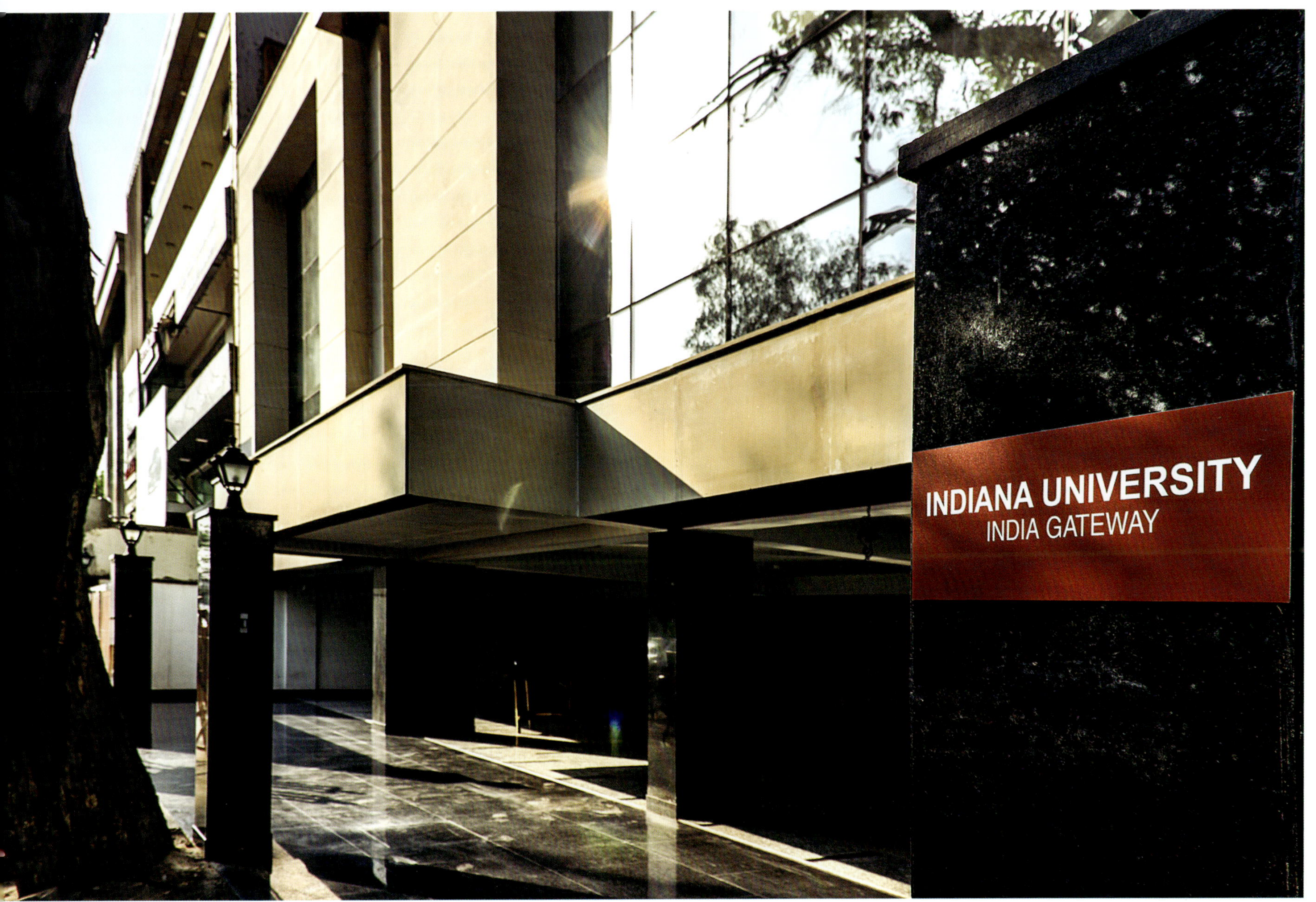
INDIANA UNIVERSITY
INDIA GATEWAY

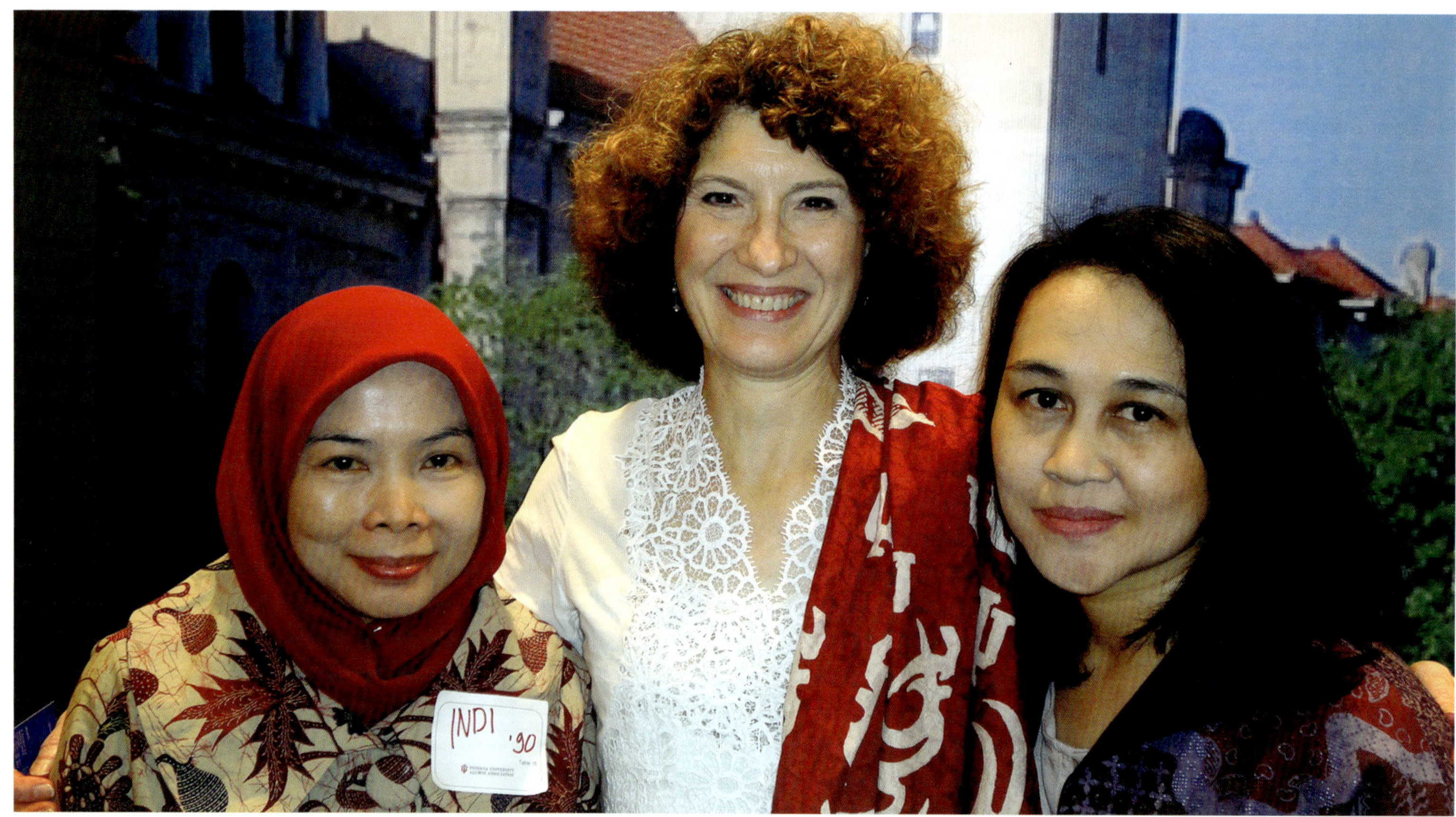

Indiana University first lady Laurie Burns McRobbie (*center*) with members of the Jakarta chapter of the IU Alumni Association, Indonesia, May 2012.
Photograph courtesy of Indiana University.

economic growth and development in Asia provides rich opportunities to expand and deepen our relationships with the best universities there. Study abroad opportunities at such universities will help prepare our students for the global future and will also serve the interests of the state of Indiana. My first visit abroad as President will be to China."[1]

At the same time, McRobbie reaffirmed his wider international commitment: "We will also work to strengthen our

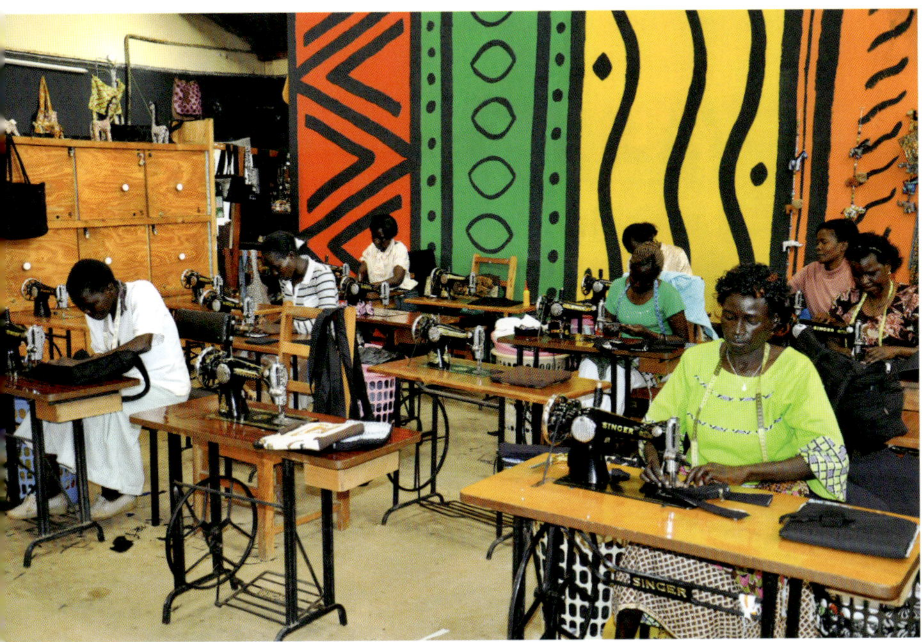

The Imani Workshops in Eldoret, Kenya, established in 2005, provide job training and income-generating activities for those affected by HIV and others in need. An Indiana University delegation to Kenya visited the workshops in 2013. *Photograph courtesy of Indiana University.*

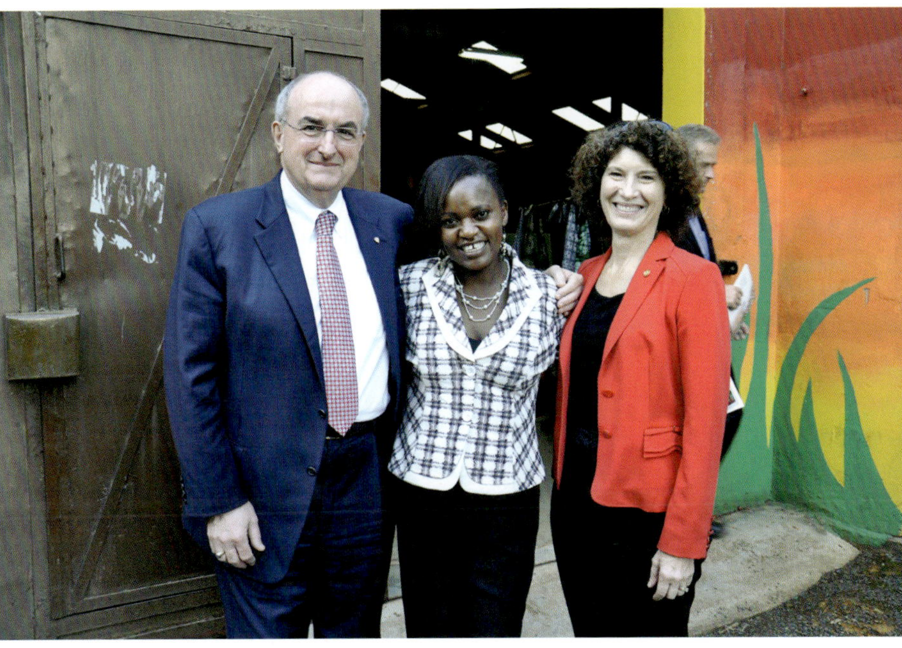

Indiana University president Michael McRobbie (*left*) and IU first lady Laurie Burns McRobbie (*right*) with Evaline Njoki, who founded the Imani Workshops. *Photograph courtesy of Indiana University.*

traditional relationships with universities in Europe and seek to identify new opportunities in Africa like IU's exceptional Nobel Peace Prize–nominated AMPATH project, carried out in collaboration with Kenya's Moi University. We must also look for new opportunities in Central and Latin America and in the Middle East. We look to our own history of change and renewal as we approach these global horizons."[2]

Over the next few years, McRobbie would reach out to colleagues, universities, and alumni on most of the continents. Meetings in Latin America in 2012 with leading officials in Brazil, Argentina, and Chile resulted in new opportunities for research as well as study abroad. Of particular note was his visit to the Academia Brasileira de Letras (Brazilian Academy of Letters) in Rio de Janeiro, where he signed an agreement of

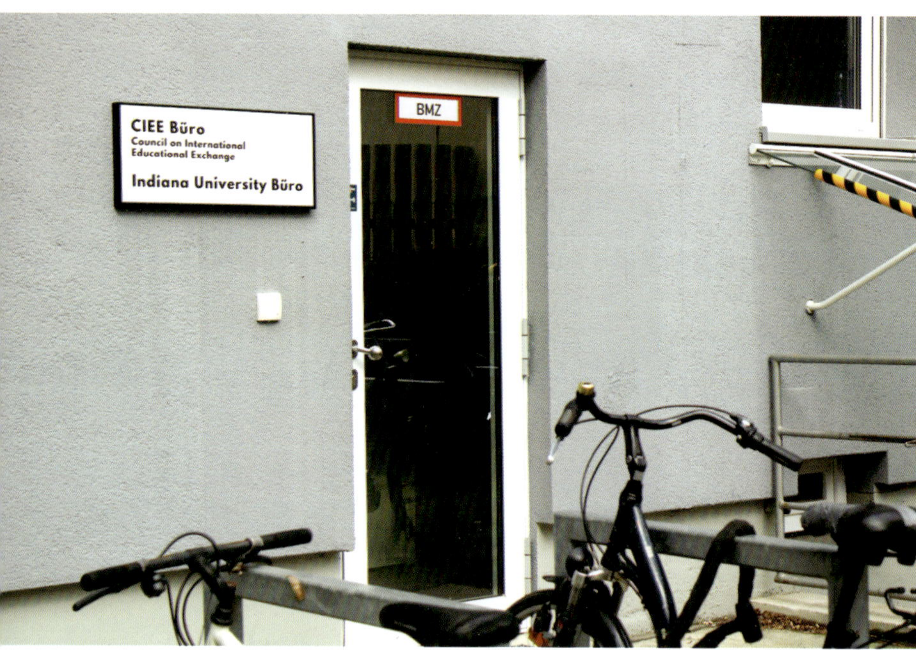

Indiana University European Gateway office in Berlin. *Photograph courtesy of Indiana University.*

cooperation. In 2013, he traveled to South Africa, Kenya, and Ghana. An important part of the journey was a series of meetings in Kenya with those involved with AMPATH and a visit to a hospital where HIV/AIDS patients were being treated. In Europe, he attended such celebrations as the fiftieth anniversary of IU's study abroad program in Bologna, Italy, in 2016; the fortieth anniversary of a partnership with the University of Warsaw in Poland in 2017; and the fiftieth anniversary of the Overseas Study program in Madrid, also in 2017. During these visits, he met with top leaders in government, education, arts and culture, and business as well as prominent IU alumni. While in Italy, McRobbie signed a historic agreement with the Uffizi Museum in Florence, one of the oldest and most renowned art galleries in the world. Under the agreement, IU's Virtual World Heritage Laboratory would create high-resolution three-dimensional digital models of the Uffizi sculptures. An important visit to Thailand took place in late March and early April 2016, primarily to celebrate the fiftieth anniversary of the National Institute of Development, Thailand's leading educational institution for graduate studies in the field of development. While in Bangkok, McRobbie held meetings with government officials, educational and business leaders, and prominent IU alumni in an effort to strengthen IU's oldest official international relationship.

McRobbie went on a special visit to Korea in 2016 to thank and recognize groups that had generously supported the establishment of a chair in Korean studies in the School of Global and International Studies. He met with the leaders of the Korea Foundation and the Academy of Korean Studies and with IU Korean alumni. He also paid a return visit to Sungkyunkwan University, Korea's oldest university with roots in Seoul going back to 1398. McRobbie had visited the Korean campus for the first time in 2008 to sign a university-wide agreement of cooperation.

While international development projects continued during McRobbie's presidency, new directions were taken in response to changing global patterns of interaction. Indiana University moved in an innovative direction with the creation of the first of its overseas centers, called Gateways. These were not degree-granting campuses like those that some US universities had set up. Building campuses abroad was a risky venture, and not always successful. The Gateways served as IU's front door in economically and culturally dynamic parts of the world; they were places for IU faculty, students, and alumni to meet and work and venues for international conferences, symposia, workshops, and other educational events. IU's China Office opened and was formally dedicated by McRobbie in May 2014. In his remarks, McRobbie commented: "Given all of these deep connections between China and Indiana University, it is fitting that we open this Gateway Office, which will help us serve our Chinese students, our many Chinese alumni, and our American students studying in China more effectively. The office will serve as an excellent home base for IU activities in China. It will support scholarly research and teaching, conferences and workshops, study abroad programs, distance learning initiatives, student recruitment activities, executive and corporate training, and alumni events."[3]

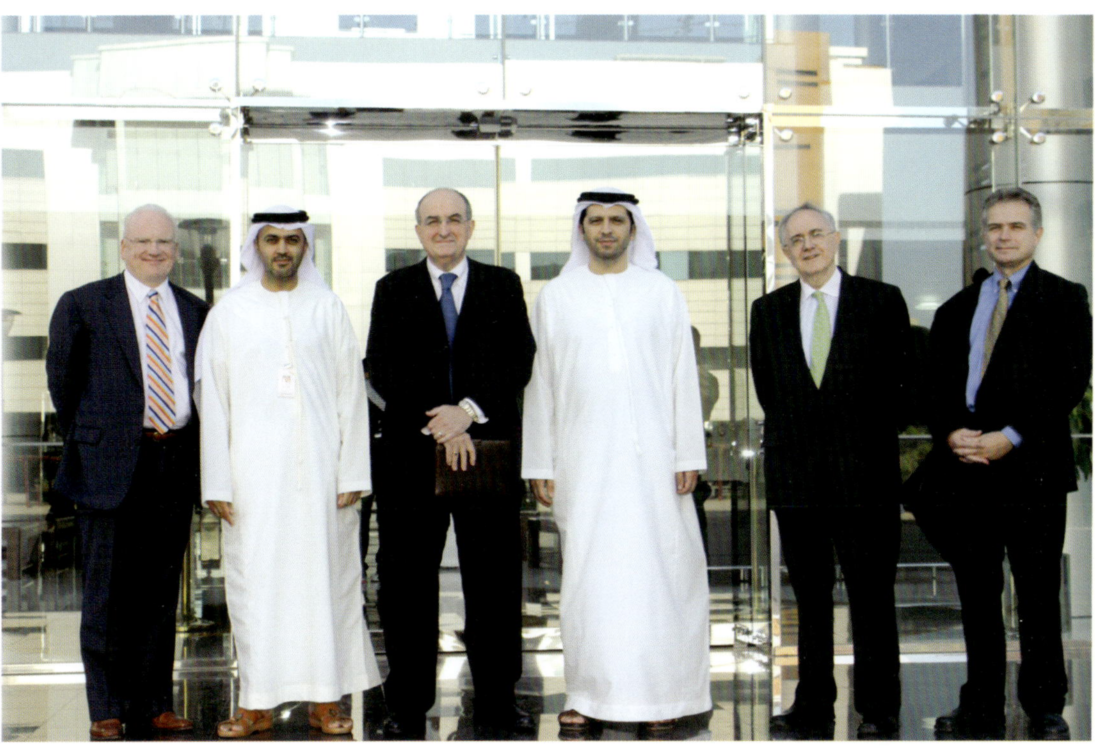

In 2009, Indiana University president Michael McRobbie (*third from left*) and vice president Patrick O'Meara (*second from right*) visit with interim president Arif Sultan Al Hammadi (*center*) of Khalifa University of Sciences, Technology, and Research in the heart of Abu Dhabi, a major Middle East center for research in science and technology. Also pictured are Richard A. Clarke, former national coordinator for security, infrastructure protection, and counterterrorism for the United States (*left*) and Shawn Reynolds, IU director of International Partnerships (*right*). The IU delegation also reconnected with IU alumni at dinner in Dubai. *Photograph courtesy of Indiana University.*

The first academic director of the IU China Gateway was Joyce Mann, a faculty member in the School of Public and Environmental Affairs with an established international reputation on China's urban and public economics and policy. Steven Yin was appointed the first manager of the center. He had

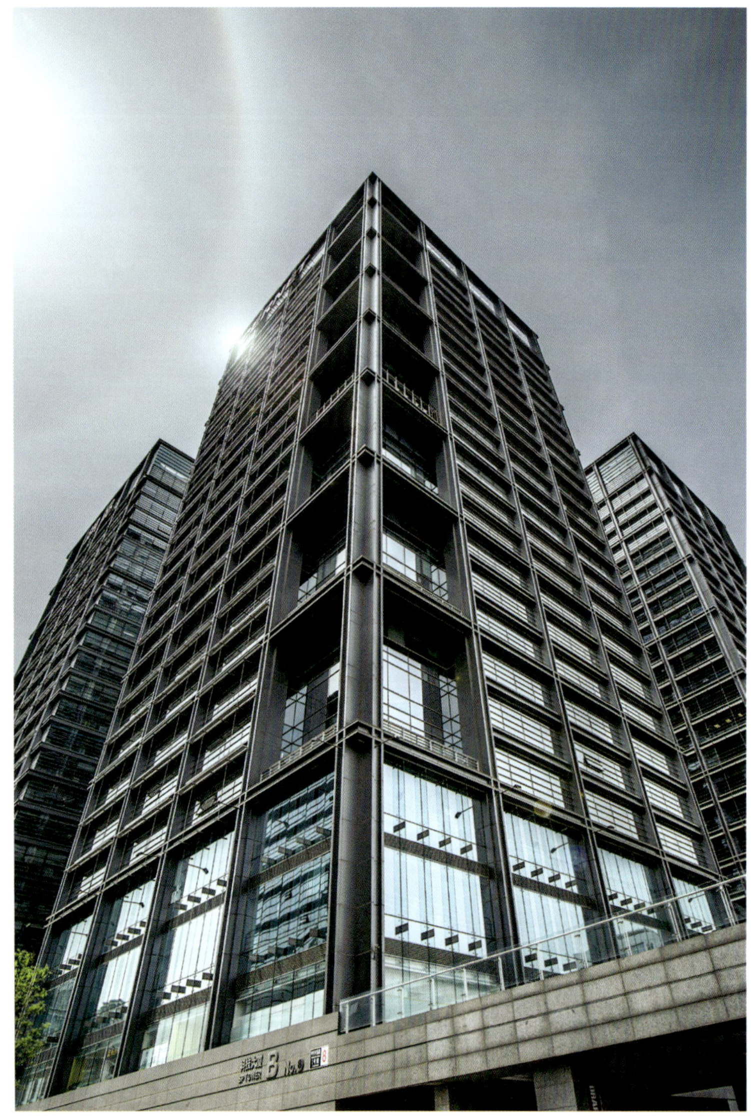

Indiana University China Gateway office in Beijing. *Photograph courtesy of Indiana University.*

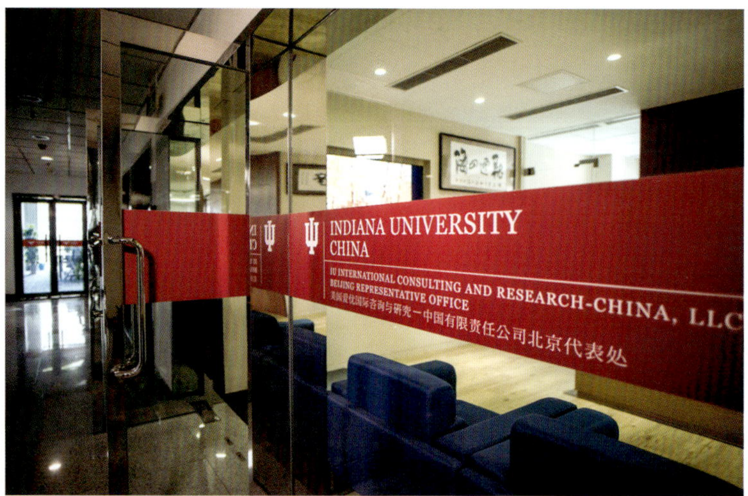

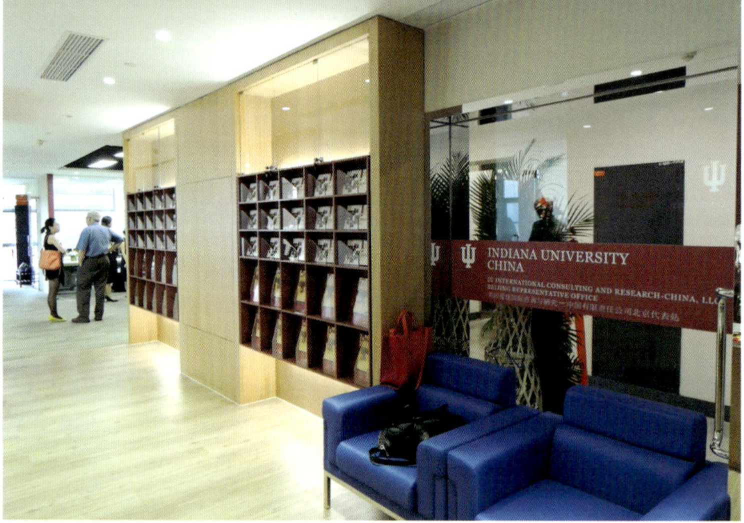

Top, Exterior lobby of the IU China Gateway office in Beijing. *Photograph courtesy of Indiana University.*

Above, Interior lobby of the IU China Gateway office in Beijing. *Photograph courtesy of Indiana University.*

previously served as the deputy director of the Education USA China program at the US embassy in Beijing. Yin described his job this way: "The Gateway is Indiana University's embassy in China, so we represent the entire university system. My job doesn't have a boundary. It can be from hosting visits of faculty or students, institutional partnership building, academic collaboration, alumni engagement, supporting international student recruitment, and meeting with Chinese university partners, helping to facilitate communication between our academic units with their counterparts all over China, to assisting IU personal visits to China."[4]

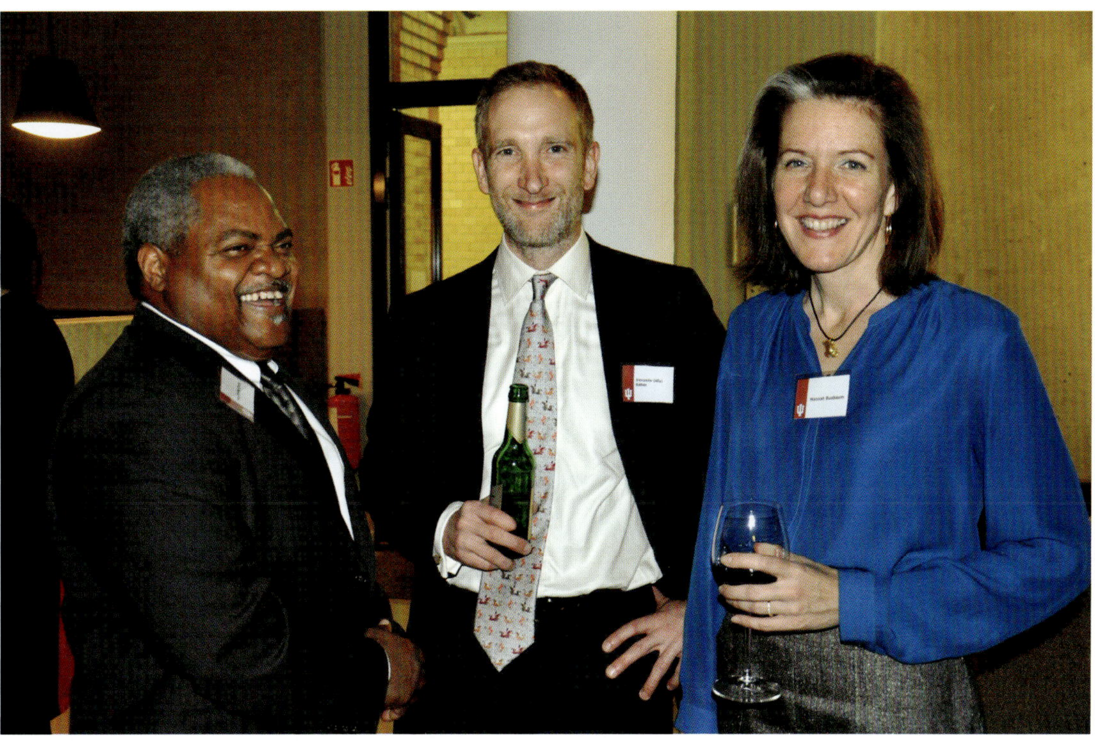

Martin McCrory, IU associate vice president for diversity, equity and multicultural affairs (*left*), Ally Batten (*center*) and Hannah Buxbaum (*right*) at the European IU Gateway office in Berlin, November 2015. *Photograph courtesy of Indiana University.*

The establishment of the IU Gateway in Gurgaon, India, a suburb of New Delhi and a leading financial and industrial center, marked the beginning of an important new era. When he opened the office in 2014, McRobbie remarked that IU's "presence in India is indicative of our desire to learn about India on its own terms and to begin an exchange that will benefit both India and Indiana and strengthen the connections between India and the United States."[5] Michael Dodson, director of the IU Dahr India Studies program, was appointed as the academic program director of the Gateway. Dodson's historical research focused on the intellectual and cultural history of northern India during the nineteenth century. The office manager, Shalini Choubey, had experience in study abroad program administration, language programs, undergraduate programs, business development, outreach,

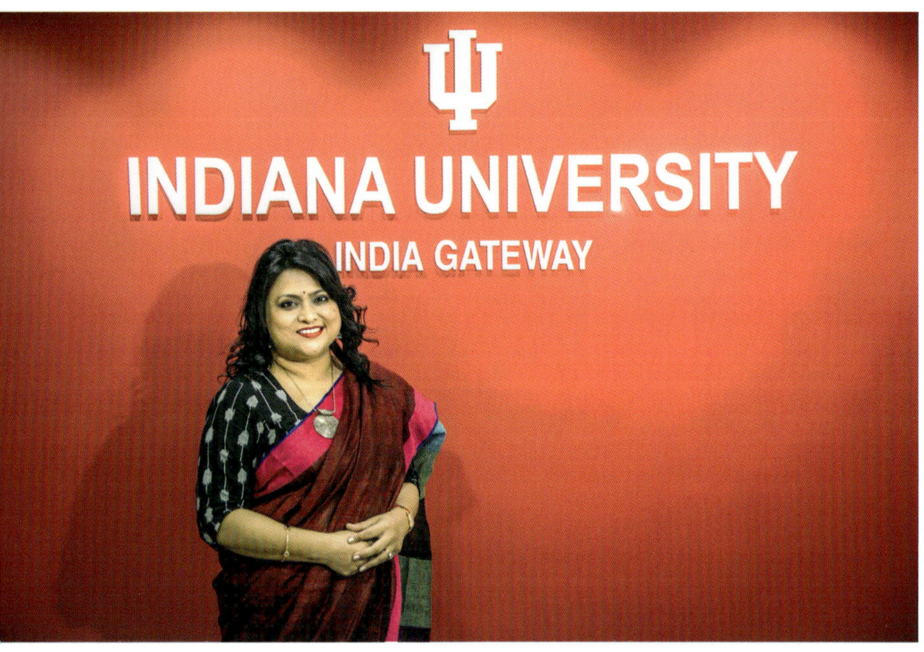

Indiana University India Gateway office administrative director Shalini Choubey at the opening of the New Delhi office, April 7, 2018.
Photograph courtesy of Indiana University.

government relations, event management, and affiliations with universities. She had previously worked as a corporate communications manager and a project coordinator with the American Institute of Indian Studies.

The IU Europe Gateway Office in Berlin opened in November 2015 in the culturally diverse Kreuzberg neighborhood of the city. Hannah Buxbaum, the John E. Schiller Chair in Legal Ethics at the IU Maurer School of Law, was appointed as the academic director, and subsequently was named the vice president for international affairs at IU in 2018. For then vice president David Zaret, the Gateway was an important IU presence in Europe. "Our new gateway office will provide IU with a physical presence in the center of Europe and a point of access to other countries of strategic interest within the region."[6]

Zaret sums up McRobbie's international commitment and significance at IU:

> I often remark that I have the most enviable position simply because all things international are one of Michael's highest priorities. When I meet with my counterparts at other Big 10 institutions, the conversation often features their laments about a lack of institutional support, a need to convince administration of this, that, and the other thing, and I look at them and I say, "I have the opposite problem. I work for a president who wants to see more and more new initiatives as well as enhancements to existing initiatives." I don't think there is another university president in the United States that places a higher priority on international engagements than Michael.[7]

As part of the continuing commitment of President McRobbie and of the Bloomington campus, in 2018, plans were announced to construct a new International Center building, which would bring together the Office of International Services, the Office of Overseas Study, and the Office of International Development. All of these units would now be in one architecturally innovative facility adjacent to the Global and International Studies Building on the IU Bloomington campus. The aim of the $17.5 million building is to centralize programs and services devoted to strengthening IU's global presence for international students and scholars, and for undergraduates studying abroad.[8]

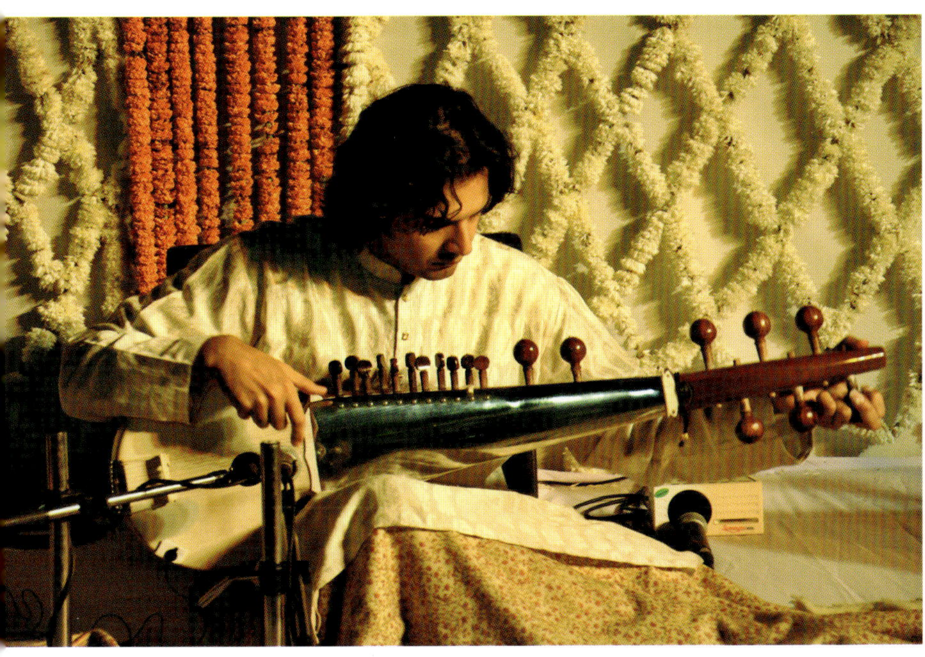

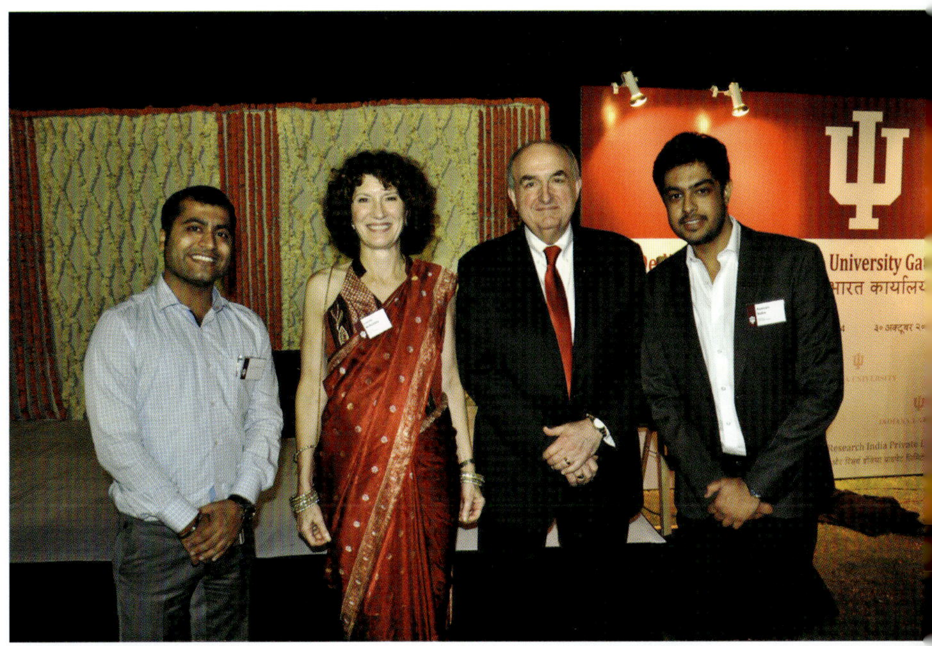

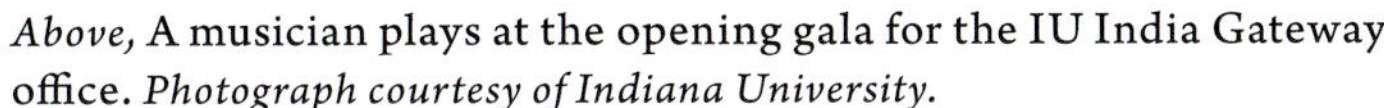

Above, A musician plays at the opening gala for the IU India Gateway office. *Photograph courtesy of Indiana University.*

Above right, India Gateway office opening party with Indiana University president Michael McRobbie (*second from left*), first lady Laurie Burns McRobbie, and IU alumni, 2013. *Photograph courtesy of Indiana University.*

Right, Prospective Indiana University students and IU alumni meet at the IU India Gateway office, 2016. *Photograph courtesy of Indiana University.*

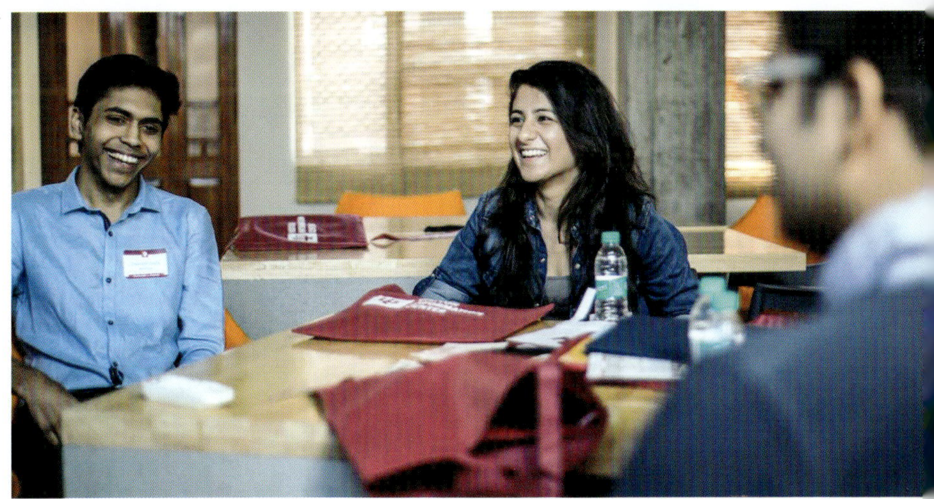

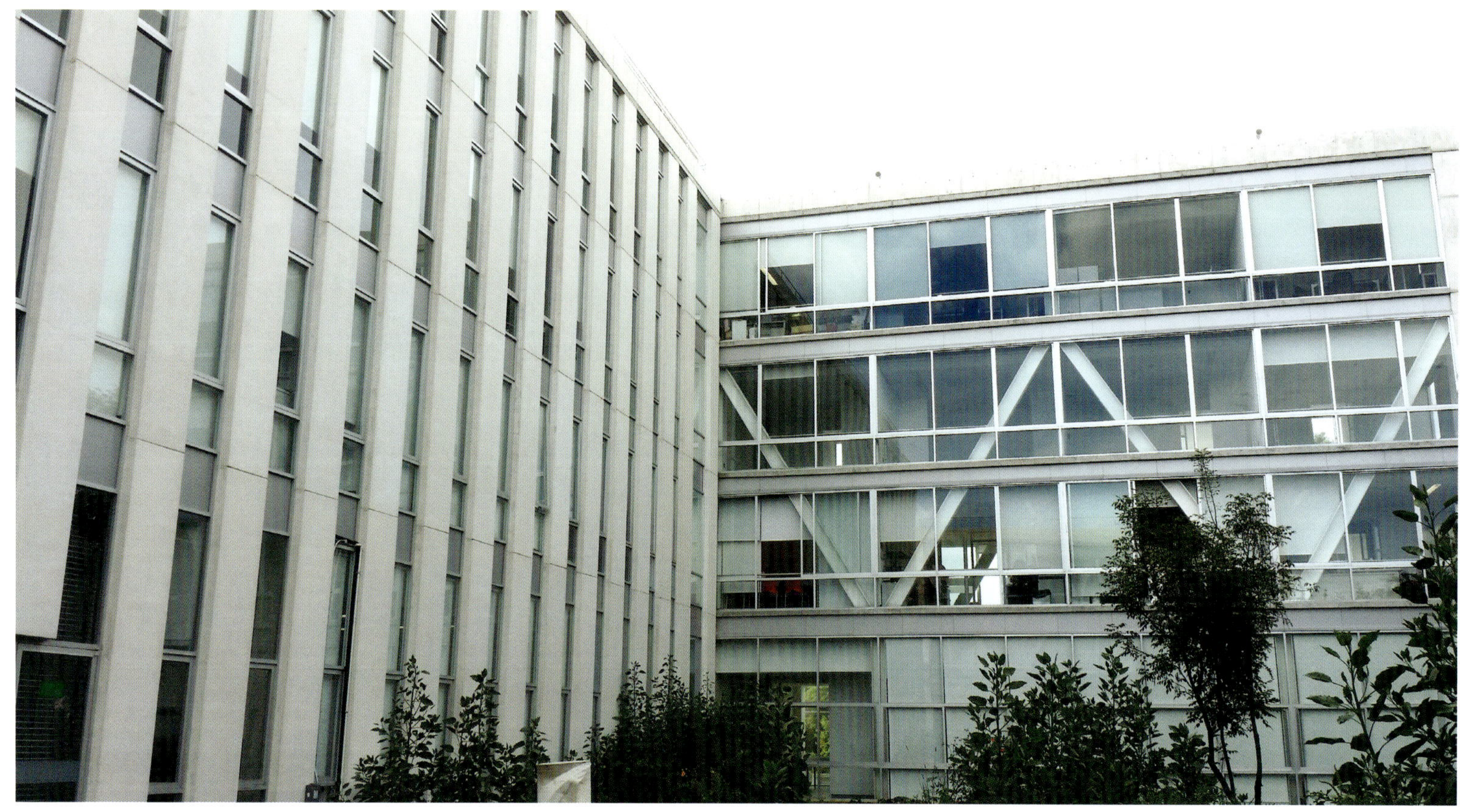

Indiana University Mexico Gateway office on the campus of National Autonomous University of Mexico, 2018.
Photograph courtesy of Indiana University.

Conclusion

This book, which has been published as part of Indiana University's bicentennial celebration, has been an excellent opportunity to reflect on the university's engagement with the wider world for over a century. At the same time, it is appropriate to speculate on whether the past can be a prologue to the future. Technology, which is patently absent from most of the chapters in this book, has already transformed the ways in which students and faculty think, communicate, and conduct research. Are there new paradigms for international cooperation on the horizon? Already, for example, the shipment of books abroad is becoming redundant because of access to materials through the internet. Many forms of face-to-face interaction can now be done electronically; courses can be taught over distance, as can the sharing of many techniques and forms of knowledge; even relevant degree programs can be completed online. Instruction by computer was already a part of the project of the Indiana University–South East European University in Macedonia, but in few other countries where IU was present.

Methodologies are now called for, as is a serious assessment of limits, pitfalls, and possibilities. Many countries do not have the basic infrastructure or resources to participate equally in development work, but over time this might improve. Of course, there are pedagogical, administrative, and technologically fundamental needs that will call for the immediacy of personal contact. It is hard to imagine a project such as AMPATH in Kenya being handled at a distance. But there are other projects where the economy of scale presented by technology will widen and enhance possible outcomes. In the end, there can be no substitute for person-to-person immersions by faculty and students in different societies and cultures, but there will also be new and creative ways to relate and interact.

When Indiana University was founded two hundred years ago, the new state of Indiana was a frontier—a developing area! There is little resemblance between the small seminary in the 1820s and the megacampuses of today. However, key principles remain immutable—the freedom to explore new ideas; what it means to be a good teacher; responding to students and societies with different needs and backgrounds; and the preparation of professionals with skills to move into the future. The tools of delivery might have changed, but the ends remain unchanged. There will be international partnerships and global connections, but the fundamentals of collaboration, exploration, and invention must remain as new technical knowledge opens up paths of access. It would be exciting to know how Indiana University embraces its international and global future over the next two hundred years.

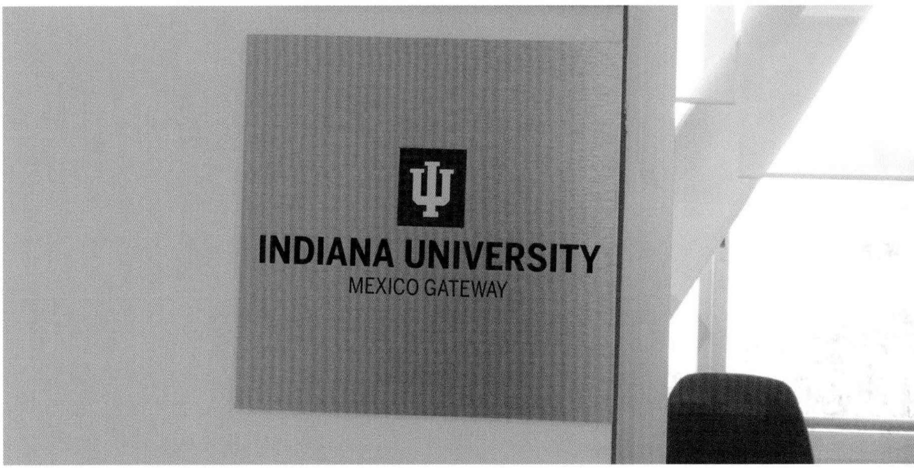

Interior placard at the Indiana University Mexico Gateway office, 2018. *Photograph courtesy of Indiana University.*

Notes

Preface

1. Kathleen Sideli and Walter Nugent, eds., *40th Anniversary Retrospective: Overseas Studies at Indiana University* (Bloomington, IN: AuthorHouse).

Introduction

1. Herman B Wells, *Being Lucky: Reminiscences and Reflections* (Bloomington: Indiana University Press, 1980), 128.
2. Ibid., 236.
3. Michael A. McRobbie, "Introduction," *International Strategic Plan* (Indiana University, March 2008).
4. David Zaret, personal interview, July 14, 2017.

1. History

1. Indiana University Office of Overseas Study, https://overseas.iu.edu/about/history.html.
2. John W. Ryan, Remarks to Alumni in the Philippines, June 1980, Office of University Archives and Records Management, http://webapp1.dlib.indiana.edu/metsnav/archives/navigate.do?oid=VAA2615-00431&pn.
3. Ibid.
4. Herman B Wells, *Being Lucky: Reminiscences and Reflections* (Bloomington: Indiana University Press, 1980), 397.
5. Ibid., 236.
6. Ibid., 252.
7. Indiana University, Board of Trustees meeting minutes, May 21–22, 1965, http://webapp1.dlib.indiana.edu/iubot/view?docId=1965-05-21.
8. Elvis J. Stahr, opening remarks for International Week, Whittenberger Auditorium, November 2, 1965, http://fedora.dlib.indiana.edu/fedora/get/iudl:1093877/OVERVIEW.
9. Indiana University, Board of Trustees meeting minutes, July 7–10, 1966, http://webapp1.dlib.indiana.edu/iubot/view?docId=1966-07-07.
10. John V. Lombardi, "Indiana University," in *Approaches to International Education*, ed. E. L. Backman (New York: ACE/Macmillan, 1984), 103–17.
11. "O'Meara Is First Vice President for International Affairs," *International News* (Indiana University Office of the Vice President for International Affairs), Fall 2007, 2, https://worldwide.iu.edu/communications/magazine/issues/2007/fall/International-Magazine-Fall-2007.pdf.
12. Indiana University, "Patrick O'Meara to Be Vice President for International Affairs," press release, July 20, 2007, http://newsinfo.iu.edu/news-archive/6041.html.
13. "Transitions," *IU International*, Fall 2011, https://worldwide.iu.edu/communications/magazine/issues/2011/fall/articles/transitions.pdf.
14. Indiana University, "Hannah Buxbaum named as IU Vice President for International Affairs," press release, November 30, 2017, https://news.iu.edu/stories/2017/11/iu/releases/30-hannah-buxbaum-international-affairs.html.
15. Indiana University, Mauer School of Law faculty profile page, https://www.law.indiana.edu/about/people/bio.php?name=buxbaum-hannah.

16. Indiana University, Office of the Vice President for International Affairs, https://ovpia.iu.edu/about/vice-president.html.

2. Indiana University in Germany

1. Jean Edward Smith, *Eisenhower in War and Peace* (New York: Random House, 2012).

2. Leah K. Peck, "Herman B Wells and the Changing Face of Higher Education in Post-war Germany," research paper presented at the annual meeting of the Association for the Study of Higher Education, Washington, DC, 2013.

3. Herman B Wells, *Being Lucky: Reminiscences and Reflections* (Bloomington: Indiana University Press, 1980), 302.

4. Herman B Wells papers, German assignment papers, 1947–1952. Indiana University Archives, C75, Box 51.

5. Peck, "Herman B Wells."

6. Herman B Wells papers, Box 50.

7. Peck, "Herman B Wells."

8. Wells, *Being Lucky*, 303.

9. Frank Banta, interview transcript, Indiana University, Center for the Study of History and Memory, History of Indiana University 1968–1981, September 19, 1980.

10. Wells, *Being Lucky*, 314.

11. Herman B Wells papers, Box 51.

12. Frank Banta, personal interview, November 22, 2013.

13. Ibid.

14. Frank Banta, interview transcript.

15. Peck, "Herman B Wells."

16. Ibid.

17. Ibid.

18. James H. Capshew, *Herman B Wells: The Promise of the American University* (Bloomington: Indiana University Press, 2012), 200.

19. Ibid.

20. James F. Tent, *The Free University of Berlin: A Political History* (Bloomington: Indiana University Press, 1988).

21. Wells, *Being Lucky*, 310.

22. Ibid., 312.

23. Herman B Wells papers, Box 50.

24. Wells, *Being Lucky*, 313

25. Peck, "Herman B Wells."

26. Ibid.

27. Michael A. McRobbie, "Press Conference and Restitution Ceremony," speech, Charlottenburg Palace, Berlin, November 21, 2011, http://president.iu.edu/speeches/archive/2011/20111121-01.shtml.

28. Ibid.

29. Ibid.

3. Indiana University in Thailand

1. Uthai Laohavichien, "The Problems and Prospects of Public Administration Education in Thailand," *Asian Journal of Public Administration* 6, no. 1 (1984): 46–60, http://hkjo.lib.hku.hk/archive/files/d750a1844c07a82653191eaef5d373a2.pdf.

2. Ibid. In 1954, Prasan Mitr became the premier campus of Srinakharinwirot University, a comprehensive institution with several campuses throughout Thailand. In that same year, IU's School of Education also established a graduate program in the Department of Education at the Faculty of Arts at Chulalongkorn University. That department later became a full-fledged Faculty of Education.

3. "Meeting on Public Administration Contract," internal IU memo, March 28, 1955, Indiana University Thailand Project records, 1953–1977. Indiana University Archives, C347, Box 2.

4. "Contract Signed Tuesday for IU-Thailand Program," *Indiana Daily Student*, May 4, 1955.

5. John W. Ryan, "Bangkok Government and Administration: Appearance and Reality" (PhD dissertation, Indiana University, 1959).

6. William J. Siffin, *The Thai Bureaucracy: Institutional Change and Development* (Westport, CT: Greenwood Press, 1976).

7. Choop Karnajaprakorn, Lawrence. E. McKibben, and William N. Thompson, *NIDA: A Case Study in Institution Development* (Bloomington: International Development Research Center, Indiana University, 1974).

8. Ibid.

9. Ibid.

10. Ibid.

11. Ibid.

12. Ibid.

13. Patrick O'Meara, "A Short History of the IU-NIDA Partnership," in *50 Years: School of Public Administration* (Bangkok: National Institute of Development Administration, 2005), 22–33.

14. Karnajaprakorn, McKibben, and Thompson, *NIDA: A Case Study.*

15. Amara Raksasataya and Chirawan Bhakdbutr, "IU-Thai Partnership," *Indiana University Alumni Magazine*, September 1986, 10–11.

16. Ibid. In addition to the NIDA relationship, there were other linkages with Thailand. In the 1990s, IU partnered with Thailand's dental schools to promote the development of graduate dental education in Thailand. Under this agreement, doctoral students trained at IU and then returned to Thailand to teach. In addition, there were faculty and student exchanges between Ramkhamhaeng University and the IU School of Optometry, and the School of Public Health and the School of Nursing both had relationships with Chulalongkorn University. There was cooperation between the School of Engineering and Technology on the IUPUI campus, the King Mongut Institute of Technology, and Mahasarakham University.

17. "IU to Present Honorary Degrees to Thai Princess and Surgeon General of the Navy," press release, December 9, 2010, http://newsinfo.iu.edu/news-archive/16611.html.

18. Michael A. McRobbie, "Universities and Global Sustainable Economic Development in the 21st Century: 50th Anniversary of the National Institute of Development Administration," speech, Bangkok, March 31, 2016, https://president.iu.edu/speeches/select-speeches/2016/2016-03-31-sustainable-economic-development.html.

19. Theodore Bowie, ed., *The Arts of Thailand* (Indiana University Fine Arts Library, Special Collections, 1960), exhibition catalog, http://iucat.iu.edu/catalog/1796520.

4. Indiana University in Pakistan

1. Herman B Wells, *Being Lucky: Reminiscences and Reflections* (Bloomington: Indiana University Press, 1980), 239.

2. "Indiana University's University of Karachi Jinnah Postgraduate Medical Center Project Records, 1955–1967," Archives Online at Indiana University, http://purl.dlib.indiana.edu/iudl/findingaids/archives/InU-Ar-VAC9611.

3. "Indiana University's University of Dacca Institute of Business Administration Project Records, 1964–1971," Archives Online at Indiana University, http://purl.dlib.indiana.edu/iudl/findingaids/archives/InU-Ar-VAC9612.

4. Wells, *Being Lucky.*

5. Ibid.

6. "Islamabad 1964–1968," May 3, 1968, Indiana University Archives, C4882.

7. Wells, *Being Lucky.*

8. "Indiana University's University of Islamabad Project Records, 1953–1974," Archives Online at Indiana University, http://purl.dlib.indiana.edu/iudl/findingaids/archives/InU-Ar-VAC9610.

9. Ibid.

10. Herman B Wells to Vice Chancellor Dr. M. Raziuddin Siddiqi, May 19, 1968, Indiana University Archives, Pakistan 7150.

11. Q. Aziz, "Pakistan's Islamabad U: Stone Designed, Ford Funded," *Christian Science Monitor,* August 5, 1967, Indiana University's University of Islamabad Project records, 1953–1974. Indiana University Archives, C48, Box 2

12. Wells, *Being Lucky.*

13. "I.U. Aids Pakistani University," April 30, 1969, Edward W. Najam papers, 1937–2005. Indiana University Archives, C391, Box 1

14. "Technical Assistance Pakistan, 1978–79," Indiana University Archives, C75.44.

15. "Indiana University's University of Islamabad Project Records."

16. Ibid.

5. Indiana University in Afghanistan

1. "Kabul University Administration Program Records, 1964–1972," Archives Online at Indiana University, http://webapp1.dlib.indiana.edu/findingaids/view?doc.view=entire_text&docId=InU-Ar-VAC8992.

2. Ibid.

3. "'The Hope of the Afghan Diaspora': IUB Hosts Conference on Higher Education Reconstruction in Afghanistan," *International News* (Indiana University Office of International Programs), May 2003, 7, 22–23, https://worldwide.iu.edu/communications/magazine/issues/2003/may/International-News-December-2003.pdf.

4. "School of Education Receives Award to Train ESL Teachers in Afghanistan," *International News* (Indiana University Office of International Programs), May 2004, 14, 26, https://worldwide.iu.edu/communications/magazine/issues/2004/spring/International-News-May-2004.pdf.

5. Mitzi Lewison and Terrence Mason, personal interview, September 15, 2016.

6. "School of Education Receives Award."

7. Lewison and Mason, personal interview.

8. Indiana University, "Education in Afghanistan: IU and 'Three Cups of Tea,'" press release, September 23, 2010, http://newsinfo.iu.edu/news-archive/15667.html.

9. "Improving Afghan Education," *IU International*, Fall 2010, 26–28, https://worldwide.iu.edu/communications/magazine/issues/2010/fall/articles/afghan.pdf.

10. Ibid.

11. Ibid.

12. Indiana University, "Education in Afghanistan."

13. "Improving Afghan Education."

14. Lewison and Mason, personal interview.

15. Ibid.

16. Indiana University, "IU Center Selected for $3.5 Million U.S. State Department Grant to Create New Master's Degree Program in Afghanistan," press release, July 13, 2011, http://newsinfo.iu.edu/news-archive/19100.html.

6. Indiana University in Poland

1. Leonard Baldyga, "The 20th Anniversary of the American Studies Center at the University of Warsaw: A Historic Overview," *Pochwala Historii Powszechnej*, 1996, 569.

2. Padraic Kenny, personal interview, September 1, 2015.

3. Robert Gosende, personal correspondence, August 7, 2011.

4. Baldyga, "The 20th Anniversary," 569.

5. Mary McGann, personal interview, September 3, 2015.

6. Bill Johnston, personal interview, September 4, 2015.

7. Ibid.

8. Ibid.

9. *Indiana University Polish Studies Center Newsletter* 21, no. 2 (January 1999), http://www.indiana.edu/~polishst/about/newsletters/jan1999.htm.

10. *Indiana University Polish Studies Center Newsletter* 18, no. 4 (September 1996), http://www.indiana.edu/~polishst/about/newsletters/sep1996.htm.

11. Kenny, personal interview.

12. McGann, personal interview.

7. Indiana University in South Africa

1. National University Continuing Education Association, "Innovations in Continuing Education: Award Winning New Programs," 1987, Indiana University President's Office records, 1976–1995. Indiana University Archives, C501, Box 113.

2. James Kilgore, personal interview, May 21, 2015.

3. Khanya College, "Khanya College 1986–1996: Ten Years of Education for Liberation, 1996, Indiana University Archives, 2006/043.9.

4. Ibid.

5. Albert Wertheim, "A Report on Khanya College," July 1990, Indiana University President's Office records, 1976–1995. Indiana University Archives, C501, Box 113.

6. Kilgore, personal interview.

7. Ibid.

8. Ibid.

9. National University Continuing Education Association, "Innovations."

10. R. Ma Newman, "The Indiana University-Khanya College Program," 1995, Indiana University Archives, 2006/043.39.

11. Personal communication between Thomas Ehrlich and Patrick O'Meara, September 10, 1990, Indiana University President's Office records, 1976–1995, Indiana University Archives, C501, Box 113.

12. The Department of Education and Training was a central government department under apartheid responsible for the education of Africans in those areas of South Africa that were not African "homelands." These schools were in primarily white territory, and attended by black students. Pam Christy and Margaret Gaganakis, "Farm Schools in South Africa: The Face of Rural Apartheid," *Comparative Education Review* 33(1989): 77–92.

13. Khanya College, "Khanya College 1986–1996."

14. Kilgore, personal interview.

8. Indiana University in Malaysia

1. Charles Reafsnyder, "Case Study: A Twinning Program in Malaysia—Lessons from the Field," in *Ambassadors of U.S. Higher Education: Quality Credit-Bearing Program Abroad*, ed. J. Deupree and M. Peace Lenn (New York: College Entrance Examination Board, 1997) 55–79.

2. Ibid.

3. James E. Weigand and John V. Lombardi, "Malaysia Program Update," December 3, 1984, Indiana University interdepartmental communication, Indiana University Archives, IU Office of International Development records.

4. Charles Reafsnyder, "ITM/MUCIA Cooperative Program in Malaysia," undated information for prospective applicants, Indiana University Archives, IU Office of International Development records.

5. Reafsnyder, "Case Study."

6. Robert H. Shaffer, (1984, November 5). "Indiana University—MUCIA Malaysian Project: Report of Field Visitation, September 20–November 5, 1984," November 5, 1984, Indiana University Archives, IU Office of International Development records.
7. Ibid.
8. Tim Diemer, personal interview, July 10, 2015.
9. Charles Reafsnyder, personal interview, January 20, 2015.
10. Diemer, personal interview.
11. Reafsnyder, personal interview.
12. Ibid.
13. Ibid.
14. Diemer, personal interview.
15. Ibid.
16. Ibid.
17. Reafsnyder, personal interview.
18. "IUPUI Forges Agreement with Malaysia's Tenaga National Institute," *IU International Programs*, May/June 1994, https://worldwide.iu.edu/communications/magazine/issues/1995/may/IU-International-May-June-1995.pdf.

9. Indiana University in Russia

1. "IU's School of Education Forms Linkage with Russian Institution," *IU International*, December 1994, 1, https://worldwide.iu.edu/interactive-map/IU-Intl-pdfs/1994-12-02.pdf.
2. Ibid.
3. Paul McNeil, "Cold War Education—Howard D. Mehlinger," January 28, 2014, Indiana University Archives, https://blogs.libraries.indiana.edu/iubarchives/2014/01/28/c271mehlinger/.
4. Ibid.
5. Don Hossler, personal communication, August 2, 2016.
6. Ibid.
7. "Current International Activities of the IU Business School: Ryazan Banker Training Program," *IU International*, January/February 1995, 2, https://worldwide.iu.edu/interactive-map/IU-Intl-pdfs/1995-01-03.pdf.

10. Indiana University in Kenya

1. Fran Quigley, *Walking Together, Walking Far: How a U.S. and African Medical School Partnership Is Winning the Fight against HIV/AIDS* (Bloomington: Indiana University Press, 2009), 35.
2. Ibid., 34.
3. Ibid., 35.
4. Jennifer Piurek, "A Rush of Hope," *Indiana University Alumni Magazine*, March/April 2007, 40–45.
5. Quigley, *Walking Together*, 7.
6. Piurek, "A Rush of Hope."
7. Quigley, *Walking Together*, 43.
8. Ibid., 48.
9. Ibid., 129.
10. Ibid., 99.
11. Ibid.
12. Ibid., 125.
13. "IU Goes to Africa," *IU International*, Spring 2014, 9.
14. Piurek, "A Rush of Hope."
15. Ibid.
16. Michael McRobbie, President's Medal for Excellence speech, October 26, 2013.
17. Piurek, "A Rush of Hope."

11. Indiana University in Ukraine

1. Charles Wise, personal interviews, August 28 and November 9, 2015.
2. "SPEA Continues to Assist Ukraine on Road to Democracy," *International Programs*, January/February 1994, 4, https://worldwide.iu.edu/interactive-map/IU-Intl-pdfs/1994-01-05.pdf.
3. Wise, personal interviews.
4. Ibid.
5. Ibid.
6. Ibid.
7. "SPEA Continues."
8. Ibid.
9. Ellie Valentine, personal interview, July 17, 2016.
10. Cassandra Howard, "IU's SPEA Receives $4.9 Million Award to Help Strengthen Democracy in Ukraine," *International News*, December 2003, 12, https://worldwide.iu.edu/interactive-map/IU-Intl-pdfs/2003-12-16.pdf.
11. Valentine, personal interview.
12. Robert Agranoff, personal interview, March 4, 2016.
13. Ibid.
14. Indiana University, "IU's Parliamentary Development Project Receives $500,000 for Ukrainian Democratization," press release, September 29, 2005, http://newsinfo.iu.edu/news-archive/2485.html.

15. Debra Kent, "Saying Yes! to Democracy," *Democracy* 28, no. 1 (Fall 2005), http://www.indiana.edu/~rcapub/v28n1/sayingyes.shtml.
16. Agranoff, personal interview.
17. Wise, personal interviews.
18. Ibid.

12. Indiana University in Kyrgyzstan

1. "IU and Other Indiana Universities Assist Kyrgyzstan's New Progressive University," *International News*, October 2000, 1–2, 14, https://worldwide.iu.edu/communications/magazine/issues/2000/october/International-News-October-2000.pdf.
2. Indiana University, "IU to Use $15 Million Grant to Establish Endowment for American University of Central Asia," press release, April 13, 2005, http://newsinfo.iu.edu/news/page/normal/2079.html.
3. Ibid.
4. Charles Reafsnyder, "Annual Report: American University of Kyrgyzstan (AUK) Faculty Development and Administrative Training," Indiana University and the Indiana Consortium for International Programs, Indiana University Office of International Development, 2000.
5. Ibid.
6. American University of Central Asia, "AUCA at a Glance," https://auca.kg/en/auca_at_a_glance/.
7. Ellen Hurwitz, personal interview, February 16, 2016.
8. Ibid.
9. Steve Hinnefeld, "Endowment Strengthens IU Ties with Kyrgyzstan; Central Asian Nation Was Scene of a Popular Uprising Last Month," *Bloomington Herald-Times*, April 13, 2005, http://newsinfo.iu.edu/news-archive/2077.html.

13. Indiana University in Macedonia

1. Leah Peck, "Building a New University in Macedonia," *IU International*, Fall 2014, 24–27, https://worldwide.iu.edu/communications/magazine/issues/2014/fall/articles/macedonia.pdf.
2. Marcin *Czapliński, Conflict Prevention and the Issue of Higher Education in the Mother Tongue: The Case of the Republic of Macedonia* (Nijmegen, Netherlands: Wolf Legal Publishers, 2008), 154.
3. Charles Reafsnyder, personal interview, February 1, 2014.
4. Paul Foster, personal interview, February 7, 2014.
5. Charles Reafsnyder, "US-Macedonia Linkage with the South East European University," Indiana University and the Indiana Consortium for International Programs, 2006. Program report evaluation report submitted to the United States Agency for International Development.
6. Dennis J. Farrington, *South East European University: The First Four Years* (Tetovo, Macedonia: South East European University, 2006) 48.
7. Reafsnyder, "US-Macedonia Linkage."
8. "Dayton Agreement," Wikipedia, 2014, https://en.wikipedia.org/wiki/Dayton_Agreement.
9. Reafsnyder, personal interview.
10. Ibid.
11. Foster, personal interview.
12. Reafsnyder, personal interview.
13. Foster, personal interview.
14. *Czapliński, Conflict Prevention*, 104.
15. Foster, personal interview.
16. Alajdin Abazi, personal interview, September 18, 2014.
17. Reafsnyder, personal interview.
18. Reafsnyder, "US-Macedonia Linkage."
19. Ibid.
20. *Czapliński, Conflict Prevention*, 107.
21. Patrick O'Meara, personal reflection, October 2014.
22. Reafsnyder, "US-Macedonia Linkage."
23. Gabrielle Goodwin and Robert Downey, personal interview, February 2, 2014.
24. Ibid.
25. Abazi, personal interview.
26. Reafsnyder, "US-Macedonia Linkage."
27. Farrington, *South East European University*.
28. Abazi, personal interview.
29. *Czapliński, Conflict Prevention*, 111.
30. Terrence Mason, personal interview, February 8, 2014.
31. Goodwin and Downey, personal interview.
32. Reafsnyder, "US-Macedonia Linkage."
33. Ibid.
34. *Czapliński, Conflict Prevention*, 112.
35. Michael McRobbie, speech at SEEU honorary degree ceremony, Tetovo, Macedonia, 2011.

14. Indiana University in Namibia

1. "Link between IU East and University of Namibia Regional Campus Thrives," *International News*, May 2004, 6, https://worldwide.iu.edu/communications/magazine/issues/2004/spring/International-News-May-2004.pdf.

2. Ibid.

3. Ibid., 16.

4. "University of Namibia Choir Performs at IU Bloomington and IU East," *International News*, December 2004, 49, https://worldwide.iu.edu/interactive-map/IU-Intl-pdfs/2004-09-11.pdf.

15. Indiana University in Liberia

1. "IU Strengthens Connections to Liberia," *International News*, Summer 2005, 8, 37, https://worldwide.iu.edu/communications/magazine/issues/2005/summer/International-News-Summer-2005.pdf.

2. Indiana University, "Liberian President Receiving Honorary Degree at IU Bloomington Commencement," press release, April 8, 2008, http://newsinfo.iu.edu/news-archive/7887.html.

3. Report. Center of Excellence for the Health and Life Sciences. University of Liberia, Indiana University, Tubman National Institute of Medical Arts, University of Massachusetts Medical School. (n.d.). USAID and HED report.

4. Indiana University, "IU Officials Travel to Liberia in Support of University Partnership," press release, November 25, 2008, http://newsinfo.iu.edu/news-archive/9356.html.

5. Report (n.d.).

6. Indiana University, "$7.2 Million Project Will Address a National Shortage of Health Care Workers in Liberia," press release, October 31, 2011, http://newsinfo.iu.edu/news-archive/19978.html.

7. Ibid.

8. Ibid.

9. Ibid.

10. Ibid.

11. Ibid.

12. Ibid.

13. "Liberian President Applauds IU Partnership with University of Liberia," *Inside IUPUI*, March 11, 2014, http://inside.iupui.edu/editors-picks/health-wellness/2014-03-11-liberian-president-iupui.shtml.

14. David Williams and Susan Williams, personal interview, November 21, 2016.

15. Ibid.

16. Ibid.

17. "Indiana University Liberian Collections," Indiana University Libraries, African Studies Guide, http://guides.libraries.indiana.edu/africanstudies/liberia.

16. Indiana University in Egypt

1. Program brochure, IUPUI McKinney School of Law.

2. Frank Emmert and Sonja Rice, personal interview, November 17, 2015.

3. Ibid.

4. Ibid.

5. Ibid.

6. Ibid.

7. Ibid.

8. Ibid.

9. Sonja Rice, "Partnering with Egyptian Law Faculties: Cooperative Agreement between USAID and Indiana University School of Law–Indianapolis," USAID Cooperative Agreement No. 263-A-00-07-00050-00, final annual program report, December 2013.

10. Emmert and Rice, personal interview.

11. Rice, *Partnering with Egyptian Law Faculties.*

12. Emmert and Rice, personal interview.

17. Indiana University in Indonesia

1. "Indonesia Public Administration Program Records, 1954–1965," Archives Online at Indiana University, http://webapp1.dlib.indiana.edu/findingaids/view?docId=InU-Ar-VAC8993.xml&brand=general&text1=Indonesia administration&startDoc=1.

2. Ibid.

3. Chemonics, "New Lessons in Indonesia's Higher Education System," https://www.chemonics.com/projects/new-lessons-indonesias-higher-education-system/.

4. Chemonics, "Who We Are," https://www.chemonics.com/who-we-are/.

5. Indiana University, "IU School of Education Dean Travels to Indonesia as Part of Higher Education Project," press release, September 10, 2012, http://newsinfo.iu.edu/news-archive/23083.html.

6. Margaret Sutton, personal interview, March 11, 2016.

7. Ibid.

8. Margaret Sutton and Mohammed. Iskander, "HELM Project: Graduate Level Education in Higher Education Leadership and Management," Indiana University report, August 10, 2012.

9. Ibid.

10. Margaret Sutton and Charles Reafsnyder, personal communication, April 13, 2015.

11. Sutton, personal interview.

12. Ibid.

13. Indiana University, "IU School of Education Dean.

14. Indiana University, "Indiana University President McRobbie to Discuss Higher Education Leadership in Bogor, Indonesia," press release, May 21, 2015, http://news.iu.edu/releases/iu/2015/05/indiana-university-president-higher-education-leadership-indonesia.shtml.

18. Indiana University in South Sudan

1. "Higher Education for Women in South Sudan," *Research IU Bloomington* (blog), posted April 16, 2013, https://web.archive.org/web/20170904161117/http://research.indiana.edu/2013/04/higher-education-for-women-in-south-sudan/.

2. Ibid.

3. Indiana University, "Redesigned USAID-Funded Project Brings South Sudan Scholars to Indiana University," press release, September 18, 2014, http://news.indiana.edu/releases/iu/2014/09/sudan-scholars-iu-bloomington.shtml.

4. Ibid.

5. Ibid.

6. Indiana University Center for Constitutional Democracy, "The Center in South Sudan," http://ccd.indiana.edu/projects/South_Sudan.

7. Ibid.

19. Indiana University in Palestine

1. LaVonn Schlegel, personal communication, November 15, 2016.

2. Indiana University, "US State Department Awards $300,000 Grant to IU Kelley School for Palestinian Economic Development," press release, June 20, 2015, http://news.indiana.edu/releases/iu/2015/06/young-entrepreneurship-livelihood-program-palestine.shtml.

3. Ibid.

4. Ibid.

5. Ibid.

6. Indiana University Kelley School of Business, Institute for International Business, "Building Entrepreneurship Excellence and Developing Economic Enterprises," https://kelley.iu.edu/IIB/ProgramsandIntitiatives/BEEADEE/page47687.html.

20. Indiana University in Latin America and the Caribbean

1. "Indiana University Peru Project Records, 1964–1969," Archives Online at Indiana University, http://webapp1.dlib.indiana.edu/findingaids/view?doc.view=entire_text&docId=InU-Ar-VAC8991.

2. Ibid.

3. Alison Reynolds, "Indiana University Travels to South America," *Blogging Hoosier History* (blog), posted April 23, 2013, https://blogs.libraries.indiana.edu/iubarchives/2013/04/23/indiana-university-travels-to-south-america/.

4. "Indiana University Uruguay Mechanical and Electronic Engineering Education Program, 1963–1967," Archives Online at Indiana University, http://webapp1.dlib.indiana.edu/findingaids/view?doc.view=entire_text&docId=InU-Ar-VAC8990.

5. Ibid.

6. "School of Optometry Remains Committed to International Humanitarian Efforts," *International Programs Newsletter*, July 1999, 5–6, https://worldwide.iu.edu/communications/magazine/issues/1999/july/IU-International-July-1999.pdf.

7. "School of Optometry Expands Its International Links," *International News*, Spring 2006, 18, https://worldwide.iu.edu/communications/magazine/issues/2006/spring/International-News-Spring-2006.pdf.

8. "Susan Sutton and Internationalization at IUPUI," *IU International*, Fall 2009, 21–24, https://worldwide.iu.edu/communications/magazine/issues/2009/fall/articles/intl.pdf.

9. Indiana University, "As State's Latino Population Grows, IU Strengthens Engagement in Mexico," press release, September 2, 2016, https://diversity.iu.edu/news-events/news/president-visits-mexico.html.

10. LaVonn Schlegel, personal communication, November 7, 2016.

11. Indiana University, "IU Kelley School of Business Awarded $1.35 Million USAID Grant to Spur Entrepreneurship in Barbados," press release, March 9, 2011, http://newsinfo.iu.edu/news-archive/17673.html.

12. Ibid.

13. Ibid.

21. Indiana University in Burma-Myanmar

1. Kay Ikranagara, "The Burmese Refugee Scholarship Program at IU Bloomington," *International News*, October 2000, 16, https://worldwide.iu.edu/communications/magazine/issues/2000/october/International-News-October-2000.pdf.

2. "Burma (Myanmar) Youth Leadership," *IU International*, Fall 2014, 28–29, https://worldwide.iu.edu/communications/magazine/issues/2014/fall/articles/burma.pdf.

3. Indiana University, "IU Kelley School of Business Awarded $1 Million USAID Grant to Support Myanmar's Economic Transition," press release, February 24, 2014, http://news.indiana.edu/releases/iu/2014/02/iu-kelley-school-awarded-usaid-grant-in-burma.shtml.

4. Ibid.

5. LaVonn Schlegel, personal correspondence, November 2, 2016.

6. Indiana University, "IU Kelley School of Business."

7. Ibid.

8. David Williams and Susan Williams, personal interview, November 29, 2016.

9. Ibid.

10. Ibid.

11. Steve Hinnefeld, "U.S. Must 'Remain on the Case' of Myanmar, Indiana University Dean Says," *News at IU Bloomington*, September 11, 2018, https://news.iu.edu/stories/2018/09/iub/inside/11-us-must-remain-on-case-of-myanmar.html?utm_source=2018-09-11&utm_medium=enewsletter&utm_content=Perilous-circumstances&utm_campaign=2018-inside-iub-distribution.

12. Lee Feinstein and Cameron Hudson, "We Are on the Verge of Extinction," *Washington Post*, August 24, 2018, https://www.washingtonpost.com/news/democracy-post/wp/2018/08/24/we-are-on-the-verge-of-extinction/?noredirect=on&utm_term=.89dd7a7d89d3.

22. Toward the Future

1. Michael A. McRobbie, "Endurance, Excellence, and the Energy of Change at Indiana University," inaugural address, October 18, 2007, http://newsinfo.iu.edu/news/page/normal/6604.html.

2. Ibid.

3. Michael McRobbie, speech at the opening ceremony for the IU China Gateway Office, May 23, 2014, Indiana University, Office of the President, https://archive.president.iu.edu/speeches/2014/20140523-01.shtml.

4. Steven Yin, personal interview, September 20, 2016.

5. Michael McRobbie, "Strengthening Indiana University's Longstanding Connections with India," speech at the grand opening of the IU India Office, October 30, 2014, https://archive.president.iu/edu/speeches/2014/20141030-02.shtml.

6. Indiana University, "IU President McRobbie Traveling to Germany to Open New IU Global Gateway Office in Berlin," press release, October 27, 2015, http://info.law.indiana.edu/releases/iu/2015/10/mcrobbie-germany-berlin-gateway.shtml.

7. David Zaret, personal interview, July 14, 2017.

8. Indiana University, "Four IU Constructed Project Requests Approved," June 15, 2018, https://news.iu.edu/stories/2018/06/iu/inside/15-four-construction-project-requests-approved.html.

Patrick O'Meara is Special Adviser to the Indiana University President, Vice President Emeritus for International Affairs, and Professor of Public and Environmental Affairs and Political Science. O'Meara greatly expanded the range and depth of international involvement at IU over the years and has published extensively in global and international affairs.

Leah K. Peck holds a PhD in higher education administration from Indiana University. Before coming to IU, she had several years of experience in university administration in Minnesota. Her research focuses on international development in higher education and various aspects of university internationalization efforts.

ACQUISITIONS EDITOR Peggy Solic

PROJECT MANAGER Darja Malcolm-Clarke

BOOK AND COVER DESIGNER Pamela Rude

COMPOSITION COORDINATOR Tony Brewer